Holocaust Monuments and National Memory Cultures in France and Germany since 1989

Holocaust Monuments and National Memory Cultures in France and Germany since 1989

The Origins and Political Function of the Vél' d'Hiv' in Paris and the Holocaust Monument in Berlin

Peter Carrier

Berghahn Books
New York • Oxford

First published in 2005 by

Berghahn Books
www.berghahnbooks.com

Library of Congress Cataloging-in-Publication Data

Carrier, Peter.
Holocaust monuments and national memory cultures in France and Germany since 1989: the origins and political function of the Vél' d'Hiv' in Paris and the Holocaust monument in Berlin / Peter Carrier.
p. cm.
Includes bibliographical references and index.
ISBN 1-57181-904-5
1. Holocaust memorials. 2. Holocaust, Jewish (1939-1945)--Influence. 3. Memory--Social aspects. 4. Denkmal fèr die ermordeten Juden Europas (Berlin, Germany) 5. Vâlodrome d'hiver (Paris, France) I. Title.

D804.3.C374 2005
940.53'1864'0943155--dc22

2005042015

British Library Cataloguing in Publication Data

A catalogue record for this book is available from the British Library.

Printed in the United States on acid-free paper.

ISBN 1-57181-904-5 hardback
ISBN 1-57181-295-X paperback

Contents

List of Illustrations

Acknowledgements

My thanks go to Jörg Beige, Etienne François, Ann Gardiner, Jonathan Huener, Eric Jacobson, Rod Kedward, Susannah Radstone, Tamar Rapoport, Elfie Rembold, Klaus Teschner and Nancy Wood for their thoughtful comments on various parts of the draft manuscript, and in particular to Gert Mattenklott for his help in defining and discussing the project.

I am grateful to the academic commission of the Senate of Berlin, whose generous NaFöG award made the research for this study at the Freie Universität possible.

Excerpts from Chapter Three and Chapter Four previously appeared in *Borec* (Slovenia, 1999), *National Identities* (UK, 2000), and *Život Umjetnosti* (Croatia, 2001).

List of Abbreviations

CDJC	Centre de Documentation Juive Contemporaine
CDU	Christlich-Demokratische Union
CRIF	Conseil Représentatif des Institutions Juives de France
CSU	Christlich-Soziale Union
DVU	Deutsche Volksunion
FDP	Freie Demokratische Partei
FN	Front National
NPD	Nationaldemokratische Partei Deutschlands
PDS	Partei des Demokratischen Sozialismus
PS	Parti Socialiste
RPR	Rassemblement pour la République
SPD	Sozialdemokratische Partei Deutschlands
UEJF	Union des Etudiants Juifs de France

Introduction

The impact of monuments and related rituals upon collective memories of the Second World War is a source of recurrent political debate in all former Allied and Axis countries. The spate of fiftieth anniversary commemorations of this event served not only to reappraise national histories in light of the end of the balance of power sustained during the Cold War, but also to symbolically compensate the dwindling number of living witnesses and victims of the war period. In both cases, public representations acquired considerable political authority as means of sustaining social memories of this period. But do representations ensure that future generations remember events of the past? And if so, do they take forms which are fitting for the events, and which do justice to victims, their relatives or even to states and societies in whose name they are created? No one would doubt today that public memorials do not guarantee remembrance and that there is no single most just form. Memorials are contingent. Their meanings may partly be deduced from their artistic composition but primarily from the many ideas and expectations with which society invests them.

Yet in spite of the inherent ambiguity of monuments, which can serve equally as catalysts for remembrance and for forgetting, political strategists continue to delegate to monuments and commemorations the moral responsibility to guarantee remembrance. How and why they do this is the topic of this book, which examines symbolic and rhetorical strategies used within institutional contexts to define the singular role of public memorials in the negotiation of new national, yet unconventional historical identities. For this reason, this study focuses on debates about monuments, in particular at the moment of their production and appropriation in the public sphere when historical information and interpretations, but also artistic forms and political interests, converge and conflict in the present. It offers insight into the process by which public art and ritual foster an understanding of the past, and consequently become instruments of political representation.

Memory cultures in European countries flourished from the 1970s following numerous openings of museums, historical exhibitions and monuments, and came to a head in the 1980s and 1990s with a series of fortieth and fiftieth anniversary commemorations of the Second World War. As witnesses of the contemporary enduring fascination with the past, we are in a position to trace the process by which such historical artefacts emerge, involving individuals, institutions and lobbies that initiate them, public reactions to them, and their resulting political function. Two monuments in particular became the focus of nationwide debate in France and Germany: the Vélodrome d'Hiver (Winter Cycling Stadium) or 'Vél' d'Hiv' in Paris, and the 'Monument for the Murdered Jews of Europe' (Denkmal für die ermordeten Juden Europas) or 'Holocaust Monument' in Berlin. The first of these monuments was built in 1994 to mark the site of round-ups of Jews prior to deportation in 1942. The second will be inaugurated in 2005 as a central symbol of the genocide against Jews. Both have been categorised as 'national' monuments, and are unique in so far as they accord central symbolic significance to the memory of crimes of the Second World War. In spite of the etymological roots of the term Holocaust in Christian theology and anti-Judaist polemic (a term originally signifying ritual sacrifices now employed to refer to the persecution and attempted destruction of Jews during the Second World War),[1] this term has become internationally accepted as a convenient but euphemistic epithet for numerous museums, memorials and commemorative days. The tacit agreement to use this euphemistic language is perhaps an expression of our incapacity to witness and represent the past. Euphemisms are a common characteristic of memory cultures as spheres of public communication and collective memory formation. Yet although they certainly foster historical misrepresentation, they also illustrate and offer insight into the very semantic and psychological distortions on which memory cultures are founded. For the purposes of this study, I will refer to the 'persecution and genocide' of the Second World War in order to refer to the event itself, to 'Holocaust remembrance' with reference to the retrospective public memories of the event inclusive of errors and ambiguities as a fact of contemporary memory cultures, and to the Holocaust in cases where this term has gained common acceptance in proper names such as the 'Holocaust Monument' in Berlin. Naturally, the monuments investigated in this study belong to the second category of manufactured memories, the complexity of which should become apparent to the reader in Part II and Part III.

The sequence and intensity of anti-Semitic persecutions during the Second World War clearly differed from one country to the next. The sculptural, rhetorical and ritual forms with which these events are represented likewise generally vary according to the nation, region or city, or to the period in which they were erected. Yet in the case of France and

Germany, the Vél' d'Hiv' and Holocaust Monument triggered analogous public responses during the 1990s. Both monuments were perceived as symbolic reparation for crimes of the nation, conditions for 'national reconciliation' in France and for 'national consensus' in Germany. At the same time, they were both unique in so far as they symbolised the integration of the potentially subversive memory of criminal acts into each national memory culture. The result in both cases was a non-conventional narrative of national heritage.

This comparison of memory cultures illustrates the complexity of collective memories of the Second World War in France and Germany and beyond, for they are both shared and distinct at the same time. On the one hand, the persecution and genocide carried out during the Second World War provide a common supranational point of historical reference, as demonstrated by the fiftieth anniversary commemorations and the increasing number of official apologies. The debate over the Vél' d'Hiv' led to one in a series of verbal public apologies for war crimes, including that of the French Catholic Church (1997), the French police force (1997), the conditional apology of the Vatican (1998), and the apology made by the Polish president Alexander Kwasniewski for crimes committed against Jews by Polish citizens (2001), to which we may add Chirac's apology to the Harkis, Algerian soldiers serving in the French army during the Algerian war, more than fifty thousand of whom were killed in reprisals (2001). On the other hand, the Second World War is generally remembered, interpreted and represented on the basis of national and local events. It simultaneously unites and divides the populations of formerly belligerent countries not only because past enmity is remembered and still felt, but because each population experienced different events or the same event differently, and has since nourished local narratives, whether of Churchill, de Gaulle and Hitler, for example, or of displacement, exile, deportation and genocide. These narratives nevertheless overlap. There exists a common shared memory of Churchill in Germany or of Hitler in France, to which the numerous works of biographical and historical literature testify. A less obvious type of cultural analogy can be observed in the structural parallels between apparently distinct national memories, almost all of which have recourse to charismatic leaders, national media, rituals and symbols, including monuments. The two monuments examined in this study likewise testify to the analogous national dimensions of official memory cultures. On this basis, the very study of the analogies and differences between mechanisms used to uphold national memory cultures might be a first step towards breaking down or rendering them less impervious to one another.

This book contains three parts. Part I defines contemporary monuments as a genre with respect to earlier monumental forms and to its political function as public art. The fact that the artistic forms and equivocal political significance of monuments have regularly been the object of public debate means that monuments merit particular attention as a form of 'discursive formation'[2] in their own right. Prior to their material existence, the Vél' d'Hiv' and Holocaust Monument existed essentially in the form of debates between people who advocated or contested their form and necessity. Petitions, conferences, speeches, public forums, press articles, parliamentary debates as well as architectural exhibitions and even everyday private conversations about monuments all constituted the discursive existence of these monuments. Thus rendered in the form of verbal narratives, contemporary monuments are subjected to varying degrees of institutionalisation. In everyday communication, for example, they may foster error and limits in historical understanding, or indifference to the past when competing alongside information and advertising on billboards or in the mass media. The goal of this first part is therefore to trace theoretically the ambivalent function of monuments as artistic sources of historical or political learning, to situate them historically with respect to current national memory cultures in France and Germany, and to offer a critique of collective discursive codes used for the interpretation of memory cultures.

Part II explores the origins of and controversies over plans for the Vél' d'Hiv' memorial and commemorations in Paris and for the Holocaust Monument in Berlin during the 1980s and 1990s. These studies draw on local sources in order to propose a comparative assessment of the languages of memory, history and nationhood employed during the debates. Since discussions in France lasted for over three years and in Germany for over ten years, it is appropriate to analyse the media debates as a form of commemoration in their own right. These commemorations and monuments functioned as a catalyst of what James Young calls 'memory-work', resulting from an *unresolved* memorial.[3] Details of these sites of memory will be examined systematically in both cases, in the following order: the architectural and urban context of the sites, and the chronology of their emergence as focal points of political controversy; the language of petitions and formal verbal responses by politicians including, in the case of the Holocaust Monument, sculptural responses by artists and architects on the basis of blueprints; the causes of the political expediency of these monuments; and the different propositions for 'national reconciliation' over the Vél' d'Hiv' and 'national consensus' over the Holocaust Monument. In this way, I explore how these sites of memory serve – via their symbolic and rhetorical constructions – to incorporate the complex and disturbing memories of collaboration, deportation and genocide into a repertoire of national symbols.

Part III strives to compare the discursive codes of nationhood employed in each debate and demonstrate how arguments of artistic, historical, pedagogical and political concern were used to legitimate memorials and underpin official models of collective memory. At the same time, it demonstrates how the monuments provided a platform to *negotiate* rhetorical codes of national self-understanding in each country. The notion of 'site of memory'[4] offers a particularly effective tool for the analysis of political symbols and will be explained in relation to its implicit political assumptions and revised on the basis of the two case studies. Since the primary aim of this study is to explain public understandings of monuments *prior* to their construction, both everyday and analytical terminology will be considered as part of the commemorative process and must be subjected to the same scrutiny as the visual symbols and commemorative rituals that it describes. The intense public participation in the debates suggests that these monuments should be taken seriously as a medium of historical understanding, which I define here as 'dialogic' sites of memory. The broader aim of this study is therefore to assess the status of these monuments as sites of memory while paying particular attention to their political expediency in relation to the language with which they are given meaning. What do the Vél' d'Hiv' and the Holocaust Monument tell us about state strategies of self-legitimisation with respect to the Holocaust after 1989? Popular narratives prior to 1989 were based on a narrative paradigm defining enemies without or heroes within the nation: anti-fascist ideology in the German Democratic Republic (GDR), anti-communist ideology in the Federal Republic of Germany (FRG), and the myth of the Resistance in France. Since these paradigms largely lost credibility in the united Germany and against the background of trials of Vichy officials in France, it is of vital importance to record how popular narratives are being restructured following the end of the East–West conflict: whether it is possible for states to operate without these inherited narrative paradigms, and therefore to integrate the memory of domestic war crimes and even of victims of these crimes within national narratives without eclipsing them anew? Accordingly, the issues broached in Part I – the historical and political function of monuments in relation to their rhetorical and symbolic elaboration – are reappraised in Part III on the basis of empirical findings in Part II.

This comparative study of monuments explores how, despite the facility of international communications and travel, and despite economic and political mergers such as European unification which undermine the cultural, political and economic sovereignty of nation-states, memory cultures continue to be maintained institutionally on a national basis. The transfer of authority to a European level, for example, appears to be evolving parallel to the maintenance of memory cultures at a national level, as if memory cultures compensated for political devolution and shifting economic loyalties by upholding cultural tradition. As the sociologist Anthony Cohen remarks, 'the symbolic expression of community and its boundaries increases in importance as the actual geo-social boundaries of the community are undermined, blurred or otherwise weakened.'[5] Nevertheless, as noted above, the Second World War remains a transnational point of historical reference that provides a wealth of monuments, debates and rituals that are simultaneously of local, national and international significance. Various forms of monuments and commemorations therefore lend themselves to a comparison of national and local public understandings of this event as well as to an exploration of the overlap and interaction of different memory cultures. How, for example, do local associations, municipal or national governments derive legitimisation by erecting monuments recalling crimes of former dictatorships? Although historical events are remembered differently on local, municipal and national levels in different countries, there remain structural analogies between commemorative forms. The Second World War could therefore be defined as a shared multipolar site of memory. It is remembered internationally as a transnational event, but appropriated in unique ways locally and nationally. Local and national war memorials in remembrance of the Second World War likewise largely conform to an internationally recognised symbolic and conceptual language that is charged with political significance according to its specific context.

Perhaps the greatest challenge facing artists, sponsors and spectators of war memorials after 1945 is the impossibility of visually or conceptually representing and therefore understanding the crimes of deportation and genocide. Whereas First World War memorials generally consisted of cenotaphs, tombs of unknown soldiers, busts of heroic victims, flags and male or female icons, Second World War memorials traditionally consisted of a list of names added to First World War memorials – stones bearing the names of fallen soldiers being a common sight on most village squares throughout Europe. It is only since the 1960s that artists and sponsors have risen to the challenge of commemorating the genocide by developing forms and concepts that reverse the traditional heroism of national memorials by striving to evoke the memory of national crimes and their victims, and to take account of the fact that people rarely identify *with* monuments but respond individually to them in a two-way dialogue.

Monuments as Focal Points of Unresolved 'Dialogue'[6]?

Intense, creative energy has been invested in the design and definition of monuments since the 1960s. 'Ephemeral', 'objectless', 'undesirable', 'counter-' and 'anti-' monuments[7] are among some of the adjectives used to describe monumental forms. Common to all these concepts is their claim to define an alternative type of monument whose qualities are measured *against* the classical model of an ornamental, figurative sculptural monument. (By reversing the above criteria, as 'enduring', 'objective', 'desirable' and 'pro-', we obtain a succinct definition of conventional monuments traditionally erected until the mid-twentieth century.) Moreover, while ephemerality and objectlessness are qualities inherent in monuments, undesirability, counteraction and opposition are qualities ascribed to the monuments but which in fact originate in the social perceptions they generate. Yet these innovative norms of the production, form and reception of monuments do not take into account the large variety of existing monumental types, including countless conventional sculptural monuments which adorn and, in spite of artistic innovations, continue to be erected in public places even today. Is there a single theoretical paradigm that permits us to comprehend the various historical, social, political and artistic dimensions of monumentality in a single concept? One of the aims of this study is to provide an analytical framework for monuments which differ radically in their form, but whose production and appropriation, that is, the social context in which they arose, reveal remarkable similarities. A basic assumption here is that monuments are focal points of a complex dialogue between past and present, between historical events, producers of monuments, and successive generations of spectators who inquire into the significance of the past on the basis of historical artefacts. At the same time, monuments are also focal points of dialogue between individuals, and between artistic, academic, religious and political institutions and their representatives in the present. Architectural blueprints, oral and textual accounts, articles, reports, speeches and petitions constitute a dialogic process which generally *precedes* the creation of monuments – a process which is founded largely on rhetorical speculation over how to commemorate rather than on the interpretation of already existing monumental forms.

The two monuments that form the basis of this study aptly illustrate such a complex process. Although the issues aired during debates over these monuments differed, focusing on the rhetoric of presidential speeches in the case of the Vél' d'Hiv' and on artistic form in the case of the Holocaust Monument, they were each the product of analogous political procedure. Both monuments occupy central urban sites in the capital cities Paris and Berlin. Their origins lay in the campaigning of citizens' action groups with public petitions, leading to demands for national reconciliation in France and consensus in Germany, and to party political disputes during presidential and parliamentary election campaigns in 1995 and 1998. These monuments also provide insight into a unique process, which integrates a nation's crimes symbolically into a repertoire of national commemorations. In contrast to conventional war memorials celebrating heroes or mourning victims lost in battle, the Vél' d'Hiv' and Holocaust Monument have challenged states to integrate the memory of innocent victims of the nation's *own* crimes into cohesive narratives of national history. The novelty, yet also the apparent incongruity, of these monuments therefore results from their use of a conventional national monumental form of commemoration in order to recall crimes of that same nation. Combined with auxiliary forms of commemorative ritual, including speeches, debates, exhibitions and conferences, they broke a national convention according to which ritual commemorations and monuments offer solace or support for the positive identification of citizens. They therefore challenge an understanding of national 'identity'[8] founded on attachments to symbols or 'sites of memory', defined by the historian Pierre Nora as 'focal points of our national heritage'.[9]

The essays collected by Nora in *Les Lieux de mémoire* propose a conception of French history founded on sites of memory recalling distant historical moments, essentially from the nineteenth century, which today possess little immediate emotional appeal, but which are still shared with a degree of pride by members of the cultural community defined as 'French': works of literature and history, geographical boundaries, architectural symbols, historical events or cultural traditions. By contrast, the debates over the Vél' d'Hiv' and Holocaust Monument have shown that the Second World War is a source of memory that continues to unite and *divide* witnesses, participants and victims, as well as younger generations that have no direct experience of the events. Partisan approaches to these monuments were not governed uniquely by conflicting interpretations of historical events in themselves, however, but by interpretations of the rhetorical or artistic means by which they should be represented and remembered. Conflict over historical memories and over their means of transmission is inherent to democratic memory cultures. This study of memorial debates therefore provides insight into the process by which contemporary national symbols emerged out of conflict, how monuments were negotiated rhetorically in political and public spheres, and finally how negotiations appeased public emotions with respect to the issue of representation. In the aftermath of these debates, the commemorations, monuments and speeches subsist as ritual, artistic and rhetorical residues of a process of historical representation and therefore appear to fulfil the function of commemorations defined by Nora as the 'regulation of conflicts'.[10]

In the following study, a close analysis of language used in the debates will highlight the way in which the articulation of conflicting interests prior to the emergence of the Vél' d'Hiv' and Holocaust Monument determined their significance. In the case of the Vél' d'Hiv', the introduction of an annual national day of commemoration in 1993 and the construction of a new monument in 1994 were the result of public controversy over the rhetoric of presidential speeches. In the case of the Holocaust Monument, the debate over its form, site and purpose meant that the very substance of this long-term non-existent monument consisted purely in verbal speculation from as early as 1988 until its official inauguration in 2005. During these preparatory periods, the material by which people experienced these monuments derived essentially from verbal or textual sources. For this reason, the rhetorical foundations of these monuments require closer analysis. For the empirical case studies in Part II, I have drawn extensively on source material such as press articles, political statements, interviews, ceremonial speeches, open letters, brochures of associations representing memorials, protocols of parliamentary debates, radio discussions with politicians and historians and also, in Germany, on public conferences and forums involving representatives from political parties and associations as well as journalists, historians and participating artists. When sculptural form became the object of political debate, as in the case of the Berlin monument, I also examined the proposed artistic forms as objects of political discourse. In this way, I have tried to give a comprehensive account of the function of national symbols as they emerge, where symbolic form and political and pedagogical interests collide, expressed via monuments and via the rhetoric with which they are sanctioned in the public sphere.

Monuments and the History of Present Time

The branch of contemporary historiography known in France as the 'history of present time' takes account not only of recent history, extending backwards in time to encompass the period remembered by people still alive at any given moment, but also of the immediate past as it is fixed and given meaning for the first time by journalists, politicians, lawyers, and historians.[11] The history of present time pays particular attention to the influence of present-day interests on our understanding of the past and to the way in which past events continue to pervade present-day thinking and actions – a process formulated by the pioneer of contemporary historiography, Marc Bloch, in terms of the necessity to 'understand the present by the past', and to 'understand the past by the present'.[12]

One of the theoretical assumptions of this study is that rhetorical and visual communication plays a central role in the formulation and transmission of the public memory of the Second World War, an event of the past that clearly pervades historical, political and social self-understanding in the present. The responsibility of the journalistic, legal, political and even artistic professions for the representation and commemoration of the past testifies not only to a plural institutional command over what we know and think about the past, but also to the dependency of these professions upon rhetorical and even visual communication in order to make the immediate past meaningful. A logical consequence of this broad 'social demand'[13] for history today is the intense international interest in public memorials and museums, whose popular appeal makes them an inevitable source of historical knowledge and experience, one which deserves a central place in the study of the history of present time alongside archival, literary and judicial sources of historical scholarship. This is particularly valid when one considers that the public memory of the Second World War will in future derive from experiences gained entirely via forms of verbal and visual representation, and that successive generations of people who have neither acquired personal experience nor indirectly inherited family experiences of persecution or deportation (such as the second generation of Algerian Jews who emigrated to France during the 1960s, or even second and third generations of Turkish immigrants in Germany) nevertheless identify strongly with the victims of the persecution and genocide of the Second World War.

The historian Henry Rousso has suggested that the public memory of the Second World War during the 1990s was marked by a process of internationalisation and 'judiciarisation'.[14] The impact of the Eichmann trial and the Six-Day War during the 1960s, for example, heralded an international interest in the persecution and genocide such that this event today acts as 'a sort of founding "negative myth" of European identity'.[15] He further argues that a judicial logic underlies the public approaches to this period, conceived in terms of judicial, financial and moral *reparation*. But although Rousso effectively demonstrates the influence of the judiciary upon the historiography of the Second World War and upon public appeals for financial and moral reparation (in the form of state apologies, for example), he overlooks other equally pervasive modes of expression of Second World War memory: the rhetoric and visual symbols on which all interventions in public memory – whether artistic, architectural, historiographical, judicial, journalistic or political – invariably draw. Since communication is indispensable to the construction of public memory, one could argue that contemporary memory cultures are characterised not only by internationalisation and judiciarisation, but also by *rhetoricisation* and *symbolisation*.

Although the discussions about the Vél d'Hiv' and Holocaust Monument were founded largely on a discourse of reparation, they were not conceived as mere auxiliary symbolisations of historical research or judicial proceedings but as vectors of public memory in their own right. Moreover, the absence of rules agreed upon to govern their implementation led to prolonged and critical debate that often questioned the legitimacy of symbolisation itself. The means by which they were implemented involved artists, architects, politicians and historians in ad hoc debates focusing on sculptural forms, the price of building materials, types of architectural competition procedures, and the wording of speeches and inscriptions. It is the very complexity of monuments and the multiplicity of actors and institutions determining their meaning that render the quest to make sense of this most complex vector of public memory all the more urgent.

Notes

1. See Giorgio Agamben, *Remnants of Auschwitz. The Witness and the Archive*, trans. Daniel Heller-Roazen, New York: Zone Books, 2000, Chapter 1.10; Odon Vallet, 'Des mots en politique: Les noms de l'innommable', *Mots/Les langages du politique* no. 56, September 1998, 138–41; Hans-Dieter Zimmermann, 'Holokauston, holocaustum, holocaust. Die Bedeutung des Wortes "Holocaust"', *Die Neue Gesellschaft/Frankfurter Hefte* no. 12, 1997, 1120–23.
2. Stuart Hall, 'The Work of Representation', in Stuart Hall, ed., *Representation. Cultural Representations and Signifying Practices*, London, Thousand Oaks & New Dehli: Sage, Open University Press, 1997, 13–64, 44.
3. James Young, *The Texture of Memory*, New Haven & London: Yale, 1993, 90.
4. Studies of sites of memory have been undertaken in several countries. In France, see Pierre Nora, ed., *Les Lieux de mémoire*, 7 vols, Paris, Gallimard, 1984–1993; idem, *The Realms of Memory: The Construction of the French Past*, trans. Arthur Goldhammer, 3 vols, New York: Columbia University Press, 1997–1998. In Germany, see Etienne François and Hagen Schulze, eds, *Deutsche Erinnerungsorte*, 3 vols, Munich: C. H. Beck, 2001.
5. Anthony Cohen, *The Symbolic Construction of Community*, Chichester, London & New York: Ellis Horword and Tavistock Publishers, 1985, 50.
6. Young, *The Texture of Memory*, 90.
7. See Michael Diers, ed., *Mon(u)mente. Formen und Funktionen ephemerer Denkmäler*, Berlin: Akademie Verlag, 1993; Felix Reuße, *Das Denkmal an der Grenze seiner Sprachfähigkeit*, Stuttgart: Klett Cotta, 1995; Walter Grasskamp, ed., *Unerwünschte Monumente. Moderne Kunst im Stadtraum*, Munich: Verlag Silke Schreiber, 1992; James Young, 'The Counter-Monument: Memory Against Itself in Germany Today', *Critical Inquiry* no. 2, 1992, 267–86; Reinhart Koselleck, 'Kriegerdenkmale als Identitätsstiftungen der Überlebenden', in Odo Marquard and Karlheinz Stierle, eds, *Identität*, Munich: Wilhelm Fink Verlag, 1979, 255–276, 274.
8. For a critique of the term 'identity', see Richard Handler, 'Is "Identity" a Useful Concept?', in John Gillis, ed., *Commemorations. The Politics of National Identity*, Princeton: Princeton University Press, 1994, 27–40.
9. Nora, 'Das Abenteuer der *Lieux de mémoire*', in Etienne François et al., eds, *Nation und Emotion*, Göttingen: Vandenhoeck & Ruprecht, 1995, 83–92, 83.
10. Nora, interview with Emmanuel de Roux, *Le Monde*, 29 November 1994, 2.
11. See Institut d'Histoire du Temps Présent, ed., *Ecrire l'histoire du temps présent*, Paris: CNRS Editions, 1993; Agnès Chauveau and Philippe Tétart, eds, *Questions à l'histoire des temps présents*, Brussels: Editions Complexe, 1992.
12. Marc Bloch, *The Historian's Craft*, trans. Peter Putnam, Manchester: Manchester University Press, 1954, 39–47.
13. Henry Rousso, *Vichy. L'événement, la mémoire, l'histoire*, Paris: Gallimard, 2001, 686.
14. Ibid., 43ff. Cf. Bloch's comparison of historical and judicial method, in *The Historian's Craft*, Chapter 4, 138–142.
15. Ibid., 45.

Part I

Monuments and Collective Memory

1

Monuments in History

The Longevity of the Monumental Genre

In his famous essay on 'Monuments' of 1927, the writer Robert Musil claims that there is nothing more invisible to the human eye than a monument. 'The remarkable thing about monuments is that one does not notice them. There is nothing in the world so invisible as a monument.'[1] The suggestion that precisely those images, figures and events that people strive to represent in public should go unheeded provokes numerous questions about the relation of individuals and groups to symbols and their impact as focal points of political communication. If familiarity with everyday objects indeed erodes the curiosity of passers-by, why do we continue to build such objects? And once built, how do these symbols influence our perception of urban surroundings and sense of belonging to a historical community, even in barely perceptible ways? Musil's radical scepticism towards the visibility of public monuments is grounded on three arguments. First, he claims that anything that endures loses its power to influence the senses of the observer, such that the familiarity of a statue seen on one's daily travels renders the statue banal. Second, at the time when Musil was writing, public monuments increasingly had to compete with media advertisements in order to capture the attention of the public. Third, everyday settings for monuments such as street corners and public squares, which are decorated with dynamic scenes of galloping horses and sword-wielding soldiers frozen in battle, render the heroic men of history ridiculous and thus, claims Musil, 'effectively precipitate them into the ocean of oblivion'.[2]

The apparent invisibility of public monuments, ensuing from their duration and familiarity, or even ridiculous appearance, is partially a consequence of the sheer longevity of this genre, since monuments have been in use as a form of social and political communication throughout history, during which their repertoire of forms has barely changed. Human and mythic icons situated in urban or natural public (rather than private or courtly) spaces are common to sepulchral art of the Middle Ages, decorative sculpture of the Renaissance and Baroque, nineteenth-century national memorials and war memorials of the twentieth century. Their function – the cohesion of social groups via the cultivation of collective memories – has likewise remained consistent even though the messages transmitted by monuments and their techniques have differed immensely. Even the Vél' d'Hiv' monument and the Holocaust Monument conform formally to monumental tradition. Although these monuments provoked unconventional conflictory modes of social remembrance, they both occupy sites of national significance in capital cities and are cast in bronze and stone. Thus the apparent invisibility provoked by the short-term familiarity of monuments, as Musil argues, is compounded by the long-term familiarity of a form of symbolic communication and cultivation of collective memory whose semantic and political function – urging us to understand and identify with, love or fear historical figures and events – harbours few surprises.

In the long term, therefore, we fail to see monuments not only because their enduring presence in our home towns is familiar, because they are overshadowed by an advertising hoarding or because they appear ridiculous, but also because the monumental genre has remained relatively unchanged over the ages while habits of human perception and communication have altered dramatically. The reason for this lies in the gulf that exists between forms of commemoration and collective narratives prescribed by state institutions on the one hand, and individual experience and understanding of commemorated events on the other. National monuments today meet with scepticism, as demonstrated by the public debates they provoke – debates that are further fuelled by the sheer number of people whose opinion is solicited by the mass media. Monuments today no longer remain the sole symbolic property of the associations or states that instigate them. They appeal to mass support while at the same time preventing genuinely plural participation in them, due to their inherently centralising symbolic function. The administrative structure of states is founded on a central hierarchy of both human and symbolic resources, and no state can claim legitimacy without recourse to a symbolic centre, as the political scientist Murray Edelman has demonstrated.[3] Political and symbolic structures are thus concomitant, in so far as they are both guided by the antagonistic principles of centricity and eccentricity. While artists and political representatives alike recognise eccentricity, they systematically return to centricity as if guided by a natural law.[4]

Art historians have amply demonstrated the longevity of this artistic and political genre. In his essay on 'Sculpture for Outdoors' from 1978,

Ernst Gombrich describes how Florentine artists and dignitaries competed during the fifteenth century to secure power in the city-state with a public display of sculptures on the Piazza della Signorina. Rival commissions attracted 'big' names among contemporary artists including Bandinelli, Donatello and Michaelangelo, provoking what Gombrich calls a 'chain reaction'[5] of projects. Sponsored by the state authorities, these projects also solicited considerable public criticism of their effectiveness and pedagogical utility, criticism that was fuelled by the very popularity of public monuments. Unlike the printed word, monuments made sense to both literate and illiterate citizens of Renaissance Florence.

The search for political legitimisation via the symbolic possession of urban spaces has been consistent from antiquity onwards. Large numbers of monuments, competition between commissioners and between artists, and complex commissioning processes and public debates also characterised waves of statuomania after the French revolution and during the rise of nationalist movements in the nineteenth century, but also during the National Socialist and communist dictatorships in the twentieth century and in new nation-states established following the dissolution of the Soviet bloc in central and eastern Europe. Today, the streets of Berlin, Moscow, Paris or Washington are littered with monuments and memorials whose inaugurations were preceded by competitions and debates and which arose as a result of chain reactions similar to those described by Gombrich in Renaissance Florence. Further long-term consistencies in the history of monuments include their ritual destruction in times of revolution (following the French revolution and the fall of communist regimes after 1989), the collection and exhibition in parks and museums of monuments belonging to defunct political regimes (also customary after 1789 and 1989), or the construction of new monuments following the foundation of new states following wars and revolutions. The securing of evidence of lost empires in urban landscapes is likewise a transhistorical phenomenon shared by major capital cities – though the securing of traces of National Socialist architecture in Berlin is motivated by entirely different intentions than, for example, those underpinning the conservation and reconstruction of sites from the Wilhelmine Empire, from ancient Rome, or from the Napoleonic era in Paris, for example. Such historical consistencies in the treatment and function of public symbols confirm the suggestion by the sociologist Norbert Elias that humankind is in essence a symbolic creature whose societies depend upon symbols in order to sustain collective communication, identification and orientation.[6]

While the generic function of historical monuments as focal points of collective identity and as carriers of historical tradition has been largely consistent over time, the specific forms of icons and their meanings have not. The works of the historian Reinhart Koselleck have demonstrated the historical evolution of monumental iconography during modernity, ranging from the dynastic effigies of the French *ancien régime*, republican icons from 1789–1870, national sites focusing on military victories and defeats in France and Germany from 1870–1945, and a more diffuse repertoire of national, local, or even anti-memorials from 1945.[7] But this periodisation is deceptive. Since there has been little formal consistency of monuments at any one time, Koselleck deduces his periodisation largely from the function of monuments as a means to legitimise the cohesion of states and societies in the present on the basis of historical interpretation. Dynastic memorials, for example, legitimise the right of individuals to inherit political offices, while republican memorials legitimise the meritocratic ideal based on just deserts of individual endeavour, most often endeavour on the battlefield by soldiers in arms embodying values considered worthy of emulation by future generations. The republican period also witnessed the democratisation of memorials now increasingly erected not in private but in public places, as well as the democratisation of memorials for the dead represented by lists of individuals' names inscribed in the name of a 'sovereign' people.[8] Koselleck further defines the subsequent nationalist period of commemorations as one in which the dead were remembered essentially as soldiers who fought in the name of national collectives, first as heroes in victory or defeat then, after the First World War, also as objects of national mourning.

We may trace an even broader history of the meanings and social utility of monuments. Beginning with the religious roots of collective memory cultures that employed symbolic icons, ritual prayer and song as a means to remembering, most historians highlight the passage from premodern to modern forms of collective remembering, which led to the increased materialisation of memory in symbolic and written recordings, to the rationalisation and individualisation of memorial practices, and to both the politicisation and democratisation of memory and memorials following the intervention of modern states in their planning – a process that has largely been accelerated by increased accessibility to monuments via printed and electronic media. Contemporary western memory cultures have certainly built upon this cultural foundation.

Closer to the present day, Sergiusz Michalski's history of public monuments begins with the 'apogee of the [monumental] tradition at the end of the 1800s'.[9] This account classifies sculptural styles in relation to their pedagogical efficacy in specific historical contexts, including the French Third Republic, the cult of Bismarck in Wilhelmine Germany, First World War memorials in Europe, monuments erected during the Nazi and communist dictatorships, the renunciation of heroic forms in favour of invisibility and 'inversion' following the Second World War, third-world memorials and, finally, developments following the fall of communist regimes in Europe after 1990. Although Michalski situates these memorial types in their respective political and historical contexts, the use of the

French Belle Epoque as a yardstick for all subsequent developments in memorial public art presupposes that subsequent monumental techniques were in decline, leading to a 'crisis of figuration' in the twentieth century and, more specifically, to 'new directions' after 1945.[10] Characteristic of Michalski's nostalgia for figurative monuments and the effective public pedagogy practised in late nineteenth-century France is his praise of the partially abstract yet militaristic Bir Hakeim memorial in the west of Paris, evoking a military charge with brandished symbolic shields and lances in the classic style of battle paintings, as 'one of the most outstanding Western war memorials created since 1945'.[11] Michalski's art-historical classification of monumental periods and styles provides a useful source of historical reference but does not adequately account for the complex process by which new, in particular non-figurative, memorials after the Second World War arose out of and provoked their political and social environment. The decline of figuration in the twentieth century should not be defined as a 'crisis', but as an innovative challenge to conventional forms of symbolic public communication. Rather than look to the past for models with which to measure contemporary developments in monumental art, one should ask: to what extent has the historical rupture of 1945 caused societies, on the initiative of politicians and artists, to abandon, build upon or modify the tradition of public monuments?

Innovations in Monumental Techniques since 1945

We may interpret monuments historically in terms of their changing styles, politically in terms of their expediency at a particular moment in time, or socially in terms of their public appeal. In reality, however, monuments require a combination of all three approaches, for they are essentially an expression of the changing means of symbolic communication about the past that is exposed simultaneously to political and social forces. The period since the Second World War has not only ushered in new monumental artistic styles alongside conventional ones but has also marked a historic formal and functional rupture in approaches to memorial practice. Several specialists of monumental art, including Aleida Assmann, Reinhart Koselleck, Peter Reichel, Richard Serra, Jochen Spielmann and Jay Winter, argue that 1945 marked a watershed in the history of monuments in terms of both style and utility. In a radical vein, Serra and Winter bear witness to the inadequacy of symbolic language as a medium of collective mourning following the persecution and genocide.[12] Reichel adopts a more compromising functionalist approach by interpreting existing monuments in relation to symbolic practices of successive political regimes, although he draws attention to the difficulty of securing social consensus after the Second World War in historical communities whose traditions had been shattered by historical discontinuity. These communities were initially reluctant to construct a common identity in relation to national memorials and, at least in the West (in contrast to the East, which saw a burgeoning of memorials of liberation after 1945), either renounced the construction of monuments or else constructed ones that did not conform to an accepted set of memorial forms or practices.[13] Spielmann interprets monuments as symptoms of an ongoing process of political communication about historical tradition, as the 'conflictory negotiation of the interpretation of history'.[14] He traces five periods in the history of monuments in West Germany: the erection of provisional monuments on historical sites during the late 1940s; the drive towards anti-socialist monuments in memory of the conservative anti-Nazi resistance constructed after the foundation of the two German states and during the 1950s; the switch from monument building to political debates about monuments during the 1960s; the increased commitment of artists to questioning the very function of public monuments during the late 1960s and 1970s; and the increasing exploitation of public monuments as focal points of political controversy during the 1980s, provoked either by local pressure groups or by state interests.[15] Assmann defines 1945 as a moment of revolution in the history of memorials, one that introduced a new 'grammar' of collective memory. The paradigms of military victory or defeat, the political utility of memory cultures for nation-states and the logic of forgetting as a basis for forgiving and remembering as a basis for honour and revenge, argues Assmann, are now being challenged by a transnational paradigm of collective remembering ensuring that memory cultures are increasingly founded on intercultural and universal ethical standards and critical self-reflection.[16] According to these functionalist approaches, postwar monuments testify to the search for a new symbolic language that may ensure meaningful political as well as social communication about history after 1945. While renouncing the quest to establish an adequate iconographic language, they consider monuments as signs of broken traditions and of the attempt to reconstruct coherent memory cultures.

Specialists of modern and contemporary public monuments unanimously suggest that the postwar period in the West heralded a radical abandonment of prewar commemorative practices. Figurative war memorials were generally renounced altogether, giving way to provisional local memorials. The sites of concentration camps were chosen by the Allies on which to erect simple obelisks. War cemeteries were established outside, not inside towns. In many cases, communities chose not to build new monuments but to modify existing First World War memorials in urban sites or on village squares with supplementary plaques, turning them into memorials commemorating victims of both wars. The local, provisional and inconsistent nature of memorial practices after 1945 is an expression of a qualitatively new type of historical consciousness. The mass industrial and meaningless killings of the Second World War could not be adequately commemorated by means of traditional ritual and monuments appealing to a sense of identification. Moreover, the realisation that the traditional vindication of military victories, victimhood or heroism in memorials was not only no longer historically but also morally untenable challenged nations like France and Germany to seek new types of monuments and rituals. This challenge culminated in what is possibly the most sophisticated response to the dilemma of national commemoration in the wake of persecution and genocide when, in France and Germany during the 1990s, local pressure groups and citizens' initiatives representing Jewish victims urged politicians to recognise the necessity of acknowledging and commemorating their own perpetrators. Prewar paradigms of collective commemoration – victory, defeat and honour – were clearly inadequate responses to public calls of this kind. The challenge of publicly acknowledging war crimes gave rise to monuments which did not primarily appeal to a sense of collective belonging but raised and provoked questions about historical meaning and about the retrospective rhetorical and visual construction and transmission of these meanings. Formal innovations of commemorative practice in this period went beyond abstraction and included such idiosyncrasies as negative representations, mostly of empty spaces in place of traditional human forms, and invisible or disappearing forms.

In light of the extent of suffering ensuing from the Second World War and the almost impossible challenge of fixing or lending this past meaning to which people can collectively relate, it is perhaps surprising that monuments continue to be used as a basis for political communication. Yet this tension increases fascination with monuments as a form of political communication, precisely because the unimaginable suffering of victims and survivors of the genocide of the 1940s defies artistic forms of commemoration. A frequent solution to the dearth of adequate styles and forms has been the use of conceptual techniques in 'counter-monuments'. These are designed not only to commemorate the past but also to encourage and provoke spectators to reflect on the process and tradition of commemoration itself. They are born out of the manipulation of everyday symbols and words in monuments, and the wider accessibility of monuments via mass printed and electronic media. They are also born out of the political commitment of individual artists who became active during the 1960s. Jochen Gerz, Esther Shalev-Gerz, Hans Haacke and Norbert Rademacher, to name just a few in France and Germany, not only refuse to celebrate military victories or glorify heroic defeats as practised in the nineteenth and early twentieth centuries, but integrate into their works an acute awareness of the inadequacy of traditional rhetorical and symbolic languages to convey or translate either the horror of events or the complexity of coming to terms with them.

How can we define monuments conceptually in the early twenty-first century? While one can look back on a relatively coherent repertoire of styles and contexts, ranging from national movements, war memorials of the First World War, the proliferation of memorials under the National Socialist and communist dictatorships, there appear at present to be no collectively accepted conventions governing the forms, motifs, themes or messages of public monuments. 'The future of the public monument', claims Michalski, 'is now more open than ever.'[17] In countries of the former Soviet Union and the eastern bloc, there is an evident trend towards the restoration and reconstruction of national symbols which existed prior to the communist regimes, as exemplified in Moscow, but also in Berlin, where the former Hohenzollern Palace, the residence of Prussian Electors, Kings and Kaisers, is due to be rebuilt from scratch. At the same time, however, there are few monuments that explicitly commemorate the negative heritage of communist regimes, just as there were few monuments erected in remembrance of persecution and genocide in the immediate aftermath of the Second World War. War crimes of either the Second World War or the Cold War clearly do not lend themselves to the conventional social practice of commemoration as a basis for the construction of memory cultures. It is for this reason that the Second World War is frequently commemorated by suspending the construction of memorials while embarking upon prolonged public debates over their forms, sites, meanings, management and costs, as witnessed in Paris and Berlin during the 1990s. The tradition of collectively commemorating the past is thus simultaneously spurred on and thwarted by negative, if not horrifying, memories.

In the face of the formal inconsistency of Holocaust monuments, whether in a local, national or international context, we may nevertheless trace consistencies in their social functions. In similar fashion to Koselleck's studies of monuments up to the end of the First World War, I will propose in this study an understanding of contemporary monuments defined not primarily in terms of form or style, but in terms of their political and social impact. Contemporary monuments are largely meaningless if encountered in isolation from their accompanying public debates. Planning and formal styles are determined by a number of agents and social forces in open conflict: politicians, artists, local and national administrators, local and national traditions, and competition procedures. A true picture of what a monument means can therefore only be attained by taking into consideration all these forces and agents. This definition of a monument as a social process, and as a meeting of symbols and words, is more equivocal than art-historical concepts of style and form, yet it does help us to appreciate the multidimensional, political and artistic, aspects of public art.

Transnational Patterns of National Memory Cultures

To what extent do contemporary war memorials represent the new or restructured national memory cultures that emerged following the end of the Cold War? Can we legitimately label them as 'French' or 'German', that is, as products of a specific place and time, or should they be subsumed to the increasingly transnational nature of Second World War commemorations? Although the fall of the socialist regimes in eastern Europe confirmed the lack of social credibility of ideological public symbols, although social memory transgresses national borders, and although monuments commemorating war crimes constitute a disturbing rather than binding force of social cohesion, states continue to draw upon monuments as an expression of national tradition. While the social perception of historical events has changed, the means of representing them has largely remained the same. In France and Germany, which both bore responsibility, albeit in different ways, for the deportation and mass murder of Jews, gypsies, political dissenters, handicapped people and homosexuals, a large proportion of contemporary public monuments are those dedicated to the memory of crimes committed during the Second World War, in particular in the capital cities of Paris and Berlin. The persecution and genocide is undoubtedly a key focal point of public war memorials and, indirectly, of French and German self-understanding, but also of a critical and transnational (though not exclusively European) memory culture. The relation between these memory cultures and their symbolic representations therefore requires thorough comparative research.

The Stockholm Forum on Holocaust Education in January 2000 testified to the keen international interest in a cooperative approach to the education of the history of genocide. Even since the 1980s, state symbolic and ritual gestures in memory of the persecution and genocide have become more frequent and widespread. A Holocaust Education Trust was set up in the United Kingdom in 1988, which introduced the study of the persecution and genocide of the Second World War into the national school curriculum, promoted projects for permanent exhibitions within the Imperial War Museum in London and Manchester, and helped to set up a national 'Holocaust Memorial Day'. In Austria, the spectre of collaboration reemerged when Jörg Haider's Freedom Party (FPÖ) joined the government coalition in October 1999 after winning 27 per cent of the vote, and following campaigning in which Haider used anti-Semitic rhetoric and legitimised National Socialist policies. Switzerland opened access to files concerning its bank deposits held during the war. In July 2001, the Polish president Alexander Kwasniewski publicly apologised for the persecution and massacre of Jews by Polish inhabitants of the town of Jedwabne in 1941. In France, successive presidents, François Mitterrand and Jacques Chirac, engaged in a prolonged debate over the necessity to recognise state crimes in the early 1990s, while in Germany associations and local and national governments committed themselves to building a national memorial dedicated to the 'murdered Jews of Europe'. And in 2003, scientific delegations discussed plans for central Holocaust museums in Paris and Brussels. A comparison of any of these memory cultures would permit us to identify local and national particularities and transnational analogies that remain less obvious in single case studies. Yet the French and German cases lend themselves especially to comparative study because they both represent processes in which national memories of war crimes were institutionalised in the form of central monuments and public debates about them. Not only were these processes of memorial institutionalisation structurally similar, involving governments, associations and the media; they also drew on comparable types of rhetoric, narrative and metaphor in order to legitimise their respective national histories. The transnational character of contemporary memory cultures therefore resides not only in the formation of communities of social memory or solidarity across political boundaries, but also in the shared structural affinities of apparently distinct cultures.

In France, during the 1990s, Second World War memorials inevitably became caught up in debates over the legacy of de Gaulle and over the public memory of deported victims. De Gaulle, leader of the Free French Forces abroad, had masterminded the myth of the French as a nation united in support of the Resistance, a myth that began to crumble during the 1970s but whose historical tenacity became fully recognised only in the 1990s. In Germany, war memorials of the 1990s also served as backdrops for sobering public discussions about the status of the Second World War in contemporary collective memory. The 'Bitburg' affair of 1985, when the US President Ronald Reagan accompanied the German Chancellor Helmut Kohl on a visit to a cemetery where SS officers lay buried, had already aroused intense public protest when Reagan stated that these officers, no less than victims of the concentration camps, were also victims of the Second World War.[18] A second public levelling of the difference between victims and perpetrators occurred in 1993 in connection with the Neue Wache ('New Guard') memorial in Berlin. The former royal guardhouse that had served during the Weimar Republic as a memorial for victims of the First World War then, in the German Democratic Republic, as a memorial for victims of the Second World War, was renovated and rededicated 'to the victims of war and tyranny' (*Den Opfern von Krieg und Gewaltherrschaft*). This memorial too became known as a label for a dubious disregard for the distinction between war victims as victims of National Socialist persecution and war victims generally, in which dead soldiers of different political persuasions and countries as well as dead victims of genocide were subsumed under the universal category of 'victim' (see Chapter Four). Feeding into both these memorial debates were polarised attitudes towards the pedagogical utility of public remembrance of the persecution and genocide in contemporary Germany, which pitted conservative historians like Ernst Nolte and Michael Stürmer against critics such as the philosopher Jürgen Habermas and the historian Hans Mommsen during the so-called Historians' Dispute (*Historikerstreit*) of 1986. This discussion had been triggered by lectures and newspaper articles in which Nolte claimed that the concentration camps were a reaction to the prison and labour camps of the Gulag, that they were not a specific historical phenomenon, and that they should therefore be relativised in relation to historical precedents such as the industrial revolution and Russian revolution. These revisionist theses questioned the specificity of the genocide against the Jews and, by implication, played down the responsibility of perpetrators.[19] Memorial politics in both France and Germany during the late twentieth century were thus governed by conflicting mythicising and demythicising forces. Notwithstanding the blunders of the Mitterrand and Kohl eras, memorial debates continued to oscillate between expressions of nostalgia for a 'normal' national identity based on the selective forgetting of war crimes, and the desire to make a clean break from the mythicising historical visions of the postwar leaders President de Gaulle and Chancellor Konrad Adenauer. In both countries, these issues were regularly negotiated in direct relation to symbolic memorial sites and to symbolic political leaders.

In spite of the distinct historical and social contexts of memorial debates in France and Germany during the 1990s, several parallels between these two memory cultures emerged. First, state representatives publicly acknowledged domestic war crimes, mourned the human loss, and thereby gave rise to national memorials and commemorations of events (war crimes) that not only did not conform to, but also indeed negated traditions of national commemoration. Second, presidents Mitterrand and Chirac, Chancellor Gerhard Schröder and Wolfgang Thierse, President of the German Bundestag from 1998, all spoke openly of national crimes while insisting that they had been in principle negated in postwar constitutions. Chirac's evocation of republican values in his speech on the site of the Vél' d'Hiv' in 1995, and Thierse's defense of human rights and dignity in the name of German people in his speech on the site of the Holocaust Monument in January 2000 are two examples of explicit references to constitutional principles. Moreover, the moral, psychological and legal commemorative discourse about the Second World War took place against a background of increased pressure to establish not only European political integration but also a common set of values based on human rights, rooted in the common memory of the genocide of the Second World War. The commemoration of domestic war crimes, the regular reiteration by state representatives of postwar constitutions, European integration and pressure for memorials from historians and associations from below are part of an international discourse of anti-nationalism, fuelled and exemplified by the public commemorations of the 1990s. The monuments erected within this context are thus ostensibly national but also demonstrate the transnational patterns within contemporary memory cultures and their representations.

Holocaust Monuments in the Context of French–Jewish and German–Jewish Relations

The significance of memorials of the Second World War emerging in the 1990s was further influenced by the status and public perception of Jewish communities. Any account of Holocaust monuments in the 1990s must acknowledge this social context, in which commemorations and monuments in memory of war crimes serve to articulate in public, sometimes even in openly pedagogical political gestures, images of the imagined 'other' with which national self-understanding is cultivated in each country. The Vichy regime not only secured the disillusionment of the Jewish community with state institutions and with the relative acculturation of French Jewry established since the revolution, but also assured a split among French Jews in search of a new identity. Zionism and domestic support for Israel flourished from its foundation in 1947 and again during the Six-Day War in 1967 alongside Richard Marienstras's Diasporism movement, founded in the 1950s in support of the recognition of minorities settled in France,[20] and alongside a number of intellectuals' defence of a return to religion (Benny Lévy), or to classical ethical values (Shmuel Trigano). Despite the immigration of some 235,000 Sephardi Jews into France in the early 1960s following the Algerian War,[21] who were not among the direct victims of France's collaboration with the National Socialists and now constitute threequarters of the French Jewish population, the persecution and genocide of the Second World War remain the most influential uniting factors of French Jewish identity. The rise of anti-Semitism during the 1970s and 1980s, the Holocaust denials of Robert Faurisson, the increased awareness of French collaboration with National Socialism as a result of legal inquiries and trials of collaborators from the 1970s onwards, not to mention the Judeophobia since the beginning of the second intifada in November 2000, have all fuelled Jewish particularism in France. In this context, the key to understanding the contribution of the Vél' d'Hiv' monument to French–Jewish relations lies in the rhetorical formulations of its campaigners. Petitioners insisted without reserve that recognition of Vichy crimes should be made by the highest state authority, namely the president. In other words, the petition was not an act of subversion but a plea soliciting a more explicit state commitment to sustaining the public memory of Vichy. The fact that the petitioners' condition for the success of their campaign was the *state institutionalisation* of the recognition of victims merely reinforced the authority of the state as the guarantor of a French national memory culture. In a historical perspective, this act was conceived as a symbolic reparation for war crimes but also, more specifically, for the wrong done by de Gaulle when he imposed an arms embargo on Israel during the Six-Day War, and when he expressed explicit resentment of French Jewish support for Israel during this war in public statements liable to fuel anti-Semitic sentiment. As will be seen in Chapter Three, much debate over the Vél' d'Hiv' during the 1990s was framed in terms of de Gaulle's symbolic distortions of the memories of the Second World War, such that the Vél' d'Hiv' only makes sense in this historical perspective: as a symbolic correction of the Resistance myth, as reparation for the handling of the Six-Day War, and as a corrective complement to Gaullist urban memorials of the Second World War that have been standing since the 1960s.

In her assessment of the status of Jews in Germany in the 1990s, the sociologist Lynn Rapaport succinctly describes how the persecution and genocide of the Second World War also continues to be the principal factor determining German–Jewish relations, 'the common experience that unites Jews and Germans today', yet one which 'simultaneously stands in the way of their readjustment'.[22] However, most historians, including Michael Brenner, Sander Gilman, Lynn Rapaport and (in France) Michel Wieviorka, agree that the 1990s were marked by an increased 'ethnicisation' of public perceptions of Jews and of the genocide. German Jews expressed their identity in terms of ethnicity either as an expression of faith[23] or as a sense of cultural belonging to a community founded on Holocaust remembrance.[24] Likewise, they are still inadvertently perceived as a measure of cultural 'difference' in Germany in spite of their relative integration.[25]

Historians of German–Jewish relations commonly argue that contemporary public attitudes towards the impact of the persecution and genocide on Jewish culture continue to be influenced by cultural representations rather than by lived experience. One could argue that memory cultures, sustained by monuments, museums and commemorative ritual, by definition reinforce the impression that the remembered culture is no longer part of the present, and thus prolongs the displacement of Jewish culture in Germany from present-day religious and cultural practices to memories of past deportation and genocide. In other words, there exists a danger that Holocaust remembrance and its recurrent echoes in contemporary anti-Semitism prevent the construction of a positive German–Jewish tradition or identity in Germany today. Gilman points out that anti-Semitic acts of aggression during the 1990s were largely directed at representations of the past such as cemeteries and memorials, rather than at the realities of Jewish life in Germany. 'Living

Jews are not seen because they are not understood to be present, even while their presence is the means by which other groups are constructed.'[26] In spite of the rapidly growing Jewish community in Germany during the 1990s, the much-debated Holocaust Monument in Berlin is primarily an expression of the search for a normalisation of national self-understanding on the basis of Holocaust remembrance and only secondarily an appeal to remember and thereby attempt to understand the historical, ethical and political consequences of the persecution and genocide of the Second World War for the life of both Jews and non-Jews in the present. It is for this reason that the journals *Jüdische Korrespondenz*, the magazine of the Jewish Cultural Association, or *Jüdisches Berlin*, of the Jewish Community in Berlin, devoted scant coverage to the memorial project. Jewish representatives in Germany initially distanced themselves from the debate, only joining in when it became the symbol of a political refusal to accept rising right-wing parties. Brenner takes up a commentary by the journalist Joseph Joffee, who in 1993 scorned Holocaust memorials in Germany, 'sites of modern idolatry', as 'alien to the principles of true Jewish memory, which only obscure authentic Jewish identity'.[27] It remains to be seen whether the growing local Jewish community in Berlin will in future welcome and adopt memorials like the Holocaust Monument or the Jewish Museum and therefore contribute not only towards the reconciliation of Jews and Germans, but also towards a memory culture that reconciles the past and a new living community of Jews in Germany, thus integrating the collective memory of the persecution and genocide into prewar and postwar German–Jewish tradition. In this sense, public conflicts over these symbols during the 1990s are paradigmatic of the national memory culture. Following the marginalisation of war crimes during the 1950s, the polarised conflict between generations and the remarginalisation of crimes perceived as a product of the capitalist economy during the 1960s and 1970s, and the relativisation of crimes committed under communist and National Socialist dictatorships during the 1980s (this was the claim of the historian Ernst Nolte in 1986, which triggered the Historian's Dispute), the symbolic debates of the 1990s partially corrected the distortions of previous decades. To this day, however, historical knowledge of the perpetration and genocide does not concur with official public commemorations or with private recollections and perceptions of family history. The former is motivated at best by the quest to establish facts, the second by moral and pedagogical principles, and the latter by a reluctance to conceive of one's own responsibility or that of one's relatives.[28] (This same reluctance was the object of criticism in Germany of the Neue Wache memorial in 1993, of Martin Walser's verbal attack on the culture of Holocaust remembrance in 1998, of the commemorations of bombing raids on German cities following the publication of Jörg Friedrich's book *Der Brand* in 2002, and of the planned Centre

Against Expulsion (Zentrum gegen Vertreibung) in 2003, dealing with the victimisation of expellees at the end of the Second World War.) Since the Holocaust Monument and the Vél' d'Hiv' only symbolically integrate the victimised 'other' into the narratives of official memory cultures, and only indirectly point towards the identity of perpetrators, it is unlikely that the monuments alone will enable such critical narratives to penetrate individual self-perceptions and thereby bridge the gap between public commemorations and private recollection of the Second World War.

Yet there are grounds for arguing that the historical narratives projected by urban memorials of the Second World War in Paris and Berlin during the 1990s will, if perceived in connection with their political and historical contexts, reduce the gap between private and public remembrance. The construction of the Vél' d'Hiv' monument, which marks the integration of the memory of Jewish victims of deportation and the end of the myth of a nation united in resistance, was the immediate consequence of political ritual and public debate from 1986 onwards. The Holocaust Monument is also more than just a monument, for it is the product of debate over the meaning of the past, and symbolises the memory of Jewish victims alongside other major memorial sites such as the Topography of Terror, the Neue Wache, the Memorial of German Resistance, the House of the Wannsee Conference and the new Jewish Museum, which form a plural 'narrative' of memories of the Second World War: mourning victims, documenting persecution, and rediscovering prewar German–Jewish traditions. The temptation to equate French and German national memory cultures with urban hardware, that is, the symbolic evidence of historical monuments and museums, overlooks preponderant commemorative software in the form of rhetorical expressions of cultural memory encountered in newspapers, political debates, academic conferences, pamphlets and private conversations that together constitute social memory. Monuments are not direct urban expressions of social memory. They do not 'reflect' the memory culture of a given group or society but only one aspect or momentary crystallisation thereof. It is in this vein that Part II of this study will undertake the interdisciplinary exploration of the rhetoric related to urban monuments.

* * *

On the basis of these preliminary remarks on the historical legacy and periodisation of monuments until the present day, what relevance do Musil's remarks about monuments in 1927 have for our understanding of the role of monuments in the constitution of national memory cultures today? Are monuments still inherently invisible or do we see or even appreciate them in ways of which we are not even aware? Musil's suggestion that invisibility is inherent to monuments requires renewed scrutiny. The question remains, for example, whether the short- and long-term familiarity of public monuments is invariably a guarantee of their invisibility, and whether these objects do in fact influence a community other than by soliciting identification and emulation. Did the competitions and public criticism of public sculpture in Renaissance Florence not educate the Florentine public to think about and debate the political necessity of historical icons beyond their mere artistic merit as public ornamentation? And did communities witnessing the destruction of the Bastille or the vandalism following the French revolution remain docile or indifferent towards 'invisible' monuments of their day? In the period following the Second World War in Europe, it is likewise difficult to remain indifferent to the challenge of collective symbolic representation following catastrophic events that defy traditional representation. Although historians like Koselleck and Winter largely agree that the historical break in tradition in 1945 brought a break in the formal language of collective symbolics, they do not explore in depth how this formal language has changed or what languages are emerging as a result. Understanding this change and responses to it in the present day is a central challenge to contemporary societies that foster historical communities on the basis of their citizens' collective communication in what Elias defines as the symbolic 'fifth dimension'.[29]

Notes

1. Robert Musil, 'Denkmale', in *Nachlaß zu Lebzeiten*, Hamburg: Rowohlt, 1957, 59–63, 59 (translations by the author).
2. Ibid., 63.
3. Murray Edelman, *The Symbolic Uses of Politics*, Urbana, Chicago, London: University of Illinois Press, 1964; idem, *Constructing the Political Spectacle*, Chicago & London: University of Chicago Press, 1988.
4. See Rudolf Arnheim, *The Power of the Center. A Study of Composition in the Visual Arts*, Berkeley, Los Angeles & London: University of California Press, 1988, Chapter 1.
5. Ernst Gombrich, *The Uses of Images. Studies in the Social Function of Art and Visual Communication*, London: Phaidon, 1999, 150.
6. Norbert Elias, *The Symbol Theory*, London, Newbury Park & New Delhi: Sage, 1989, 57.
7. Reinhart Koselleck, *Zur politischen Ikonographie des gewaltsamen Todes. Ein deutsch-französischer Vergleich*, Basel: Schwabe, 1998; idem, 'Kriegerdenkmäler als Identitätsstiftungen der Überlebenden', in Marquard and Stierle, eds, *Identität*, 255–75.
8. See Koselleck, *Zur politischen Ikonographie*, 20.
9. Sergiusz Michalski, *Public Monuments. Art in Political Bondage 1870–1997*, London: Reaktion Books, 1998, 9.
10. Ibid., 8, 154.
11. Ibid., 169. Michalski is referring to Albert Féraud and Marc Landowski's 'Homage to Marshal Koenig and His Troops' at Porte Maillot, Paris, 1984.

12. See Hamburger Kunstverein, ed., *Richard Serra: Zum Holocaust-Mahnmal in Berlin*, trans. Barbara Uppenkamp, Hamburg: Hamburger Kunstverein, 1998, 8; Winter, *Sites of Memory, Sites of Mourning: The Great War in European Cultural History*, Cambridge: Cambridge University Press, 1995, 9.
13. Peter Reichel, *Politik mit der Erinnerung. Gedächtnisorte im Streit um die nationalsozialistische Vergangenheit*, Munich: Hanser, 1995, 41.
14. Jochen Spielmann, *Entwürfe zur Sinngebung des Sinnlosen. Zu einer Theorie des Denkmals als Manifestation des 'kulturellen Gedächtnisses'. Der Wettbewerb für ein Denkmal für Auschwitz*, Ph.D. dissertation, Freie Universität Berlin, 1990, 3.
15. Spielmann, 'Steine des Anstoßes – Denkmale in Erinnerung an den Nationalsozialismus in der Bundesrepublik Deutschland', *Kritische Berichte* no. 3, 1988, 5–16.
16. Aleida Assmann, 'Individuelles und kollektives Gedächtnis – Formen, Funktionen und Medien', in Kurt Wettengel, ed., *Das Gedächtnis der Kunst. Geschichte und Erinnerung in der Kunst der Gegenwart*, Frankfurt am Main: Hatje Cantz Verlag, 2000, 21–27, 23f.
17. Michalski, *Public Monuments*, 10.
18. Geoffrey Hartmann, *Bitburg in Moral and Political Perspective*, Bloomington: Indiana University Press, 1986, xiv.
19. See *Forever in the Shadow of Hitler*, trans. James Knowlton and Truett Cates, Atlantic Highlands: Humanities Press International, 1993.
20. See Paula Hyman, *The Jews of Modern France*, Berkeley: University of California Press, 1998, 205f.
21. See Esther Benbassa, *The Jews of France. A History from Antiquity to the Present*, trans. M. DeBevoise, Princeton: Princeton University Press, 1999, 187f.
22. Lynn Rapaport, *Jews in Germany after the Holocaust. Memory, Identity, and Jewish–German Relations*, Cambridge: Cambridge University Press, 1997, 261.
23. Michael Brenner, *After the Holocaust. Rebuilding Jewish Lives in Postwar Germany*, trans. Barbara Harshar, Princeton: Princeton University Press, 1977, 156.
24. Rapaport, *Jews in Germany*, 259.
25. Sander Gilman, *Jews in Today's German Culture*, Bloomington & Indianapolis: Indiana University Press, 1999, 38.
26. Ibid., 32.
27. See Brenner, *After the Holocaust*, 154.
28. See Harald Welzer et al., *Opa war kein Nazi. Nationalsozialismus und Holocaust im Familiengedächtnis*, Frankfurt am Main: Fischer Verlag, 2002; Herfried Münkler, 'Unter Abwertungsvorbehalt', *Frankfurter Rundschau*, 24 September 2003, 9; Achatz von Müller, 'Volk der Täter, Volk der Opfer', *Die Zeit*, 23 October 2003, 35.
29. Elias, *The Symbol Theory*, 47.

2
History in Monuments

Monuments as Historical Prisms

A monument may never lay claim to artistic autonomy from its social and historical context. It is necessarily a product and reflection of its time, derived from the initiative of an individual, group or state. The production and reception of monuments are determined by three diachronic historical moments. First, the moment of the historical event or figure which it represents or denotes. Second, the moment at which the monument was conceived and constructed. Third, the moment(s) of its reception, when subjected to interpretation or debate due to its renewed political relevance, a decision to renovate or demolish the monument, or even vandalism. Monuments may therefore act as a prism for understanding successive historical and political contexts in which memory cultures evolve. Just as a prism filters and deflects light, monuments act as a medium between the (historical) event and the spectator's eye. They must therefore be carefully read as coded historical interpretations based on their form, size or situation. Figurative monuments appeal to a sense of identification with the represented figure, while counter-monuments of the sort produced by artists like Edward Kienholz or Jochen Gerz invite the spectator to call into question the very process of monumental representation.

Since the meanings ascribed to monuments are themselves conditioned by the social and political contexts in which successive spectators formulate interpretations, they are prone to historical relativism. Meaning is not fixed in stone, but varies according to subjective criteria. Interpretations formulated by individual spectators or critics depend upon prior knowledge of both history and the history of the monuments, and upon the degree of personal and emotional involvement resulting from their participation or lack of participation in events as witnesses. Direct participants naturally respond to events differently from those who learn about them retrospectively exclusively via monuments, books, photographs, films or witness accounts. Further relativism occurs when monuments acquire a new function in a political context different from the one in which they were erected. This occurs when political regimes change. After 1989, many monuments erected in the German Democratic Republic were demolished. However, the Commission on the Handling of Political Monuments of the Postwar Years in Former East Berlin decided that some monuments from the GDR that were ideologically incompatible with the political culture of the new Federal Republic should be left intact. They were converted or equipped with an additional inscription – either in order to modify their political content, or else to turn them into ironic public citations of the former state ideology by highlighting their origins as an ideological product of a defunct regime. Two conspicuous examples of these in Berlin are the memorial for German members of the International Brigade during the Spanish Civil War in the Friedrichshain Park (converted 1994), and the Marx-Engels monument in the Marx-Engels-Forum near Alexanderplatz.[1]

The triad of historical reference points that converge in a monument – the historical moment referred to, the moment of production, and the moment of reception – serves as an interpretative framework for most monuments. Yet the task of decoding monuments is rendered more complex by the network of auxiliary rhetorical and visual media via which commemorative performances are conveyed to a broad public.[2] Recurring debates over monuments in France and Germany since the 1990s have primarily been about the forms in which history is made accessible to a wide public and only indirectly about the represented historical events. They do not recount the past, but analyse the means of representing and understanding history in the present. While the debate over the Holocaust Monument in Berlin focused extensively on the sculptural form it should take and the very necessity and utility of such a monument, for example, the debate over the Vél' d'Hiv' in Paris focused on the rhetorical form of speeches at the annual commemoration staged on the site of the monument from 1992. The artistic form of the sculpture nearby the site of the cycle stadium in Paris played no direct role in public debate; yet the fact that it was built resulted directly from demands formulated by pressure groups, so that it became a focal point of public controversy over the role of presidents François Mitterrand and Jacques Chirac in commemorations and television interviews, and over the wording of verbal statements. In this way, both monuments surpassed their quality as stone sculptures and inscriptions on urban sites by becoming objects of political controversy over forms of historical representation. In short, these monuments became sites of memory of the deportation and genocide of Jews in

France and Germany, but also of public and state responses to the challenge of transmitting historical memories as a process in its own right. The debates accompanying the inception of these monumental projects offer a historical document of the conception and construction of a historical medium in its phases of production and initial reception.

Commemorative ceremonies such as wreath laying, anniversaries, official inaugurations or modifications of monuments constitute both official expressions of and appeals to historical memory. The forms in which they are performed, embodied and transmitted reveal intentions underlying their instigation in relation to the context in which they are interpreted. Sociologists of art and literature have already warned against the ideological roots of 'production' and 'reception' as interpretative models. Pierre Zima locates the meaning of artistic products in an 'interdiscursive consensus', achieved via the tacit collaboration between producers and 'recipients' of art.[3] Pierre Bourdieu likewise derives his interpretation of art from the interaction of structural relations between producers of art (including institutional contexts such as competitions, prizes and associations) on the one hand with formal structural relations within art works on the other.[4] Although the status of public monuments is, in contrast to works of 'pure' art, explicitly political, the relation between artistic forms, intentions of their producers and audiences, and the social context in which they arise is no less complex. In order to take full account of the artistic, political and social criteria at stake in the interpretation of public art, the case studies of the Vél' d'Hiv' and Holocaust Monument in Part II will therefore be structured according to analyses of form (sculptural and rhetorical), intention (of commissioning agents, leading to both the construction and deconstruction of memorials), and context (governing parties, institutions and local tradition).

Another reason for methodological caution is the fact that the sequence of production and reception of monuments does not always take place in linear succession. In the case of the Holocaust Monument in Berlin, production was dogged for over eleven years by the conflicting opinions and interests of the organising association, of local and federal governments, as well as of architects, artists, journalists, intellectuals and the general public. In this way, the reception of this monument appeared to take place in anticipation of, that is, *before* its production. The large size and symbolic location of this monument in central Berlin (between Leipziger Platz and the Brandenburg Gate) raised essential questions not only about the forms in which the past may be represented in plastic form, but also about the status of the genocide in German national heritage, the role of symbols in the united Germany, and about the function of monuments as such. This final theoretical question on the political function of monuments posed perhaps the greatest challenge to those people responsible for selecting a monument and brought into doubt the very utility of ritual forms conventionally used to sustain memory cultures. Do monuments provide plausible supports for social memory? Not only are monuments man-made constructions representing specific interpretations of the past, but the very *use* of monuments is a construction or conventional aid to social cohesion inherent in western societies, albeit one which is not indispensable for social cohesion as such.[5] The debates over memory cultures in the 1980s and 1990s therefore testify to a dual phenomenon: the intensity both of monumental commemorations and of scepticism towards their function. In light of the persistent use of monuments and commemorations, which are relatively archaic forms of public commemoration in an age of digital telecommunications, we must ask, why and how states do today continue to sanction monuments?

The Convergence of Art, History and Politics in Monuments

When artists and architects are invited to design a monument they face the challenge of devising a form of historical representation which combines both factual documentation and artifice. All monuments, even counter-monuments that reduce to a minimum or eliminate symbolic elements, contain what the architect Salomon Korn calls a 'residual aesthetic' ('*Rest-Ästhetik*').[6] According to this simplified dichotomy, monuments are technical hybrids extending across disciplines. As historical documents, they testify to past events: dates, names, statistics and motives. As art, they testify to the intervention of individual artists and spectators in the mediation and transmission of historical information, and to their attempts to recognise, understand and draw moral lessons from events of the past.[7] By transmitting information about the past, yet also conveying the interpretations of their creators and critics, monuments fulfil both a documentary and artistic function. The art historian Jochen Spielmann has succinctly defined a monument in all its facets, and deserves to be quoted in full:

> A monument is an independent work of art reminding us of people or events. It is erected in a public space by a specific group on a specific site and is designed to endure. In this process, a monument fulfils a function of identification, legitimisation, representation, anticipation, interpretation and information. It acts as a symbol in so far as it sustains political and historical discussion in a society, provides a link between cultural formation and institutionalised communication, and is both a manifestation of cultural memory and historical consciousness. ... A monument is the result of a communication process involving conflictory negotiation of the interpretation of history. Discussion, development and reception are an integral part of the monument itself. In order to be and remain a monument, it must be subjected to ritual reception.[8]

Spielmann here exposes the essential hybridity of monuments. He describes them as primarily functional, fulfilling a political purpose of 'identification, legitimisation and representation' as catalysts for a community's debate about its past, and whose very existence is dependent upon their social reception. However, he also emphasises the artistic intention of their creators in so far as they are designed to 'endure over time' and solicit emotional adherence necessary for effective identification.

By transmitting and fostering collective historical memories, monuments operate parallel to and even challenge scientific works of history in the task of establishing collective historical memories. Although the medium of public art addresses passers-by, whereas historiography addresses readers and students of history, they nevertheless both appeal to broader overlapping audiences via auxiliary mass media. The key difference between public art and history lies in their distinctive forms and criteria of communication. Unlike historical scholarship, monuments do not adhere to criteria of proof and plausibility demanded of the social sciences. Their meanings are subject rather to the formal criteria of art and the contingency of their politically and socially determined production and reception. The disciplinary tightrope embodied in historical monuments therefore subjects history to art and politics, albeit without renouncing the function of transmitting information about history. According to strict definitions, the function of a monument is diametrically opposed to that of a document: a monument is a symbol of the past designed to 'perpetuate memory', whereas a document is a form of 'proof' claiming a degree of objectivity as historical testimony.[9] Monuments are generally not bound by the regime of proof and objectivity and leave the spectator greater room for interpretation than works of history. And whereas historical writings render documentary evidence via narration and argumentation, monuments are not bound to employ documentary evidence and may incorporate plastic forms, inscriptions, rhetoric and ritual, making them more open to interpretation and vulnerable to manipulation.

However, neither monuments nor documents ever totally elude the influence of the other. Monumental objects created in remembrance of the past and erected in public places both denote past events and evoke interpretations of events in the present. Yet documents also both denote and evoke events, in so far as they only make sense following the intervention of the historian in their selection, organisation and narrative elucidation. The philosopher Ernst Cassirer aptly describes this interpretative dilemma as a conflict between objects and their function. 'The decisive question is always whether we attempt to understand the function on the basis of the object [*Gebilde*] or the object on the basis of the function, whether we "justify" the latter with the former, or the former with the latter.'[10]

Many existing studies of monuments are founded on a normative definition of a single type such as ephemeral, counter-, undesirable or objectless. The historians Michael Geyer and Sybil Milton defend a more constructivist standpoint by suggesting that monuments are today perceived primarily via secondary forms of media such as photographic and filmic media.[11] Milton claims that 'the new aesthetic trend of photographing Holocaust memorials' testifies to an ongoing search for an optimal sculptural form which would solve the quest to design a monument providing an 'appropriate' testimony to genocide. 'We are still,' claims Milton, 'confronted by the issue of defining appropriate memorial art for public spaces designed in fitting memory of all victims of … the Holocaust'.[12] Yet Milton's allusion to an ideal, normative artistic standard detracts from the fact that numerous monuments are in fact erected in memory of genocide regardless of artistic trends and regardless of the quest for a most appropriate or optimal form. However unsatisfactorily they appear to fulfil their function as historical representations, memorials in memory of the genocide, whether figurative, abstract or makeshift, are still regularly installed without regard for contemporary norms. In spite of innovations in contemporary art, which have been incorporated into so-called counter-monuments and which question the utility of monuments as such, conventional figurative and non-figurative stone monuments continue to be built, and still capture public attention. It appears that the social and political function accorded to monuments depends less on their forms than on the contexts in which they are conceived, erected and perceived.

Both monuments examined in Part II of this study are conventional forms of commemoration in so far as they mark with stone a site in capital cities in remembrance of the past. Both were also preceded by debates over what most 'appropriate' rhetorical or sculptural form the commemoration should take. This study does not take up the issues of these debates in order to establish a solution to the quest for a commemorative norm, but attempts instead to assess and compare the consequences of these monuments and their accompanying debates for the national memory cultures of France and Germany during the 1990s. In both cases, symbolic forms acted as mediators of political interests and historical understanding. On the one hand, they demonstrated the political dimension of art. Sculptural forms conveyed a specific political and historiographical meaning, in particular via didactic inscriptions, and when political messages were associated with them during the course of commemorative speeches or public debates. On the other hand, they also demonstrated the artistic dimension of politics, for political leaders appealed for public support by informal means: by inaugurating monuments, performing ritual commemorations or delivering commemorative speeches. This phenomenon was particularly apparent during the French commemorations of Vichy between 1992 and 1997, which were marked by reactions to the rhetoric of commemorative speeches made by political leaders on the occasion of ceremonies held on the site of the Vél' d'Hiv'.

In general, commemorations and monuments constitute a point of convergence for the aestheticisation of politics and the politicisation of art, an interaction between two practices often considered to be distinct. When examining monuments and commemorations, it is not possible to distinguish entirely between a purely political message and the means with which it is expressed, between didactic 'content' and autonomous 'form'. The power of commemorations and monuments lies in their ambiguity and openness to interpretation; they are an informal means of political communication whose prime function is to promote consensus or the cohesion of as large a section of society as possible by integrating diverse political standpoints within a community of historical memory, or even by urging people to adhere to collective symbols whose political legitimacy is not founded on explicit political significance.

It is commonly assumed that monuments directly express or reflect the political interests of the institutions which sponsor them. While this may be true at any one time, one must not forget that the inherent contextuality and historicity of monuments means that they are often the products of a clash of multiple conflicting interests and institutions and, moreover, that they may become the object of different politically motivated institutional clashes as political contexts change over time. Associations that erect monuments in order to sustain the memory of deportations, for example, cannot guarantee that such measures will fulfil their aims. Likewise, the presence of monuments of the German Democratic Republic in the new Federal Republic after 1989 clearly does not indicate that the government of the new Federal Republic of Germany supports communist ideology, for the often pompous forms of these monuments serve as an ironic reminder that the regime which gave rise to them no longer exists. Again, the meaning of monuments is not inherent in their forms alone, but dependent on the context of their production and reception. In liberal societies, we cannot equate the strictly institutional political interests of governing parties or nations with the alleged messages of monumental objects. We should therefore be wary of using the term 'instrumentalisation' in order to define the political function of monuments such as the Vél' d'Hiv' or Holocaust Monument. Moreover, the interdisciplinary nature of monuments solicits the expertise of artists, art historians, historians, political scientists and politicians who together must determine the credence of monuments as supports for memories of historical events. The decision over the form of the Holocaust Monument, for example, was delayed by dispute not only over an appropriate form, but also over theoretical questions pertaining to the practice of commemoration itself: whether a monument was the most appropriate form of commemoration and what procedure was required to reach a decision on these issues. In short, monuments must be conceived of as gestures of intention that are subject to contextual, historical and disciplinary contingency.

Monuments as Vehicles of Historical Ambivalence

The fiftieth anniversary commemorations of the Second World War took place within the context of the public and political fascination with memory cultures that began in the 1970s, a period characterised by an inflation of the number of historical commemorations, exhibitions, new museums and works of historical literature. The intensity and frequency of commemorative events led some critics to warn of the industrialisation, commercialisation, ritualisation and trivialisation of history. Robert Hewison deplored the 'heritage industry'[13] in Britain, Bernhard Schulz warned against 'monument tourism'[14] in Germany, while Dirk Schümer suggested that the inflation of historical commemorations might, in extreme cases, lead to a public aversion or even indifference to historical tradition, a 'blunting' (*Abstumpfung*)[15] of historical curiosity.

The potential trivialisation, commercialisation, or even misrepresentation of history in monuments merit criticism on the grounds that the uninhibited popularisation of history undermines scientific criteria of historical knowledge and the corrective role of historians. However, the very fact that monuments, as artistic objects of non-scientific historical value, make a contribution to the sum of historical knowledge within their immediate social context merits analysis in its own right. Popular representations reach more people than scientific studies. At the same time, they lend themselves to the public articulation of history while drawing on complex mechanisms of artistic, historical and political representations to do so. These mechanisms of representation should be taken seriously. David Lowenthal describes the phenomenon of heritage in the 1990s, arguing that historical *mis*representations should be observed and analysed as legitimate forms of historical transmission. 'Heritage is often criticised for failing to abide by the tenets of historical evidence. I argue that this charge is correct but pointless, for the sources, aims and modes of persuasion employed by heritage are closer to those of memoirists than historians.'[16]

How do monuments sustain social memory? Traditionally, they are experienced as a concrete form or sculpture in a public place evoking partial and vague memories of historical events or figures that require complementary information in an inscription or commentary. On the one hand, they fulfil a heuristic function by reminding passers-by of something they already know or by imparting information about a previously unknown event. On the other hand, monuments may be inert if passers-by either do not see them, or see them but remain oblivious to, and therefore neither remember nor forget the event being commemorated. They may serve as a source of historical instruction or else, in the words of Musil, become 'invisible' and generate indifference towards their political relevance. However, the phases of conception, production and reception or even demolition of monuments have been regularly monitored in public debates of the 1990s with such fervour that the relative heuristic effect or degree of inertia of a monument is governed by media, including the mass media, photography and forms of political representation, which surpass its immediate aesthetic effect. Some monuments remind us not only of the history to which they refer, but also of the history of their own tumultuous origins. We should therefore ask not whether a monument is visible or invisible, a spur for either memory or forgetting, but how it took effect, when and why, and what monuments convey to us today, whether history or the history of their own making in the present.

The habitual means for reappraising the history of most nations are judicial and historical. Crimes of the past are dealt with before courts, while the research of professional historians serves as a corrective for public knowledge of and opinion on the past. However, the intense and prolonged public debates over national heritage or over monuments commemorating the Second World War in France and Germany during the 1990s constitute a third form of historical representation that merits interpretation at two further levels. First, as an artistic, non-scientific medium that nevertheless contributes to general historical knowledge. Second, as the rhetoric of ritual speeches and critical interpretation conveyed via the mass media. Such plastic and rhetorical forms of communication, as opposed to scientific and judicial communication, ensure popular participation in history and heritage and in the critical apprehension of modes of representation.

Monuments as Spurs to Participate in History through its Formal Mediation

Having established that the significance of monuments is dependent not only on sculptural, but also on auxiliary rhetorical, photographic and filmic means of communication by which they are reproduced, one must ask how the multiple 'translations' of history, first into stone and then into visual and rhetorical media, impinge on our understanding of the past. The ritualisation of memory by means of its repeated representation in photographic and narrative reproductions made during procedures for the selection of sites and forms of monuments or during annual ceremonies, can effectively thwart the function of commemoration: to call up or preserve the past in the present by means of memory. Rituals are by nature repetitious and reductive. Moreover, their function approaches that of the mass media by rendering history banal, for just as monuments reduce history to a specific genre by marking a site with a tangible object and a fixed repertoire of forms such as statues, plaques, inscriptions, crosses, cenotaphs, or archways, the mass media reduce different historical events in different places and from different times to a single form, whether a journalistic report or television screen.[17]

According to Pierre Nora, the mass media reduce historical events to the status of information and spectacle, and therefore negate the intended function of commemoration. 'Information itself secretes antibodies, and the written or spoken press as a whole rather has the effect of limiting the outbreak of unfettered opinion.'[18] Nora's idea of the neutralising effect of 'antibodies' inherent in the transmission of information spotlights the essential paradox of commemoration, where the intention to foster historical consciousness results in the effective promotion of historical indifference. On the one hand, such indifference may be generated by the very familiarity and persistence of commemorative forms, sustained either by the physical presence of monuments or by the regular succession of ceremonies, newspapers, or media broadcasts over time. On the other hand, indifference may also be nurtured by the fact that commemoration, as historical representation, is in essence a medium separating events from spectators, who are condemned to what Nora calls a state of 'participation without participation'.[19] Traditional forms of monumental or ceremonial commemoration and the mass media transmission of the past share the role of calling to mind an event that is either *irretrievable in time*, or *contemporary but too distant* to impinge directly on the spectator's experience. Both forms appeal to participation, yet stand as tangible evidence of its impossibility. In this respect, citizens' action groups which initiated debates over the Vél' d'Hiv' memorial in Paris or the Holocaust Monument in Berlin effectively participated in commemorative events, but not in historical events, except in so far as these monuments have themselves become part of contemporary history. Although spectators of monuments are inevitably passive spectators and do not participate in history, they do participate in historical interpretation, in particular in the interpretation of the media of historical transmission. Monuments and commemorations are therefore contrived rather than actual embodiments of the past, hallmarks of modern societies reliant on symbolic 'sites', in the form of written records, archives, artefacts and traces.

The Relation of Monuments to Fiftieth Anniversary Commemorations of the Second World War

Recent commemorations of the 1500th anniversary of the baptism of Clovis in France (1996), the 750th anniversary of the foundation of Berlin (1987), or the 500th anniversary of the birth of Luther (1983), all of which represented political interests and triggered public debate in the present, suggest that historical events that took place several hundred years ago are not necessarily less effective objects of commemoration than those which took place only a few years ago. Is there an optimum moment for the inauguration of a monument? The effectiveness of a monument or commemoration is determined less by the lapse of time between a historical event and its commemoration than by the ideological benefit gained by evoking the event in the present.

One could similarly ask, what is the shortest lapse of time between an event and its commemoration for the commemoration to be effective? Again, commemorations of the recent past depend on the continuing political relevance of the event to which they refer. An obvious example is the collapse of the Berlin Wall, which has been commemorated annually since the first anniversary of this event in 1990. Perhaps the shortest lapse of time for a commemoration is the period of one hundred days, which is traditionally celebrated as a moment to take stock of a political leader's or party's first hundred days in power, as in the case of the British, French and German governments. These are examples of what David Lowenthal calls 'instant tradition',[20] where even the very recent past is turned into an object of retrospection and deemed worthy of commemoration.

The literary historian Heinz Schlaffer observes that, in contrast to previous epochs such as the eighteenth century, when antiquity was held up as a cultural model, or the early nineteenth century, when the Middle Ages took priority, periods commemorated in the twentieth century have been eclectic. The sole criterion for the selection of periods to be commemorated today, claims Schlaffer, is a 'zero' in the number of years passed since the original event.[21] However, his claim that the process of selecting events and epochs to be commemorated in the 1980s was 'gratuitous' and plagued by 'indifference'[22] is not entirely plausible, for there also appears to exist a hierarchy of periods governing the selection of monuments and commemorations within contemporary memory cultures. The proliferation of fiftieth anniversary commemorations of the Second World War in the 1980s and 1990s may not be ascribed solely to the zero in the figure '50'. For commemorations also mark stages in the process of historicisation of an event – its fixation in works of historiography and historical symbols – which begins at the same time as the event itself, in particular via the medium of photographic and literary journalism, and continues as long as people write about or represent the event. In particular, fifty years marks the passing of a generation, a biological lapse in time after which the generation of participants in and witnesses of the historical events begins to disappear. This process effectively seals the transition from one type of historical medium to another, from the oral sources of witnesses to written or recorded sources. Representations therefore play a significant role in fixing impressions and interpretations of the past as a society's relation to its past becomes increasingly reliant on recorded or 'archival' material.[23]

Another factor governing the frequency, rhythm and intensity of European commemorations of the Second World War in the 1980s and

1990s was the urgency with which political leaders sought to integrate this controversial period into national memory following the collapse of regimes in the eastern bloc. Following the resurgence of national traditions in Europe after 1989, the monuments and commemorations instigated in the 1990s help to remind us of the continuing relevance of the Second World War – as a primary rupture in tradition and moment of political regeneration – for the creation of social consensus in countries where consensus over the common aversion to communism was weakened after the end of the Cold War. In other words, western memory cultures founded on anti-communist consensus before 1989 but destabilised by the rapid demise of the communist regimes were in a position after 1989 to found a new social consensus in relation to the Second World War, albeit not an anti-fascist consensus as in the GDR but an anti-Holocaust consensus cultivated by an institutionalised memory culture via memorial symbols and the mass media.

Commemorations of the Second World War as a catastrophe and rupture in national traditions also served to underscore, by negation, the benefits of a new beginning after 1945. In the postwar years, both Germany and France introduced new constitutions: in Germany, the creation of the German Democratic Republic and Federal Republic in 1949, and in France the creation of the Fourth Republic in 1946. Even the U.K. saw the introduction of radical political reform with the introduction of the welfare state in 1945.[24] The commemoration of this event therefore rekindles memories not only of catastrophe, persecution and genocide, but also of the origins and the relative continuity of the present political constitutions since this rupture. Commemorations in the 1980s and 1990s were therefore not determined by consensus over the zero in the fifty-year time lapse, but by a social demand for meaningful representations and a political demand for a reorientation of public attitudes to the Second World War and the Cold War. Since there is not a linear proportional relation between the intensity of public interest in a commemoration or monument and the elapse of time between an event and its commemoration, one must assume that these factors were the essential motors of postwar commemorative customs.

Notes

1. See Report of the *Kommission zum Umgang mit den politischen Denkmälern der Nachkriegszeit im ehemaligen Ost-Berlin*, 15 February 1993, 51–53; Dieter Rulff, 'Ernst Thälmann fällt, Marx und Engels bleiben', *Die Tageszeitung*, 16 February 1993, 17.
2. Cf. Dietmar Schiller, '"Geschichtsbilder" im Fernsehen: Zur Militarisierung des öffentlichen Raums im vereinten Deutschland durch staatlich inszenierte Symbolpolitik', *Kritische Berichte* no. 1, 1997, 39–54.

3. Pierre Zima, '"Rezeption" und "Produktion" als ideologische Begriffe', in Zima, *Kritik der Literatursoziologie*, Frankfurt am Main: Suhrkamp, 1978, 72–112, 96.
4. See Pierre Bourdieu, *The Rules of Art*, trans. Susan Emanuel, London: Polity Press, 1996, 369.
5. Cf. David Lowenthal, 'Identity, Heritage, and History', in John Gillis, ed., *Commemorations. The Politics of National Identity*, Princeton: Princeton University Press, 1994, 41–57, 45.
6. Salomon Korn, 'Holocaust-Gedenken: Ein deutsches Dilemma', *Aus Politik und Zeitgeschichte* no. 4, 1997, 23–30, 28.
7. Jacques Le Goff, 'Documento/monumento', *Enciclopedia Einaudi*, Turin, 1978, vol. 5, 38–48, 44.
8. Spielmann, 'Der Prozeß ist genauso wichtig wie das Ergebnis', in Neue Gesellschaft für Bildende Kunst, ed., *Der Wettbewerb für das 'Denkmal für die ermordeten Juden Europas'*, Berlin: Verlag der Kunst, 1995, 128–45, 129f.
9. This opposition is established by Le Goff, 'Documento/monumento', 38.
10. Ernst Cassirer, *Philosophie der symbolischen Formen*, Darmstadt: Primus Verlag, 1977, 10.
11. Michael Geyer, 'The Place of the Second World War in German Memory and History', *New German Critique* no. 71, 1997, 5–40, 6.
12. Sybil Milton, 'The Memoralisation of the Holocaust', in Milton, *In Fitting Memory. The Art and Politics of Holocaust Memorials*, Detroit: Wayne State University Press, 1991, 7–18, 17.
13. Robert Hewison, *The Heritage Industry. Britain in a Climate of Decline*, London: Methuen, 1987.
14. Bernhard Schulz, 'Denkmal ist, was vorhanden ist', *Der Tagesspiegel*, 8 September 1996, 25.
15. Dirk Schümer, 'Erlebnisraum Holocaust', *Frankfurter Allgemeine Zeitung*, 11 November 1994, 41.
16. David Lowenthal, 'Fabricating Heritage', *History & Memory* no. 1, 1998, 5–24, 9.
17. Cf. Peppino Ortevola, 'Storia e mass media', in Nicola Gallerano, ed., *L'uso pubblico della storia*, Milan: Franco Angeli, 1995, 63–82, 64.
18. Nora, 'Le retour de l'événement', in Jacques Le Goff and Pierre Nora, eds, *Faire de l'histoire*, vol. I, Paris: Gallimard, 1974, 210–228, 215.
19. Ibid.
20. Lowenthal, *The Heritage Crusade and the Spoils of History*, London: Viking, 1997, 17ff.
21. Heinz Schlaffer, 'Gedenktage', in *Merkur* no. 479, 1989, 81–84, 83.
22. Ibid.
23. Nora, 'Entre mémoire et histoire', in Nora, ed., *Les Lieux de mémoire*, vol. I, *La République*, Paris: Gallimard, 1984, xvii–xlii, xxviii.
24. See Sarah Benton, 'The 1945 "Republic"', *History Workshop Journal* no. 43, 1997, 249–57.

Part II

Paris and Berlin as Sites of Memory of the 1990s

The national monuments in memory of deportations and genocide carried out during the Second World War, known as the Vél' d'Hiv' and Holocaust Monument, arose from distinct political and cultural contexts and did not result from a policy of Franco-German reconciliation. Comparison of these monuments does not reveal direct interaction between the two memory cultures, therefore, but transnational analogies between local commemorative customs and discourses as well as local specificities.[1] It is precisely with such investigations of commemorations on the basis of analogies and specificities that it is possible to establish the degree to which the focal points, narrative structures and metaphors of memory cultures are local, national or transnational. In France and Germany, for example, the Second World War is a transnational object of commemoration in so far as it represents a shared historical caesura and the origin of postwar political cultures. Historical memories of this event are also fixed in comparable commemorative media such as central monuments or rituals and promoted by similar institutions and forms of communication: petitions, the mass media, architectural competitions, exhibitions, public conferences and debates. At the same time, political leaders generally speak in the name of a nation, and war memorials in towns and villages generally represent local communities by naming individual (usually military) victims or the number of dead. The complexity of this socially, politically and geographically defined memory culture is compounded by the multiplicity of channels of symbolic communication, which guarantee the contingency of symbols on the basis of which historical events are discussed in the public sphere. In the face of the multiple social, political and geographical strata of memory cultures, the plurality of institutions governing public discourse on memory, and the resulting contingency of memorial symbols, one of the aims of this part will be to explore grey zones of memory cultures within or beyond the nation, and to enquire whether the audiences connected with these monuments can in fact legitimately be described as 'national'.

It is often impossible to establish the exact scope of the memory culture to which symbols belong. If we ask to whom a monument belongs, for or by whom it was built, we naturally provoke a number of different answers. The Vél' d'Hiv' and Holocaust Monument were initiated by associations, but then erected in a local urban setting in the name of the nation on behalf of Jewish victims of deportation and genocide, or rather on behalf of the memory of them sustained by their families or survivors. Although construed as national, they are in fact a product of the political will of a multitude of individual members of associations, institutions, political parties, states and intellectual elites. The putative national character of collective symbols is rather deduced as a consequence of their central site in a capital city, state involvement, their emotional appeal to a broad section of society, or their repeated rhetorical definition as 'national'.

Among the symbolic, ritual and institutional factors contributing to the emergence of the Vél' d'Hiv' and Holocaust Monument, rhetoric proved to be the single most influential element in their national construction. The origins of the French controversy, which led to the introduction of a national day of commemoration in 1993, the inauguration of the monument in 1994 and Chirac's speech in 1995, lay in the appeal to the president by the Comité Vél' d'Hiv' 42 for an explicit verbal recognition of Vichy crimes. The origins of the German controversy likewise lay in the verbal appeal and petitions of the citizens' action group Perspektive Berlin for a sculptural recognition of the genocide against Jews. These sites were rendered public not by their physical presence but by rhetorical speculations on the forms in which deportation and genocide may be commemorated and remembered. The Holocaust Monument in particular existed only in the forms of an empty building site, a series of architectural blueprints, and rhetorical speculation on modes of historical commemoration which focused attention on a succession of public controversies. Although the immediate aims of each campaign differed, the resulting controversies consisted in a verbal conflict of interpretations expressed by rival political communities and individuals striving to achieve social acceptance of their vision of the past. In order to understand how these elaborately contrived symbols acquired national significance in the 1990s, we must therefore analyse the rhetorical strategies employed in petitions for the commemorations, in statements and speeches of political representatives, and in ensuing media debate, as well as the significance of this rhetoric in relation to the political context in which it emerged. Since both debates lasted for several years, it is appropriate to analyse the media debate as a form of commemoration in its own right.

The origins of the study of rhetoric go back to Aristotle's famous treatise on the art of persuasion and to Latin texts on the art of oratory such as the *Rhetorica ad Herennium*. Today, this discipline has been adapted in the fields of cultural studies, in linguistics, and even in political science in analyses of the influence of political communication on the 'construction' of what is commonly referred to as cultural identity, collective memory, self-understanding, or the public mind. Analyses of discourse in these fields help us in particular to understand the way in which verbal and visual communication influences the nature of the communities in which we live.[2]

The monuments and memory cultures under examination here are specific to the period following 1989. This year marked not only the end of the Cold War, but also the beginning of extensive fiftieth anniversary commemorations of the Second World War. These commemorations were also part of the international intensification of public ritual and recorded communication. In addition to the release of state archives after 1989, there occurred an increase in artistic and ritual communication in the public sphere that provoked debate over the transmission and pedagogical function of history. This transition of the means of formal transmission of Second World War history in the public sphere was partly provoked by the sense that recordings and rituals would compensate the gradual disappearance of people with personal memories of the historical event. Although recordings, rituals, monuments and historiography relating to this period had already emerged immediately after the event (and thereby not only complemented but also influenced the emerging memories of witnesses), the 1980s and 1990s were marked by an inflation of recorded commemorations. Monuments erected at this time in memory of the Second World War only make sense within the context of the symbolic reassertion of national identities following the post-Cold War destabilisation and in anticipation of an increasingly integrated world economic and communication system. The reinforcement of traditional local and national memory cultures may be seen as a reaction following the recognition that memory cultures share common focal points and commemorative customs. Although the monuments in Paris and Berlin were initiated in similar conditions in each case and 'from below' by citizens' action groups, the subsequent participation of state representatives in their interpretation demonstrated the central function of art in the attempted 'nationalisation' of collective memory.

The following two case studies do not aim to situate the monuments historically in relation to earlier commemorations and monuments,[3] but to examine how they served to incorporate the complex and disturbing memories of deportation and genocide into a repertoire of national symbols appealing to a cohesive collective self-understanding. Each study focuses on four issues, in the following order: 1. The relation of the monuments to other Second World War memorials in Paris and Berlin and the history of their emergence; 2. The discursive strategies employed in petitions and in the responses of artists, critics, historians and politicians; 3. The political context in which the projects unfolded, linking issues of the 1940s to those of the 1990s; 4. The various means undertaken to achieve 'national reconciliation' or 'national consensus', and the way in which protagonists of the commemorations thus appealed to national identity during the debates.

Notes

The text of notes 1–3 appears at the end of Chapter Three.

3

Paris: the Vél' d'Hiv' and the Promise of National Reconciliation 1992–97[4]

Controversial ceremonies on the site of a central monument commemorating the deportation of Jews from Paris in 1942 became the focus of presidents Mitterrand and Chirac's attempts to secure national reconciliation from 1992. Memories of state persecutions and victims of national policy presented an obstacle to the representation of conventional national identity. The monument and related commemorations of Vichy were nevertheless used to legitimate a cohesive official state memory: by rhetorical appeals to humanist traditions and to nationhood as an ideal, almost religious vocation.

The introduction of a parliamentary bill to instigate a 'National Day of Commemoration of the Racist and Anti-Semitic Persecutions'[5] in 1993 and the construction of a monument in 1994 as a site at which to perform an annual wreath-laying ceremony on this day in Paris, marked a turning point in the official state interpretation of French collaboration. Whereas victims of anti-Semitic persecutions and deportations had previously been mourned in private ceremonies or, when public, subsumed to republican ritual,[6] the introduction and immediate implementation of the annual day of commemoration in 1993 appeared to satisfy both Jewish and state interests[7] and was generally sanctioned by historians and all political parties except the extreme right. The commemoration had been initiated in 1992 by President François Mitterrand on the occasion of the fiftieth anniversary of the internment of 13,152 Jews on 16 and 17 July 1942 in the Vélodrome d'Hiver (Winter Cycling Stadium) or Vél' d'Hiv' in Paris, before deportation. This event rapidly became a focal point of nationwide attention when Mitterrand refused to respond to the petitions of the citizens' action group Comité Vél' d'Hiv' 42 requesting him to make a speech in the name of the Fifth Republic acknowledging responsibility for crimes of the Vichy regime. Mitterrand's silence, and otherwise ambiguous statements about his activities as a journalist for the pro-Vichy press, as a short-lived collaborator of the pro-Vichy French Legion of War Veterans (Légion Française des Combattants), but later also his support of the Resistance and criticism of the Vichy regime's policy with respect to his work for the reintegration of prisoners of war from 1943, deepened public mistrust. The controversy over this commemoration culminated three years later when the newly elected President Chirac responded positively to the demands of petitions by giving a historic speech, the first in which a president of the French Republic officially acknowledged the responsibility of the Vichy regime for the deportations and therefore indirectly for the genocide of the Second World War. The new commemoration and monument thus secured – with symbolic means – 'national reconciliation' between the republican state and those who demanded symbolic reparation for the crimes of the French State of Vichy.[8] Yet despite the 72 per cent popular support for Chirac's speech in opinion polls, it is impossible to attribute to this single gesture the 'moral reparation' of which the historian Esther Benbassa talks.[9] The renewed Judeophobia in France since 2000, but also the ambiguities inherent in the Vél' d'Hiv' site and commemoration, suggest that reconciliation was certainly approached but not achieved.

The novelty of this rhetorical gesture consisted in its solemnity and explicitness. Although numerous collaborators had already been tried, sentenced and often executed in the purge or 'purification' (*épuration*) measures from 1944, Chirac's speech was perceived as a primary gesture of historical enlightenment and national reconciliation which would radically revise the Gaullist myth of a nation united in resistance. The speech of 1995 was therefore compared to official verbal and symbolic measures of reconciliation made in the Federal Republic of Germany, in particular Chancellor Willy Brandt's act of kneeling before the Warsaw Ghetto Monument in 1970 and President Richard von Weizsäcker's speech before the German parliament marking the fortieth anniversary of the end of the Second World War in 1985. In reality, however, these symbolic acts of reparation were not void of ambiguity, since they reveal on closer inspection Chirac's implicit reassertion of Gaullist national self-understanding, and von Weizsäcker's reassertion of the self-understanding of German people as victims of National Socialism.[10]

Rousso has already demonstrated historically the mutations of political interpretations of Vichy after 1944 in his pioneering study *Le Syndrome de Vichy* and, in collaboration with Eric Conan, in *Vichy, un passé qui ne passe pas*. Yet both these studies interpret the public preoccupation with Vichy since the 1970s in terms of a collective pathology, an 'obsession' – an issue that Rousso himself has since revised by defining three phases of the 'contents of representations': a cultural and historiographical reevaluation of the Vichy regime; the emergence of the 'memory of the Shoah'; and the concomitant reparation, internationalisation and 'judiciarisation' of Vichy.[11] Instead, this chapter attempts to show that the rhetorical, artistic and ritual representations themselves (which are inseparable from their 'contents'), as embodied in the controversy over the Vél' d'Hiv', mark the transition of the memorial legacy of Vichy from collective 'obsession' to a period of *relative* reconciliation. Moreover, the very techniques of representing memory cultures (narrative, ritual and symbolic paradigms) reveal striking structural and thematic analogies on the basis of which a comparison of different memory cultures is possible and the internationalisation of memories of the Second World War is taking place. Parallel to the trial of the Vichy official Paul Touvier in 1994, the Vél' d'Hiv' marked the symbolic institutionalisation of the Vichy regime and its crimes – a process compounded from the late 1990s by the increased institutionalisation of the study and implementation of reparation measures within the Mattéoli Commission (founded in 1997) and of research and publications within the Foundation for the Memory of the Shoah (founded in 2000). It is debatable whether this process of institutionalisation faithfully reflects contemporary French self-understanding, for the trial and conviction of the last surviving Vichy official, Maurice Papon, in 1997 and 1998 for complicity in crimes against humanity (Papon ordered the arrest for deportation of 1,560 Jews from 1942 to 1944), and the belated restitution of Jewish property confiscated during collaboration, reopened painful memories of the Vichy regime. It is nevertheless likely that the Papon trial and calls for financial reparations did not reverse the process of institutionalisation and historicisation of the war period in France, but that they too, by opening the past to public negotiation and rearticulation, contributed towards the end of a compulsive preoccupation with this period and the beginning of its integration into a complex national legacy of both 'positive' and 'negative' sites of memory. It is in this sense that the commemorations and monuments of the 1990s in France surpassed traditional national paradigms (conceived in terms of the alternative between either collective remembrance or collective forgetting of a historical event) by integrating the memory of war crimes into the contemporary 'French' memory culture on the path towards an increasingly postnational self-understanding (see Part III). Whereas reconciliation was sought until the 1970s on the basis of pardon or institutionalised amnesia, the tendency today, as exemplified by the Vél' d'Hiv', is to seek reconciliation on the basis of public awareness and recognition of war crimes. Whereas amnesia and national mythology may have been considered a social necessity during the postwar years in order to ensure a smooth transition of the administration to republican order, it is now accepted that reconciliation may only be achieved through campaigns of historical awareness raising, of which political gestures, rituals and commemorations constitute an essential symbolic component alongside educational programmes and historiography.

The Emergence of the Vélodrome d'Hiver as a 'Site of Memory', 1992–97

i. The Site and its Urban Context

Visitors at the site of the Vél' d'Hiv' in Paris encounter three, if not four elements. The site of the former cycle stadium (an office block now stands in its place belonging to the Interior Ministry) is marked with a stele with an inscription recalling the events of 1942, a street sign marking the Square of Jewish Martyrs (Place des Martyrs Juifs), and a figurative sculpture nearby on the Quai de Grenelle. This monumental ensemble draws on five types of commemoration. The first, the original historical site, is authentic and exists only in photographs or in the imagination, while the other four types draw on different degrees of formal mediation of the site. The street sign literally inscribes the memorial into the urban geography of the city. The stele, a small stone surrounded by grass and a railing, is engraved with an inscription recalling the history and numbers of victims of the deportations and naming the perpetrator as the 'Nazi occupiers'. The sculpture includes an inscription recalling the event, the need for remembrance, and the reasons for the persecutions, while identifying perpetrators as the 'de facto authority called the "government of the French State"'. It also offers a visual sculptural rendering of the events of 1942 by depicting a group of people seated, waiting with suitcases. An additional form of mediation is the ritual state ceremony, where speeches are held and wreaths laid, either in front of the stele until 1994 or in front of the sculpture from 1995.

The events of 1942 were initially marked by a plaque installed in 1946 by an anti-racist association at the entrance to the Vél' d'Hiv' building on 8 boulevard de Grenelle, where private commemorations were held. The site began to acquire national significance on the occasion of the fortieth anniversary commemoration in 1982 when Jacques Chirac, in his function as mayor of Paris, attended the ceremony. This fortieth anniversary was overshadowed by the Israeli intervention in Lebanon, and critics marked the event by calling for vigilance against contemporary racist sentiments in France.[12] The site of the stadium has been marked by a monument since 1986 when Chirac, now prime minister, unveiled a stele marking the site of the stadium (Fig. 1) and the street sign naming the square between the Bir Hakeim bridge and the boulevard de Grenelle as the Square of Jewish Martyrs. On this occasion, the gathering included major dignitaries from the Jewish community, the Israeli ambassador, rabbis Joseph Kaplan and René Sirat, as well as an estimated 1,500 spectators.[13] It was not until 1992 that the site became a focus of media attention following the controversy over Mitterrand's handling of the commemoration. The bronze sculpture depicting a seated group with suitcases was finally erected in a small park on the adjacent Quai de Grenelle in 1994 (Fig. 2). Since 1992, either the president or prime minister in person has attended this ceremony at the site of the monument, which has become an established date in the calendar of national commemorations. At the same time, plaques with identical inscriptions have been erected in several provincial towns and on the sites of internment camps, at which municipal representatives hold ceremonies commemorating the deportations at the same time as the Vél' d'Hiv' ceremony each year.

The novelty of this memorial consists not only in its explicit recognition of Jewish victims, but also in the symbolic link it creates between deportation, genocide, the French State of Vichy and, as a result of the subsequent commemorations, the Fifth Republic. In contrast to the inscribed stele inaugurated in 1986, which imputes responsibility for the deportations to 'the police of the government of Vichy under the orders of Nazi occupiers',[14] the inscription on the new monument directly accuses the French State: 'The French Republic pays homage to the victims of racist and anti-Semitic persecutions and crimes against humanity committed under the de facto authority called the "government of the French State" 1940–1944'.[15] However, both the inscription on the monument of 1994 and President Chirac's speech of 1995 distinguish clearly between the French State of Vichy and the republic; the term 'de facto authority' and the use of inverted commas to define the "French State" also underscore a willingness to disassociate in legal terms the Vichy regime from the republic and thus deny elements of social continuity; and by paying 'homage' to the victims, they testify to the moral, not the political responsibility of the republic. Although the Vél' d'Hiv' commemorations and 1994 monument acknowledge in general terms the responsibility of French authorities in the deportations of 1942, and thereby contradict the Gaullist myth of a nation united in resistance, they do not disqualify either the moral, social or political integrity of the postwar republic. In other words, the first inscription represents the perpetrator of the specific events of July 1942 as an external authority, while the second inscription represents the event in general terms as 'racist and anti-Semitic persecutions' and the perpetrator as French, but illegitimate. Moreover, by flaunting the disgrace of collaboration as a negative model (the deportations of 1942 had not previously been commemorated by heads of state on this large scale), this memorial reinforces an alternative, 'positive' republican tradition.

The fact that the site of the Vél' d'Hiv' today consists of a diffuse ensemble of elements, dispersed within an area of two to three hundred square metres, is testimony to the somewhat improvised evolution of the site. This monument is not the result of a calculated decision to erect a monument, as in the case of the Holocaust Monument in Berlin or the Jewish memorial in Vienna, but rather an accidental accumulation of minor commemorative events since 1946, and more intensively during

Figure 1: Stele marking the site of the Vél' d'Hiv' (inaugurated in 1986)

the thirteen years between 1982 and 1995. The Vél' d'Hiv' is not a monument in the traditional sense, for the elements of the ensemble emerged in staggered intervals over time and are scattered in space. They nevertheless have the collective quality of a monument in so far as they remind us of a single event of the past, are used as a backdrop for annual national commemorations, and triggered explosive public debates. As a result, Vél' d'Hiv' has become a household name in France.

The figurative style of the centrepiece sculpture of the Vél' d'Hiv' is strikingly anachronistic in comparison to innovations in monumental art since the 1960s. The bronze Vél' d'Hiv' sculpture designed by Walter Spitzer depicts a group of seven figures including two women, one holding a child, a child and baby playing together, an old man, and a middle-aged woman, who all appear seated, waiting beside suitcases in a scene depicting the hours of detention prior to deportation. The figures are

Figure 2: Monument for victims of the Vél' d'Hiv' round-ups of 16 and 17 July 1942, by Walter Spitzer (inaugurated in 1994)

slightly smaller than life-size and the entire group, raised on a concrete platform representing the curved planks of a cycle track, is approximately three metres long, two metres wide and two metres high. The selection of the monument added in July 1994 was made behind closed doors by a commission comprising members of survivors' organisations, of the Ministry of Veterans Affairs and of the Ministry of Culture in the town hall of Paris, and competition among artists was minimalised.[16] At no time in the evolution of the site did the public debate focus on this selection procedure or on artistic questions of form and layout, neither before nor after it was built. Instead, debate centred exclusively on the peripheral political rituals taking place on the site of the monument.

The lack of debate over the artistic dimension of and selection procedure for the monument in France and the relative intensity of debates over the form of equivalent monuments to the memory of the fate of Jews during the Second World War elsewhere, is significant in its own right. According to conventional procedure, demands for a memorial are followed by lobbying and often by a competition designed to secure a most 'appropriate' consensual memorial form. Public debate over the form of the Holocaust Monument in Berlin prior to the parliamentary resolution to build it lasted eleven years, and another six years will have elapsed before its official inauguration in 2005; comparable debate over the Yad Vashem Memorial in Jerusalem lasted twelve years. The challenge of reaching agreement on a single visible sign was also an absolute condition of the success of the project for a memorial in Vienna in the 1990s. Any calls to abandon either the Berlin or Vienna projects were interpreted as an invalidation of competition procedures, a dent in the authority of associations and politicians and therefore of deep-seated assumptions about the origins of state monuments. In these cases, the artistic challenge was closely linked to political processes of negotiation, such that the success or failure of the artistic project was interpreted as a measure of the success or failure of political protocol.[17] Unlike the Berlin and Vienna monuments, the political deliberation and negotiation of monumental forms, involving architectural competitions, parliamentary committees and debates, and the creation of charity foundations, are conventions which were not adopted for the Vél' d'Hiv'.

It should be stressed that the diffuse, improvised nature of the five monumental elements and the artistic banality of the central sculpture constitute the peculiar logic of this monument. The quest for an ideal artistic representation of history was not a condition for the Paris monument, which instead emerged piece by piece over time *incidentally* to ritual ceremonies. The Vél' d'Hiv' monument is rather a by-product of political attempts to ritually commemorate historic dates. In retrospect, its elements serve as a backdrop for symbolic political representation. They were not the planned goal, but remnants or traces of successive commemorations that involved the presence of political representatives, gestures of wreath laying, and political speeches. They therefore remind us not only of history in the 1940s but of the history of their making in the 1980s and 1990s, including concomitant procedural shortcomings, and ideological manipulations. In contrast to many central memorials of its kind, the Vél' d'Hiv' was not planned as a central national monument, and did not pose the absolute challenge of graphically representing history in a single object. The lack of debate over its form therefore results from its singularly contingent origins as a site at which state rituals could be performed. Another striking aspect of the Vél' d'Hiv' monument is its use of inscriptions rather than abstract plastic forms. The inscribed stele, street sign and sculpture fulfil a largely denotative function marking the site with terse rhetorical rather than elaborate sculptural interpretation. The monumental elements are dominated by inscriptions containing essentially historical facts, such that the function of stone and steel materials is not sculptural, but primarily to act as a durable support for words.

In addition to its inherent sculptural significance and its expediency as a support for inscriptions and political ritual, the Vél' d'Hiv' monument has become part of an urban narrative in combination with the city's historical architecture and monuments and with existing national memorials of the Second World War in Paris. These include numerous street plaques marking the site of the homes or the assassination of members of the Resistance, as well as street names. Most existing Second World War memorials in Paris commemorate events or figures associated with de Gaulle. There are two Gaullist memorials in the immediate vicinity of the Vél' d'Hiv'. First, the bridge across the Seine close by the Vél' d'Hiv' has been named the Bir Hakeim bridge, after the military victory of the Free French Forces in northern Africa in May and June 1942. In the centre of the bridge stands the statue France Coming to Life Again (La France renaissante) by the sculptor Wederlink which, since its construction in 1930, has been complemented by a plaque with an inscription recounting the military glory at Bir Hakeim and interpreting this victory as a symbol of the continuity of the French government in exile and in resistance against occupation. 'France,' says the inscription, 'has never stopped fighting'. Another Gaullist memorial is situated two hundred metres upstream from the Vél' d'Hiv', a stone memorial (approx. six metres long, one metre wide and three metres high) to General Diego Brosset who is said to have responded to de Gaulle's historic radio appeal of 18 June 1940 to the 'Free French' by leading the military campaign in central Africa and the battle at Bir Hakeim. The most famous Gaullist monument in the west of Paris is the tomb of the unknown soldier and eternal flame installed beneath the Arc de Triomphe in 1920 in honour of dead soldiers of the First World War. Like the Cenotaph in London and the Neue Wache in Berlin, this memorial was later adapted as a joint memorial to victims of both world wars. It consists not only of the tomb of the unknown soldier but also of a group of six bronze plaques set in the ground, three of which are dedicated to Gaullist memories of the Second World War: to the campaign in North Africa, to de Gaulle's radio broadcast of 18 June 1940, and to all soldiers who died fighting for France during 1939-1945 (the other three plaques address the proclamation of the Third Republic in 1870, the repossession of Alsatia and Lorraine in 1918, and the victims of the Indochinese war). An additional bronze statue of de Gaulle walking down the Champs Elysées after the liberation of Paris in 1944 was erected on 9 November 2001. In contrast to this predominantly Gaullist symbolic presence in Paris, the Vél' d'Hiv' is a memorial anomaly, for it represents the Jewish rather than the Resistance memory of the Second World War. The Vél' d'Hiv' and its surrounding topography therefore embody in stone the two most pervasive public memories of Vichy – the Gaullist perspective dominant until the 1970s, and the more recent Jewish perspective. This architectural contradiction graphically embodies the as yet unresolved conflict between these two modes of social memory, a conflict that intensified during the 1990s.

In contrast to the west of Paris, the eastern sector of the city contains monuments that do not adhere to the Gaullist vision of the Second

World War. Two monuments in particular tell an alternative story to the glorification of military victories. First, the Memorial of the Unknown Jewish Martyr (Mémorial du Martyr Juif Inconnu) in the Marais district, erected in 1956, which combines a specifically Jewish memory of genocide with elements of traditional war memorials of universal appeal. In the courtyard of the Centre for Contemporary Jewish Documentation (Centre de Documentation Juive Contemporaine) stands a large concrete cylinder bearing the names of concentration camps and containing ashes of victims from Auschwitz, while the crypt contains the tomb of an unknown victim and an eternal flame.[18] Only retrospectively does this combination of symbols of the genocide with universal symbolism characteristic of First World War memorials appear contradictory. Its historical site in the Saint-Paul area, where Jewish immigrants from eastern Europe first arrived during the nineteenth century, was not interpreted as a site of Jewish resistance against or victimisation by the state, but as a place of reconciliation where immigrants arrived and were successfully integrated into French society.[19] This monument therefore commemorates the genocide in combination with the national integration of Jews during the nineteenth century in the vicinity of the monument in Paris by cleverly externalising or detaching the genocide from national concerns, for the names of concentration camps and universal symbols locate this event in distant concentration camps far from both French territory and responsibility. The second monument for victims, the Memorial of the Martyrs of Deportation (Mémorial des Martyrs de la Déportation) designed by Georges-Henri Pingusson consists of a massive concrete monument situated on the eastern tip of the Ile de la Cité and inaugurated in 1962 by de Gaulle. Like the Vél' d'Hiv', this site is devoted to the memory of deportations. However, it contains no specific reference to Jewish victims, and its dedication to 'the two hundred thousand *French* martyrs who died in the deportation camps' (my italics), identifying victims as French nationals, distorts the historical record by suggesting that victims died willingly for a *national* cause rather than as victims of state persecution. Moreover, in spite of the monument's official title, inscriptions on the interior walls of the memorial account not for the conditions of departure but for the destinations of deportees. Like the Memorial of the Unknown Jewish Martyr, the Memorial of the Martyrs of Deportation therefore symbolically assimilates the specific Jewish memory of the Second World War into national memory.

The centrepiece of both monuments is a crypt containing remains of an unknown deportee. Unlike the unknown soldier traditionally used in national war memorials to associate military endeavour and patriotic self-sacrifice as national ideals, however, the unknown individuals in these monuments are not victims who died in combat, but innocent victims of persecution. Again, these tombs of unknown deportees subordinate the memory of alleged foreign victimisation to national belonging by exhibiting victims in a symbolic form traditionally reserved for national heroes. The authority responsible for their fate is not named. Instead, a panoply of dramatic abstract symbols evokes the fate of the victims in terms that transcend the specific historical causes of the events. In the Memorial of the Martyrs of Deportation, for example, impressions of imprisonment are evoked with a long dark corridor, narrow passageways, iron railings and a spiked portcullis, and inscriptions include the names of concentration camps and quotations by well-known French writers. In short, the Memorial of the Unknown Jewish Martyr recalls the genocide against Jews in general, and the Memorial of the Martyrs of Deportation recalls deportation in general. Both deny the paradox that deportees were largely victims of the very nation in whose name they are commemorated.[20]

In contrast to existing monuments, the Vél' d'Hiv' breaks new ground by not representing victims as 'unknown' individuals and victimisation in general regardless of the identity of persecutors or those persecuted. Instead, it evokes historically identifiable Jewish victims in association with a specific date and specific place, as well as a specific perpetrator, the 'French State'. Renouncing the universalist claims of the former two monuments, the Vél' d'Hiv' creates a unique link between historical specificity and monumentality. The physical proximity of the Vél' d'Hiv' monument to a number of urban ornaments reminding us of de Gaulle's military victories further establishes a dialectical relation between the 'positive' myth of the Resistance and the 'negative' commemoration of deportation and genocide. The Vél' d'Hiv' monument is therefore a symbolic anomaly, but also a complement to its immediate memorial surroundings. It challenges the traditionally celebratory function of commemoration by pinpointing the historical responsibility of the French state and society.

How, in light of the criminality of the nation implied by the Vél' d'Hiv' monument, does the nation commemorate the memory of its own crimes in an artistic and ritual form which has traditionally been the domain of national glorification? The significance of a monument cannot be deduced from its architectural and urban characteristics alone. In order to assess the question whether the monumental, rhetorical and ritual innovations of the Vél' d'Hiv' site genuinely redressed the previous memorial and commemorative imbalance, in which Gaullist ideals pervaded official state representations of Vichy, we must examine more closely the reasons why this commemorative site acquired symbolic significance leading to the introduction of the national day of commemoration in 1993, the construction of the monument in 1994 and Chirac's historic speech of 1995.

ii. Phases of the Commemorative Debate

On 16 and 17 July 1942, 13,152 Jews were rounded up and interned in the winter cycling stadium (Vél' d'Hiv') in Paris prior to their deportation to camps elsewhere in France and then to camps in the East. On 16 July 1992, President François Mitterrand attended the fiftieth anniversary commemoration of the round-ups at the site of the Vél' d'Hiv', the first official ceremony which brought together the highest state representatives including the president, the presidents of the National Assembly, the Senate and the Constitutional Council, as well as ministers, the chief of police and church leaders. The ceremony gained added symbolic significance because a group of intellectuals calling themselves the Comité Vél' d'Hiv' 42 had previously urged Mitterrand to make a speech recognising the persecution of Jews under the Vichy regime (Fig. 3). However, Mitterrand refused to comply with their petition, explaining his motives in the annual television declaration on 14 July that year. Instead, Robert Badinter, President of the Constitutional Council, delivered an unofficial speech recalling the history of the events of 1942 in which he insisted that 'my words are in no way linked to my official function'.[21] Public outrage ensued, which was only quashed three years later when Chirac, shortly after being elected president on 7 May 1995, delivered a speech at the annual Vél' d'Hiv' commemoration which, in accordance with the demands of the Comité Vél' d'Hiv' 42, expressed official recognition of the crimes of the Vichy regime (see Appendix).

The evolution of this commemorative debate may be traced chronologically from 1992 to 1997, where debates largely took place either in anticipation of or in response to the Vél' d'Hiv' commemorations in July each year. The arguments of petitioners and politicians revolved around the consequence of the speech, that is, whether the president, in the name of the Fifth Republic, should recognise the responsibility of the Vichy regime and of French people at that time for war crimes. The petition of the Comité Vél' d'Hiv' 42 on 17 June 1992 demanded 'that the President of the Republic, the head of state, officially recognises and declares that the French State of Vichy is responsible for persecutions and crimes against Jews of France'.[22] Mitterrand responded by refusing to recognise responsibility on behalf of the Fifth Republic, claiming that postwar France, 'the Resistance, then the de Gaulle government, then the Fourth Republic and others were founded on the refusal of this French State',[23] and therefore that one must ask for an explanation not from the republic, but from the 'French State' (of Vichy) itself. A second petition of the Comité Vél' d'Hiv' 42 on 16 July (Fig. 4) reinforced the first by claiming that 'of all the things that have been done in the name of France, the French State is today accountable' and that the act of recognition is one 'involving the whole nation'.[24] The official speech given by Robert Badinter contained factual information about the events of 1942,

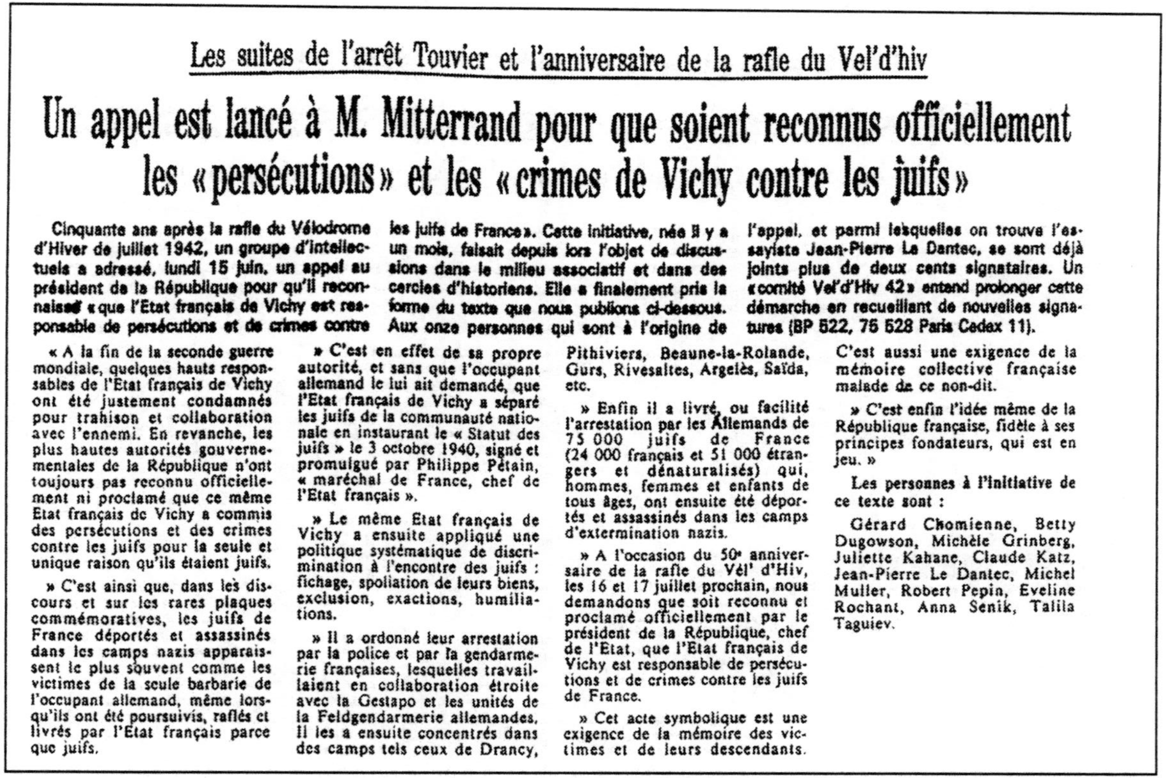

Les suites de l'arrêt Touvier et l'anniversaire de la rafle du Vel'd'hiv

Un appel est lancé à M. Mitterrand pour que soient reconnus officiellement les «persécutions» et les «crimes de Vichy contre les juifs»

Cinquante ans après la rafle du Vélodrome d'Hiver de juillet 1942, un groupe d'intellectuels a adressé, lundi 15 juin, un appel au président de la République pour qu'il reconnaisse «que l'Etat français de Vichy est responsable de persécutions et de crimes contre les juifs de France». Cette initiative, née il y a un mois, faisait depuis lors l'objet de discussions dans le milieu associatif et dans des cercles d'historiens. Elle a finalement pris la forme du texte que nous publions ci-dessous. Aux onze personnes qui sont à l'origine de l'appel, et parmi lesquelles on trouve l'essayiste Jean-Pierre Le Dantec, se sont déjà joints plus de deux cents signataires. Un «comité Vel'd'Hiv 42» entend prolonger cette démarche en recueillant de nouvelles signatures (BP 522, 75 528 Paris Cedex 11).

« A la fin de la seconde guerre mondiale, quelques hauts responsables de l'Etat français de Vichy ont été justement condamnés pour trahison et collaboration avec l'ennemi. En revanche, les plus hautes autorités gouvernementales de la République n'ont toujours pas reconnu officiellement ni proclamé que ce même Etat français de Vichy a commis des persécutions et des crimes contre les juifs pour la seule et unique raison qu'ils étaient juifs.

» C'est ainsi que, dans les discours et sur les rares plaques commémoratives, les juifs de France déportés et assassinés dans les camps nazis apparaissent le plus souvent comme les victimes de la seule barbarie de l'occupant allemand, même lorsqu'ils ont été poursuivis, raflés et livrés par l'Etat français parce que juifs.

» C'est en effet de sa propre autorité, et sans que l'occupant allemand le lui ait demandé, que l'Etat français de Vichy a séparé les juifs de la communauté nationale en instaurant le « Statut des juifs » le 3 octobre 1940, signé et promulgué par Philippe Pétain, « maréchal de France, chef de l'Etat français ».

» Le même Etat français de Vichy a ensuite appliqué une politique systématique de discrimination à l'encontre des juifs : fichage, spoliation de leurs biens, exclusion, exactions, humiliations.

» Il a ordonné leur arrestation par la police et par la gendarmerie françaises, lesquelles travaillaient en collaboration étroite avec la Gestapo et les unités de la Feldgendarmerie allemandes. Il les a ensuite concentrés dans des camps tels ceux de Drancy, Pithiviers, Beaune-la-Rolande, Gurs, Rivesaltes, Argelès, Saïda, etc.

» Enfin il a livré, ou facilité l'arrestation par les Allemands de 75 000 juifs de France (24 000 français et 51 000 étrangers et dénaturalisés) qui, hommes, femmes et enfants de tous âges, ont ensuite été déportés et assassinés dans les camps d'extermination nazis.

» A l'occasion du 50e anniversaire de la rafle du Vél' d'Hiv, les 16 et 17 juillet prochain, nous demandons que soit reconnu et proclamé officiellement par le président de la République, chef de l'Etat, que l'Etat français de Vichy est responsable de persécutions et de crimes contre les juifs de France.

» Cet acte symbolique est une exigence de la mémoire des victimes et de leurs descendants. C'est aussi une exigence de la mémoire collective française malade de ce non-dit.

» C'est enfin l'idée même de la République française, fidèle à ses principes fondateurs, qui est en jeu. »

Les personnes à l'initiative de ce texte sont :

Gérard Chomienne, Betty Dugowson, Michèle Grinberg, Juliette Kahane, Claude Katz, Jean-Pierre Le Dantec, Michel Muller, Robert Pepin, Eveline Rochant, Anna Senik, Talila Taguiev.

Figure 3: First petition of the Comité Vél'd'Hiv 42, appealing to President Mitterand to make a commemorative speech at the Vél'd'Hiv memorial in 1992. Text initiated by Gérard Chomienne, Betty Dugowson, Michèle Grinberg, Juliette Kahane, Claude Katz, Jean-Pierre Le Dantec, Michel Muller, Robert Pepin, Eveline Rochant, Anna Selik, Talila Taguiev (*Le Monde*, 17 June 1992)

Le Comité Vel' d'Hiv' 42 : l'Etat est « sourd »

« On savait l'Etat muet, on le découvre sourd. » Interrogé à la télévision au sujet de l'appel du comité Vel' d'Hiv' 42 pour « la reconnaissance officielle des persécutions et des crimes de Vichy contre les juifs », *le président de la République a répondu aujourd'hui qu'il était sans objet. On n'a pas, selon lui, à demander des comptes à la République puisque c'est elle qui, en 1790, a intégré les juifs de France comme citoyens de plein droit, elle qui, se fondant sur la Déclaration des droits de l'homme et du citoyen, a exclu toute discrimination religieuse ou raciale.*

« Mais comment le président de la République peut-il sérieusement soupçonner les milliers de signataires de l'appel du comité Vel' d'Hiv' 42 d'ignorer tout cela ? A l'entendre, nous souhaiterions que la République s'accuse de crimes qu'elle n'a pas commis. Mais rien dans le texte de l'appel n'autorise cette confusion. On sait bien qu'avant de perpétrer ses crimes, Vichy a commencé par abolir la République et par supprimer sa devise. De même, personne n'a pensé que le geste de Willy Brandt s'agenouillant à Auschwitz était dirigé contre la République de Weimar ni contre la République fédérale.

» On nous dit que la République n'est pas engagée par les agissements de Vichy, et que cet Etat n'avait de français que le nom. Mais pourtant il était servi par des administrateurs français, des magistrats français, des policiers français, qui ont accepté en masse de prêter serment à Pétain, d'exécuter des ordres inhumains et parfois de prendre eux-mêmes des initiatives criminelles, oubliant qu'ils avaient été nommés à leur poste par un Etat républicain. De tout ce qui s'est fait au nom de la France, l'Etat français est aujourd'hui comptable.

» Le proclamer solennellement est une façon de rester fidèle à l'idéal républicain et à la mémoire de tous ceux qui ont résisté aux nazis et à leurs complices. Qui mieux que le président de la République peut mettre un terme au silence officiel qui dure depuis cinquante ans à propos d'une des pages les plus sinistres de l'Histoire de France ?

» C'est pourquoi nous réitérons notre appel pour que le président de la République, chef de l'Etat, prononce une déclaration solennelle le 16 juillet sur les lieux mêmes de la rafle du Vel' d'Hiv'. Ni le dépôt d'une gerbe lors de cette cérémonie ni même d'éventuelles condamnations judiciaires d'individus ne sauraient tenir lieu d'acte politique engageant la Nation tout entière. »

► Le comité Vel' d'Hiv' 42 a été constitué après un appel à M. Mitterrand publié dans notre journal (*le Monde* du 17 juin) par onze personnes, dont l'essayiste Jean-Pierre Le Dantec, auxquelles se sont joints depuis plusieurs centaines de signataires.

Figure 4: Second petition of the Comité Vél' d'Hiv' 42 (*Le Monde*, 16 July 1992)

a condemnation of the involvement of the French police, an affirmation of the necessity of commemorative events for 'teaching truth and the power of justice', but also that the republic 'should not be held accountable for crimes committed by the men of Vichy'.[25] The Comité Vél' d'Hiv' 42 responded critically in a further communiqué (Fig. 5) by insisting that the president in person should have held the speech as an act of 'national representation'. Its call for the introduction of a 'national day of commemoration of the persecutions and crimes perpetrated against the Jews by the French State of Vichy',[26] was nevertheless fulfilled by Mitterrand in December.

Le Comité Vel' d'Hiv' 42 s'adresse aux parlementaires

Le Comité Vel' d'Hiv' 42 a commenté la cérémonie officielle organisée le 16 juillet boulevard de Grenelle, à Paris, en diffusant le communiqué suivant :

« Enfin, la vérité sur les crimes de l'Etat français de Vichy est sortie au grand jour dans la presse et les médias. Enfin, après cinquante ans de silence officiel, les plus hautes autorités de l'Etat assistent à l'hommage rendu aux victimes de la rafle du Vel'd'Hiv'et le président de la République appuie de sa présence la dénonciation de ce crime.

» Le Comité Vel' d'Hiv' 42, qui s'est associé à la cérémonie par le dépôt d'une gerbe au nom des milliers de signataires de son appel « pour la reconnaissance officielle des crimes de l'Etat français de Vichy contre les juifs », a écouté avec émotion le discours de Robert Badinter dénonçant justement la responsabilité de l'Etat français de Vichy.

» Ce que Robert Badinter a exprimé à titre personnel, c'était, selon nous, au président de la République de le proclamer à titre officiel. Cet acte symbolique tant attendu reste donc inaccompli.

» Le Comité Vel' d'Hiv' 42 en réaffirme la nécessité et, maintenant l'objectif de son appel, s'adresse aujourd'hui à la représentation nationale et invite chaque parlementaire à œuvrer afin que soit votée par l'Assemblée une loi faisant du 16 juillet une journée nationale de commémoration des persécutions et des crimes perpétrés contre les juifs par l'Etat français de Vichy. »

▶ Comité Vel' d'Hiv' 42, BP 522 75 528 Paris Cedex 11.

Figure 5: Communiqué of the Comité Vél' d'Hiv' 42, in response to the ceremony at the Vél' d'Hiv' in 1992, when President Mitterrand attended, but did not hold the speech requested by the association (*Le Monde*, 20 July 1992)

Petitions by other associations followed in 1993 and 1994. The Union of Jewish Students of France (UEJF) launched a petition in January 1993, repeating the demands of the Comité Vél' d'Hiv' 42, while also requesting the president to end the ritual of laying a wreath at the grave of Philippe Pétain.[27] Then, in 1994, the civil representatives of the Jewish community at the trial of Paul Touvier claimed that national reconciliation could only be implemented if the highest state authorities stated that they were willing to accept the crimes of collaboration.[28] Finally, President Chirac held his historic speech at the Vél' d'Hiv' commemoration in 1995, in which he claimed that 'we still owe an imprescriptible debt to the Jews deported from France', and that French people shared a 'collective fault'.

Two years later in 1997, the newly elected prime minister Lionel Jospin delivered the speech at the Vél' d'Hiv' commemoration in which he insisted that the crimes of 1942 should leave a mark on French collective consciousness. Although Olivier Biffaud of *Le Monde* interpreted this speech as a reiteration of Chirac's speech of 1995, Jospin had in fact adopted a less emotional, more historical, approach than Chirac by underlining not that France or the nation in general, but that 'a government, an administration of our country, then carried out irreparable deeds'.[29] He avoided referring to the nation as a vague transhistorical entity and defined instead individuals and institutions – political decision-makers, administrators, judges, police officers and gendarmes – insisting that recognisable individuals and their actions made it impossible to confuse Vichy and the republic.[30] Jospin thus combined both Chirac's and Mitterrand's perspectives by acknowledging responsibility and differentiating historically between France, the republic, Vichy, and between the institutions of both regimes and the individuals working on their behalf. The former president of the National Assembly, now chairman of the Gaullist party Rassemblement pour la République (RPR), Philippe Séguin, claimed to be tired of the repeated trials of prominent French officials of the Vichy regime, and deplored the spectacle of what he called 'this spirit of self-flagellation, ... this obsession with collective atonement' conveyed by both the trial of Papon and Chirac's Vél' d'Hiv' speech of 1995.[31] Séguin argued that Chirac's expression of collective guilt or 'debt' appeared to equate Vichy with France and therefore to contradict Gaullist doctrine and encourage national criticism that might fuel the more patriotic discourse of the Front National. Séguin's dissatisfaction also spurred Prime Minister Jospin to take a public stance against Chirac's Vél' d'Hiv' speech of 1995 by denying that France is 'guilty' 'because ... Vichy was the negation of France'.[32] Chirac in return responded to these criticisms by defending the arguments he expressed in 1995 in another speech given on 5 December 1997 at the Memorial of the Unknown Jewish Martyr during a ceremony to open a permanent exhibition of files used for the census of Jews in France from 1940.[33]

Between 1992 and 1997, the commemoration of a single event of 1942 evolved alternately from a divisive into a consensual, and again into a divisive vector of political and public opinion towards Vichy. Moreover, it spurred politicians and intellectuals to take a public stand on ethical, historical, legal and psychological questions concerning collective guilt, the continuity of state and society before and after 1940 and 1944, and the role of Vichy in French social memory in the 1990s. The public was given the apparently arbitrary choice between Mitterrand, Séguin and Jospin on the one hand, and Chirac on the other, that is, between the denial of continuity between Vichy and the republic and the acknowledgement of their interconnectedness. These two visions of national history became an object of political debate, condensed in the symbol of the Vél' d'Hiv'.[34] As politicians temporarily adopted the stance of historians, however, they did not lay claim to scientific method. Their debate was governed by laws of symbolic representation, involving a stark polarisation of opinion between political figures, parties, factions within the RPR and between the readiness to acknowledge (Chirac) or not acknowledge (Mitterrand) moral responsibility of the French State of Vichy for war crimes. The outcome of this debate over national symbolics was therefore determined only partly by the historical accuracy of statements made by either of the presidents and essentially by the effectiveness with which symbols, ritual and rhetoric were used in appeals to uphold existing national traditions and public emotions. In 1992, Mitterrand bluntly refused to make an official verbal recognition of war crimes in order not to soil the name of the Fifth Republic whereas, in 1986 and 1995, Chirac acknowledged the memory of Vichy as a negative example of republican values of liberty, justice and solidarity precisely in order to honour these values. Both presidents were concerned primarily with the pro-republican pedagogical effect of their speeches.[35] This polarisation of the two heads of state with respect to the historical symbol repeatedly divided public opinion and fuelled debate. The Vél' d'Hiv' commemorations were not a source of consensus, therefore, but of sustained political and social division.

Changing political and historical circumstances have confirmed the place of the Vél' d'Hiv' in the institutional commemorative calendar. The bill introduced in 1993 to establish the first Sunday following the 16 and 17 July each year as an annual day of commemoration become law in 2000. During the same year, the parliament introduced a new bill to guarantee financial reparations for orphans of deported victims, and set up the Foundation for the Memory of the Shoah, while Chirac continued unabashedly to honour de Gaulle by opening the Charles de Gaulle Museum in the Invalides military museum. Commemorations of the Vél' d'Hiv' in 2001 and 2002 took place under the shadow of the intensified Israeli–Palestinian conflict following the declaration of the second intifada in November 2000. The wave of violent attacks on Jewish cemeteries, schools and synagogues in France between 2001 and 2002 was not an expression of traditional anti-Semitism but of a limited, extreme sense of social deprivation by Arab youths in poor suburban areas that translated into a diffuse feeling of hostility towards Israel and Jewish symbols which the political scientist Pierre-André Taguieff has defined in terms of a generalised 'judeophobia'.[36] The Vél' d'Hiv' speech of July 2001 therefore focused explicitly on the theme of ethnic and religious tolerance among young people. The following year, the sixtieth anniversary of the deportations of 1942, was overshadowed not only by continuing acts of violence but also by the scandal of the victory of the leader of the right-wing Front National party, Le Pen, in the first round of the presidential election in April. The speech of the Prime Minister Pierre Raffarin then reinforced the sense of Chirac's speech of 1995 by laying claim to the compatibility of and even equating republican values with minority interests, arguing that 'an aggression against the Jewish community is an aggression against France'.[37] The town hall of Paris hosted a series of related films and discussions at the central video library, the TV5 television channel broadcast a series of documentary films about the deportations of 1942, and an exhibition about the Vél' d'Hiv' round-ups was hosted in the entrance of the St Lazare railway station before travelling to a further eleven venues. Most significantly, almost all speakers commemorating the deportations have, since 1995, quoted Chirac's historical speech of 1995, thus entrenching the legacy of this historic symbolic gesture in spite of its inherent contradictions.

How are we to understand the conflicting interpretations of Vichy and French nationhood on the basis of the political usage of the Vél' d'Hiv', expressed in particular via presidential speeches? And how did the speeches reflect commemorative and rhetorical strategies designed to relate the Vél' d'Hiv' monument to a sense of national belonging, to present this site as a consensual historical symbol? The Vél' d'Hiv' monument became a national symbol in the course of its symbolic and rhetorical enhancement in spite of historians' claims that there existed other, more representative national sites of memory. The persistently controversial nature of this monument and commemoration heightened its symbolic and emotional value for all political representatives involved in the dispute, whether they were for or against the presidential acknowledgement of war crimes. The symbolic potency of this monument as a specifically national site of memory increased in proportion to the intensity and duration of the debate as such, which were in turn fuelled by the clash of interpretations of those involved. The monumentality of the Vél' d'Hiv' is not only an architectural quality, but a social construction within a specific 'semiosphere' or 'communicative field'[38] comprising political interests, ritual commemorations, media publicity and public debate. Furthermore, the emergence of this monument as a national monument was not a result of social consensus over its meaning, but precisely the lack of consensus in a debate whose participants were united in their certainty over which symbols were worth disputing!

The 'nationalisation' of the site and symbol of the Vél' d'Hiv' was therefore motivated by contemporary political expediency. Swamped in a succession of presidential speeches, wreath-laying ceremonies, and overshadowed by political disputes among and within parties regarding their stance towards the Front National, it is not surprising that the Vél' d'Hiv' site or monumental ensemble – the ostensible focal point of the original commemoration – was entirely omitted from public debate, except on the occasion of the official inauguration of Walter Spitzer's bronze sculpture in July 1994, when the sculpture was mentioned and illustrated, but not discussed in French newspapers. The Vél' d'Hiv' site and commemoration therefore represent a case of both the politics of art (the political use of symbolics), and the art of politics (expressed in oratory) defined by Edelman as the 'symbolic use of politics'.[39] In the first case, public art and peripheral commemorative rituals relating to the site give rise to political gestures and are the object of debate over historical interpretation. In the second case, art, including rhetorical appeals to a sense of belonging and of tradition, is a means to achieve effective political communication employed during commemorations.

* * *

In contrast to monuments such as street plaques, the Memorial of the Unknown Jewish Martyr or the Memorial of the Martyrs of Deportation in Paris, which were erected between the 1940s and 1960s, the Vél' d'Hiv' monument has, in the course of public debate, acquired a particular status as a national monument to French collaboration. In addition to gaining nationwide attention, it was officially classified as a central monument on 3 December 1993 when selected by decree as the site of the annual National Day of Commemoration of the Racist and Anti-Semitic Persecutions. As one of the most well-known and most controversial sites of memory of the Second World War in France during the 1990s, its monumentality is less a material, architectural category than one of political expediency.

The relatively limited political impact of this monument prior to the controversies of the 1990s makes the highly emotional tone of the controversies, once they broke out, more remarkable. The public invisibility of this site before 1992 is compounded by the fact that there remain very few visual documents of the round-ups of 1942.[40] The political scientist Pierre Birnbaum, writing shortly before the Vél' d'Hiv' commemoration in 1992, claimed that physical, urban sites of Jewish memory had become very rare.[41] However, Birnbaum overlooked the fact that the stele and Square of Jewish Martyrs in memory of victims of the Vél' d'Hiv' round-ups existed as early as 1986 in addition to a plaque and private memorial ceremonies from 1946. It would be more accurate to say that memorials at the sites of the Vél' d'Hiv' round-ups and the French internment camps did exist before the 1990s, but that the mass media and public largely ignored them.[42] Within only a few years the relative lack of interest in sites of memory of the Jewish community in France, which Birnbaum interprets as outright scarcity, has been reversed.

The reason for this remarkable transformation of public perceptions of victims as French victims of foreign powers to Jewish victims of both foreign and indigenous powers is rooted in the awakening of a Jewish memory culture in France in the 1960s. This transformation found expression in the transition from universalised representations of victimhood and externalised representations of sites of perpetration (in the Memorial of the Unknown Jewish Martyr and the Memorial of the Martyrs of Deportation) on the one hand, to the historical recognition of particular indigenous acts of persecution (in the Vél' d'Hiv' monument) on the other. Silence over the fate of Jewish victims had been brought about in part by French survivors' own desire to downplay their identity as victims and to integrate into French society after 1944, but also by the overwhelming power of the myth of a nation united in resistance, a myth broken by the suspension of laws on the prescription of war crimes in 1964, by the explosive public impact of cultural representations such as Marcel Ophuls's film *The Sorrow and the Pity* (*Le Chagrin et la pitié*) in 1971, the arrival of Jewish immigrants from North Africa, and not least the international awareness of the instability of the state of Israel following the Six-Day War in 1967.

Historians have repeatedly questioned whether the Vél' d'Hiv' possesses characteristics of a site of memory of the Vichy regime in the sense asserted by Nora, as a 'focal point of our national heritage'.[43] This monument, and the national day of commemoration performed there each year, convey a somewhat one-sided image of Vichy history in so far as they focus attention exclusively on the state persecution of Jews and therefore detract from the fate of prisoners of war or forced labour workers sent to Germany in exchange for the release of prisoners of war, and from both the 'interior' and 'exterior' Resistance, that is, of clandestine communist groups inside and de Gaulle's forces outside France. Until the 1970s, two of the strongest myths of postwar France were founded on the memory of the Resistance – either of the democratic ideals and patriotism promoted by de Gaulle, or of an extensive popular movement of 'national insurrection',[44] both of which have since been relativised by the rise of Jewish memory and the realisation, promoted by historiography, exhibitions, films, commemorations, trials and debates since the 1970s, that a large section of French society not only actively collaborated with the occupiers but also supported indigenous anti-Semitism, as well as state anti-Semitism introduced in the legislature of 1940–41.[45]

Eric Conan, Henry Rousso and Théo Klein suggest alternative sites of memory of Vichy which, they claim, convey a more balanced understanding of the motives for and consequences of French collaboration. Conan and Rousso suggest that the introduction of laws on the status of Jews, passed between July 1940 and summer 1941, would better represent the function of the regime because these laws highlight an indigenous form of anti-Semitism, 'a principle of political and social exclusion ingrained at the heart of a certain French tradition',[46] and because they reveal how racism was written into common law, and therefore not only arose in extreme situations such as the Vél' d'Hiv' round-ups. The Vél' d'Hiv' symbolises an act of state collaboration which was not related to Vichy policy, for the French police were responding to orders from the Gestapo. These round-ups exemplify an extreme, exceptional form of persecution that contains no elements of the everyday social consequences of xenophobia. Klein suggests that 10 July 1940 would be a more plausible national day of commemoration since on this day the National Assembly of the Third Republic voted to promulgate a new constitution and thereby granted Pétain the legal means, in the name of the republic, to enforce his programme of 'National Revolution'.[47] Such a commemoration would lay blame for the existence of the Vichy regime on representatives of the Third Republic, suggest a strong political continuity between the republic and the Vichy regime, and therefore undermine the Gaullist doctrine that Vichy was a brief interruption, an illegal 'parenthesis' in French history.

From a historical point of view, therefore, the Vél' d'Hiv' represents Jews as victims of state collaboration with Germany rather than of indigenous French anti-Semitic laws and xenophobia. One must nevertheless inquire precisely how and why this symbol of state collaboration was in fact perceived and constructed as one of the most explosive national sites of memory of this period during the 1990s. In spite of its limited historical pertinence as a national monument, the impact of the Vél' d'Hiv' merits examination in its own right as an illustration of contemporary social and political constraints leading to the public understanding of the past.

The Rhetorical Construction of the Vél' d'Hiv' Site

The Vél' d'Hiv' site was not conceived as a national monument prior to its construction, but acquired such significance over time due to peripheral symbolic and ritual reinforcement. Hence the discrepancy between its inconspicuous architectural qualities (it is located on a raised garden barely visible from the street) and its conspicuous social impact. In addition to the architectural forms and elaborate ritualisation of this monument, we may also examine more closely the terminology and phrasing of the commemorative speeches made by political leaders, for these speeches constituted the very focus of petitions and the subsequent debate leading to the politicisation and therefore to the social construction of the Vél' d'Hiv' as a site of memory.

The ceremony of 1995 was widely applauded by historians in the press because no president had previously given verbal acknowledgement of crimes committed in the name of the Vichy regime in this frank manner. 'For the first time,' claimed Conan and Rousso, 'a President of the Republic used language void of ambiguities, verbal contortions and roundabout means which previously characterised most presidential speeches – and they were altogether rare – dealing with the question of Vichy.'[48] According to Henri Hajdenberg, president of the Representative Council of the Jewish Institutions of France (CRIF), Chirac's declaration amounted to a turning point marking the very first recognition of responsibilities of the Vichy state.[49]

Three versions of the petition by the Comité Vél' d'Hiv' 42 appeared in *Le Monde* between 1992 and 1994, including an additional petition by the Union of Jewish Students of France (UEJF) in 1993. The uncompromising campaigning of citizens' action groups for a verbal gesture raised public expectations to such an extent that verbal acknowledgement by the president was construed as a single exclusive condition of the commemoration, a moral imperative which suggested that a verbal statement would not only recognise the nation's responsibility, but even make amends for crimes committed during the Second World War. Petitions and speeches both employed the moralistic vocabulary of 'debt', 'affliction', 'accountability' and 'atonement'. The petition of 17 June 1992 called for the speech as a gesture recognising the memory of individual victims but also as a symbolic reaffirmation of republican values and as 'a necessity for French collective memory, which is afflicted with this unspoken fact'.[50] Moreover, the petition of 16 July 1992 not only claimed that 'the French State is now accountable', but that neither a wreath-laying ceremony nor legal proceedings would be an adequate substitute for a verbal symbolic gesture by the president![51]

The emotive appeals contained in petitions nevertheless led to some confusion. References to the '*Etat français*', that is, the state generally without distinguishing clearly between either the Vichy regime or the republic, threw doubt over precisely who and what was held to be accountable: the French State (of Vichy) or the French (republican) state. Although there are historical grounds on which to demonstrate the legal and social interdependence of the French Republic and the Vichy regime (the parliament of the Third Republic voted for its own dissolution in 1940, and several members of administrative elites of Vichy including the police and judiciary continued to operate after 1944), the moralistic tone of petitioners and politicians who inculpated the '*Etat français*' in general, as a homogeneous ahistorical community extending into the present, accentuated the emotive nature of the debate. The contrast between Mitterrand's refusal and Chirac's willingness to fulfil the demands of the petitions further polarised the perceived attitudes of the two presidents and the moralistic judgements made on them, such that Mitterrand was surrounded by scandal and Chirac's gesture understood, as Hajdenberg's response shows, as a form of reconciliation. Although Chirac's rhetorical acknowledgement of 'collective error' and 'imprescriptible debt'[52] in 1995 belongs to the realm of *informal* politics (the speech was purely symbolic and had no direct bearing on policy), and is historically untenable (collective fault and imprescriptible debt are legal and moral categories hardly applicable to an entire social group as large as a nation, except by association), it nevertheless put a temporary end to controversy over the allegedly ambiguous attitudes of postwar political leaders towards Vichy.

i. The Petitions: a Verbal Act as an Exclusive Condition of Moral Reparation?

The sequence of rhetorical exchanges between petitioners, political leaders, journalists and historians over a period of more than three years transformed the debate over the Vél' d'Hiv' into a debate over the most appropriate terminology to describe the nation. The Comité Vél' d'Hiv' 42 had initially provoked this preoccupation with terminology in 1992 by refusing all types of commemorative gesture other than the president's rhetorical statement acknowledging Vichy crimes. However, the terminology used in this exchange was fraught with confusion, since it was not clear precisely for what, and in the name of what, the president was being asked to recognise responsibility. 'Who is accountable for the crimes of Vichy?' ask Conan and Rousso, 'France? The French? The state? The nation? The republic?'[53] Confusion was increased by the number of terms used during the debate to describe the French nation, which included the Gaullist term 'a certain idea of France',[54] 'the de facto authority',[55] and 'the de facto authority called "the government of the French State"' (term used for inscriptions on the Vél' d'Hiv' and a number of other monuments unveiled throughout France in 1994), as well as related expressions such as 'national reconciliation' or 'civil peace'. The wealth of expressions used to describe the nation in relation to the Vél' d'Hiv' commemorations therefore reflects the multiple ideological dimensions acquired by this site during the debate. The Vél' d'Hiv' served as a focal point for lobby groups, politicians, journalists and historians to demonstratively interpret history in the public sphere by attaching appropriate rhetorical labels to the nation. Attention was diverted from the monument and the commemorations to the specific problem of how to name the nation in relation to Vichy.

The progressive 'nationalisation' of this site of memory may be best observed if we analyse the dynamics of the commemorative debate, which were determined by the identity of political agents in the past and present, that is, the question posed by Conan and Rousso concerning *who* commemorated *what* in the *name of what*? The answer to the question 'who?' is fairly straightforward, since it almost invariably involved a president or prime minister, the heads of government representing the political authority of the nation in the 1990s. 'What?' refers to the historical events being commemorated in the 1940s, and poses the challenge of naming the nation at that time as Vichy or 'the French State'.[56] 'In the name of what?' refers to the society, on behalf of which the commemoration takes place, that is, present-day France. In reality, however, the latter was referred to in various terms as 'France', 'the nation', 'the republic', 'the government', or 'the French State', such that confusion arose over whether the 'the French State' was being used extensively to denote the state in general over time, or whether it referred specifically to the Vichy state or to the Fifth Republic.[57] Chirac, Hadjenberg, Rousso used the term extensively, while Mitterrand, Jospin and Badinter used it to distinguish specific historical dimensions. It therefore became difficult to understand the precise meaning of the Vél' d'Hiv' speeches when any of these terms were used ambiguously, or when the use of apparently ahistorical terms such as 'France' or 'a certain idea of France' glossed over the precise historical period of the nation in question. These terms led to the rhetorical amalgamation of different historical periods, presenting the nation as an eternal transhistorical entity. In order to dissipate the confusion surrounding terminology defining the nation, and to understand the political uses of such confusion, it is worthwhile examining in more detail the political function of historical rhetoric in commemorative speeches at the Vél' d'Hiv'.

The first petition of the Comité Vél' d'Hiv' 42 set the tone of the debate:

> On the occasion of the fiftieth anniversary of the round-ups at the Vél' d'Hiv' on 16 and 17 July, we demand that it be recognised and officially proclaimed by the President of the Republic, the head of state, that the French State of Vichy is responsible for persecutions and crimes against the Jews of France. This symbolic act is required for the memory of the victims and their descendants. It is also required for French collective memory, afflicted with this unspoken fact. Ultimately, the very idea of the French Republic, faithful to her founding principles, is at stake.[58]

The purpose of this petition was to urge President Mitterrand to recognise officially, in the name of the Fifth Republic in 1992, the moral responsibility of the 'French State of Vichy' for anti-Semitic persecutions of the 1940s, with the stated goal of appeasing 'the memory of the victims and their descendants' as well as 'French collective memory' by sustaining the 'idea' of the republic and its 'principles'. From the beginning, therefore, the petition focused upon the presidential commemorative speech as the single means by which the French state could make amends for acts of the French State of Vichy. Both the moral and political dimensions of the petitions were formulated in general, absolute terms. In moral terms, for example, the petitions supposed that crimes of the French State may be repaired or 'cured' by means of formal verbal recognition; the petition presented the nation as an organic, personified whole capable, in religious terms, of achieving personal redemption by contrition and confession. The petitions thereby overstated the symbolic authority of the word of the president by demanding a verbal recognition as an *exclusive* condition in order to end the 'afflicted' or 'ill' ('*malade*') state of the nation. Non-verbal symbolic acts such as the presence of President Mitterrand at the Vél' d'Hiv' commemoration, the construction of a monument there and of a museum on the site of the Izieu internment camp, or the introduction of a national day of commemoration in 1993, were considered insufficient. The petition was based on the combined political and religious assumption that the president's verbal recognition of an apparently unspoken fact would be equivalent to moral reparation for the entire nation.

This insistence on a verbal gesture characterised all subsequent symbolic gestures and statements relating to the Vél' d'Hiv' commemoration. Moreover, by making verbal utterances the sole condition for the success or failure of the commemoration, the debate over the Vél' d'Hiv' revolved not around the most appropriate rituals or sculpture, but around the wording of commemorative speeches and definitions of the French nation as a collective whole: either as the nation under Vichy (the object of commemoration), or the nation under the Fifth Republic (the commemorative agent drawing legitimacy in the present from the commemoration). The issue of defining adequately the French nation with respect to the Vél' d'Hiv' commemoration was determined by distinctions between France and Vichy, and thus became the main condition for the perceived success or failure of subsequent commemorations. Chirac's speech of 1995, which acknowledged in unambiguous terms - in the same moral vein as the petition – the crimes of the Vichy regime, was therefore applauded as a form of redemption or 'final stroke' which verbally reconciled the French nation of the 1990s to its recent history.[59]

ii. Mitterrand's Reticence: 'The Fifth Republic is not Vichy'

In the annual presidential television interview on 14 July 1992, Mitterrand refused to comply with the petition of the Comité Vél' d'Hiv' 42 on ideological grounds. A verbal acknowledgement of 'debt' by the president, pronounced in the name of the Fifth Republic for acts occurring under the Vichy regime, would have evoked symbolically a moral, historical and political continuity between the Vichy government and the republic of 1992, that is, between the France of 1942 and the France of 1992. According to Mitterrand, the republic had traditionally respected citizens' rights including those of Jews, and had purged a large number of collaborators after 1944, so that solely the 'French State' should be held accountable.[60] Moreover, the act of recognition as demanded in the petitions would have brought into question two key aspects of French political culture to which Mitterrand alludes in the interview. First, citizens' rights and republicanism, implying the founding constitutional principles of the republic, the Universal Declaration of the Rights of Man, which were officially denied under Vichy.[61] Second, such a recognition would have contradicted the Gaullist perception of Vichy as an anomaly or form of 'parenthesis' in French political tradition, an interpretation that both overestimates the role of the Resistance and underestimates political, legal and social continuities between Vichy and the republic before and after 1944.

The petitions were also based on premises that could lead to historical misrepresentation. The stringency of the appeals of 1992 implied that crimes had never before been recognised whereas, in reality, they had been recognised both symbolically and legally during the purges of collaborators immediately after the war, which led to trials of over 120,000 collaborators, over 700 executions and some 4,500 summary executions by the Resistance.[62] Films and literature had documented the period from the 1970s. According to Conan and Rousso, the petitioners had rekindled an anachronistic controversy by evoking a generalised collective guilt and by singling out the state as the sole responsible agent of the crimes.[63] The novelty of the petition lay not in its content, therefore, but in the fact that it demanded a purely *verbal* form of reparation as a symbolic act by the head of state.

Exclusive emphasis on verbal declarations, which was set in motion on the initiative of the Comité Vél' d'Hiv' 42, characterised the entire sequence of commemorations. Public controversy over Mitterrand's refusal to make a formal declaration of recognition was intensified by indignation over the biographical entanglement of the president himself, and inflated the significance of the symbolic gesture as if it were a mirror of national self-understanding as such. Although speeches are an integral component of most historical commemorations, they are rarely singled out in this way as exclusive conditions of public and political acceptance. The focus on the wording of speeches was therefore unique to the Vél' d'Hiv'. In contrast to Mitterrand, Chirac accepted the challenge of making a speech in 1995. Yet despite the fact that Chirac's speech at the Vél' d'Hiv' commemoration of 1986 contained precisely the same themes, narrative structure and arguments as that of 1995, only the later speech was subject to close scrutiny in the press.[64] We must assume, therefore, that controversy over the Vél' d'Hiv' in the 1990s resulted from contextual political and historical conditions. Without the insistence of the Comité Vél' d'Hiv' 42 on a verbal gesture, it is possible that Mitterrand's non-verbal gestures of attending the ceremony, laying a wreath, introducing a day of national commemoration and implementing the new Vél' d'Hiv' monument would have been accepted as signs of recognition and reconciliation. But the political impact of this monument was determined not by architectural qualities or commemorative ritual, but by lobbying and petitioning for a verbal gesture, with which Chirac complied in 1995 and thus secured broad social acceptance.

iii. Chirac's Oratory: the Myth of Universalism

President Chirac's commemorative speech at the Vél' d'Hiv' in 1995 initially created 'very broad consensus'[65] among representatives of Jewish associations, intellectuals, politicians from both the left and the right, and from governments abroad. This speech also appeared, at least in terms of its rhetoric, to break with the controversial Gaullist notion that Vichy was illegal, a notion that had been implicitly sanctioned by Mitterrand's silence in 1992. It therefore brought the public debate to a temporary halt. The press reflected overall support for Chirac, with only muted criticism. Gilles Bresson, writing in *Libération*, alluded to the conflict between the two presidents over the Vél' d'Hiv' by reporting that 'Jacques Chirac has well and truly moved a step beyond Mitterrandism'[66] while Henry Rousso claimed that 'Jacques Chirac is leaving behind the myth and approaching History'.[67] The first thorough critique appeared only several weeks later in *Le Monde*, when the political philosopher Blandine Kriegel exposed some philosophical and historical fallacies of the speech.[68] This was followed by a critique of the ethical implications and rhetorical inconsistencies of the speech by the sociologist Nathalie Heinich.[69] In short, Chirac scored a political success by responding to demands to assuage controversy on the basis of the assumption that the verbal recognition of crimes fifty-three years after their occurrence in some way compensated or, in moral terms, repaired them. But what was the precise wording, and what historical and political meanings did the speech attribute to memories associated with the Vél' d'Hiv'? Closer examination of the terminology reveals ambiguities suggesting that public consensus won by the president's gesture may be imputed to the skilful rhetorical manipulation of the issues at stake. This speech couched the recognition of crimes in rhetoric of the nation, where the affirmation of collective moral fault served as a negative model for the reaffirmation of nationhood as a transcendent, abstract ideal.

One reason why Chirac's speech won widespread approval is its timely response to a mounting sense of anticipation which the petitions had created by turning the question of verbal recognition into an exclusive condition, and which had been intensified by the prolonged dispute over Mitterrand's silence. Expressions of the desire to overcome the enduring controversy surrounding Mitterrand had been sounded early in the debate. The repeated petitions of Jewish associations emphasised a sense of impatience over the continuing controversy. The second petition called on the president to 'put an end to the official silence that has lasted for fifty years. ... This is why we are reiterating our appeal' (Fig. 4).[70] Moreover, prognoses such as that of Pierre Bérégovoy, then prime minister, who was reported to have announced in November 1992 that President Mitterrand would finally perform a 'significant act'[71] of recognition that year, were *not* fulfilled and thus both aggravated and frustrated assumptions among associations that Mitterrand would indeed comply with demands of the Comité Vél' d'Hiv' 42.[72] The subsequent nonfulfilment of such expectations reinforced indignation about the behaviour of Mitterrand and ensured approval of the behaviour of Chirac. In other words, accumulated criticisms of Mitterrand's involvement in Vichy and his handling of the Vél' d'Hiv' commemorations ensured that Chirac's fulfilment of Mitterrand's omission, that is, the breaking of silence with respect to the demands of the Comité Vél' d'Hiv' 42, increased public satisfaction when it was finally fulfilled. In this way, the speech acquired intense symbolic proportions. The debate over the wording of this speech offers insight into official understandings of Vichy in relation to traditional Gaullist paradigms of the French memory culture. For if we accept, as proposed above, that the means by which the Vél' d'Hiv' monument was politically appropriated and represented were governed less by the architectural character of the site than by the peripheral claims to interpret the site by naming the nation, then we must look more closely at the precise wording of Chirac's speech of July 1995, which marked a historic moment in the state's appropriation of the legacy of Vichy.

This speech was organised according to a stringent narrative structure and employed complex terminology conveying an equally complex portrait of the nation. The thematic sequence of the speech may be divided into five segments, each conveyed in a specific rhetorical mode of lament, history, appeal, warning and prognosis, in the following order: (a) a lament on the injury done to the memory of France by the Vichy regime, and on the inadequacy of words to account for the events being commemorated; (b) a historical account of these events emphasising the fact that France was directly implicated in the deportations of Jews; (c) an appeal to remember these events as a moral duty, both because Jewish theology lays emphasis on memory, and because these crimes represent an 'imprescriptible debt' for French people; (d) a warning against the persistence of racism, anti-Semitism, fear and 'exclusion', combined with an appeal to memory and 'vigilance' in order to counteract enduring 'obscure forces' (a lightly veiled reference to the Front National); (e) a prognosis that hope for the future is based on the lessons of history and conscious resistance to xenophobia in the name of humanist values. These five themes were couched in highly stylised rhetoric containing a number of references to the nation, some of which evoked and therefore invested the Vél' d'Hiv' with traditional Gaullist paradigms of national self-understanding.

The four rhetorical tropes on which Chirac's speech is founded may be summarised as follows. First, he *personifies* the nation. The speech opens with the words, 'There is, in the *life* of a nation …',[73] and France is subsequently evoked as a wilful agent, one which 'accomplished irreparable acts'. Repeated references to four complementary subjects of the nation as 'I', 'France', 'you' (the first person plural *vous*) and 'we' creates a further rhetorical bond of solidarity between the person of the president ('I'), the person 'France', the vaguely defined collectivity of spectators ('you') and the all-encompassing collectivity 'we'. This conception of the nation as a person is reinforced throughout the debate by reference to the moral integrity of society, referred to in petitions of 1992 as 'afflicted'[74] and 'accountable'.[75] These linguistic expressions of the personified nation, conceived in non-political terms as a community bound by history, are reinforced by references to two communities of social memory, that of the 'Jewish community' and that of 'France': 'The Jewish community remembers, and the whole of France along with it.' Although Chirac does not subsume the memory of Jews to that of the nation, and avoids the assimilationist rhetoric used in his speech of 1986, where he spoke of the Jewish community's 'rootedness in the national community', he nevertheless evokes the integrative force of the nation in apolitical, ideal terms that reinforce the idea of a personified nation endowed with the human faculty of memory.

Second, Chirac equates the nation with an abstract ideal, and therefore reiterates one of the most celebrated and quoted phrases of de Gaulle, 'a certain idea of France'. He appeals to this ideal nation, 'honest, generous, faithful to its traditions, to its genius' as an alternative to Vichy, one which offers a positive moral foundation for collective emotional allegiance. Universal humanist values – 'values of freedom, justice, tolerance on which French identity is founded' – are affirmed in contrast to Vichy, which is thus evoked as a negative model, the rejection of which serves to reassert French republican traditions. In this way, the speech effectively evokes the rejection of Vichy as a basis for the affirmation of the set of *apolitical* timeless values of honesty, generosity and loyalty to tradition. The very abstraction of nationhood as a set of apolitical ideas thus appeals more effectively to social consensus: the moral conceptualisation of the nation here leaves the political significance of the Vél' d'Hiv' site open.[76] Such appeals to national consensus on the basis of moral ideas are consistent with the core Gaullist doctrine of national unity (*rassemblement*).

Third, Chirac's speech *relativises* the significance of Vichy by contrasting its relatively short historical duration of four years with timeless national traditions. First, he evokes the lifespan of the personified nation as one interrupted intermittently by 'moments' of tragedy or shame, exemplified by the deportations of July 1942. This timescale is surmounted by more or less extensive historical timespans: the past is conceived of as open, if not eternal, in references to 'our traditions' and 'our past', or else as having originated in the Enlightenment ('an idea of mankind, of his freedom and his dignity') and in the Resistance ('spirit of vigilance'); the future is evoked as 'hope' based on the 'lessons' of history. Both these references to distant origins in the past and to an open future are transcended by repeated invocations of immeasurable atemporal 'values'. The speech therefore evokes a nation under the threat of 'obscure forces continually at work', yet capable of hope and progression from bad to good via the affirmation of values from earlier traditions. This multiple time sequence is consistently reproduced in Chirac's official declarations relating to Vichy: in the speech at the Vél' d'Hiv' commemoration in 1986, the declaration on Jewish Community Radio (Radio Communauté-Judaïques) in 1992,[77] in the Vél' d'Hiv' speech of 1995, as well as in two commemorative speeches given in November and December 1997.[78] Here Chirac repeatedly declared that we may learn from history in order to prevent its repetition, and that we may come to terms with and learn from the past in order to seek guidance for the future: 'Accepting the past involves developing means to construct the future.'[79]

Fourth, the speech presents the nation as one simultaneously *divided and united*. Although, as Rousso points out, the duality or 'division' (*clivage*)[80] of French history conveyed in the speech reflects an authentic historical division between collaborators and supporters of the Resistance, it also constructs the image of a nation united in ideas and values, which is bolstered by references to the nation as a transcendental, ideal community, '... one and indivisible, in the heart of these French people'. The statuses of 'Vichy' and of 'France' are therefore not presented in equal terms in the speech, for Vichy is described as a historical 'moment' which interrupts or 'soils' the ideal continuity of timeless republican values. They do not constitute, as Rousso argues, a 'double necessity' or a 'division', but a historical principle on the one hand (Vichy), and a *transcendental* principle on the other (France). The rhetorical construction of a nation divided between historical responsibility for a collective fault and pride in a certain idea of France in fact reaffirms the unity of the national community. The affirmation of division is, by definition, affirmation that something whole is divided, therefore divided yet intact. This rhetorical double bind, employed by Chirac and defended by Rousso, may only be sustained if we distinguish clearly between the terms in which the French nation is here understood: as divided in history, and united in an atemporal transcendental set of values.

iv. Reparation with Rhetoric?

The petitions of 1992–93 were based on the assumption that a rhetorical gesture would constitute a form of reparation of the nation's memory. The second petition of 16 July 1992 even insisted that neither a symbolic gesture such as a wreath-laying ceremony nor judicial forms of reparation such as the trials of Vichy officials would equal the solemnity of a presidential speech. Petitioners insisted that state rhetoric constituted a distinct form of reparation, and therefore summoned the presidential authority to speak in the name of the conscience of the nation.

The dispute over the president's participation in the Vél' d'Hiv' commemorations of the 1990s consequently revolved around the rhetorical problem of naming the nation, as noted above. The initial petition of the

Comité Vél' d'Hiv' 42 defined the nation in holistic terms, where 'French collective memory' was described as 'ill' or 'afflicted', the French state as 'responsible' and 'accountable', and where the president was required to act on behalf of 'the entire nation'. It did not take into account historical or social discrepancies within the nation, including differences over time between the Vichy regime and the republics and between successive generations, or between differences in various sections of society at any one time, whether bystanders, prisoners of war, forced labour workers, members of the Resistance, collaborators, or (in Mitterrand's case) collaborator then Resistance worker in succession. The petition of June 1992 set this holistic notion of the nation as a condition for the most appropriate rhetorical accompaniment to the Vél' d'Hiv' commemoration. As a result, the ensuing debate focused less on the events of 1942 than on each president's relative capacity to find adequate words to commemorate Vichy in relation to the holistic conception of the French nation defined and demanded in the petitions. The debate was coloured by a persistent desire to name, and therefore categorise the nation in a singular noun. As Murray Edelman observes, however, categorisation in itself – of political communities, interests and beliefs – fosters an understanding of political communities in almost religious terms. 'The continuous evocation of problematical beliefs through categorizations and figures of speech that are not recognized as symbolic at all makes terms like "society" and "the national interest" look like calls to a higher duty rather than public relations ploys.'[81] Mitterrand's silence, in spite of his readiness to bear witness to history with symbolic gestures, was understood by petitioners as a refusal to officially recognise the deportations of 1942. By contrast, Chirac complied with the petitions' appeal to repair or, in accordance with the metaphor conveyed in the petition of 17 June 1992, 'cure' French memory 'afflicted with this unspoken fact'. In reality, however, the difference between the behaviour of the two presidents lay in their degrees of readiness to categorise the nation in the holistic and personified terms stipulated by the petitions.

Perhaps the only means of overcoming the dilemma of how to verbally acknowledge historical events without explicitly associating the present-day nation with a former regime is to avoid the rhetoric of nationhood altogether; to break down the nation into its component parts, for example: institutions, corporations, and individuals. Prime Minister Jospin's Vél' d'Hiv' speech of 1997 in fact did this by conspicuously avoiding naming the nation with a singular noun, referring instead to particular sections of society which collaborated and which continued to exercise authority after the war under a republican government: 'politicians, administrators, judges, the police and gendarmes'.[82] Retrospectively, therefore, one may ask why participants in the debate over the Vél' d'Hiv' from 1992–95 insisted on naming the nation in holistic terms, and why this resulted in a lack of consensus over the terminology of the nation. The act of naming the nation in relation to historical commemorations serves to lend a firm identity to states as agents of history and thereby simplifies the task of remembering them as collectivities. During the debate over the Vél' d'Hiv' commemoration, however, historical terms such as 'the Resistance', 'France', 'republic' and 'French State', which had previously been taken for granted, were revealed to be contradictory, and therefore ceased to be categories which fostered consensual historical points of reference. The Vél' d'Hiv' debate brought into question the authority normally enjoyed by established historical terminology, and therefore triggered a crisis of French national identity on the basis of a crisis of what Bourdieu calls the 'power to name'.[83]

The Vél' d'Hiv' and the Discourse of National Integration in the 1990s

The Vél' d'Hiv' commemoration speech of 1995 was the first act of state symbolics performed by Chirac in his role as head of state and occurred at the peak of his career after two previous attempts to become president. In anticipation of the commemoration, one month before the first round of the presidential election on 9 April 1995, Chirac gave a speech to a gathering of several thousand young people in Paris which underscored a deeply felt sense of history based on the idea that a new age would begin following the election and the end of the fiftieth anniversary commemorations of the Second World War. 'Next May, an era will come to an end, one generation will hand over to the new men. The next French president will take up his function in the wake of the fiftieth anniversary commemoration of the end of the Second World War. A new chapter in our history will begin. We are going to write this chapter together.'[84]

This conscious link between the presidential election of 1995 and the commemorations of the Second World War offers a key to understanding the political intentions underlying the handling of the Vél' d'Hiv' commemoration. Chirac's preelection speech drew on key tenets of Gaullist doctrine: political personalism, skilful rhetorical appeals to the nation as a vocation and transcendental 'idea', and to national renewal, described as 'a new chapter'. Evocations of the 'social fracture' fuelled fears of an apparent national division and emphasised the need to voluntarily reassert national unity, conveyed by the Gaullist principle of *rassemblement*. The Vél' d'Hiv' commemoration was thereby conceived and articulated within the context of the president's quest to secure national consensus following his election victory and to assure political legitimisation by appropriating a symbol of one of the most controversial issues of contemporary French history.

Conan and Rousso interpret Chirac's speech of 1995 as a necessary tactical response to the prevailing public understanding of Vichy. Just as de Gaulle, claim the authors, was skilled in responding to public expectations by expounding 'judicial fictions', Chirac's speech responded accurately to public expectations in the 1990s.[85] In his time, de Gaulle was responding to the profound division of public opinion in the turbulent postwar years by forging social cohesion around the myth of a nation united in resistance. In the 1990s, Chirac responded to a nation which had since rejected the Gaullist myth but which continued to pursue public incriminations of collaborators and war criminals in similar fashion to the immediate postwar years. Despite the absence of a credible national myth, Chirac succeeded in parrying apparently unpatriotic public sentiment by acknowledging French war crimes while appealing to the restoration of republican tradition in a dual image of the nation – one guilty and therefore indebted to victims from the past, yet capable of hope in the future and belief in a common idea. He thereby upheld the Gaullist 'rise-fall' myth, of national renewal emerging from national decline.[86]

Although Chirac's speech provided a fitting judicial fiction to respond to the climate of public opinion surrounding the commemorations of Vichy, it should not be forgotten that the origin of this controversy was not public opinion itself, but particular interventions by pressure groups such as the Comité Vél' d'Hiv' 42 which contributed to the formation of such public opinion. The account presented in the speech was primarily reactive, conceived in response to demands of the Comité Vél' d'Hiv' 42 and subsequent petitioners, who had all appealed primarily for the state recognition of the memories and experiences of Jewish deportees. If we assume that the dual narrative of Chirac's speech, depicting a hopeful nation emerging from a guilty, criminal nation, indeed served to placate what Conan and Rousso call the popular 'obsession' with Vichy crimes in the 1990s, it did so by appealing to a deeper sense of history and patriotism designed to bind society as a national community of values which transcends the criminal past and minority differences. The consensus achieved by Chirac was not, as Rousso suggests, based only on public satisfaction with the historical accuracy of his speech, depicting a society divided between collaborators and supporters of the Resistance, between 'a France under the authority of Vichy' and 'the home of the rights of Man'.[87] Although we may applaud the relatively high degree of historical truth expressed by Chirac, it is more likely that public adhesion to this speech was founded on a spontaneous sense of allegiance to the values it evoked. As Conan and Rousso observe, the Vél' d'Hiv' debate was an anachronism, motivated by interests of the 1990s rather than those of the 1940s, which are reflected in the formulations of petitions demanding 'rights' of the Jewish 'community'. Public acceptance of Chirac's speech of 1995 cannot be imputed to historical accuracy alone, therefore, but to the skilful appeal to interests and values of the present day via ritual and rhetorical representations. Explaining the consensus surrounding this speech as a response to an 'obsession' with Vichy in the 1990s does not account for its success, since it is not proven to what extent French society was in reality collectively obsessed. In contrast to Conan and Rousso, the historians Chris Flood and Hugo Frey argued that French society was not in fact 'obsessed' with but rather indifferent to the guilt of its parents' generation, basing their analysis on opinion polls conducted by *Le Figaro* newspaper.[88] The logic of the speech in fact pursued a dual redemptive logic based on the recognition of victims and the acknowledgement of war crimes, but also the celebration of republican values.

Chirac appealed to social consensus and patriotism by negating Vichy and affirming common identification with a presidential leader, with a personified nation conceived as an organic whole harbouring collective memories, and with a transcendental or timeless sense of nationhood based on humanist values. Vichy therefore played a central role in a strategy of verbally acknowledging unpleasant memories in order to appeal anew to patriotic sentiment. By simultaneously evoking the anti-Semitism of Vichy and xenophobia of the 1990s in conjunction with timeless values, Chirac used the commemoration to political ends by a process of association or *historical grafting*, whereby political issues from the past were raised as a model or warning for the present. According to the historian Robert Frank, 'collective memory represses, transforms and revives certain aspects of the latent civil war that divided the French from 1940 to 1944, and grafts them onto political battles of the Fourth Republic.'[89] Historical grafting of the past and present unfolded in the speech in the following sequence. First, after recalling the deportations of 1942, Chirac underscored the need of the Jewish community and the whole nation to remember the events in order to guard against their repetition. Second, switching into a vocabulary of the 1990s, he suggested that the memory of Vichy serves a directly pedagogical function in the present to combat 'Muslim fundamentalism, … fear and exclusion' in general, and the right-wing Front National party in particular, which was not named but referred to unmistakably as 'certain groups, certain publications, certain teachings, certain political parties, … obscure forces constantly at work'. Third, he proposed a solution to the conflicts of the 1940s and 1990s by praising the Resistance and ideal humanist values 'on which French identity is founded and to which we are bound in the future'. The three elements of this speech – first a tribute to the memory of the French Jewish 'community' (minority rights), second a warning against 'integrationism' (extreme minority groups) and 'obscure forces' (racism and the Front National) and, third, an appeal to national republican traditions – offer an account of history in which the dilemma of confrontations between minorities and forces of persecution, whether in 1942 or 1995, may be overcome by adhering to traditional republican values. In short, Chirac's speech conveys an appeal to national integration on the basis of republican values as a compromise between minority demands and racial persecution.

The affirmation of the policy of national integration as a negation of Vichy is a characteristic example of the interpretation of the past in light of present concerns, and of the use of memories of the past to legitimate policies in the present. Chirac's speech achieved this in part by means of a rhetorical amalgam of policies of social and ethnic integration on the basis of the single word 'exclusion'. While 'exclusion' in 1942 was a consequence of racial laws against Jews, Gypsies, or the mentally handicapped, for example, 'exclusion' in 1995 referred primarily to the social exclusion resulting from unemployment. 'Exclusion' was one of Chirac's main slogans in the presidential election campaign of 1995, used in conjunction with the slogans 'social fracture' and 'France for everyone' to convey the issues on which the election of 1995 was fought.[90] At the same time, 'exclusion' also describes the situation of immigrants living in France without a legal residence permit: essentially African asylum-seekers coined as the sans *papiers* (without papers) who were refused the right to acquire French nationality following new laws on naturalisation introduced in 1993.[91]

By simultaneously calling for the respect of minority identities and the rejection of both extremist minority movements ('Muslim fundamentalism') and parties with racist programmes ('obscure forces'), Chirac links the racial tensions of the 1940s with those of the 1990s while appealing in both cases to the common alternative of universal Enlightenment values. However, this historical amalgam of racism of the 1940s and 1990s derives from a purely rhetorical allusion via the homonym 'exclusion'. In reality, the extent to which the racism of the 1940s against Jews can be related to the racism of the 1990s against Algerian and African immigrants is questionable in so far as the deportations of 1942 are historically unrelated to the immigration issue of the 1990s resulting from the nationality code of 1993. However, this rhetorically induced historical and political amalgam reinforced the emotional effect of the speech by equating indignation at the treatment of Jews in the past with indignation at the treatment of immigrants and unemployed people in the present.[92] The evocation of multiple meanings of the term 'exclusion' in order to allude to two or three political issues in different historical periods is justified on moral grounds, but obscured historical distinctions between the issues. The use of this single term in order to simultaneously allude to both the xenophobia and racial laws of Vichy and to xenophobia and social exclusion of the present day compounded the sense of moral indignation deriving from different sources and encouraged a sense of *general* indignation detached from its precise political and historical causes. For this reason, where the grafting of different histories of injustice by Chirac solicited general indignation, spectators were made to be more receptive to a general and exclusively *ideal* (rather than complex political) solution like the one proposed in the speech. The force of this speech lies in its concise definition of a problem for which it offers an equally concise, albeit rhetorical, solution.

In the aftermath of the Vél' d'Hiv' commemoration, Chirac's speech took on a further political dimension in so far as the commemorations of Vichy became an object of dispute between major political parties, including the Front National, over the legitimacy of their respective claims to promote national heritage. Following Chirac's speech of 1995 Le Pen, the leader of the Front National, accused the president of having sought to settle an 'electoral debt' towards the Jewish community, and of having 'soiled our nation and its memory'.[93] Le Pen had previously attempted to undermine the authority of Chirac in 1995 by suggesting that his party is controlled by Jewish organisations.[94] He made a third attack on the Gaullist party in 1997 by condemning the trial of Maurice Papon and bringing into question the reputation of de Gaulle by insinuating that his wartime exile in London invalidated his status as a figurehead of the Resistance.[95] Though trivial in content, Le Pen's acts of verbal aggression were timed to undermine the credibility of the RPR following its failure to win a majority of seats in the parliamentary elections of July 1997.

By condemning Chirac's Vél' d'Hiv' speech and the Papon trial as an affront to patriotic sentiment, the Front National presented itself as the genuinely national party, and even adopted the Gaullist campaign slogan 'neither right nor left but French!'.[96] Fears that the Front National would thus gain electoral advantage, by condemning official state recognitions of Vichy or the Papon trial, drove the president of the RPR Philippe Séguin to condemn the trial as a pretext to put on trial both de Gaulle and Gaullism, and France.[97] Vichy therefore became a point of conflict between right and extreme-right parties, and between factions of the Gaullist party itself, a conflict which Séguin dramatised as a threat to the stability of both Gaullist tradition and of the very nation. While Chirac distanced his party from the racist policies of the Front National by deploring xenophobia and racism in his Vél' d'Hiv' speech, Séguin attempted to distance the same party from Chirac's stance in order to avoid offering ideological ammunition to Le Pen with which he could condemn the president or the RPR as unpatriotic. On close inspection, however, the Gaullist precepts maintained in Chirac's speech suggest that the protests mounted by Gaullist colleagues like Séguin against Chirac's handling of Vichy were not entirely justified. The dispute provoked in 1997 by Séguin was a purely sectarian response to verbal attacks made by Le Pen on de Gaulle and Gaullist tradition. In reality, the Vél' d'Hiv' commemorations did not negate, but revised and restated Gaullist principles of nationhood.

The Vél' d'Hiv' commemorations were exploited as a strategic response to the 'obsession' with Vichy crimes by reasserting the Gaullist vision of nationhood as a transcendental ideal, and as a response to the issue of minorities and immigration in the 1990s. Both issues fuelled party-political dispute over claims to national heritage. The Vél' d'Hiv' was therefore a catalyst for a sobering reappraisal of history which was immediately subordinated to the public negotiation of national political traditions, in particular Gaullism and republican integration, and to the claims of various parties to best represent these traditions.

'National Reconciliation'? The Shadow of the Gaullist Vision of History over Presidents Mitterrand and Chirac

Although presidents Mitterrand and Chirac both advocated 'national reconciliation' during the fiftieth and fifty-third anniversary commemorations of the Vél' d'Hiv', Mitterrand was embroiled in controversy, while Chirac's handling of Vichy, just two months after being elected president, met with broad public approval. Within only a few years, the Vél' d'Hiv' became a site of memory of Vichy, a symbolic focal point for the national memory of this period. However, the close connection between this symbol, the presidential personalities and their historical statements, all of which were overshadowed by de Gaulle's vision of history, suggests that the national memory of Vichy associated with the Vél' d'Hiv' is largely a political construction founded on biographical, symbolic and rhetorical strategies. By analysing these strategies, I have attempted to explain the transition from controversy in 1992 to relative reconciliation in 1995.

Many observers of French politics agree that there have been few public figures more skilful in the art of political symbolics during the twentieth century than Charles de Gaulle. The common precepts of Gaullism – national sovereignty, an ideal historical mission, national consensus, and the integrative symbolic function of the president[98] – were sustained in conjunction with a simple but strong image of French history whose origins extend back to Clovis, the ancient Gauls, and the Capetian dynasty.[99] De Gaulle also established new national symbols such as his radio appeal of 18 June 1940 to civil resistance within French territory. Since 1944, the public understanding of Vichy has either been defined by Gaullist doctrine or, since the seventies, in reaction to de Gaulle.

Having organised the Free French Forces in London during the occupation, de Gaulle was regarded as the successful alternative to both the Vichy regime and the politically fragmented Resistance. However, he promoted a myth of the Resistance as a coherent nationwide movement, a myth now broken since the passing of de Gaulle himself and the proliferation of historical studies of this period revealing that fewer people than formerly assumed participated in Resistance activities, and that the Resistance was not a united movement, but composed of multiple factions.[100] Central to Gaullist historiography is the idea that the Vichy regime was illegal, and that it therefore represents an interruption in French history, disconnected from the Third and Fourth Republics preceding and succeeding it. According to the French Committee of National Liberation (Comité Français de Libération Nationale), a fusion of the French provisional governments in London and Algeria founded by de Gaulle in June 1943, Vichy was a 'de facto authority' and its acts 'null and void'.[101] The political origins of the Fourth Republic were therefore assumed to lie in the Resistance and the Free French Forces in London. However, the dismissal of the political and historical legitimacy of Vichy as an interruption of republican political tradition overlooks the extent to which elements of legislation, institutions as well as judicial and police personnel continued beyond the duration of the Vichy government. Not only did the National Assembly of the Third Republic legally accord full powers to Pétain in July 1940, but some Vichy officials, members of the judiciary and high civil servants, as well as some legislation introduced under Vichy, continued to operate under the Fourth Republic after 1944.

In light of the preponderance of the Gaullist understanding of Vichy prior to the watershed of the 1970s, it is common for political representatives to refer to or play on Gaullist imagery even today. The relative continuity and discontinuity of the state before and after collaboration therefore remains a measure of the relevance of this period for French political traditions. For this reason, when Mitterrand justified his refusal to acknowledge responsibility for Vichy crimes in 1992 on the grounds that the French state in 1940 was not the republic but Vichy, he was criticised for adhering to de Gaulle's understanding of Vichy as a form of parenthesis, as a political system entirely detached from the republican traditions preceding and following it.[102] His refusal to accede to demands of the Comité Vél' d'Hiv' 42 indeed partially adhered to de Gaulle's vision of the political illegitimacy of the Vichy regime. However, he cannot be accused of sustaining the Gaullist myth merely on the grounds that he refused to verbally acknowledge the Vichy regime on behalf of the Fifth Republic, for he also made significant symbolic gestures in recognition of the deportation of Jews in 1941–42 which went beyond those made by de Gaulle: by attending ceremonies, introducing the national day of commemoration, having the Vél' d'Hiv' monument erected, ceasing to lay a wreath at Pétain's grave, and by inaugurating the memorial to the internment camp at Izieu. Prior to the 1970s, commemorations in memory of Jewish victims were largely performed in traditional republican style.[103] Whereas de Gaulle inaugurated the Memorial of the Martyrs of Deportation in Paris, for example, which commemorates the deportations of the 1940s in general and names 'French martyrs' as victims, Mitterrand instigated commemorations of crimes against Jews in particular, which inculpate the 'French State' as *perpetrator*.

Chirac's speech of 1995, in contrast to Mitterrand's silence, was interpreted as a radical break with Gaullism. The public recognition of crimes, the declaration of 'collective error' and 'imprescriptible debt' evoked not only moral and judicial continuity between Vichy and the republic, but also implied moral and political accountability continuing into the present in 1995. The assertion that error and debt are inherited by successive generations constitutes a radical break with de Gaulle's understanding of Vichy. Nevertheless, Chirac did not abandon but reaffirmed the holistic notion of France as a community bound by common universal values, if not a myth of universalism.[104] By projecting the dual history of a nation first 'soiled' by crime then redeemed in 'ideal' values, referring to the topos of a single personified nation as if it were capable of rehabilitation, he even revived an archetypal Gaullist metaphor of national history, one which alternates between catastrophe and renewal,[105] and transposed this metaphor onto present-day commemorations of Vichy. This evocation of contradictory political traditions, of exclusionary or xenophobic versus Enlightenment values sustained within the same nation, appealed to a political culture based on the wilful recognition and negation of Vichy. When Chirac made a verbal recognition of moral debt on behalf of the nation, therefore, he did not discredit the nation, since an expression of collective error and responsibility in the 1990s for events of the 1940s necessarily presupposes a personified notion of nationhood with a morality spanning fifty years – analogous to that of an individual, who may be forgiven after acts of remorse and confession. The metaphor of the nation as a single organism with an integral and relatively coherent memory like that of a human individual, presents the faults of the nation as *human* faults: while the nation is discredited with the crimes of Vichy, it is simultaneously credited with the faculty of overcoming these faults.

The speech of 1995 thus adopted Gaullist doctrine by appealing to the nation as an organic community whose members are bound by an abstract 'certain idea', a sense of solidarity conveyed by the communitarian rhetoric of 'we' and 'you', common memories and a common future. Its location was not described in geographical terms, but as the 'heart' of all French people, such that Frenchness was conceived as something exceptional and incommunicable: a 'certain', and therefore indescribable idea of the nation.[106] The sense of community was reinforced by the challenge of combating xenophobia on the basis of a collective voluntary reassertion of the ethical values of republicanism. By conveying a strong sense of nationhood and national continuity on the basis of these values, Chirac did not refute but restated the Gaullist doctrine of Vichy as a parenthesis in French history. Whereas de Gaulle is reputed to have denied the legitimacy of the Vichy state in legal terms ('null and void'),

Chirac denied Vichy in moral terms, where national traditions were momentarily 'soiled' by Vichy. And while the pedagogical thrust of Chirac's invocation of republican political culture as the negation of dictatorship was sound, his appeal to Enlightenment values in abstract and somewhat bombastic terms (the nation as person, as timeless and as an idea, a nation 'one and indivisible, in the heart of French people') reinforced a romantic view of nationhood founded on redemptive *voluntarism*.

Just as Mitterrand cannot be categorised as wholly 'Gaullist', therefore, Chirac cannot be categorised as having wholly broken with Gaullist doctrine because, as indicated above, his Vél' d'Hiv' speeches (of 1986, 1995, as well as commentary on the Vél' d'Hiv' in 1992 and related commemorations in 1997) consistently reiterated the narrative of a nation progressing from the recognition of debt to the reaffirmation of universal humanist values and the restoration of 'a certain idea of France'. Although the attitudes of presidents Mitterrand and Chirac were polarised by critics with regard to their differing receptions of popular Gaullist historiography during the Vél' d'Hiv' commemorations, it is essential to guard against equating Mitterrand's attitude with that of de Gaulle while interpreting Chirac's response as a form of emancipation from de Gaulle. In reality, Mitterrand appears to have partially revised the Gaullist vision of Vichy by promoting non-verbal symbols of the French State's responsibility for deportations, whereas Chirac conveyed a revision of de Gaulle's vision while upholding orthodox Gaullist rhetoric of the ideal nation. In both cases, the latent political tradition of Gaullism determined the ideological criteria in which the symbolic rituals of successive presidential leaders were couched. However, as already indicated, Mitterrand's interpretation only partially conformed to de Gaulle's interpretation. Likewise, Chirac's interpretation only partially revised it. In light of the general adherence to Gaullist historiography by both presidents, therefore, one may suppose that the polemicisation of the differences between their handling of the commemoration was founded not on historical arguments but on the political inclination to define or reinforce the binary opposition between the presidents and their parties. The controversy over the Vél' d'Hiv' commemorations was likewise motivated less by the desire to present an accurate historical account of the events of July 1942 than by the desire to uphold Gaullist tradition. The extent to which Gaullist tradition continues to overshadow political culture in France in the twenty-first century is reflected in controversies over the reduction of the duration of the French presidency from seven to five years in 2000, the cessation of the annual RPR party pilgrimage to de Gaulle's grave to commemorate his death from 2000, and the erection of a monument of de Gaulle on the Champs Elysées on 9 November 2000. Although living memories of de Gaulle are fading over time, although the Gaullist vision of history and myth of the Resistance have been revised, and although some Gaullist institutional establishments are under review, deep-seated political customs such as a charismatic leadership style in conjunction with Gaullism as a reference point for political and social values continue to structure French political culture and, as the case of the Vél' d'Hiv' has proven, French memory culture.

One of the main paradigms of political discourse in postwar France has been the quest to establish 'national reconciliation'. Having emerged during conflict between left and right as early as the Dreyfus affair, it evolved during the 1950s and 1970s in connection with the campaign by adherents of Philippe Pétain, who attempted to rehabilitate the architect of the armistice with Germany in 1940 as the hero of Verdun and the armistice of 1918 by having his ashes transferred from the island of Yeu to Douaumont, that is, from the sanctuary of the prison where he spent the last years of his life to the cemetery for fallen soldiers of the First World War.[107] Georges Pompidou likewise advocated national reconciliation in 1972 by granting a legal pardon to Paul Touvier, former head of the militia in Lyon. During the 1980s, Mitterrand continued the ritual, initiated by de Gaulle, of annually laying a wreath on Pétain's grave, a gesture which symbolically reconciled the conflicting images of the First World War hero and the architect of the tragic 1940 armistice with the republic via the figure of de Gaulle, who had styled himself as the architect of the liberation. However, by putting an end to this ritual in 1993, and by initiating the Vél' d'Hiv' annual ceremony, monument, and national day of commemoration, Mitterrand made a symbolic break with previous presidents' policies of national reconciliation. In the 1990s, the Vél' d'Hiv' commemoration was initiated with the promise of establishing moral reconciliation of the nation and the absolution of French 'collective memory' – not by means of amnesty, however, but by explicitly recognising fault, as demanded in the petitions of pressure groups from 1992. The broad consensus won by Chirac following his speech of 1995 was primarily due to his positive response to expectations raised by the repeated petitions of the Comité Vél' d'Hiv' 42, which insisted on a verbal proclamation of responsibility on behalf of the republic. However, this consensus may also be imputed to the rhetorical force of his speech which, while ostensibly breaking with Gaullist doctrine of the illegality of Vichy, skilfully appealed to universal moral values in the name of republicanism, to public indignation at the policies of 'exclusion' of both the 1940s and 1990s, and presented the nation as a person, one therefore capable of self-improvement.

Reconciliation is a topos of political communication that promises to foster patriotism by resolving historical inconsistencies. The cases of Pétain and Touvier, for example, illustrate politically motivated attempts to veil shameful memories of persecutions. By contrast, the Vél' d'Hiv' illustrates a shift in the meaning of national reconciliation in the 1990s and therefore a potential modification of collective historical self-understanding. Two modes of reconciliation crystallised and evolved in connection with the debate over the Vél' d'Hiv' between 1992 and 1995, and were echoed in 1997 in relation to the Papon trial. Mitterrand advocated reconciliation by insisting verbally on the strict distinction between Vichy and the republic, although at the same time he performed non-verbal acts of recognition at ceremonies at the Vél' d'Hiv' from 1992. Chirac devised a second form of reconciliation, an appeal for reparation via a solemn act of recognition of historical facts and universal moral responsibility. Public critiques of these commemorations were measured largely by standards set by de Gaulle: Mitterrand's refusal to make the speech in 1992 was interpreted as a Gaullist vision of the Vichy regime, as a parenthesis in French history, in spite of his symbolic gestures of recognition; Chirac's inculpation of the 'French State' in 1995 was interpreted as an abandonment of Gaullist historiography; and Philippe Séguin publicly condemned the trial of Maurice Papon in 1997 and Chirac's use of the notion of 'imprescriptible debt' in the Vél' d'Hiv' speech as a 'trial against Gaullism'.[108]

The controversy surrounding this commemoration culminated in 1997 when Jospin, responding to Séguin's public protest, contested Chirac's speech of 1995 by resorting to Mitterrand's interpretation of the relation between Vichy and the republic. 'France,' according to Jospin, 'is not guilty because … Vichy was the negation of France and at any rate the negation of the republic.'[109] Jospin's speech before the National Assembly was greeted with an ovation. This sequence of commemorations of Vichy by political leaders thus evolved from Mitterrand's controversial negation of the identification of Vichy with the republic, through Chirac's acknowledgement of war crimes while upholding Gaullist values to Jospin's recognition of individual responsibility, but refusal to either identify the Vichy regime with the republic or to pay homage to Gaullist values.

The holistic understanding of the nation is based on the integrative power of the Gaullist movement, the symbolic leadership of the president, and a vaguely defined historical mission of the nation. In their handling of national history and social memory during the commemorations of the Vél' d'Hiv', both Mitterrand and Chirac upheld a revised Gaullist vision of the French nation. The polemic polarisation of the positions of Mitterrand and Chirac towards Gaullist doctrine – as the adhesion of the former and the emancipation of the latter – may not be deduced from the commemorative strategies pursued by the two presidents. The polemic appears rather to have been motivated by contemporary political concerns: dissatisfaction with Mitterrand's personal involvement in Vichy prior to his Resistance activities from 1943; indignation over his belated and ambiguous verbal statements concerning this involvement, particularly during the historic television interview in September 1994; and a concern to take a clear public stance against the racist discourse of the Front National. In reality, however, both presidents appealed to national reconciliation by adhering to Gaullist historiography and universal republican values.

The quest for national reconciliation is a symptom of political uncertainties about national identity, which have been reflected in the increased public support for the Front National since 1983. In this respect, the debate surrounding the Vél' d'Hiv', which crystallised a number of moral and political issues relating to the interpretation of Vichy history in the 1990s, shows how controversy resulting from the 'difficult' memories of this period was effectively instrumentalised in order to reassert republican tradition. The Vél' d'Hiv', initially a symbol of a specifically Jewish social memory, was subsequently, in particular from the 1990s, integrated as a national form of commemoration. Both Mitterrand and Chirac used this single monument or site of memory in their pursuit of national reconciliation by appealing to a groundswell of consensus over republican ideals, reinforced by first exposing then deploring Vichy as a negative ideal.

The relative success and failure of Chirac and Mitterrand in promoting reconciliation may only partially be imputed to the generation gap between the two presidents (Mitterrand was born in 1916, Chirac in 1932). Although Mitterrand, unlike Chirac, was directly involved in positions of political responsibility during the years of occupation, an explanation of each president's response to petitions on the basis of biographical experience alone would suggest that their historical interpretations were determined, and therefore would detract from the deliberate commemorative strategies undertaken by each president with respect to rhetoric and symbols. Just as this conflict resulted primarily from their divergent understandings and rhetorical renderings of the continuity of the state before, during and after collaboration, its resolution lay in Chirac's rhetorical astuteness in relativising positive and negative traditions.

This campaign to urge reconciliation between the French republican state and Jewish victims of the French State must be interpreted within the context of prevailing political interests of the 1990s. It was not only a traditional conflict between left and right, however, but between the broader issues of inclusion in and exclusion from public life. One could even read this monument as the embodiment of two opposed interpretations of French political culture since the end of the economic and social upheavals known as the trente *glorieuses* in the 1970s. On the one hand, the monument and commemorative day testify to the recognition of 'exclusion' in both the 1940s and 1990s. In this case, the Vél' d'Hiv' could be said to symbolise the partial 'fragmentation'[110] of French society in the face of ethnic or regional movements, for example, heralding the dissolution of consensus based on the classical model of republican integration. On the other hand, the explicit verbal negation of 'exclusion' by the presidents during commemorations of the Vél' d'Hiv' testifies to the voluntary reassertion of national unity or *rassemblement* on the basis of consensual republican values.[111] These two interpretations of contemporary French political culture – one sceptical, the other faithful towards the continuing validity of republicanism – underpinned the ideological conflict over the Vél' d'Hiv'.

The suspension of debate after the speech by Chirac in 1995 suggests that the Vél' d'Hiv' effectively fulfilled the function of a site of memory as a stabiliser or regulator of conflicts. However, this process of historicisation did not result merely from the passage of time (implied by the selection of already 'regulated' sites from the nineteenth century for the seven-volume *Les Lieux de mémoire*). It would be similarly misleading to suppose that the Vél' d'Hiv' marked the transition of Vichy from the realm of 'real' to 'mythic' memory, terms used by Benedict Anderson to explain how the memory of distant crimes, such as the Saint Barthélémy massacres of Huguenots in 1572, was integrated as 'French' or 'our own'.[112] By contrast, the preliminary historicisation of Vichy experienced during the 1990s was only partially a result of structural changes such as the passage of time and generations, or the transition to myth; the Vél' d'Hiv' served primarily as a backdrop for the politically motivated reinterpretation of deportations in the form of an architectural symbol and speeches appealing to the historical grafting of the issue of exclusion and the rehabilitation of Gaullist ideals.

Since no positive identification with the crimes of the Vichy regime is possible, and since these crimes cannot be integrated into a coherent narrative of the nation or canon of national symbols or sites of memory, Chirac solemnised the nation's crimes as a negative example in order to persuasively reaffirm alternative positive traditions. He thus reasserted republican values and the myth of the nation's origin in 1789 as the negation of the violation of these values in 1942. By further defining the presidential election of May 1995 as the end of an era and the beginning of a new generation,[113] he interpreted 1995 as a historic moment: as the end of the fiftieth anniversary commemorations, as the arrival of a generation of political leaders too young to have been personally involved in the Vichy regime, and therefore as a signal to turn attention away from the Vichy past. The Vél' d'Hiv' nevertheless remains an ambivalent site of memory. Today, the annual wreath-laying ceremony at the Vél' d'Hiv' monument on the first Sunday following 16 and 17 July occurs immediately after the celebrations of 14 July. This ritual juxtaposition of two of the most memorable historical origins of the French nation – one positive and celebratory (the storming of the Bastille on 14 July 1789), the other negative and grievous (the round-up and deportation of Jews from occupied Paris on 16 and 17 July 1942) – poignantly recalls the debate over the Vél' d'Hiv' as a memorial process of reconciliation in its own right.

Notes

1. See Heinz-Gerhard Haupt and Jürgen Kocka, eds, *Geschichte und Vergleich. Ansätze und Ergebnisse international vergleichender Geschichtsschreibung*, Frankfurt am Main: Campus, 1996, 10f.
2. See M. Lane Bruner, *Strategies of Remembrance. The Rhetorical Dimensions of National Identity Construction*, Colombia: University of South Carolina Press, 2002; Murray Edelman, *Political Language. Words That Succeed and Policies That Fail*, New York: Academic Press, 1977; Chaim Perelman, *The Realm of Rhetoric*, trans. William Kluback, Notre Dame: University of Notre Dame Press, 1982.
3. This has already been done. In the case of France, see Serge Barcellini and Annette Wieviorka, *Passant, souviens-toi! Les lieux du souvenir de la Seconde Guerre mondiale en France*, Paris: Plon, 1995; and Eric Conan and Henry Rousso, *Vichy, un passé qui ne passe pas*, Paris: Fayard, 1994. In the case of Germany, see Stephanie Endlich and Thomas Lutz, *Gedenken und Lernen an historischen Orten. Ein Wegweiser zu Gedenkstätten für die Opfer des Nationalsozialismus in Berlin*, Berlin: Edition Hentrich, 1995; Ulrike Puvogel and Martin Stankowski, *Gedenkstätten für die Opfer des Nationalsozialismus. Eine Dokumentation*, Bonn: Bundeszentrale für politische Bildung, 1995; and Eva-Maria Klother, *Denkmalplastik nach 1945 bis 1989 in Ost- und West-Berlin*, Münster: Lit Verlag, 1996.
4. This chapter is a revised and enlarged version of the essay: '"National Reconciliation?" Mitterrand, Chirac and the Commemorations of Vichy 1992–95', *National Identities* no. 2, 2000, 127–144: http://www.tandf.co.uk.
5. 'Journée nationale commémorative des persécutions racistes et antisémites commises sous l'autorité de fait dit "gouvernement de l'Etat français" (1940–1944)', marked annually from 1993 by a wreath-laying ceremony at the Vél' d'Hiv' monument (see Fig. 2) on the first Sunday following 16 July. This day of commemoration became law on 29 February 2000, under the new official title of the 'National Day in Memory of the Victims of Racist and Anti-Semitic Crimes of the French State and with Homage to the "Righteous" People of France' ('Journée nationale à la mémoire des victimes des crimes racistes et antisémites de l'Etat français et d'hommage aux "justes" de France').
6. See Annette Wieviorka, *Déportation et génocide. Entre la mémoire et l'oubli*, Paris: Plon, 1992, 356.
7. Rousso speaks of a tension between the claims of the 'national and international collectivity' and of 'communitarian' interests. See Rousso, in an interview with Philippe Petit, *La Hantise du passé*, Paris: Textuel, 1998, 33.
8. In order to avoid confusion between the generic term 'Etat français' (French state) and the official name of the Vichy regime (also 'Etat français': French State, the term used in state documents from 1941 instead of 'French Republic'), most commentators speak of 'l'Etat français de Vichy'. References to 'l'Etat français' during discussions in the 1990s were therefore often ambiguous.
9. Esther Benbassa, *The Jews of France*, 192.
10. See Bruner, *Strategies of Remembrance*, 19–24.
11. Rousso, *Vichy. L'événement, la mémoire, l'histoire*, 36ff.
12. See Special dossier on this issue, *Le Quotidien de Paris*, 12 July 1982, 1–8.
13. See brochure of the Commission du Souvenir du C.R.I.F., *Inauguration de la Place des Martyrs Juifs du Vélodrome d'Hiver. Grande Rafle des 16 et 17 juillet 1942*, July 1986.

14. Full inscription: 'Les 16 et 17 juillet 1942/ 13152 Juifs furent arrêtés dans Paris et sa banlieue/ déportés et assassinés à Auschwitz/ Dans le vélodrome d'hiver qui s'élevait ici/ 4115 enfants/ 2916 femmes/ 1129 hommes/ furent parqués dans des conditions inhumaines/ par la police du gouvernement de Vichy/ sur ordre des occupants nazis/ que ceux qui ont tenté de leur venir en aide/ soient remerciés/ passant, souviens-toi.' Cf. Barcellini and Wieviorka, *Passant, souviens-toi! Les lieux du souvenir de la Seconde Guerre mondiale en France*, 477.
15. Full inscription: 'La République française/ en hommage aux victimes/ des persécutions racistes et antisémites/ et des crimes contre l'humanité/ commis sous l'autorité de fait/ dite "gouvernement de l'Etat français" (1940–1944)/ N'oublions jamais.'
16. See Caroline Wiedmer's account of the selection procedure, in *The Claims of Memory. Representations of the Holocaust in Germany and France*, Ithaca: Cornell University Press, 1999, 72–78.
17. See Volker Müller, 'Der lange Weg zum Mahnmal', *Berliner Zeitung*, 17 November 1997, 11.
18. Ashes, unknown individuals and eternal flames belong to a repertoire of symbols used in First World War memorials internationally. Cf. Ken Inglis, 'Entombing Unknown Soldiers: From London and Paris to Baghdad', *History & Memory* no. 5, 1993, 7–31.
19. See A. Alperine, 'Les Martyrs juifs ont leur monument à Paris' (1956), in Serge Klarsfeld, ed., *Mémoire du génocide*, Paris: Centre de Documentation Juive Contemporaine and Association 'Fils et Filles des Déportés Juifs de France', 1987, 15–16.
20. N.B. In the case of the Memorial of the Unknown Jewish Martyr, this paradox applies only to the symbolic aspect of the crypt and memorial: the same building houses the Centre for Contemporary Jewish Documentation which contains invaluable archives on all aspects of Vichy including, since December 1997, the files used from 1940 to register Jews resident in the occupied zone of France.
21. Robert Badinter, 'M. Badinter: nous devons aux victimes "l'enseignement de la vérité et la force de la justice"', *Le Monde*, 18 July 1992, 9.
22. 'Un appel est lancé à M. Mitterrand pour que soient reconnus officiellement les "persecutions" et les "crimes de Vichy contre les juifs"', *Le Monde*, 17 June 1992, 10.
23. *Le Monde*, 16 July 1992, 7.
24. Ibid.
25. Badinter, *Le Monde*, 17 July 1992, 9.
26. 'Le Comité Vel' d'Hiv' '42 s'adresse aux parlementaires', *Le Monde*, 19/20 July 1992, 6.
27. See 'Vichy: les étudiants juifs attendent un geste de Mitterrand', *Libération*, 14 January 1993, 5.
28. 'Les parties civiles juives s'indignent des propos de M. Mitterrand', *Le Monde*, 21 April 1994, 7.
29. Lionel Jospin, 'Un gouvernement, une administration de notre pays, ont alors commis l'irréparable', *Le Monde*, 22 July 1997, 8.
30. Ibid.
31. Philippe Séguin, 'Assez! Assez! Assez!', *Le Figaro*, 21 October 1997, 6.
32. Quoted in Jean-Baptiste de Montvalon, 'Pour Lionel Jospin, la "France" n'est pas coupable de Vichy', *Le Monde*, 23 October 1997, 6.
33. Chirac, 'Quatre années de menace et d'exclusion programmée', *Le Monde*, 6 December 1997, 11.

34. According to Edelman, 'condensation symbols ... condense into one symbolic event, sign, or act patriotic pride, anxieties, remembrances of past glories or humiliations, promises of future greatness'. Edelman, *The Symbolic Uses of Politics*, 6.
35. Chirac's Vel' d'Hiv' speech of 1986 is published in the brochure of the Commission du Souvenir du C.R.I.F., *Inauguration de la Place des Martyrs Juifs du Vélodrome d'Hiver. Grande Rafle des 16 et 17 juillet 1942*.
36. See Pierre-André Taguieff, *La Nouvelle judéophobie*, Paris: Fondation du 2 mars/Mille et une nuit, 2002; and Nonna Mayer, 'La France n'est pas antisémite', *Le Monde*, 4 April 2002.
37. Quoted in Anna Bitton and Stéphane Jordain, 'Vél d'Hiv: Raffarin entre passé et présent', *Libération*, 22 July 2002, 2.
38. Andreas Dörner, *Politischer Mythos und symbolische Politik. Sinnstiftung durch symbolische Formen am Beispiel des Hermannsmythos*, Opladen: Westdeutscher Verlag, 1994, 45, 49.
39. Edelman, *The Symbolic Use of Politics*, 64.
40. Surviving photographs are reproduced in Serge Klarsfeld, *Le Mémorial de la déportation des juifs de France*, Paris: Centre de Documentation Juive Contemporaine de Paris, 1979.
41. Pierre Birnbaum, 'Grégoire, Dreyfus, Drancy et Copernic', in Nora, ed., *Les Lieux de mémoire*, vol. III, *Les France* 1, Paris: Gallimard, 1993, 561–613, 561f.
42. The 40th anniversary of Vel' d'Hiv' in 1982 was characteristically uncontroversial and largely ignored by the national press. See Annie Kriegel, 'Ce jour-là, j'ai quitté mon enfance', *Le Figaro*, 16 July 1982, 11.
43. Nora, 'Das Abenteuer der *Lieux de mémoire*', 83.
44. Rousso, *Le Syndrome de Vichy*, 316, 319.
45. See Conan and Rousso, Vichy, un passé qui ne passe pas, 271f.
46. Ibid.
47. See Théo Klein, 'Une manière d'être juif', interview with Théo Klein, *Le Débat* no. 82, 1994, 117–28, 126.
48. Conan and Rousso, *Vichy, un passé qui ne passe pas*, 2nd edn, Paris: Gallimard, 1995, 451.
49. See Gilles Bresson, 'Chirac: la France complice des nazis', *Libération*, 17 July 1995, 10–11.
50. 'Un appel est lancé à M. Mitterrand', *Le Monde*, 17 June 1992, 10.
51. 'Le Comité Vél' d'Hiv' 42: l'Etat est "sourd"', *Le Monde*, 16 July 1992, 8.
52. All references to Chirac's Vél' d'Hiv' speech of 1995 are from *Passages*, July–August 1995, 35–40 (see Appendix).
53. Conan and Rousso, *Vichy, un passé qui ne passe pas*, 46.
54. Charles de Gaulle, *Mémoires de guerre*, 6 vols, Paris: Plon, 1976, vol. 1, L'Appel 1940–1942, 1.
55. Official term used by the Comité Français de Libération Nationale (CFLN) from 1944. See Robert Paxton, *Vichy France. Old Guard and New Order*, London: Barrie & Jenkins, 1972, 330.
56. Official term used instead of 'République Française' to define the Vichy state from January 1941, as recorded in official documents such as the *Journal Officiel*, the protocol reports of governmental proceedings.
57. Cf. Nathalie Heinich, 'En guise de clarification', *Le Débat* no. 89, 205–206.
58. 'Un appel est lancé à M. Mitterrand', *Le Monde*, 17 June 1992, 10.
59. Unreserved commendations were expressed by public figures such as Joseph Sitruk, Henri Hajdenberg, Serge Klarsfeld, Jean-Marie Lustiger and André Rossinot. See 'Le président du CRIF salue "le discours que l'on n'attendait plus"', *Le Monde*, 18 July 1995, 6.

60. Annual presidential declaration of 14 July by Mitterrand, 'De Mauvaises moeurs se sont répandues partout, y compris dans la justice', *Le Monde,* 16 July 1992, 7.
61. For example, the republican motto 'Liberté, Egalité, Fraternité' was replaced by 'Travail, Famille, Patrie'. See Mona Ozouf, 'Liberté, Egalité, Fraternité', in Nora, ed., *Les Lieux de mémoire,* vol. III, *Les France* 3, Paris: Gallimard, 1993, 583–629, 623.
62. Figures cited in Paxton, *Vichy France. Old Guard and New Order,* 329. Peter Novick's earlier work of 1968 cites two statistics collected by local prefects in 1948 and 1952 of either 9,673 or 10,822 summary executions. See Novick, *The Resistance versus Vichy. The Purge of Collaborators in Liberated France,* London: Chatto & Windus, 1968 (appendix).
63. Conan and Rousso, *Vichy, un passé qui ne passe pas,* 39.
64. In 1986, Chirac aimed to 'pay homage to those who suffered so cruelly', to draw a lesson from the memory of 1942 as a 'boost to national consciousness', and therefore to reaffirm republican values on the basis of this lesson: 'Such is the lesson that we should draw from the tragic events being commemorated today. The debt we are in towards these victims is imprescriptible: that of being faithful to the values of freedom and justice which, in the eyes of all humanity, are the message and the very legitimacy of our country.' See brochure of the Commission du Souvenir du C.R.I.F., *Inauguration de la Place des Martyrs Juifs du Vélodrome d'Hiver. Grande Rafle des 16 et 17 juillet 1942.*
65. Rousso, 'Sortir du dilemme: Pétain, est-ce la France?', *Le Débat* no. 89, March/April 1996, 198–204, 199.
66. Bresson, *Libération,* 17 July 1995, 10.
67. Rousso, interviewed by Annette Lévy-Willard, *Libération,* 17 July 1995, 11. Caroline Wiedmer also interprets Chirac's gesture as a 'clear break with Mitterrand's de Gaulle-inspired position on the Occupation', in Wiedmer, *The Claims of Memory,* 54.
68. Blandine Kriegel, *Le Monde,* 8 September 1995, 14.
69. See the debate between Heinich and Rousso, in *Le Débat* no. 89.
70. 'Le Comité Vél' d'Hiv' 42: l'Etat est "sourd"', *Le Monde,* 16 July 1992, 8.
71. 'Vichy: les étudiants juifs attendent un geste de Mitterrand', *Libération,* 14 January 1993, 5.
72. The phenomenon of the 'generation of assumptions' in the public sphere has been examined in detail by Edelman in *Political Language. Words That Succeed and Policies That Fail,* 35–37. This technique was applied by Serge Klarsfeld in 1993 in order to provoke public indignation over Mitterrand's wreath laying at the tomb of Pétain. See Klarsfeld, 'M. Mitterrand ne fera plus fleurir la tombe de Pétain', *Le Monde,* 22 July 1992.
73. My italics. All references are to Chirac's speech (see Appendix).
74. 'Un appel est lancé à M. Mitterrand', *Le Monde,* 17 June 1995, 10.
75. 'Le Comité Vél' d'Hiv' 42: l'Etat est "sourd"', *Le Monde,* 16 July 1992, 8.
76. The political usages of ambiguity in political symbolics is explored in depth by Robert Meadow, in *Politics as Communication,* New Jersey: Ablex Publishing Corp., 1980, 35.
77. See 'M. Chirac souligne "le devoir de nous souvenir des atrocités du nazisme"', *Le Monde,* 17 July 1992, 9.
78. See 'Le message du chef d'Etat', *Libération,* 3 November 1997, 16; 'Quatre années de menace et d'exclusion programmée', *Le Monde,* 6 December 1997, 11.
79. 'Quatre années de menace et d'exclusion programmée', *Le Monde,* 6 December 1997, 11.

80. Rousso, 'Le débat continue…', *Le Débat* no. 89, 206–207, 207.
81. Edelman, *Political Language. Words That Succeed and Policies That Fail*, 154f.
82. Jospin, 'Un gouvernement, une administration de notre pays, ont alors commis l'irréparable', *Le Monde*, 22 July 1997, 8.
83. Bourdieu, 'Espace social et genèse des "classes"', Actes de la recherche en sciences sociales, 52–53, 1984, 3-12.
84. Quoted in Jean Charlot, *Pourquoi Jacques Chirac?* Paris: Fallois, 1995, 144f.
85. Conan and Rousso, Vichy, un passé qui ne passe pas, 2nd edn, 455.
86. Cf. Hugo Frey, 'Rebuilding France. Gaullist Historiography, the Rise-fall Myth and French Identity 1945–58', in Stefan Berger et al., eds, *Writing National Histories. Western Europe since 1800*, London: Routledge, 1999, 205–216, 213; Kenneth Mouré and Martin Alexander, eds, *Crisis and Renewal in France 1918–1962*, New York & Oxford: Berghahn, 2002.
87. Rousso, 'Sortir du dilemme: Pétain, est-ce la France?', 200f.
88. See Flood and Frey, 'The Vichy Syndrome Revisited', *Contemporary French Civilisation* no. 2, 1995, 231–49, 240f.
89. Robert Frank, 'A propos des commémorations françaises de la deuxième guerre mondiale', in Alfred Wahl, ed., *Mémoire de la Seconde Guerre Mondiale*, proceedings of conference from 6 to 8 October 1983, Metz: Centre de Recherche Histoire et Civilisation de l'Europe Occidentale, 1984, 281–90, 290. In the same vein, Emmanuel Sivan and Jay Winter refer to 'retroactive interference' in their essay 'Setting the Framework', in Winter and Sivan, eds, *War and Remembrance in the Twentieth Century*, Cambridge: Cambridge University Press, 1999, 6–39, 34.
90. See Charlot, *Pourquoi Jacques Chirac?* 54, 77–78.
91. The debate over the sans papiers began in 1996 when a group of asylum-seekers occupied the St. Bernard Church in Paris. For details of the nationality code of 1993, see Danièle Lochak, 'Usages et mésusages d'une notion polémique. La référence à l'identité nationale dans le débat sur la réforme du code de la nationalité 1985–1993', in C.R.I.S.P.A. and C.U.R.A.P.P., eds, *L'Identité politique*, Paris: Presses Universitaires de France, 1994, 306–23.
92. Cf. Frank, 'A propos des commémorations françaises de la deuxième guerre mondiale'. One cannot underestimate the political implications of innuendo (e.g. 'exclusion') in this speech, where Chirac rhetorically grafts racism against Jews in the 1940s onto racism against Muslims in the 1990s. According to Benjamin Stora, the debate over Vichy (in particular the Papon trial) intensified the issue of the rights of French Muslims, while Farhad Khosrokhavar suggests that Muslims have today effectively substituted Jews in a process of 'displacement of racism'. See Benjamin Stora, 'Vergangenheit, die wiederkehrt', *Die Zeit*, 14 November 1997, 13; Khosrokhavar, 'L'universel abstrait, le politique et la construction de l'islamisme comme forme d'altérité', in Wieviorka, ed., *Une société fragmentée? Le multiculturalisme en débat*, Paris: La Découverte, 1996, 113–72, 148.
93. Quoted in Stéphane Trano, 'Le Grand Pardon', *Tribune Juive*, 27 July 1995, 14–17, 16f.
94. See interview with Le Pen in Nicolas Domenach and Maurice Szafran, Le Roman d'un président, Paris: Plon, 1997, and report by Douglas Johnson, 'French Anti-Semitism Revisited', *The Spectator*, 15 March 1997, 18–19.
95. Le Pen was quoted in the media as having said that 'it was more convenient to resist in London than to resist in Paris'. See Pascale Robert-Diard, 'Philippe Séguin se distingue de Jacques Chirac au sujet de Vichy', *Le Monde*, 21 October 1997, 6.
96. Quoted in Jonathan Marcus, 'Advance or Consolidation? The French

National Front and the 1995 Elections', *West European Politics* no. 2, 1996, 303–320, 316. See note 250.
97. Séguin, 'Assez! Assez! Assez!', *Le Figaro*, 21 October 1997, 6.
98. Cf. Jean-Christian Petitfils, *Le Gaullisme*, Paris: Presses Universitaires de France, 1977 (Chapter I); Bernhard Schmidt et al., eds, *Frankreich Lexikon*, Berlin: Erich Schmidt Verlag, 1981, 323–29.
99. See Maurice Agulhon, 'De Gaulle et l'histoire de France', *Vingtième Siècle* no. 53, January / March 1997, 3–12, 6.
100. See Jean-Pierre Azéma, 'Des Résistances à la Résistance', in Jean-Pierre Azéma and François Bédarida, eds, *La France des années noires*, 2 vols, Paris: Seuil, 1993, vol. 2, *De l'Occupation à la Libération*, 241–70, esp. 242–47.
101. Quoted from an ordinance published on 9 August 1944. See Paxton, *Vichy France*, 330.
102. E.g., Edwy Plenel, 'La République et l'oubli', *Le Monde*, 19 / 20 July 1992, 1, 6.
103. See Annette Wieviorka's description of the republican style of Jewish commemorations of the 1950s, in *Déportation et génocide*, 356.
104. The notions of transcendance, voluntarism, historical action and social unity in a projected future are not unique to Gaullism, but occur in universalist ideologies elsewhere. Cf. Bernhard Giesen and Kay Junge, 'Der Mythos des Universalismus', in Helmut Berding, ed., *Mythos und Nation*, Frankfurt am Main: Suhrkamp, 1996, 34–64, 40.
105. Maurice Agulhon refers to a Gaullist 'dialectic' of national history, 'alternating between catastrophes and recoveries'. See Agulhon, 'De Gaulle et l'histoire de France', 7. See also Frey's analysis of the 'rise-fall myth' in 'Rebuilding France. Gaullist Historiography, the Rise-fall Myth and French Identity 1945–58'.
106. Cf. Gaffney, 'Language and Politics: the Case of Neo-Gaullism', in J. Gaffney and E. Kolinsky, eds, *Political Culture in France and Germany*, London: Routledge, 1991, 91–129, 95.
107. See Rousso, *Le Syndrome de Vichy*, 54–61.
108. Séguin, 'Assez! Assez! Assez!' *Le Figaro*, 21 October 1997, 6.
109. Quoted in De Montvalon, 'Pour Lionel Jospin, la "France" n'est pas coupable de Vichy', *Le Monde*, 23 October 1997, 6.
110. Michel Wieviorka, ed., *Une société fragmentée? Le multiculturalisme en débat*, Paris: La Découverte, 1996.
111. The political scientist Serge Bernstein directly opposes Michel Wieviorka by arguing that a 'renaissance of republican culture' has occurred in France since the 1980s. Cf. Bernstein, 'Le retour de la culture républicaine', *Vingtième Siècle* no. 44, October / December 1994, 113–20, 117.
112. Benedict Anderson, *Imagined Communities. Reflections on the Origin and Spread of Nationalism* (1983), London & New York: Verso, 1991, 199–201.
113. See Charlot, *Pourquoi Jacques Chirac?* 144.

4

Berlin: the Monument for the Murdered Jews of Europe and the Promise of Consensus 1988–2000[1]

Plans for a 'Monument for the Murdered Jews of Europe' or 'Holocaust Monument'[2] in Berlin gave rise to one of the most intense and prolonged debates over the memorial legacy and representations of the Second World War in the history of the Federal Republic of Germany. Following the renaming of streets and the removal or modification of monuments in the eastern sector of the city from 1989, and parallel to negotiations over the possible reconstruction of the Hohenzollern Palace, the debate over the planned Holocaust Monument exemplified the problematical cultural and symbolic transformation of this city prior to and following its reinstatement as the seat of government in 1999.

The campaign was marked by two issues. What is the most adequate form of monument? And is the monument as a genre (in contrast to other forms of ritual commemoration such as wreath-laying, demonstrations, public speeches or national holidays, for example) an effective medium of commemoration? Confusion and prolonged debate over the first issue of form led immediately to the second issue of the very desirability of such a monument. These issues suggest that the various designs proposed for this monument should be systematically analysed in relation to their specific social context – in relation to the origins of the project following the campaign of the citizens' action group Perspektive Berlin from 1988, the role of intellectuals and politicians involved in the debate, the arguments of artists and architects expressed in public forums and conferences, as well as the political mechanisms employed in the process of decision-making. The architect Robert Kudielka has defined the dual function of the monument as the rendering of information from the past on the one hand ('bearing witness') and serving the memorial needs of the present and future on the other ('maintaining consciousness').[3] At no time was this monument intended to represent artistically the historical theme of genocide indicated in its title. Nor was it to directly represent politically a sense of national self-understanding, although many people ascribed to it this function, including Chancellor Kohl.[4] Instead, if we recognise the Holocaust Monument as a product of its social environment and as a focus of public debate with respect to both its artistic and political representative function, we must ask: for whom was the monument built, and what understanding of history does it underpin? The meaning of the monument as a contribution to historical understanding thus results from the interaction of artistic and political forms of representation.

Political strategies undertaken to appropriate this allegedly national symbol, which are the object of this chapter, strove to forge consensus against a climate of dissent. As a result of prolonged controversy, the project for this monument has a history of its own. It is even possible that it will stand less as testimony to the victims of genocide than as testimony to the difficulty of selecting and agreeing upon an adequate medium with which to commemorate them. The project gave rise not only to a large number of architectural and artistic blueprints, but also to a wealth of highly politicised discourse on contemporary history and the role of commemoration. By examining prize-winning models, but also initial petitions, instructions briefing artists on how to submit a model, conferences, press reports, interviews documenting responses of artists, architects and their critics, as well as political statements and the Bundestag debates of 9 May 1996 and 25 June 1999, we may better understand the way in which the Holocaust Monument became a focal point of contentions over Germany's memory culture from unification in 1989.

This chapter attempts to explain the problems arising from this project in comparison to the debate over the Vél' d'Hiv' in France by examining the conditions established for the monument, the responses of artists, politicians and intellectuals, and the political consequences of the project. The four main sections focus on: the site and emergence of the Holocaust Monument as a focus of political controversy from 1988; the proposed monuments and discourse of artists and political leaders; the relation of the monument to current political issues (the reinstatement of Berlin as the capital city, and the parliamentary election campaign of 1998); and the extent to which the quest to achieve national 'consensus', analogous to the quest in France to achieve 'reconciliation', was fulfilled during the process of selecting a monument.

The Emergence of the Holocaust Monument as a 'Site of Memory', 1988–99

i. The Site and its Urban Context

The planned Monument for the Murdered Jews of Europe differs in several respects from the large number of existing sites in Berlin recalling the

National Socialist dictatorship and its victims,[5] and therefore breaks with a tradition of commemorative forms used in both the Federal Republic and the German Democratic Republic. It is not designed to mark and trace the history of a specific authentic site or event on a specific day, but recalls the genocide as a whole. It is larger than any previous monument (on a site of twenty thousand square metres). And unlike most memorials and documentation centres, this monument consists primarily of a sculpture, complemented, according to the parliamentary resolution of 25 June 1999, with an information centre. Its symbolic significance is heightened by immediate urban surroundings: the new governmental zone, the Reichstag building and Brandenburg Gate to the north, the Potsdamer Platz, Leipziger Platz and the documentation centre called the Topography of Terror to the south. By occupying a location on the former no-man's land between East and West Berlin close to these existing sites (Fig. 6), it acquired national symbolic significance that neutralised discrepancies between separate commemorative traditions of the former East and West Germanys. Before unification in 1990, styles of and inscriptions on monuments ranged between largely 'anti-fascist' memorials celebrating heroes and heroic acts of resistance in the East, and anti-communist memorials, ones commemorating victimhood generally, and in particular memorials designed to give meaning to specific historical sites in the West, such as plaques on historical buildings, memorials on the sites of former synagogues, museum exhibitions, monuments in cemeteries and on sites on which acts of persecution, deportation and resistance took place.[6] The East German cultural authorities adopted a distinctly ideological policy towards memorials, inaugurating the Neue Wache in Berlin as a 'memorial for victims of fascism' in 1956 and a national memorial on the site of the former Buchenwald concentration camp in 1958. The tradition of central memorials common in the East was foreign to the West. Plans for a national monument in Bonn initiated in 1977 led to a competition between 1984 and 1985 but not to its realisation.[7] West Germany possessed no central memorial to the Second World War, but rather countless local commemorative projects.[8] In this respect, the Holocaust Monument is designed as a new all-German site, and as a complement to other memorials installed since 1989. This essentially artistic, abstract sculpture is dedicated specifically to Jewish victims of Europe. It thus complements existing memorials in Berlin such as the Topography of Terror (which exposes the foundations of the former Gestapo headquarters and exhibits documentation about the site), the House of the Wannsee Conference (where the conference leading to the 'final solution' took place in 1942), the Jewish Museum (documenting the history of German Jewry), the German Resistance Memorial and the Neue Wache memorial. At the same time, however, the Holocaust Monument differs *qualitatively* from many of the existing memorials. It gives priority to abstract form rather than pedagogical documentary exhibits. Its dedication to Jewish victims counteracts the unspecific dedication 'to victims of war and tyranny' of the Neue Wache memorial. And it does not draw attention to the significance of the former uses of its historical site.

The monument consists of a trapezium field of 2,700 grey concrete steles between fifty centimetres and five metres in height that are arranged in straight rows, albeit slightly tilted at irregular angles (Fig. 7). The four rooms of the subterranean information centre provide visitors with access to witness accounts, to documentation of the history of persecuted individuals, families and communities and of the destruction of Jewish life in Europe, to lists of names of victims and their personal tragedies presented audibly and projected onto the walls (an exhibit in collaboration with the Yad Vashem Memorial in Jerusalem), to films and databanks about the types of persecution suffered, and to details of other memorials in Germany. The floor of the monument sinks towards the centre such that, despite the increasing height of the steles, the monument rises only slightly above ground level. Some critics have likened this design to a Jewish cemetery, although its designers, the American architect Peter Eisenman and artist Richard Serra (who withdrew from the project in March 1998), deny any symbolic content, interpreting their work instead in purely abstract terms as a 'zone of instability'[9] acting on the subjective perception of visitors as they walk into the narrow ninety-centimetre-wide passageways and find themselves symbolically engulfed by the steles. According to the original plan, this monument was to have contained four thousand steles. Following the visit of Chancellor Kohl to the exhibition of shortlisted models, however, the designers were requested to reduce the size of the field of steles and integrate trees and parking spaces into the border between the monument and surrounding streets. The visitor therefore encounters a monument in the city centre that is very broad, low, and framed by trees and a constant stream of traffic on three of its four sides.

The monument is integrated into its urban surroundings as an extension of the public space of the Tiergarten park to the west, and as an extension of the urban grid structure of apartment and office blocks, embassies and governmental buildings to the east. By linking the park in the west and the urban grid in the east, it also links the two halves of the formerly divided city. In contrast to most existent monuments and memorials commemorating the Second World War in Europe, the site of the Holocaust Monument in Berlin was not determined from the outset by its historical significance. Unlike the Vél' d'Hiv', for example, which was established as a site for small-scale public commemorations of a precise historical event of 16 and 17 July 1942 before it acquired national political significance in the 1980s, the significance of the site of the Berlin monument was consistently perceived in general and imprecise terms. On the one hand, its dedication – either to Jewish victims of the genocide in particular, or to

Figure 6: Location of the Holocaust Monument on the former no-man's land between East and West Berlin (1998)

Figure 7: Model for the Holocaust Monument by Peter Eisenman and Richard Serra (1997): modified version (1998) with trees, parking spaces and 2,700 instead of 4,000 steles

all victim groups – was a constant source of dispute. Moreover, its publicly accepted name, 'Holocaust Monument', understood as a commemoration of the Holocaust in general, detracted from historical detail. And although references to the site employed during the debate – 'minister gardens', 'strip of land on which the wall stood', 'Prussian Ministry for Nutrition and Agriculture', near to the 'former Imperial Chancellery' and 'Hitler's bunker' – described the past uses of the site, the very multiplicity of terms demonstrated how perceptions of its historical significance differed. Whereas the form of a memorial on an 'authentic' historical site like that of the Vél' d'Hiv' is largely determined by the significance of the site itself, the perceived historical insignificance of the Berlin site accentuated the anticipated universality of the monument – a universality accentuated yet further by the public's espousal of it as a monument dedicated to all victims of the persecution rather (as its official name indicates) than to Jews alone. The decision of petitioners to disregard the specific historical significance of the site and to claim that it should have national appeal was therefore coherent with the unspecific popular appropriation of the monument as a 'Holocaust Monument'. The fact that the idea to build a monument preexisted any agreement on what to build and precisely where and why to build it (for whom and in the name of what), suggests that the intentions of the organisers were primarily political, and that their preconceptions about Germany's memory culture prevailed over the concern to explore and interpret the history of the site and people's memories relating to it. Motivations for the construction of this monument therefore contrasted starkly with the historical guiding principle underlying memorials on sites like the Topography of Terror or the Memorial of German Resistance.

The Holocaust Monument was therefore characterised from the start by historical indeterminacy resulting from its organisers' pretension to universality: the attempt to bear witness to the genocide of the Second World War with a single symbol. Although the site of the Holocaust Monument is historically significant, this was underplayed during the debate. By giving priority to a general symbolic rather than specific historical significance of the site, organisers exacerbated the difficulty of deciding what monument to build. A monument designed to represent 'a duty for all Germans in East and West'[10] and an 'all-German act'[11] inevitably reduced the possibility of realising the conditions for this commemoration in a single monument.

ii. Phases of the Commemorative Debate

In order to clarify the multiple issues associated with the monument, I propose to briefly outline chronological phases of the commemorative debate associated with this monument. The origins of the project may be traced back to negotiations undertaken by the association Initiative for Dealing with the Gestapo Grounds (Initiative zum Umgang mit dem Gestapo-Gelände) in 1980 to build a memorial on the site of the Prince-Albrecht Palace, the location of the Gestapo headquarters from 1933. Perspektive Berlin, the citizens' action group founded by the journalist Lea Rosh and historian Eberhard Jäckel, joined in the quest to design a permanent memorial for this site in 1988 following the opening of the provisional documentation centre (the Topography of Terror) there in 1987.

This project was controversial from its inception in 1988. Perspektive Berlin intervened in the existing project to construct a memorial, and aroused media interest by polemicising the necessity of a monument as a form of moral reparation for Jewish victims. An open statement of the association Active Museum of Fascism and Resistance (Aktives Museum Faschismus und Widerstand) in Berlin, which had participated in the search for an adequate commemorative usage of the Prince-Albrecht site throughout the 1980s, even criticised Perspektive Berlin for attempting to usurp the existing project. According to the statement, members of Perspektive Berlin were practising a 'form of lobbying with expensive advertisements designed to win over a public which is not fully aware of the state of the discussion'.[12] Hans Dingel, also of the association Active Museum, accused Perspektive Berlin, which had solicited the support of local politicians, of bypassing measures previously taken by associations to develop the site.[13] A key point of contention was the type of memorial. The Active Museum association had been campaigning for a heuristic rather than purely aesthetic memorial, one in which 'people can think about the persecutors, about the structures in which they worked and about the ongoing effect of these structures to this day',[14] by drawing people's attention to the historical significance of sites with techniques defined by the art historian Christine Fischer-Defoy as 'marking, researching, remembering, learning, teaching, warning, commemorating, creating, mediating, meeting'.[15] In March 1990, the local state-appointed commission debating the future use of this site[16] finally decided to accept the proposal of the association Active Museum to build a documentation centre rather than a monument. Perspektive Berlin (whose activities were delegated to the association Support Group for the Construction of a Monument for the Murdered Jews of Europe (Förderkreis zur Errichtung eines Denkmals für die ermordeten Juden Europe) in 1989 then sought a new site for a separate Monument for the Murdered Jews of Europe. In November 1992, the Berlin Senate finally approved the site between the Brandenburg Gate and Leipziger Platz, which had been previously occupied by the ministerial gardens adjoining the Prussian Ministry for Nutrition and Agriculture and the presidential residence and, after 1945, by the no-man's land of the Berlin Wall.

The debate entered a second phase in 1991 and 1992 when representatives of the Roma and Sinti community campaigned for the representation of other victim groups in a collective monument. This provoked representatives of the Jewish community and historians to insist on the specificity of the genocide against Jews and therefore exclude the possibility of a monument mentioning Jews together with other victim groups. This issue was settled provisionally by proposing separate monuments for each group, although precise plans for the location, size and form of these monuments were left unresolved.[17]

Next followed two architectural competitions, which focused public interest on the artistic form of the monument. Reputed artists familiar with the problem of memory and memorial representation were invited to submit proposals, including Christian Boltanski, Gerhard Merz, Richard Serra in 1995; followed by Jochen Gerz, Rachel Whitehead and the architects Daniel Libeskind and Peter Eisenman in the second competition of 1997. Some 528 models were submitted in 1995 followed by 28 models (by invitation only) in 1997, which led to the selection of two prize models in 1995 and four in 1997. A large number of intellectuals, including architects, artists, art critics, historians, journalists and political scientists, joined in the debate on the cultural pages of daily newspapers, but no agreement was reached over a single model. The shortlisting of multiple prizewinners, followed by exhibitions and conferences, prolonged the debate and offered the public an opportunity to become informed about, if not involved in the selection process. However, hopes that public involvement would lead to the negotiation of a more broadly based social consensus were not fulfilled, for the debate promoted conflict rather than consensus.

The much publicised cancellation of the first competition in 1995 by Chancellor Kohl, allegedly due to a lack of consensus over the winning models, has been a subject of much speculation. The artist Richard Serra suggests that Kohl had, until this moment, suspended judgement on the project in order to woo the right wing of the CDU,[18] while his histrionic cancellation of the competition was, as the historian Hans-Georg Stavginski argues, probably influenced by the president of the Central Council of Jews in Germany, Ignatz Bubis,[19] whose opposition to the shortlisted models prompted the chancellor to woo the left wing of his party without alienating the right, who were only too pleased to see the project flounder. Kohl's decision was almost certainly motivated by all these factors, as well as the need to turn the page on the commemorative blunders committed at Bitburg and with the Neue Wache memorial. In any case, the cancellation certainly marked a turning point in the debate in so far as it led to the introduction of institutional measures to build social consensus: a special parliamentary committee was established, a Bundestag debate staged in May 1996, and three conferences each involving over ninety experts and politicians were organised, followed by exhibitions of the proposals submitted in each competition, a series of six public hearings of the artists and architects early in 1998, meetings organised by religious and political associations, as well as a series of hearings of the parliamentary cultural committee in 1999. State measures taken to precipitate a decision culminated in the Bundestag ballot on 25 June 1999, in which members of parliament approved the model by Eisenman. Ballots were cast in the following manner: 439 out of 559 MPs present at the sitting voted in favour of the basic motion to build the monument; 325 voted in favour of a monument dedicated exclusively to Jewish victims rather than to all victim groups collectively; 314 voted for the modified model by Eisenman, 209 for Richard Schröder's proposal to build a simple monument bearing the inscription 'Thou shalt not murder' in German and Hebrew. In short, the decision fell on the second version of Eisenman and Serra's model with 2,700 steles, modified with an information centre and dedicated to the 'murdered Jews of Europe'.

The second exhibition gave rise to even more controversy when a number of intellectuals, including successive presidents of the Academy of Arts Walter Jens and György Konrád, and politicians, including Berlin's governing mayor Eberhard Diepgen, called for a halt to the project in February 1998. Richard Serra resigned from his cooperation with Peter Eisenman, and Jochen Gerz withdrew his model from competition. The direct intervention of Chancellor Kohl from 1995 and Michael Naumann, the Social Democrat representative for cultural affairs prior to the parliamentary elections in September 1998, even turned the search for an adequate monument into an affair of state. Prior to the elections of September 1998, the competition was postponed in order to avoid turning the monument into a party political issue during election campaigning. Following the election, however, which led to the formation of a coalition government with the Social Democratic Party (SPD) and the Green Party, debate not only intensified but also became increasingly political and legal in character. Naumann, now appointed as the Federal Cultural Representative (Bundeskulturbeauftragter), whose status was later muted by decree to State Minister for Culture in the Chancellor's Office (Staatsminister für Kultur im Kanzleramt),[20] ceased to appeal for the cancellation of the project and suggested alternative monuments: the modification of Eisenman's project by integrating video screens into the steles showing recordings of witnesses from Steven Spielberg's Survivors of the Shoah Visual History Foundation; the substitution of the monument with a building containing the same video collection; or its substitution with a Holocaust museum. Andreas Nachama, chairman of the Jewish Community of Berlin, also proposed a University for Jewish Studies including a collective programme of Catholic, Protestant and Islamic theology. These proposals were systematically criticised in the press.

Naumann finally negotiated a fourth project in collaboration with Eisenman, who agreed to integrate into his original model an institutional building containing a library, a branch of the Leo Baeck Institute, a research centre and Shoah Foundation videos, thus further reducing the number of steles from 2,700 to 1,500. This proposal, presented at a parliamentary press conference on 18 December 1998, was sanctioned by the media and two of the organising bodies: Naumann on behalf of the federal government, and Lea Rosh on behalf of the association. Apparent consensus was therefore reached momentarily in a compromise model combining art with a pedagogical institute. However, artists and politicians did not endorse this decision. The artist Jochen Gerz and architect Daniel Libeskind accused Eisenman of plagiarism, because the revised model contained an information centre similar to the building proposed in Gerz's proposal shortlisted in the competition of 1997, and a field of steles similar to those in the grounds of Libeskind's Jewish Museum.[21] Moreover, members of the Christian Democratic Union (CDU) and Christian Social Union (CSU) parliamentary parties in both the federal and regional Berlin governments rallied against the decision reached by Naumann.

The final preparatory phase of the debate was heralded by the government's approval of Lea Rosh's plan to delegate the ultimate responsibility for selecting a monument to the Bundestag, as expressed in a press conference on 9 September 1998. This plan was ultimately realised on 25 June 1999, after the competition procedure had collapsed. The competition procedure had been effectively violated on three occasions. First, when Naumann presented the modified Eisenman model or 'Eisenman III' in December 1998 without consulting the organising committee responsible for decision-making, comprising the association, the Berlin Senate and federal government, in collaboration with the commission of experts. Second, when the media and organising committee gave consideration to a proposal that had received no credit during the official competitions: a proposal by the theologian Richard Schröder to erect a simple monument bearing the inscription 'Thou shalt not kill'. Third, when the Berlin Senate voted in favour of a motion put forward by the governing mayor Diepgen to postpone the competition on 16 March 1999.

By bypassing the rules of the competition, Naumann's compromise proposal triggered protest from artists, representatives of existing memorials in Berlin, and from members of the CDU, CSU and Free Democratic Party (FDP) in both local and federal parliaments, transforming the monument project into a party political issue and spurring debate over rules of procedure required to reach a decision. Parties had previously been divided over the monument issue. The local SPD in Berlin and the federal CDU in Bonn had largely favoured the project, while the local CDU in Berlin and federal SPD in Bonn opposed it. Following the elections of

September 1998 and Naumann's sudden and undiplomatic intervention in the competition procedure, however, and despite the general insistence that party whips should *not* encourage members of parliament to vote in accordance with party policy, a degree of party cohesion between local and national governments did evolve. The new federal SPD representatives ceased to voice outright protest at the project, and the CDU parliamentary party in Berlin invited directors of existing memorials there to a hearing on 8 February 1999 in order to articulate protest against the plan to construct a combined monument and institution. They argued that costs, estimated at 180 million deutschmarks, were unjustified at a time when existing memorials were underfunded, and appealed for priority to be given to memorials on 'authentic' historical sites, such as the Topography of Terror or the Memorial of German Resistance.[22] Parliamentary discussions resulted in greater party cohesion. A majority of CDU MPs favoured the model by Richard Schröder. A majority of SPD MPs favoured the hybrid 'Eisenman III' model combining a sculpture and information centre. And members of all groups recommended the model by Eisenman without an information centre.[23] Three Bundestag group motions were consequently put forward in April 1999. In addition, the motion for a complete abandonment of the project was likewise proposed by fifty-eight members of the CDU and CSU parliamentary parties.

Confusion over the number and complexity of issues under consideration and the repeated disregard of established competition procedure finally legitimated the recourse to purely institutional decision-making measures. Following a series of hearings organised by the parliamentary cultural committee and the formulation of group motions to be voted on in 1999, authority for selecting a monument was transferred from the three organisers to the Bundestag alone then, following the resolution of 25 June 1999, to a new Foundation Monument for the Murdered Jews of Europe (Stiftung Denkmal für die ermordeten Juden Europas), designed to implement and administrate the memorial project.

From this moment on, the debate over this monument entered a new phase. The artistic form had been settled and was no longer an issue. Under the auspices of the Foundation Monument for the Murdered Jews of Europe, officially established in April 2000, the monumental project became increasingly institutionalised. The foundation set up an elaborate internet site, which marginalised the controversies of the 1990s by focusing on technical questions of finance, administration, architecture and on the calendar of events leading up to the official inauguration of the site on 8 May 2005. Proceedings were initially delayed by uncertainty over sources of funding, before the federal government pledged funds of over fifty-three million euros for the project until 2005. The foundation appointed a work group responsible for the form and content of the information centre, as well as a twenty-two-member board of trustees representing the citizens' action group, the federal government, political parties, the Central Council of Jews in Germany, the Jewish Community of Berlin, the Jewish Museum, the Topography of Terror Foundation, and members of memorials on the sites of former concentration camps. Five-metre-high banners were raised on the site illustrating and explaining its future use, and an information platform constructed in June 2002 with diagrams visualising the future monument, thus turning the still-empty site into an ephemeral monument of the anticipated stone monument. Peripheral public relations activities organised by the foundation included a series of talks on 'Sites of Persecution – Sites of Memory' in 2003, an exhibition of paintings by the Israeli artist Pinhas Golan, a musical concert on the site to mark the official beginning of construction on 30 April 2003, as well as publications including a regular information bulletin, 'Monumentinfo' (*Denkmalinfo*), and the first in a series of books, 'Papers of the Foundation' (*Schriftenreihe der Stiftung*).[23] The monument was further popularised in relation to the growing cult of the architect Peter Eisenman, who regularly visited Berlin to hold lectures, examine the progress of the construction site, publish press articles, and even engage in public gestures of reconciliation such as publicly thanking Martin Walser for having polarised public opinion and inadvertently encouraged public support for the monument in 1998 by criticising it as an example of moral intimidation of the German population![24]

The empty site was also used for commemorations. On 27 January 2000, the German government supplemented its annual commemorative speeches, held in parliament in memory of the liberation of the Auschwitz concentration camp in 1945, with an additional speech on the empty memorial site, held by the president of the Bundestag. The still incomplete plans for an information centre accompanying the monument and the veto of the governing mayor Diepgen meant that the planned ceremony for the laying of the foundation stone could not be held, but associations and government ministers assembled there nevertheless to hold commemorative speeches under the gaze of the media in defiance of continuing postponements. This symbolic event prolonged the series of commemorative gestures associated with this monument, which for a period of seventeen years (between its inception in 1988 and official inauguration in 2005) will have consisted essentially of rhetorical and ritual gestures and media campaigns. On the same day, members of the Jewish community used the site for a collective reading of all names of deportees listed in the Berlin Commemorative Book (*Berliner Gedenkbuch*), a ceremony previously staged at the Grunewald train station from which deportations had taken place, and thus reinforced the trend towards the centralisation of commemorative ritual. Meanwhile, associations representing non-Jewish victims became increasingly active. A Memorial to the Memory of the Victims of National-Socialist Crimes of Euthanasia was inaugurated on 14 October 2000 on the grounds of the Max Delbrück Centre for Molecular Medicine in the north of Berlin.[26] In September 2001, the Roma and Sinti held public meetings in order to plan the construction of a memorial next to the Reichstag and thus replace the temporary memorial there. These negotiations also met with conflict when a request by the Central Council of Roma and Sinti to include an inscription, a quotation of the former president Roman Herzog in which he equated the persecution of Jews and gypsies, was opposed at a scientific symposium in late 2003.[27] In December of the same year, members of parliament also voted in favour of a decision to build a central monument for homosexuals persecuted and murdered under the National Socialist regime, and approved a site for this in the Tiergarten park in central Berlin.

Parallel to the institutional activities of the foundation from 1999, the Holocaust Monument continued to provide a source of sporadic public debate. The fencing surrounding the building site served as a support for graffiti and posters displaying alternative designs and protest slogans. Representatives of handicapped people took legal action against the foundation in 2002 in order to ensure the accessibility of all people to the monument. In particular, the citizens' action group continued to stage provocative publicity stunts. Intense controversy erupted again in 2001 when the association campaigning for the Holocaust Monument launched an advertising campaign to solicit public donations. The advertising poster appearing on hoardings throughout Germany (Fig. 8) showed a photograph of snow-topped mountains and a lake superimposed with the statement in large letters and in inverted commas, 'The Holocaust never took place' ('*Den Holocaust hat es nie gegeben*'). Small letters at the base of the image explained that the purpose of the poster was to collect donations for the association's financial share of the monument's costs. Once again, the monument was a source of division. Alexander Brenner, chairman of the Jewish Community of Berlin, supported the campaign. Paul Spiegel, president of the Central Council of Jews in Germany from 2000, vehemently opposed it.[28] Historians joined Spiegel and successfully campaigned to have the posters removed with the aid of a petition to collect signatures in daily newspapers and via the internet.[29] Historians claimed that the poster's statement, despite its use of inverted commas, would reinforce prejudices rather than provoke questions about Holocaust denial. Their critics emphasised that people would indeed grasp the ironic message of the poster on the basis of its combination of image and words in a deliberately ambiguous advertising technique. They further criticised the collection of signatures via the internet as ineffective, appealing instead for a campaign against negationism in schools, public places, institutions and associations. Nevertheless, the poster campaign had by this time already fulfilled the aim of the citizens' action group – to revive debate about the monument and collective memory.

Figure 8: Poster campaign launched by the 'Support Group for the Construction of a Monument for the Murdered Jews of Europe' to raise funds in 2001

Further publicity stunts organised by the citizens' action group included an invitation to the model Claudia Schiffer to appear in television advertisements appealing for donations towards the costs of the monument in October 2002. The chairwoman of the group, Lea Rosh, also repeated the street collections of donations with which she had initiated the project in 1988, and now appeared in August 2003 alongside political figures such as the former Berlin mayor Walter Momper and the member of parliament for the Party of Democratic Socialism (PDS), Petra Pau. The aim of the citizens' action group was to exploit popular opinion, in particular via the mass media, in favour of a single issue, the monument. However, it is questionable whether the use of advertising techniques effectively provokes or sustains historical consciousness of persecution and genocide. One of the sharpest critics of the project, the journalist Henryk Broder, claimed that the primary motivation of the citizens' action group was to erect a monument in memory of its own members' personal ambitions. The fact that the extreme right-wing party, the National Democratic Party of Germany (NPD), adopted exactly the same phrase for its poster during the local election campaign in October 2001 in Berlin, and even pasted this poster on the boundary fence of the construction site of the monument, confirms Broder's suggestion that the poster of the citizens' action group indeed lent support to revisionism.[30]

The protective coating 'Protectosil', designed to be painted on the steles in order to repel graffiti, provided a further source of debate in late 2003. One of the subsidiaries of the Degussa company producing the protective coating, Degesch, was discovered to have produced the poisonous Zyklon B gas used in the gas chambers during the war. Although the company had already engaged economic historians in investigations of its past ventures, and was a founder member of the foundation 'Memory, Responsibility and Future' (Erinnerung, Verantwortung und Zukunft) set up in 2000 to organise reparations for victims of slave and forced labour on behalf of German industry, opinions were characteristically divided over the question whether to suspend construction proceedings and seek a new product or else accept the Degussa product as one more expression of the historical contradictions exposed by the prospect of the Holocaust Monument. The controversy was exacerbated by the revelation that a Swiss company's bid to supply a similar protective coating ('PSS') for half the cost of that quoted by Degussa had been rejected, revealing that the contract had been granted to Degussa under suspicious circumstances and, moreover, that companies had been competing to win contracts for the monument as an effective platform for informal advertising. Rosh, initiator of the monumental project, favoured a suspension of construction, whereas Eisenman accepted the contradictions and urged to proceed with the construction. Alexander Brenner, on behalf of the Jewish Community of Berlin, favoured suspension, while Paul Spiegel, of the Central Council of Jews in Germany, argued for continuation. One of the fiercest criticisms came from the former State Minister for Culture and now publisher, Michael Naumann, who derided the calls to suspend the construction of the monument as an act of 'political hygiene', a false attempt to symbolically purify the recent past of Germany with a demonstrative gesture of piety towards an industrial product. Not only was the company and the contemporary German state not identical with the company and state of the 1940s, but suspension of the construction would have implied that those responsible for the monument were striving to ensure that the monument would veil undeniable historical contradictions, continuities and ruptures in German history. 'Transference of guilt onto industrial products,' claimed Naumann, 'serves a new kind of role play.'[31] He was thus referring to the recurrent tendency in Germany to extract oneself and one's forefathers from historical responsibility by externalising this responsibility, that is, by projecting culpability onto the figure of Hitler for example or, in this case, onto industry. News that a second subsidiary of Degussa called Woermann Construction Chemicals had already supplied liquefaction chemicals for the concrete used to build the steles further deepened the controversy, leading the board of trustees to decide in November 2003 to continue construction with the tainted products while agreeing to integrate documentation about the controversial construction process into the memorial itself as a realistic pedagogical example of the historical contradictions in German history. This monument thus testifies both to the events of the 1940s and to the history of the monument's own making as an event in its own right.

During this final phase of discussions preceding the official inauguration of the monument, the Holocaust Monument, like the Vél' d'Hiv', became a constant and automatic reference point in public discourse whenever the nation was evoked in relation to war crimes. This phase of the project was characterised by the elaborate institutionalisation of political communication generated by the monument (within the Foundation Monument for the Murdered Jews of Europe, for example), and by displacement of discussion about the past and about people's understanding of this past in the present onto objects of substitution. In the first phase of discussions about the monument, these objects included the artistic form of the monument and the search for an adequate selection procedure. In the final phase, they included the controversial poster campaign, public personalities such as the architect and the initiator of the citizens' action group, anxiety over anticipated vandalism of the monument with graffiti, and the producers of industrial paint.

The Rhetorical and Artistic Construction of the Holocaust Monument

The conditions for a monument established in the series of petitions and media campaign from 1988 were followed by responses in the form of blueprints of monuments, and public and political debate over these responses. Knowledge about the planned monument was therefore transmitted by a complex discursive system based on rhetorical demands of the organisers, sculptural responses of artists and architects (discourse *of* art), and rhetorical responses in the form of artists' and architects' justifications of their works and subsequent interpretations and critiques by intellectuals and politicians (discourse *on* art). This system relied on a network of media communication in the form of press reports, exhibitions, conferences and panel discussions. From the beginning, this debate or 'discursive event'[32] was characterised by the remarkable incongruity, expressed in petitions and instructions to participants in the competitions of 1995 and 1997, between the distinct political purpose of the monument and the entirely open formal solutions expected of artists and architects. The discrepancy between the prescribed purpose and open means with which to realise this purpose was the prime cause of confusion and controversy over the project.

Aufruf

der Bürgerinitiative „Perspektive Berlin" an den Berliner Senat, die Regierungen der Bundesländer, die Bundesregierung:

Ein halbes Jahrhundert ist seit der Machtübernahme der Nazis und dem Mord an den Juden Europas vergangen. Aber auf deutschem Boden, im Land der Täter, gibt es bis heute keine zentrale Gedenkstätte, die an diesen einmaligen Völkermord, und kein Mahnmal, das an die Opfer erinnert.

Das ist eine Schande.

Deshalb fordern wir, endlich für die Millionen ermordeter Juden ein unübersehbares Mahnmal in Berlin zu errichten. Und zwar auf dem ehemaligen GESTAPO-Gelände, dem Sitz des Reichssicherheitshauptamtes, der Mordzentrale in der Reichshauptstadt. Die Errichtung dieses Mahnmals ist eine Verpflichtung für alle Deutschen in Ost und West.

Willy Brandt
Klaus Bednarz
Volker Braun
Margherita von Brentano
Eberhard Fechner
Hanns Joachim Friedrichs
Günter Grass
Heinrich Hannover
Christof Hein
Dieter Hildebrandt
Hilmar Hoffmann
Alfred Hrdlicka
Eberhard Jäckel
Inge Jens, Walter Jens
Beate Klarsfeld
Udo Lindenberg
Egon Monk
Heiner Müller
Uta Ranke-Heinemann
Horst-Eberhard Richter
Otto Schily
Helmut Simon
Klaus Staeck
Franz Steinkühler
Klaus Wagenbach
Christa Wolf

Für die PERSPEKTIVE BERLIN e.V.:

Lea Rosh, Ada Withake-Scholz, Christian Fenner, Arnt Seifert, Ulrich Baehr, Tilman Fichter, Rolf Kreibich, Leonie Ossowski, Monika und Rainer Papenfuß, Jakob Schulze-Rohr.

Unterstützer dieser Aktion werden gebeten, ihre Unterschrift zu schicken an:
PERSPEKTIVE BERLIN e.V., Tempelhofer Ufer 22, D-1000 Berlin 61

Spenden bitte auf das Konto: Bank für Sozialwirtschaft Berlin, Konto-Nummer: 3 071 700, BLZ 100 105 00.

Bestätigungen über Zuwendungen gemäß § 10 b EStG werden zugesandt.

Figure 9: Petition of the citizens' action group 'Perspektive Berlin' (*Frankfurter Rundschau*, 30 January 1989)

i. The Petitions: Conditions for the Monument

The controversies over the Vél' d'Hiv' commemoration and Holocaust Monument owe their existence to citizens' action groups. In both cases, petitions were published repeatedly in national newspapers and widely discussed, and therefore created a broad public expectation that the demands of the petitions be fulfilled. The type of response demanded by the petitions nevertheless differed in each country. Debate in France was about political rhetoric, in Germany over political art. Those published in France between 1992 and 1994 called for the president to make a verbal declaration at the Vél' d'Hiv' commemoration, and therefore created a direct rhetorical link between the conditions laid down in the petition and the terms of the presidential speeches. In Germany, they called for a response in the form of a monument: an artistic or architectural object with 'central' and 'national' symbolic significance (Fig. 9).[33]

Although the political legitimacy of both sites may be imputed to active petitioning, the intervention of state leaders, parliamentary elections and the symbolic status of capital cities, and although each project triggered analogous public disputes over national memory cultures, the formal object of dispute differed in each country. In short, although the Berlin monument differs from the Paris monument in so far as they each address distinct political communities, and give priority to the artistic form of the monument on the one hand, and accompanying ritual on the other, the end product of these controversies was in each case a monument. Yet the monuments themselves are mute, for they offer only partial insight into the events they commemorate, and almost no insight into their origins.

a. The Projected Community

The petitions of Perspektive Berlin contained presumptions about the identity of people to whom the petition was addressed and for whom the monument was intended. The written guidelines for the architectural competition similarly stipulated the identity of those who gave the commission, of the commissioned artists and architects, and of the public for whom the monument was commissioned. This debate therefore adopted a structure similar to that over the Vél' d'Hiv', where presidents were summoned to define who commemorated what (historical event) how (with a speech or monument) and in the name of what (political community). In contrast to the Vél' d'Hiv', however, where the president was summoned to commemorate a specific event of 1942 with a speech in the name of the nation, conditions for the Holocaust Monument were more complex. In this case, petitions were formulated in the passive mode and thus named no specific agent ('who') to perform the commemoration. 'Therefore we call for … a conspicuous monument to be constructed in Berlin' was the key message of the petition published in January 1989.[34] The event to be commemorated – the genocide against Jews in Europe during the Second World War – was also conceived in general terms. And the means of commemoration were not prescribed in petitions precisely as a verbal recognition of state responsibility, as in the French case, but as a monument or memorial whose significance should be conveyed by its artistic form.

The essential analogy between the campaigns in Paris and Berlin lay in the definition of their political purposes as specifically national monuments. The fact that questions of 'who', 'what' and 'how' were specified in petitions for the Vél' d'Hiv' but left open in petitions for the Holocaust Monument was perhaps one cause of the relative brevity of the first debate, and the long duration and complexity of the second. Yet although the object and degree of specificity of the two petitions differed, the conditions of both campaigns focused on the analogous political intentions of the organisers of each project: the national scope of the political community, and the primacy of the memory of deportation and genocide as a foundation of values and collective memories for each community. The petitions of 1989 in Germany referred to the monument in political and moral terms as 'central' and as 'a duty for all Germans in East and West'. Instructions to artists described the goal of the competition of 1995 in similarly moral and political terms. The nation is mentioned five times as 'Germany', 'the Germans' and 'German' in conjunction with the monument, which in turn is conceived as a 'duty', as the symbol of a historical 'burden', and as a location linking 'both halves of the city'.[35]

Instructions for participants in the second competition of 1997 described the purpose of the monument in less moral terms, reverting instead to jargon of a personified nation that expresses 'experiences' and 'self-idealisation', and where each nation harbours particular 'aesthetic traditions'. According to the instructions,

> The monuments of each country embody the experiences of the nation, its self-idealisation, political necessities and aesthetic traditions. This is why the forms of monuments in America, Poland, Israel or Holland differ so remarkably. ... Germany's national Monument for the Murdered Jews of Europe will necessarily define Germany's own present memory of the Holocaust, a complex and difficult memory.[36]

By establishing conditions for a monument which should have 'central' symbolic significance for Germany and express national 'ideals', 'experiences' and 'traditions', these petitions and briefings ensured that the designs, their authors' justifications and critical responses were accompanied by controversy not only over the form, but also over the political means required in order to reach a decision and over the very feasibility of charging a single monument with meaning for a group as large as a nation. These conditions were exacerbated following the cancellation of the first competition in July 1995, when Chancellor Kohl expressed disapproval of the prize-winning model on the grounds that social consensus was lacking. From this moment, consensus was projected as the sole condition for a conclusion to the debate over the monument. Expressing indignation and impatience over the long duration and complexity of the discussion, the chancellor's spokesman urged all people involved to rapidly reach broad consensus.[37] Hence the almost oppressively consensual terms in which the invitation to participants in the second official competition of 1997 was formulated.

The competition of 1997 was therefore handicapped from the start by an ideological burden, based on the demand that a single monument should embody the whole nation's memory of the genocide against the Jews during the Second World War, and on the consistent demand for consensus. In both cases, the identity of the group of people presumed to identify with the monument and therefore to engage in communal 'consent' was described not as members of the commissioning body, the jury of specialists, the local community or relatives of victims, for example, but as the nation. The petitions highlighted the indeterminate and therefore problematic social appeal of this political symbol. Can a nation be conceived as a coherent community that identifies collectively with or engages in a sense of emotional allegiance with a single central symbol? And are monuments politically legitimate forms of cultural expression that reflect the values or consciousness of a national community?

b. Document or Monument?

Monuments situated in public places invariably possess both artistic values and political functions akin to works of architecture. 'Works of architecture', according to the philosopher Albrecht Wellmer, 'are only works of art in so far as they are also 'real' and useful objects which, as aesthetic objects, belong at the same time to a certain social, historical and practical context.'[38] The Holocaust Monument exemplifies the inherent interdisciplinarity of monuments. Petitions published by Perspektive Berlin and the Support Group called specifically for a site with 'national' political significance, but which should be occupied by an artistic monument. Whereas the initial petition of January 1989 called for a '*Gedenkstätte*',[39] the second petition of April 1989 called for a '*Mahnmal*',[40] and the third, in 1990, for a '*Denkmal*'.[41] Although these terms are often interchangeable in practice, their precise meanings reflect the dual documentary and artistic functions of memorials. The term *Gedenkstätte* generally refers to a memorial museum exhibiting historical documentation, characterised by its 'arranged'[42] character. A *Mahnmal* often conveys a moral message urging remembrance as a guide for future action and as a form of prevention, that is, a monument 'which should retain something in one's memory which one hopes will not happen again'.[43] *Denkmal* refers more generally to representations of a historical event or person.

Following these early petitions, subsequent statements made by the organisers called more explicitly for a purely sculptural model. The official invitation to participants of the first competition of 1994 was entitled

'Artistic Competition', which offered 'the possibility of relating sculpture to built space', yet where 'art itself should determine the form of discussion'.[44] In a statement on the aims of the association, Joachim Braun referred to the 'artistic task' and the obligation to invite 'the best artists of the day' to submit designs.[45] Eligible to take part, as defined in the invitation of 1994, were 'men and women artists and artists from related areas',[46] although they were recommended to collaborate with writers, historians, architects and urban planners.

The two main issues governing the decision-making process – the question of what form the monument should take, and whether it should be built at all – were a direct consequence of the incompatible conditions described in the petitions of 1989 and reiterated in guidelines for the competitions of 1994 and 1997 – stipulating that an open artistic form should fulfil closed political conditions. The expectation that one monument should provide a 'central' and 'national' focus of identification invested the site with an intense symbolic significance that no single monument or memorial could realistically fulfil. These conditions provoked perceptions of the monument as something absolute. The historian Peter Steinbach suggested that public acceptance of the monument could only be achieved via additional forms of translation,[47] that is, with historical information not inherent to the monument itself but about people and their primarily political motivations for instigating the commemoration in the present day. Such forms of translation or mediation between the monumental object and the public indeed occurred in the institutional forms of conferences, exhibitions, political hearings and media debate. Prior to its construction, this monument was not an inert artefact, but the focus of discussion on public symbols and their artistic, historical and political functions. In this way, rhetorical 'translation' lent the monument additional documentary value – albeit not in the form of information about the past, but about the process of understanding the past in relation to national symbols in the 1990s.

ii. Discourse on Art as a Political Issue

When members of the citizens' action group Perspektive Berlin campaigned for a Holocaust monument, they claimed to be conforming to the examples of other nations, in particular to the Yad Vashem Memorial in Jerusalem and the United States Holocaust Memorial Museum in Washington.[48] The justification of the monument by its organisers Lea Rosh and Eberhard Jäckel on the grounds that Germany would suffer 'disgrace' ('*Schande*') so long as it did not possess a central memorial comparable to those in Jerusalem or Washington[49] suggests that their exclusive focus on the need for a monument was not based on political or cultural necessity, but on convention, sustained by the conviction that nations require stone memorials, and that different nations should possess similar modes of cultural representation. Petitions and competitions for the Berlin site called not for a museum like those in Jerusalem and Washington, however, but for a monument, a means of expression characteristic of national movements of the nineteenth and early twentieth centuries. The inherent anachronism of the chosen mode of commemoration is an additional cause of the controversy and sluggish selection procedure. Why did organisers insist on a monument rather than on numerous alternative forms of historical commemoration: state speeches, ritual wreath-laying ceremonies, demonstrations, annual commemorative days, the renaming of streets or a museum, for example? And why were appeals for other forms of commemoration not given serious consideration? Several critics called for a smaller monument, or suggested alternatives, such as the setting up of a charity foundation for survivors, or the transfer of funds to underfunded existing memorials on the sites of concentration camps.[50]

In light of the enduring fierce public debate it is unlikely that the project could have been implemented without the intervention of parliament in 1999. The organs of political deliberation, including parties, the citizens' action group, the media and associations did not bring about the formation of a coherent public opinion about either the form, site or purpose of the monument. Parties were divided over this issue for three reasons. First, opinions over the official status of the Second World War and the genocide in present-day national self-understanding differed. Although the dominant parties of the Federal Republic had been refounded (in the case of the SPD and FDP) or founded (in the case of the CDU) after 1945, and although they pledged allegiance to an essentially liberal constitution, and therefore share a common history anchored in the Federal Republic and distinct from both the National Socialist regime and the Weimar Republic, they have traditionally projected different visions of contemporary history. Willy Brandt, chancellor and symbolic figurehead of the postwar SPD, famously knelt in a gesture of humility in honour of the victims of persecution at the Warsaw Ghetto Monument in 1970. The CDU chancellor Kohl repeatedly demonstrated a relative lack of humility following the Bitburg affair and his coining of the adage according to which his generation, born too late to have participated actively in the Second World War, enjoyed the 'mercy of a late birth'. Chancellor Schröder similarly argued in favour of a normalisation of German self-understanding and declared publicly in a speech in November 2001 that the Holocaust Monument should be a place that people 'like to visit'.[51] Second, the inherent structure of the political system of the Federal Republic encouraged disagreement between local and national representatives. Although cultural policies in the Federal Republic are the responsibility of ministries of culture within the regional governments of each

Land, the federal government reserves the right to determine framework policies, concerning film or the mass media for example, under the auspices of the 'permanent conference' of regional cultural ministers. This largely stable distribution of responsibilities became less reliable after 1990 due to the polarisation of interests between the old *Länder* of West Germany and the new ones on the territory of the former East Germany, and due to the increasing centralisation of cultural administration following the transfer of the capital city from Bonn to Berlin in 1999 and the appointment of a federal cultural minister without portfolio in 1998. Third, what most caused division within and between parties in relation to the Holocaust Monument was the nature of the unconventional issue of art within the political arena. The monument not only addressed a core component of historical self-understanding of state and society in postwar Germany. More significantly, it placed the quest to find an adequate artistic form at the centre of negotiations about this self-understanding, as if the artistic representation were a substitute for the representation of state and society. The divisive issue of the monument thus exposed weaknesses but also strengths of political culture in Germany. It is true, as the cultural historian Caroline Wiedmer explains, that the bureaucratic decision-making process, during which the citizens' action group or 'Support Group' was included in the organising committee and jury members selected from the same committee, was unfair. Neither the committee nor the jury could lay claim to a neutral decision while their members included the very people who had lobbied for the monument from 1988.[52] At the same time, however, the media exposure, discussion of and even protests over these contradictions prior to the intervention of parliament in 1999 testify to a degree of openness, spontaneity and plurality of the opinions exchanged and arguments aired in the public sphere. In spite of the increased institutionalisation of the monumental project since 1999 in close collaboration with the government within the Foundation Monument for the Murdered Jews of Europe under the chairmanship of the president of the Bundestag, we should not lose sight of this element of spontaneity and openness that marked the first phase of deliberation.

The insistence on an artistic monumental form of commemoration accorded political responsibility to artists and architects to fulfil the stated conditions. At the Bundestag debate of May 1996, members of parliament readily spoke of the moral and political purpose of art, but refrained from describing how this should be implemented. Rupert Scholz of the CDU pleaded for a monument which would expose and make people aware of 'the primary causes of the crimes committed against the Jewish people',[53] and Anton Pfeifer (CDU) supported the project as a symbolic reinforcement of 'basic values of freedom, justice, solidarity'.[54] Moreover, six out of the ten participants in this debate emphasised the necessity of an artistic monument while simultaneously denying their personal competence in artistic matters. Scholz insisted on the 'artistic autonomy of the jury',[55] Burkhard Hirsch of the FDP disclaimed any 'form determined by the state',[56] and Ludwig Elm, Thomas Krüger, Anton Pfeifer and Cornelia Schmalz-Jacobsen underscored the necessity of art in spite of their incapacity to judge or prescribe the final model. The instigators Lea Rosh and Eberhard Jäckel likewise called explicitly for a monument while denying their personal competence in the field of art.[57]

On the one hand, the reserve of the politicians and organisers responsible for implementing this project, reflected in their reluctance in 1996 to put this issue to a vote in the Bundestag, was politically motivated; the three-member commission, and the public competitions, conferences and exhibitions were the result of a political effort to maintain the *plebiscitary* nature of the decision-making procedure. On the other hand, the emphasis laid on the necessity of an artistic monument, combined with the delegation to artists and architects of the entire decision over the form of the monument, fuelled a misunderstanding of art as a field of practice inaccessible to ordinary people or politicians. Why, if they genuinely possessed no competence in the field of art and monumental form, did organisers adhere to the convention of a monument and refuse to yield to public demands for alternative forms of commemoration? Their conventionality consisted in the delegation of responsibility for the design of the monument to artists and architects, based on the strict division of labour between art and politics. The simultaneous insistence on the interconnectedness of art and politics and the refusal to acknowledge overlapping competencies in each field, testifies to politicians' reluctance to bear direct responsibility for the controversial project and consequently to the mystification of the task of transmitting historical knowledge of the genocide.

Efforts to neutralise the explosive political nature of this project by relegating it to the apparently unpolitical sphere of art nevertheless served precisely to politicise the role of art as a medium for the transmission of historical knowledge and values. Prior to the final Bundestag vote in June 1999, scrupulous care was taken by the parliamentary cultural committee to ensure that MPs would not have to vote on a question of aesthetics. The five group motions were formulated with respect to the following questions: whether to go ahead with the project to build a monument, whether to construct the model proposed by Richard Schröder bearing the inscription 'Thou shalt not murder', whether to construct the revised model proposed by Eisenman combined with an information centre or 'house of memory', whether to dedicate the site to Jewish victims alone or to all victim groups, and whether to set up a foundation to preside over the construction and administration of the monument. Speakers at the final Bundestag debate in June 1999 indeed generally evaded the subject of sculptural forms and addressed instead the topics of civil responsibilities with respect to national history (Wolfgang Thierse, SPD), the necessity of an artistic monument in general as an 'art of bringing forth' (Wolfgang Gerhardt, FDP),[58] or the need to annul the project in order to maintain the inviolability of existent national memorials such as the Neue Wache (Martin Hohmann, CDU). Those who discussed the merits of the model of a stele bearing the inscription 'Thou shalt not murder', including Eberhard Diepgen (CDU), Annette Fugmann-Heesing (SPD) or Hartmut Koschyk (CSU), addressed the sense of the fifth commandment as a token of relations between Judaism and Christianity. Only Diepgen cautiously broached the relative artistic merits of the field of 2,700 steles and the single inscribed stele, arguing that the 'mass' and the 'simulation of horror' of the first proposal do not increase but thwart the emotional effect of a monument.[59] However, in light of the approaching regional parliamentary election in Berlin on 10 October 1999, the blatant political interest underlying the mayor's criticism of the field of steles detracted from the credibility of his arguments.

The Bundestag vote was the final stage in a cumulative decision-making process involving the parliamentary cultural committee, parliamentary parties at federal and regional levels, but also the official competition jury, the organising committee, artists, and in particular the intervention of Chancellor Kohl and Michael Naumann in the competition procedure. Although formal questions were deliberated extensively in the press and by the jury, which led to the shortlisting of two models in 1995 and four models in 1997, neither public opinion nor jury members were united, and the selection of the model by Eisenman and Serra was ultimately determined by the decision of Chancellor Kohl when he intervened in competition procedures in 1995 and 1997. The addition of an information centre was determined by the political strategy of politicians and lobbying directors of existent memorials in Berlin. Their judgment was guided not by the artistic form of the monument but by finance and by their scepticism towards a purely sculptural model. Moreover, a combined sculpture with an information and documentation centre ensured that existent memorials in Berlin would not be neglected as a result of increased centralisation of Berlin's cultural memorial policy. The Holocaust Monument was henceforth considered as a starting point for tourists visiting the city's historical sites, offering orientation with respect to the pedagogical memorial sites of the National Socialist era.

No consideration was given here to formal questions or to the merits of various artistic and non-artistic means of transmitting historical understanding. Art was a condition of the project expressed in petitions and by politicians, but formal criteria were nevertheless delegated entirely to artists and architects participating in the two competitions. According to Hermann Rudolf, editor of the Berlin daily *Der Tagesspiegel*, the selection of the 'Eisenman II' model combining a sculpture and information centre testified to the continuing social utility of monuments in the 1990s, but also to a lack of public trust in the 'silent message' of art alone.[60] Other critics of this compromise decision to combine art and information likewise claimed that only a purely sculptural monument open to multiple interpretations would have been free of dogma and thus 'democratic'.[61] Wolfgang Gerhardt argued in his speech that the aesthetic principle of Eisenman's model would be neutralised if combined with an information centre, that is, if the expressive language of plastic form was superseded by explanatory rhetoric.[62] The political discourse on art during this debate therefore testifies to a fascination with artistic symbols and the continuing political legitimacy of historical monuments as a genre, but also to a misunderstanding and mistrust of the heuristic function of art itself.

iii. Discourse of Art: Blueprints Submitted by Artists and Architects in the Official Competitions of 1995 and 1997

a. Competition Results

The conditions of centrality, national appeal and consensus established in the petitions, competitions and conferences determined the issues of debate over the monument from 1995. The following analysis of some of the models submitted in the competition explores the extent to which the monuments and their authors' verbal justifications were conceived in direct response to appeals for consensus from 1995. Although debate about the monument was repeatedly displaced by debate about the means required to secure a decision on its behalf, the adequacy of the monumental form was consistently cited as a condition for realising the project. The question of 'what monument?' was therefore inseparable from the questions of 'whether' a monument should be built and 'how' to implement it in practice.

The first architectural competition in 1994 attracted 528 entries, from which two joint winners were selected. For the second competition in 1997, 25 artists and architects were invited to submit a model, of which four were shortlisted and exhibited along with the other models. Although it is not possible to examine all of the official designs or additional unofficial proposals individually, it is worthwhile looking more closely at the shortlisted models in order to identify formal characteristics and motifs, the verbal justifications of their authors, and the critical responses of the public, all of which may be read as contributions to the quest to establish social consensus on the basis of the monument following the cancellation of the first competition in 1995.

This subsection contains descriptions of the prize-winning models in the official competitions of 1995 and 1997, and an inventory of common monumental motifs that reflect a degree of formal unity between them. Although no single model provided a basis for the identification of a cohesive community of memory, the intentions expressed by artists and architects revealed an implicit consensus over the general purpose of commemoration: as a link between individuals' memories and public commemoration; and as a medium for the promotion of historical understanding, a medium that inevitably draws on traditions of monumental representations in the form of quotations of other monuments and symbolic types.

My intention is not to argue for or against particular models, but to analyse those selected by the juries as well as the accompanying discourse of artists, architects and their critics. Designs that were not shortlisted received minimal public attention and therefore did not trigger debate contributing to the construction of a memory culture. However, it is worthwhile acknowledging some of the remaining proposals from the first and second competitions, as well as the countless alternative designs suggested throughout the course of the debate, for they testify to the extensive creative impulse triggered by the search for an adequate monument. Among the most remarkable of these suggestions include: a monumental bus-stop from which visitors could travel to historical memorial sites in Germany and beyond (Renata Stih and Frieder Schnock); the substitution of a kilometre-long section of the A7 motorway near Kassel with cobblestones and the use of funds raised from the sale of the plot of land in Berlin to create a foundation for persecuted minorities (Rudolf Herz and Reinhard Matz, a model that won approval among visitors to the exhibition of the competition of 1997);[63] the mock sale of the plot of land in a newspaper advertisement in May 1998 (this enterprise, by Horst Hoheisel and Andreas Knitz, effectively attracted potential buyers);[64] the substitution of one of the pillars of the Brandenburg Gate with an artificial pillar (Salomon Korn);[65] the erection of four billboards on each side of the plot, bearing a short text referring to the failure of efforts to erect a monument on the site (by the SCALA group, Rolf Storz and Hans-Jörg Wöhrle); the annulment of the project altogether and the use of funds for a scientific foundation similar to the Nobel Prize (Christina von Braun);[66] or even the declaration of the visitors' book from the exhibition of projects in 1998 as a monumental testimony to the public response to the commemorative process in its own right (Fig. 10).[67]

The large number and variety of unofficial suggestions for this monument almost all subverted or dispensed with the traditional stone monument, revealing a broad and vibrant public interest in the exploration of alternative methods of commemoration. The insistence of organisers and politicians on the need to mark the site with a monumental object won mitigated public support and therefore exacerbated the debate. A revocation of these strict conditions (of a central national monument) imposed by the association in petitions and press reports, might possibly have opened a new opportunity for an entirely different, non-sculptural, form of commemoration.

Figure 10: The visitors' book from the public exhibition of projects for the Holocaust Monument in 1998

In light of the highly politicised context in which the Holocaust Monument project evolved, we should examine the models selected during the competitions of 1995 and 1997 in relation to both their form and function. How did the artists and architects justify their designs? And how did critics respond to the designs and to their creators' arguments in light of consistent demands for consensus and a rapid end to the debate?[68] The political conditions established in petitions and official instructions issued to artists during the selection process suggest that the source of controversy lay not in the proposed monuments themselves but in the incommensurable relation between the conditions, which created a fixed idea of the anticipated function of the monument, and the medium chosen to fulfil them. In practice, some consistencies in the motifs shared by different shortlisted monuments nevertheless suggest that the artistic proposals did in fact provide a potential formal consensus over the means of commemorating the genocide in stone. The reluctance of the jury, political representatives, critics and the wider public to rally to any of the common motifs of the prize-winning models, however, may be imputed to the difficult task of 'doing justice to *all* dimensions of the mass murder with a *single* monument',[69] one whose thematic generality called for an abstract monument and a vague form of remembrance.

The first competition resulted in a joint first prize, awarded in March 1995 for the designs submitted by Simon Ungers and by the group of

Figure 11: Model for the Holocaust Monument by Simon Ungers (1995). Monuments bring together the world of politics, the intelligentsia and art under the public eye. Here, the Berlin Minister of Culture Thomas Nagel (left) and the President of the Academy of Arts Walter Jens (right) discuss the merits of the prize-winning model for the Holocaust Monument. The artist listens attentively while a member of the public looks on in consternation © Landesarchiv Berlin

artists and architects led by Christine Jackob-Marks. The model by Ungers (Fig. 11) consists of four one-hundred-metre-long, six-metre-high steel girders (evoking railway lines) arranged in a square and supported at the corners by concrete blocks. The girders are perforated with the names of concentration camps in five-metre-high letters that can be read from the inside of the square, and which are projected by sunlight onto the ground – either positively inside the square, or negatively outside it – onto the surrounding streets and buildings. The centre of the square contains a 2.5-metre-high plateau from which visitors can read the names. The jury is reported to have favoured its suitability for both private remembrance and official commemorative ceremonies, and its unambiguous meaning, from which no external verbal or written explanations are required to complete its meaning.[70]

The model by Jackob-Marks's group (Fig. 12) was selected as the overall winner in June 1995, but met with continued public controversy and was finally overruled by Chancellor Kohl in July 1995. This model consists of an eighty-five-metre-square concrete panel tilted to a height of eleven metres on the south side, and on which the 4.5 million names of known Jewish victims are engraved, while space for the remaining 1.5 million unknown names is left empty. The cost of engraving the names

Figure 12: Model for the Holocaust Monument by Christine Jackob-Marks, Hella Rolfes, Hans Scheib, Reinhard Stangl and Felix Theissen (1995). © Landesarchiv Berlin

would require ongoing public participation in the form of additional sponsorship – a process intended to engage the public in a process that 'would never be completed'.[71] Eighteen stones from Masada are placed in irregular positions on the panel to represent the countries from which Jews were deported. Like Maya Lin's Vietnam Veterans Memorial in Washington, the engraving of each victim's name individually is intended to neutralise their anonymity. Unlike the Vietnam memorial, however, which serves the community of survivors to honour their dead relatives, the Holocaust Monument evokes not the honour of known soldiers of one's own country but shame towards entirely unknown civilian victims of a persecuted community. The formal similarity between this model and the Vietnam Veterans Memorial therefore veils their historical discrepancy. Salomon Korn suggested that, in the case of the Holocaust Monument, the inscription of each individual's name would in fact entrench the anonymity of victims by symbolically evoking a false solidarity between victims, 'as if the murdered – including soldiers – had died for a common cause, a higher goal'.[72]

The competition was formally postponed in July 1995 due to controversy over the form of the model by Jackob-Marks's group - over the technique of naming all victims, its ambiguous historical significance, and high costs. The rejection of this prize-winning model led supporters and critics of the project to either justify or question new measures to establish consensus over the monument. Subsequent discussions were devoted not only to the question of form but also to size, the suitability of the site, the method of decision-making and therefore the very legitimacy of the project. These discussions led to the resignation of some members of the panel at the conferences in 1997. Some feared that a monument dedicated solely to victims could encourage excessive identification with victims instead of an awareness of the historical means of perpetration, as promoted in the Topography of Terror exhibition.[73] Others feared that it may represent a symbolic 'final stroke' ('*Schlußstrich*') ending the West German tradition of critically appropriating the history of the Second World War.[74]

Following the second competition, four joint first prizewinners were announced in November 1997: for the proposal by the architect Peter Eisenman and artist Richard Serra, the artist Jochen Gerz, and the architects Daniel Libeskind and Gesine Weinmiller respectively. One single model had to be selected. The form and intentions of these projects may be summarised as follows.

Peter Eisenman and Richard Serra (Fig. 7): a field of 2,700 concrete steles (0.92 metres wide and 2.3 metres long) slightly tilted at irregular angles and arranged in regular rows 0.92 metres apart, the heights of which rise and fall between fifty centimetres and five metres. The base of the monument dips towards the centre, so that the tops of the steles rise only slightly above ground level. When Chancellor Kohl requested the artists to modify their design in 1998, the number of steles was to be reduced to 2,500 and trees and bushes added as a frame. At the public hearing of the artists in January 1998, Serra defined the monument as 'sacred' and 'open', one that may be experienced similarly by visitors regardless of their nationality, race or religion.[75] Their proposal described the design as the 'search for instability in an apparently stable system', one which would physically destabilise visitors and thus entail 'the destruction of the illusion of security given by the order of the grid and the surrounding framework of streets'.[76] This model therefore bears comparison with 'experiential'[77] museums designed to plunge visitors into reconstructed scenes of the past, and which regained popularity in the 1980s. In this monument, however, the visitor's empathy with the past is not fostered by lifelike reconstructions of scenes with everyday objects, smells and sounds from the past, but by arousing a physical sense of oppression in an unfamiliar enclosed space. A Japanese tourist, claims Eisenman, 'would perhaps feel what it is like to go into a gas chamber'.[78] The architect later nuanced this inappropriate remark by describing the monument as a place in which visitors would not be urged to learn about historical facts or collective historical processes, but be forced to contemplate their individual understanding of the past by working backwards from traces of memories in the present. 'Each reaction here,' claimed Eisenman, 'will be the substratum of German culture.'[79]

Two architectural principles underlie this attempt to 'destabilise' the visitor. First, the structure is intended to evoke 'incomprehensibility'[80] by the following means: the apparent order of the grid of steles is incompatible with the actual sense of disorder which overcomes the individual once inside the grid. The visitor is forcibly isolated; the linear axes do not, as in functional buildings, lead anywhere, nor does the grid have a centre; the grid echoes that of the surrounding urban housing and office blocks, but with radically different and irregular proportions; and the organisation of space – the relative disproportion between the regularly spaced steles and their varying heights – is intended to evoke an incongruent experience of time as one walks into the grid. Second, the model is intended to evoke what Eisenman and Serra call a 'new idea of memory'[81] by commemorating the past without recourse to symbols. In this way, they intend to dispense with the simultaneity of experience and understanding customary in traditional symbolic monuments: like a maze without a centre and without the purpose of getting out again, this grid is designed to arouse a sense of instability by defying the spectators' natural desire to understand the monument.[82] By allusion, therefore, the incomprehensibility induced by the structure of the monument may be compared to the incomprehensibility of genocide. Serra withdrew from the competition when Eisenman agreed, on the advice of Chancellor Kohl, to reduce the number of steles to 2,700 and to add trees. The vote by the Bundestag in June 1999 in favour of this model with the addition of a small information centre or 'house of memory' in order to supply documentation about the site thus complemented but also contradicted the original intention of the artists.

Jochen Gerz (Fig. 13): a flat smooth concrete field containing thirty-nine lampposts bearing the word 'Why?' in the thirty-one languages spoken by persecuted Jews. The site includes a building called 'The Ear' containing three rooms: the 'room of memory' in which Steven Spielberg's planned collection of thirty thousand video recordings of survivors of persecution and genocide may be viewed; the 'room of answers' in which visitors are invited to discuss and write down their responses to the question 'Why did it happen?' in a short sentence, which is then inscribed into the concrete ground of the site over a period of thirty years or more to form a collective text; the 'room of silence' in which visitors may meditate while listening to the music 'eternal e' by La Monte Young. On the north side, a glass bridge enables visitors to view the site from above. Eighteen signs carry information about the monument. A memorial foundation would be launched to employ researchers and monitors to explain the purpose of the monument to visitors. This monument draws on elements of Gerz's earlier countermonuments by largely dispensing with symbolism and inviting passers-by to participate actively in its construction. According to Gerz, 'the monument and memorial must serve the discussion and therefore be conceived as part of the latter … The "central" work can only be the visitors' own contribution, their own answer. Nothing can represent this in its place … One's own life becomes one's own answer. This is the only way of preventing the victims from being banished to the rituals of forgetting.'[83] The function of Gerz's monument is not to render the past in a symbol, but to trigger memory in conjunction with reflection on the process of commemoration in relation to the present. 'People are memory, not the objects,'[84] claims Gerz. He proposes a radical notion of monumentality, according to which the visitors should themselves become living memorials.

Daniel Libeskind (Fig. 14): Libeskind's model, called 'Stonebreath' (*Steinatem*),[85] consists in a row of fragmented perforated concrete wall segments 21 metres high and 115 metres long which represent a solid casting of the so-called 'voids' (inaccessible empty enclosed sections) of the Jewish Museum, also situated in central Berlin. The wall cuts diagonally across the base of the site, which is defined by white concrete, and which extends beyond the designated area of the monument across the adjacent Ebertstrasse. Libeskind conceived his monument as a space integrated architecturally into its urban surroundings, and integrated symbolically by multiple references to historical sites elsewhere in Berlin: the white concrete base corresponds exactly to the surface area of the Reichstag; an inscribed stone referring to the monument is installed in front of the Reichstag in order to evoke a link between parliament and history; passing traffic and the adjacent Goethe memorial are incorporated into the site; the wall segments point in the direction of the House of the Wannsee Conference; and their height corresponds closely to the facades of surrounding buildings. The wall segments are intended to reflect, according to Libeskind, 'the obliterated and submerged aspect of Berlin', the oblique holes 'draw the sky and air into the surrounding urban space',[86] while their sculptural character and surrounding trees create 'an important urban meeting place'.[87] Libeskind's model therefore employs a traditional architectural language of vertical and horizontal planes and symbolic quotations that are gently subverted by the oblique angle of the wall with respect to the surrounding urban grid, and by the irregular holes in its facade.

Gesine Weinmiller (Fig. 15): a broken Star of David made of eighteen panels between two and seven metres high situated on a concrete incline such that the tops of the panels are horizontal and level with the stepped platform on the north, south and east sides of the monument. Each panel is made of a different type of stone from the regions from which victims were deported. The visitor approaches the monument down the incline and can leave via steps situated at the bottom from an opening in the wall enclosed by a row of columns. Weinmiller describes the broken star as 'an image of the scattered and murdered people', and intends the site to be used as a 'place of quiet in which each visitor can find associations and images in order to commemorate in a personal way',[88] one where stones, candles but also (on official occasions) wreaths may be laid. Weinmiller's use of an explicit symbol of Judaism met with criticism because it excludes commemoration of other victim groups, whether those of political discrimination, euthanasia victims, Roma and Sinti or homosexuals, for example, and also because this reversal of a symbol of victimisation stigmatised by the National Socialists implicitly sustains the reductive symbolic language established at that time while obscuring the multiple meanings of this symbol throughout history.[89]

b. Conflicting Uses or Consensual Motifs?

In a conference debate at the Berlin Academy of Arts in November 1998, the architect Florian von Buttlar defined three semiotic categories into which the models for the Holocaust Monument fell: pictorial (Weinmiller), affective (Eisenman, Serra and Libeskind) and conceptual (Gerz).[90] These categories serve as an enlightening interpretative aid, suggesting a limited artistic repertoire of contemporary monuments to which a large number of the proposals conformed. However, this formal interpretation of the monuments overlooks the influence of the political context on the forms and meanings of the monuments, and on the prolonged and inconclusive decision-making process. Instead of arguing deductively from the form of proposed models, I propose here to assess the significance of models inductively in relation to conditions and expectations established before and after the two competitions.

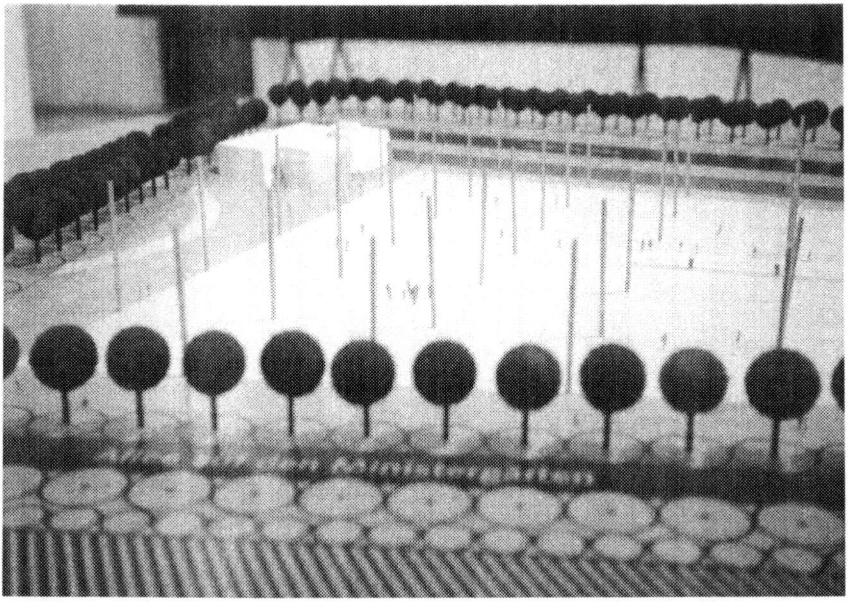

Figure 13: Model for the Holocaust Monument by Jochen Gerz (1997)

Figure 14: Model for the Holocaust Monument by Daniel Libeskind (1997)

Figure 15: Model for the Holocaust Monument by Gesine Weinmiller (1997)

As von Buttlar shows, there were consistent grounds on which consensus over the form of the monument could effectively have been reached, on the basis of pictorial, affective or conceptual criteria. The recurrent motifs of 'emptiness' (*Leere*) and the sublime, for example, confirm von Buttlar's identification of semiotic consistencies between different models. The fact that no agreement was reached on the basis of these consistent motifs therefore suggests that the roots of dissent lay elsewhere, in the discrepancy between the anticipated political function of the monument and the formal means available to fulfil this function. The formal briefing addressed to competition participants defined precise conditions for the monument's function, but no indication of how this should be implemented. While we may applaud the openness of the briefing, permitting all possible artistic techniques, the combination of strictly defined political conditions and open formal conditions put pressure on artists alone to shoulder the incommensurable political burden of creating this new national monument. As a result, the models shortlisted in 1995 and 1997 may be interpreted as formal responses to the conditions of centrality and nationality established in the petitions, conditions subsequently echoed in instructions for participants in the competitions and ensuing debates. The political function of the proposed monumental forms was reflected in the ways in which individuals and the state were intended to use the monument, and how they were each expected to relate to it as the basis of a symbolic contract between the state, artist and individuals.

In reality, however, this symbolic contract, promising the reconciliation of individual, social and state memories, was fraught with contradictions. The field of steles by Eisenman and Serra, for example, aimed to isolate visitors in order to arouse in them a sense of disorientation or fear, whereas the proposals of Libeskind and Weinmiller offered an open space in which to rest, reflect and talk. By inviting visitors to compose an answer to the question 'Why?', Gerz's model aimed to involve the public in the active construction of a necessarily incomplete monument. Each of these three models prescribed a specific type of sociability: radical isolation, casual public communication, and formal written testimony. Moreover, theoretical statements of the artists and architects described the public to which the monument appeals in an indeterminate fashion, defined variously as supranational, national or local. According to Gerz, the monument was to appeal to 'a community beyond the nation',[91] although he described it as 'a place of German identity'.[92] Hermann Rudolf warned against burdening the monument with the task of 'national-pedagogical reform', a task better implemented by individual witnesses and the scientific community, while simultaneously pleading for the monument as a necessary 'public presence ... in the centre of public life, in the centre of the capital city'.[93] Michel Friedman, then vice chairman of the Central Council of Jews in Germany, defined the monument essentially as an expression of local culture.[94] The local appeal of the monument was reinforced by the dominance of local over national media in the treatment of this topic, and by the key role played by the Berlin Senate in postponing the decision following conflicts of opinion between local and national governments in 1998 and 1999. Indecision was a consequence not only of the difficulty of selecting an appropriate form of monument, therefore, but also of the conflicting opinions over the public usage and the social and political function of the monument, and of the complex decision-making procedure involving the association and federal and local governments.

The shortlisted models likewise projected very different assumptions about the state. Libeskind described his model as a 'gateway to the governmental zone', a monument which is 'supportive of the state' (*staatstragend*).[95] By contrast, Eisenman claimed that his model left no area free for ritual wreath-laying ceremonies, and therefore resisted state appropriation.[96] According to the art critic Eduard Beaucamp, this model 'prevents inappropriate collective mourning rituals, public demonstrations, representative state occasions' – a function radically revised in 1998 when Eisenman agreed to reduce its size, add trees, parking spaces and an information centre.[97] Finally, Gerz attempted to displace responsibility for the creation of the monument from the artist and the state to the public. He brought into question the traditionally distinct roles of the commissioning authority and the commissioned work of art carried out by an artist for a specific audience. The invitation to answer the question 'Why?' not only delegated creative activity to the audience by requesting it to compose a collective text inscribed onto the concrete base of the monument, but also demonstrated the freedom of contemporary artists to work for commissions which do not predetermine the content or form of the work, a contractual relationship which Gerz defines as a 'non-commission'.[98] Precisely this political understanding of the role of the artist led him to withdraw his model from the competition in July 1998 on the grounds that his model had been plagiarised by subsequent proposals, and that the continuing controversy over the project proved the failure of state and society to fulfil the conditions of the commission.[99] It is indeed Gerz who suggested complementing the monument with an additional building and supplementary media, inviting visitors to respond actively to the project.

In spite of the disparities between the proposed usages of these monuments by the individual, society and the state, they revealed some consistent formal and semantic motifs that constituted a potential basis for consensus over the Holocaust Monument. Most blueprints proposed a low-lying structure (Libeskind's was an exception). Almost all models demonstrate varying degrees of abstraction by avoiding the representation of human or natural figures, and none except Gerz incorporated an inscription.[100] It is perhaps significant that the most abstract of the short-listed models, the field of steles by Eisenman and Serra, was favoured by the specialist commission and by the chancellor. Abstraction is less likely to alienate sectors of the public for ideological reasons and thus facilitates greater social consensus. Also consistent to most models were the composite references to existent symbols and monuments in what the literary specialist Gert Mattenklott calls 'monuments of monuments'.[101] Libeskind's model, for example, served as a symbolic focal point for quotations of at least five existent symbols in Berlin: the Jewish Museum, Reichstag, Goethe memorial, the House of the Wannsee Conference and the facades of city houses. Weinmiller's model cited the Star of David, classical pillars and even the Wailing Wall. Jackob-Marks's proposal to name all victims adopted the technique of the Vietnam Veterans Memorial, while Gerz's principle of asking citizens to compose a script for the monument repeated a technique already used for his counter-monuments in Biron, Harburg and Saarbrücken. Moreover, the models of Eisenman and Serra, Gerz and Weinmiller all employed elemental monolithic forms as an ironic reproduction and multiplication of the basic form of traditional sculptural monuments.

The most consistent theme during the debates over these models was the problem of representation itself. In the third of a series of conferences organised by the Berlin Senate in 1997, on the 'Typology and Iconography of the Monument', discussion focused on the motif of emptiness. 'The heart of a German monument,' claimed James Young, 'will have to contain an emptiness, which the artist must somehow represent as an inspiration or as a concept.'[102] Yet the architect Robert Kudielka warned against the 'false pathos of an awesome emptiness',[103] and appealed instead to the example of counter-monuments which commemorate the past not with focal points of collective identification, but by exploring the very process of commemoration. 'Of course,' claimed Kudielka, 'it is about the "unrepresentable", yet this does not involve theatrical capitulation in the face of excess … but rather the precise articulation of the relation between the capacity of the means of representation and the limits of their adequacy.'[104] In practice, only Gerz incorporated elements of the counter-monument genre, where the lampposts and concrete base functioned as a mere support for questioning visitors and recording their responses. By dispensing almost entirely with sculptural form, this proposal provided a non-symbolic rhetorical basis for perpetually negotiating the process of commemoration as such. Its open character did not call for consensus over a fixed monumental form or meaning, but readiness to interrogate the very principles of commemoration.

Other models directly echoed the previous theoretical discussions on emptiness. Ungers's construction of perforated steel girders enclosing an empty concrete platform indeed put an empty space at its centre, described by the art historian Tilman Buddensieg as 'monumental nothingness' ('*das monumentale Nichts*').[105] Libeskind likewise intended to make emptiness visible and spur reflection by casting the empty spaces or 'voids' of the Jewish Museum in concrete, with the aim, according to the art critic Harald Fricke, of 'making emptiness intelligible'.[106] Moreover, all these models, in particular the arrangements of concrete panels and steles by Weinmiller, Eisenman and Serra, corresponded closely to the definition of a cenotaph – a monument in the form of an empty grave, or one in memory of lost dead people or those buried elsewhere. One could even argue that the Holocaust Monument conforms to the definition of a cenotaph regardless of its particular sculptural form, in so far as it marks a geographical site in memory of dead people not buried on the site of the monument. A monument of this sort – empty, abstract, in memory of absent dead, dedicated to all Jewish victims of the Second World War genocide, a representation dedicated to something unrepresentable – is perhaps an architectural translation of the sublime, which the art historian Dieter Hoffmann-Axthelm defines in terms of hollowness, a lack of (human) scale, abstraction, enormity, and inaccessibility.[107] The motif of the cenotaph and, by implication, the sublime, which was inherent to several of the monumental projects and to the project itself regardless of individual models, suggests that consensus over the monument presupposed consensus over the principle of constructing a cenotaph. Some critics argued that even counter-monuments are also grounded in an aesthetics of the sublime, due to the renunciation of sensible effects in favour of the conceptualisation of representation.[108] However, the direct appeal to the spectator's active participation in the continuous rhetorical construction of counter-monuments in fact displaces their effect from the realm of aesthetic experience to the rational conceptualisation of its function.

Formal consistencies between the proposed models suggest that consensus over this monument should have been sought less in the precise *form* of one monument than in the *mode* of commemoration, whether that of a cenotaph, a memorial museum, a counter-monument designed to sustain the critique of representations, or ritual forms of commemoration such as a national holiday, a regular political wreath-laying ceremony or demonstration, for example. However, the inconclusive competitions to build a central Holocaust Monument suggest that there was no basis for agreement over either the form or mode of commemoration. The unyielding insistence on a national monument from the beginning of the campaign in 1988 – a form of commemoration favoured by national movements of the nineteenth century following the French revolution, the Napoleonic Wars, or the unification of Germany in 1871, for example – was perhaps one reason why no consensus was established. The anachronism of both the chosen form (a monument) and its symbolic potency (representative of the nation) were the prime causes of the repeated postponement of this project until, following increased political pressure, the authority for reaching a decision was transferred to the Bundestag in 1999.

The Holocaust Monument and the Discourse of National Integration in the 1990s

The Holocaust Monument was conceived by petitioners in anticipation of a new national memory culture of the unified Germany after 1990, and in defiance of public dissent over its form, site and dedication, as a historical symbol with which citizens of both former German states, as well as younger members of the new state, could identify. In reality, competitions, exhibitions and media responses to the monument provided a forum for a less consensual site of national memory. In its early stages, from 1989, the project was a source of controversy over the pedagogical benefits of commemorating either perpetrators or victims on the Prince-Albrecht site. The association Active Museum advocated documentation about persecutions, the citizens' action group Perspektive Berlin a monumental commemoration of victims. Even more controversial was the debate over the question whether victims should be commemorated with a single collective monument or separate monuments. Critics feared that a single monument would blur historical distinctions between motives for persecutions, but also that separate monuments would foster the symbolic segregation of the memory of victim groups according to a hierarchy established within the system of perpetration itself. Although the decision fell in favour of a central monument specifically for Jewish victims, plans for the location and site of additional monuments initially remained unresolved. Why was this monument, like the Vél' d'Hiv', a source of intense and prolonged political controversy? And are we justified, like Habermas, Young and even Chancellor Kohl, in interpreting this monument as a direct reflection of Germany's memory culture and national self-understanding? According to Habermas, 'the monument will be a sign that memory of the Holocaust is a fundamental element of the ethical-political self-understanding of the Federal Republic.'[109] Yet opinion polls carried out in August 1995, stating that only 46 per cent of interviewees 'knew about the project' and 37 per cent 'had heard about the debate', dissuade us from drawing conclusions about a genuinely national memory culture on the basis of the Holocaust Monument.[110] A more accurate interpretation of the political consequence of this monument can instead be made on the basis of the rhetorical constructions of intellectuals and politicians engaged in the debate, where references to the nation reflect the multiple and often contradictory political and artistic understandings of a specific social group rather than general characteristics of a genuinely collective national memory culture.

Opinions towards the monument among politicians on both regional and federal levels were divided regardless of their party allegiance. The approaching parliamentary elections of September 1998 and the local governmental election in Berlin of October 1999 nevertheless polarised the monument into an issue of party politics. Resistance within the Berlin Senate, and vociferous campaigning against the monument by the governing mayor Diepgen hindered a final decision. Prior to the parliamentary elections, at the local level, the CDU had emerged as opponents, the SPD as supporters of the project. At a national level, however, CDU representatives had generally supported the project behind Kohl while the SPD opposed the project. The controversial statement against the monument made by the SPD cultural representative Naumann in July 1998 served to further polarise the debate into a party political issue at a national level. Backed by the SPD candidate for chancellor, Gerhard Schröder, for whom polls predicted an election victory, Naumann's statement put pressure on the coalition government (then comprising the CDU, CSU and FDP) to push through a decision for the monument before the election in order to prevent the SPD, in the event of their election victory, from reversing the project. In this way, the emotional issue of the Holocaust Monument and impatience over the longstanding indecision was exploited by party representatives in order to project an illusory resolve and cohesion of party policy where none existed, for individual opinions of MPs and the public rarely coincided with party allegiances. Genuine attitudes towards this issue were motivated not by party political allegiances but by understandings of the efficacy of monuments as carriers of historical information, as media of historical understanding, and as supports of a coherent memory culture.

The political expediency of the Holocaust Monument in the parliamentary elections of September 1998 is symptomatic of issues of cultural policy in Germany since unification in 1990. These include the treatment of monuments erected under the German Democratic Republic by destruction, alteration or integration, and countless new architectural constructions in Berlin in connection with its reinstatement as the capital city in 1999.[111] In this context, Naumann's provocative criticism of the monument project was not based on architectural or historical criteria, but served to draw attention to the SPD's policy of reforming the administration of culture in Germany. The proposal to nominate a state minister for cultural affairs within the federal government (previously unheard of in the Federal Republic, where culture had traditionally been the responsibility of local government) pointed towards an authoritative national alternative to the previous decentralised cultural policy. Naumann's decisive rejection of the monument and simultaneous approval of the reconstruction of the Hohenzollern Palace in Berlin supposed an end of intractable debates over national symbols such as the Holocaust Monument, which had spurred sustained conflict between local and central governments.[112]

The Holocaust Monument was embroiled in further controversy in October 1998 when the writer Martin Walser, on receiving the Peace Prize of the German Book Trade (Friedenspreis des Deutschen Buchhandels), spoke out against the monument. Walser argued not only against the symbolic ritualisation of history, but also for the 'normalisation' of the Federal Republic's memory culture, in which Auschwitz would no longer play a central role as a 'permanent presentation of disgrace', or even a 'means of intimidation', 'moral cudgel', 'compulsory exercise' or 'moral pistol' in the hands of 'soldiers of opinion'.[113] Walser's sweeping polemic had little to do with the monument, which here served as a 'projection surface'[114] for moral and political arguments. By equating the historical event 'Auschwitz' with the monumental medium of transmission in his plea to end the ritual presentation of the former by renouncing the latter, Walser overlooked the distinction between the function of artistic media and their alleged moral messages. Social memory is not directly sustained by or dependent upon the physical presence of a monument. The destruction of monuments is likewise not automatically an expression of a society's desire to eliminate memory.[115] Likewise, the construction of new monuments does not guarantee the maintenance of social memory. The relation between the physical presence of monuments and social memory is not causal but subject to the relatively arbitrary play of public and political interests, which constitute the social context in which the monument emerges. However, many participants in the debate, including those who initiated the project such as Lea Rosh and Eberhard Jäckel, shared the 'realist' and moralistic arguments of Walser by equating the monument with the continuing primacy of the genocide in German memory culture.

Although monuments are not a direct expression of an integral social memory, they do reflect the memory culture of a society to which the makers of monuments aspire, and thus fulfil a heuristic rather than socially representative function. In similar fashion to the Vél' d'Hiv' in Paris, which added a new dimension to an urban landscape dominated by Gaullist memorials of the Second World War, the Holocaust Monument modifies the memorial urban landscape of the city of Berlin. Prior to 1989, Berlin possessed two ideologically distinct groups of memorials, one that paid homage to a largely anti-fascist resistance in the East, and one that exposed the traces of sites of persecution in the West. Since the fall of the Berlin Wall in 1989, the reconstruction of the city has been guided by a policy of 'critical reconstruction', a policy recognised by the regional government in response to lobbying by the Historical Berlin Association (Gesellschaft Historisches Berlin), which advocates architectural reconstruction of the city in accordance with the plots and structures of the prewar period while making concessions to technological advances and financial restrictions.[116] The reconstruction of the city, reinstated as the capital city from 1999, has been motivated by financial speculation and the quest to reverse the traces of the National Socialist and communist dictatorships by reverting to prewar city planning, that is, a cityscape reminiscent of the Wilhelmine Empire in accordance with the advice of the Historical Berlin Association. Within this restorative context, the Holocaust Monument is, like its French counterpart, part of a central, integrated architectural landscape and charged with a politically motivated heuristic function – to symbolise the war crimes of the nation in the centre of that same nation.

'National Consensus' on the Basis of Art?

There are at least two reasons why the debate over the site, dedication, and above all the form and selection procedure for this monument lasted eleven years, between the inception of the project in 1988 and the parliamentary vote in June 1999. First, the complexity of the means and the multiplicity of organs of communication dogged the decision-making process. There were several purely structural political reasons why neither of the competitions led to a satisfactory decision. The multiple institutions involved, including the three commissioning bodies and sponsors

– the Berlin Senate, parliamentary committee and association – were unable to reach a unanimous agreement. The large number of (over five hundred) competition entries surpassed the organisers' administrative capacity. The inconclusive and open nature of the competitions, both of which led to joint first prizes and exhibitions, rendered opinions in conferences and in the media even more irreconcilable. Finally, the controversial intervention of Chancellor Kohl in the cancellation of the first competition and in the selection of the model by Eisenman and Serra in the second competition rekindled controversy over the chancellor's somewhat autocratic influence over the new design of the Neue Wache war memorial in 1993.[117]

Second, the failure to achieve consensus over the Holocaust Monument in spite of the common motifs of proposals submitted in 1995 and 1997 may be imputed to the prodigious number of usages prescribed by the models for individuals and the state, but also to the problematic principle of constructing a 'central', 'national' symbol. The conditions of the campaign and issues of debate suggest that the failure to reach consensus over the Holocaust Monument was partly due to the coercive nature of the very demand for consensus. The call for a central national monument in the initial petitions, in competition instructions, and in discussions following the annulment of the first competition in 1995 created an irreconcilable discrepancy between the expected political *conditions* and the artistic *medium* required to realise these conditions. Can the appeal for such a monument be fulfilled in a single site? Although the architectural competitions focused public attention on the specific question of form, the root of the controversy in fact lay in the social, political and moral presuppositions projected onto the monument. Resistance to the project was triggered not only by the inadequacy of the artistic medium in relation to the subject matter of persecution and genocide. Not, that is, because the technical means to 'represent' genocide realistically had not been mastered. Rather, resistance arose (i) because the reduction of a historical event which exceeds our imagination to a single, largely abstract, form breaks a historiographical taboo, entailing a disregard for historical detail which could foster relativism,[118] both in the interpretation and public usage of the monument; (ii) because the political conditions of centrality and national representativeness surpass the capacity of a *single* symbol to commemorate the genocide in the name of the *whole* German nation; (iii) because the conspicuous central site contradicted a longstanding policy of constructing decentralised historical memorials in Germany. This project was hampered not only by the problem of form, therefore, but by doubts over whether the conditions required for such a national symbol dedicated to all victims could be realistically fulfilled.

Calls for consensus did not feature in petitions at the start of the campaign in 1989, but six years later in reaction to controversy following the first architectural competition in 1995, when Chancellor Kohl's intervention halted the plan to build the monument designed by Christine Jackob-Marks on the grounds that too little consensus had been established.[119] Among the ten speakers at the Bundestag debate on this issue in May 1996, six explicitly pleaded for broad social consensus and subsequently announced a series of major conferences for early 1997 devoted to the question of how to achieve this on the basis of the monument. However, the very insistence on consensus exacerbated debate over how to establish it. By calling for social consensus as a single condition for the realisation of the monument, without identifying the precise procedure by which consensus could be built on the basis of a monument, members of parliament aggravated the discrepancy between the stringent political conditions and artistic monumental means for fulfilling them.[120] Dispute occurred at three levels – over the most suitable form and site of the monument, the very necessity of a central national monument, and the appropriate political means required to secure a decision on behalf of the jury, joint organisers (parliamentary committee, Berlin Senate and the Support Group), the chancellor, parliament, intellectuals and the wider public. In other words, three types of consensus were sought over the questions of *what* to build, *whether* it should be built, and *how* to reach a decision. And the fact that the debate focused largely on the first question of form reflects the unique political legitimacy accorded to art, as well as a reluctance to involve the state in the decision-making process. Paradoxically, the fixation of political representatives on the necessity for the consent of as large a portion of society as possible[121] supposed the voluntary elimination of political mechanisms in the choice of a monumental form – a call for a type of plebiscite or direct democracy over the unorthodox issue of artistic form The observations of the journalist Bernhard Schulz reflect how this project for an artistic monument became the focus of a political dilemma, where a single object was called upon to embody an entire society's relation to its complex history. Inquiring whether a work of public art can convey the meaning of a past event and evoke the historical consciousness of it in the present day, he responded negatively in the face of 'the difficulty of making an unambiguous and clearly understood statement with a monument built according to contemporary formal language'.[122] The organisers' plans to involve the public in the process of selecting a design by means of competitions, conferences and media debates failed due to the nature of the prescribed monument, where a single site and form referring to the genocide in general were expected to fulfil a 'national purpose'[123] as the 'core of our self-understanding as a nation'.[124]

These plans also failed because consensus was sought first and essentially in the monumental form, without previously establishing whether the public consented to the more fundamental issues of whether to build such a monument and how to reach a decision. Petitions and briefings had dictated conditions for a monument without discussing other types of commemoration. Moreover, the insistence on establishing broad social consensus over the sculptural form of the monument, as well as the abrupt intervention of the chancellor, delayed the implementation of other decision-making authorities such as the parliamentary cultural committee or even parliament itself. One reason why no common decision was reached according to the terms of the petitions and briefings to artists and architects is that direct national consensus over a single central monument as described above would have approached an ideal or 'pure' consensus.[125] Only when the decision-making process was delegated to parliament in 1999 did other forms of consensus take priority and facilitate a vote by MPs. These included *issue* consensus, regarding the necessity of such a monument, and *fundamental* or *procedural* consensus regarding the rules and mechanisms required to reach a decision.[126]

It was during this final stage of the selection procedure following the failure of the competition process and prior to the parliamentary vote that decision-making processes were discussed openly, including the legitimacy of the various political institutions available to reach a decision beyond direct public consent over monumental form. While the monument alone appeared to offer no reliable foundation for agreement in spite of conferences and exhibitions facilitating public participation, alternative forms of state authority were taken into consideration and implemented. When Chancellor Kohl's decision to cancel the competition in 1995 and select the model by Eisenman and Serra in 1998 were dismissed as autocratic, alternative appeals were made for a direct parliamentary ballot on the issue.[127] Finally, the appointment of Naumann as the State Minister for Culture in the Chancellor's Office introduced a new platform for cultural representation comparable to the French Minister of Culture and British National Heritage Secretary.

Yet the complex political function of art prevented a decision over the Holocaust Monument even when organisers began to consider new methods of institutional decision-making beyond the competition procedure. Following inconclusive attempts to implement a plebiscitary decision by inviting the public to participate via exhibitions, conferences, public hearings and extensive press coverage, MPs were called to vote on five motions that precluded any discussion of artistic forms. The challenge of resolving the incongruous relation between politics and art posed from 1988 by this project for a specifically artistic national monument therefore remained unresolved throughout the debate. Characteristic of this persistent dilemma were remarks by Volker Beck and Wolfgang Gerhardt in the debate of 25 June 1999. Both MPs questioned the legitimacy of the decision to include an information centre within the monument. Beck suggested that a monument is democratic only if 'open', while Gerhardt argued that supplementary documentation would effectively neutralise both the artistic expressiveness of the field of steles and violate the principal criterion of the petitions and competition, whose purpose was to select a monument rather than an information centre.

The failure of the quest to select a purely 'artistic' monument void of rhetorical aids is one reason why the proposal by the theologian Richard Schröder to erect a monument dispensing with artistic form and serving merely as a support for the inscription 'Thou shalt not murder' was perceived as a fitting response to an apparently irresolvable debate over sculptural form. However, by displacing the object of dispute from plastic form to rhetoric, and by overriding the monument's dedication to Jewish victims of the genocide with a universal moral dedication from the Fifth Commandment, Schröder's proposal also invalidated the premises of the competitions and petitions, which had called for a monument dedicated specifically to the 'murdered Jews of Europe'. If realised, this model would have displaced the signifying function of the monument from sculptural form to its inscription, from an artistic to a rhetorical form of commemoration. Members of parliament favoured neither of these solutions in June 1999. Eisenman's purely abstract solution left the signification of the monument open to multiple interpretations of history, whereas the rhetorical precision of Schröder's model divided the public over the aptness of its meaning. The inscription was criticised for being too general to evoke the genocide against Jews, because it evoked a false affinity between Christianity and Judaism, and because the Hebrew letters would be readable only for descendants of victims or else have a merely decorative function for people unable to read Hebrew. This dilemma over the inadequacy of both pure abstraction and one-dimensional rhetorical signification, between the openness of Eisenman and Serra's model and the closed nature of Schröder's model, was solved with a compromise. The final decision to complement Eisenman's model with an information centre had the advantage of compensating an artistic medium of history with pedagogical information *about* history and about other memorials on authentic historic sites. In this way, information is not fixed in stone or subject to multiple interpretations, but can be modified over time and thus controlled by the organising foundation in collaboration with scientific advisers.[128]

The challenge to select a single appropriate form of monument was therefore skirted. The information centre, somewhat like an institutional guardhouse, offers the public an intellectual access to the political context and historical significance of the monument and provides pedagogical orientation beyond the scope of the monument. Social consensus was not achieved directly over the issue of the Holocaust Monument but on the basis of a complex combination of petitions, media debate, competitions, public forums, conferences and exhibitions, followed by the intervention of Chancellor Kohl and the State Minister for Culture, Michael Naumann, and with the aid of formal political institutions, including the citizens' action group, the Berlin Senate, the parliamentary cultural committee and all MPs who voted in June 1999. This monument is therefore not a representation of national self-understanding but the visible consequence of an exercise in the political negotiation of a symbol perceived as national.

The call for a central, national monument immediately raises the questions, 'Central to what?' and, 'Who belongs to the nation?' The terms in which the debate over this monument was conducted reflect how advocates of the project attempted to define the collective self-understanding of a social group in relation to a symbol designed to sustain memory of the genocide beyond the lifespan of eyewitnesses. The Holocaust Monument is therefore a medium which operates alongside other types of literary and filmic media and museums, but which is charged with an additional representative function as a focal point of national historical consciousness. In reality, it is questionable whether symbols can effectively represent a society's 'self-understanding'. Such a premise may only be fulfilled in the unlikely event that the memories harboured by individual citizens correspond to those evoked by symbols constructed on their behalf, or which they confront in daily life.

The attempt to equip the nation with a central symbol of an emotional bond derived from a sense of collective responsibility could foster a degree of complacency by the mere fact that it subsumes this emotional, albeit problematical, attachment to the past to the construction of a national common bond in the present. Several critics expressed doubts about the Holocaust Monument in these terms. The deliberately provocative claim by the essayist Eike Geisel, writing for the left-wing journal *Junge Welt* (formerly the official paper of the East German Socialist Youth Organisation, the Freie Deutsche Jugend), that 'even dead Jews may serve to bind the national collective',[129] echoed widespread critiques of the Holocaust Monument as a form of 'alibi' which 'delegates' memory to objects, such that the significance of the remembered events is subordinate to the contemporary expediency of commemoration. Monuments are a form of social convention which inevitably historicises events by rendering them in a mode common to all other monumentalised events of different historical periods. Their artistic or ornamental value, their usage as urban landmarks, and their traditional function as foci of positive patriotic identification,[130] even make them inherently suspect as a means to acknowledge the historical legacy of the genocide against Jews.

These doubts, and the failure of the competitions to culminate in a clear decision over what form and whether to build the monument, underscored its social undesirability. The project was too big – both physically, as if a big crime is compensated by a big monument, and emotionally, bordering on pathos. During the debate, this national monument acquired a status as an absolute, if not as the national monument for all time. It reflects an ideal holistic notion of nationhood which cannot accommodate the historical complexity of its theme, and which only detailed documentation, such as that displayed in the information centre and on local memorial sites, can convey. When Jens publicly opposed the project in February 1998 by asking the question 'It is easy to talk about the death of millions – but how did Selma Kohn go into the gas?',[131] he highlighted an essential incongruity between history and its medium, between the facts of historical experience and the ideal, ideological function imposed on this single, allegedly national monument.

Notes

1. This chapter is a revised and enlarged version of the essays: 'Monumentalizacija Nacije? "Spomenik umorjenim Židom Evrope" v Berlinu, 1988–98' ('National Monuments? The "Monument for the Murdered Jews of Europe" in Berlin, 1988–98'), trans. Lev Kreft, *Borec* no. 575–6, 1999, 6–27; and 'Fiksiranje sjećanja. Spomenik ubijenim europskim židovima u berlinu' (Memorial Fixation. The Monument for the Murdered Jews of Europe in Berlin), trans. Suzana Jukić, *Život Umjetnosti* no. 2, 2001, 118–131.
2. This monument has two names. The parallel usage of the official title 'Monument for the Murdered Jews of Europe' (*Denkmal für die ermordeten Juden Europas*) and the shorter and more common term 'Holocaust Monument' (*Holocaust-Denkmal*) demonstrates the discrepancy between the organisers' intentions and the popular understanding of the monument. Cf. Salomon Korn, 'Mit falschem Etikett', *Frankfurter Rundschau*, 4 September 1997, 6.
3. Robert Kudielka, 'Das falsche Gewicht der Betroffenheit', *Freitag*, 5 September 1997, 13.
4. Kohl described the monument as a matter concerning 'the core of our self-understanding as a nation'. Quoted in 'Helmut Kohl schließt Verzicht aus', *Berliner Zeitung*, 18 September 1998, 10.
5. For a comprehensive survey of present-day monuments in Berlin, see Stephanie Endlich and Thomas Lutz, eds, *Gedenken und Lernen an historischen Orten*; Martin Schönfeld, *Gedenktafeln in West-Berlin*, Berlin: Aktives Museum, vol. 6, 1993; vol. 4, 1991.
6. See Spielmann's historical assessment of memorials constructed in Berlin between the 1950s and 1980s, 'Gedenken und Denkmal', in Berlinische Galerie and Senatsverwaltung für Bau- und Wohnungswesen, eds, *Gedenken und Denkmal. Entwürfe zur Erinnerung an die Deportation und Vernichtung der jüdischen Bevölkerung Berlins*, Berlin: Berlinische Galerie, 1988, 7–46.
7. See Freimut Duve, ed., *Mahnmal für die Opfer des Krieges und der Gewaltherrschaft in Bonn*, Bonn: SPD Bundestagsfraktion, 1985.
8. See Lothar Gall, 'Brauchen wir eine Mitte?', in Helmut Engel and Wolfgang Ribbe, eds, *Hauptstadt Berlin – Wohin mit der Mitte? Historische, städtebauliche und architektonische Wurzeln des Stadtzentrums*, Berlin: Akademie Verlag, 1993, 229–236.
9. Peter Eisenman and Richard Serra, *Materialien für die erste Beurteilungssitzung*, press release, November 1997.

10. First petition published by the association Perspektive Berlin, 'Aufruf', *Frankfurter Rundschau*, 30 January 1989, 4.
11. Lea Rosh, quoted in a letter dated 6 November 1989 from the 'Initiative zum Umgang mit dem "Gestapo-Gelände"', in Bürgerinitiative Perspektive Berlin, ed., *Ein Denkmal für die ermordeten Juden Europas. Dokumentation* 1988–1995, Berlin, 90–93.
12. Statement by the association 'Aktives Museum Faschismus und Widerstand in Berlin', in ibid., 55–58, 56.
13. Interview with Hans Dingel, 'Der Tod jedes einzelnen ist singulär!', *Die Tageszeitung*, 29 April 1989.
14. Statement of April 1989 by the association 'Aktives Museum Faschismus und Widerstand in Berlin', in Bürgerinitiative Perspektive Berlin, ed., *Ein Denkmal für die ermordeten Juden Europas. Dokumentation 1988–1995*, 56.
15. Quoted in Stephanie Endlich, *Die Zukunft des Berliner 'Prinz-Albrecht-Geländes' ('Gestapo-Geländes')'*, Berlin: Senatsverwaltung für Kulturelle Angelegenheiten & Berliner Festspiele, 1990, 16.
16. *Fachkommission zur Erarbeitung von Vorschlägen für die künftige Nutzung des 'Prinz-Albrecht-Geländes'*.
17. See the petition of the Central Council of German Roma and Sinti, Zentralrat Deutscher Sinti und Roma, 'Aufruf', *Der Tagesspiegel*, 11 April 1989. See also the correspondence between the Central Council of Roma and Sinti and the Central Council of Jews in Germany, in Bürgerinitiative Perspektive Berlin, ed., *Ein Denkmal für die ermordeten Juden Europas. Dokumentation 1988–1995*, 113–16.
18. See Hamburger Kunstverein, ed., *Richard Serra: Zum Holocaust-Mahnmal in Berlin*, 4.
19. Hans-Georg Stavginski, *Das Holocaust-Denkmal: der Streit um das 'Denkmal für die ermordeten Juden Europas' in Berlin (1988–1999)*, Paderborn: Schöningh, 2002, 113.
20. A new post for a minister without portfolio created on 3 February 1999 following a provisional status as Federal Cultural Representative from 27 September 1998. Cf. Jürgen Kolbe, 'Michael, der tapfere Ritter', *Frankfurter Rundschau*, 13 November 1998, 10.
21. See Gerz's open letter to the chairwoman of the Bundestag cultural committee Elke Leonhard, 'Systematischer Ideenklau', *Frankfurter Allgemeine Zeitung*, 29 January 1999, 18.
22. Cf. '"Künstliches Gebilde"', *Berliner Zeitung*, 9 February 1999.
23. According to the report, '"Schröders Mahnmal-Idee einbeziehen"', *Der Tagesspiegel*, 1 April 1999, 33.
24. Sybille Quack, ed., *Auf dem Weg zur Realisierung. Das Denkmal für die ermordeten Juden Europas und der Ort der Information. Architektur und historisches Konzept*, Stuttgart: Deutsche Verlags-Anstalt, 2002.
25. See Alexander Kluy, 'Der Raum als therapeutisches Gedächtnis', *Frankfurter Rundschau*, 25 October 2003, 16.
26. See Frank Ebbinghaus, 'Nie wieder? Die Angst der Bioenergetik: ein Euthanasie-Mahnmal in Berlin', *Frankfurter Allgemeine Zeitung*, 16 October 2000, 54.
27. See 'Sinti und Roma rufen zu Aktion für NS-Mahnmal auf', *Frankfurter Rundschau*, 15 August 2001, 4; 'Konflikt um Sinti-Mahnmal', *Frankfurter Rundschau*, 20 November 2003, 4.
28. See Katja Füchsel, 'Provozieren erlaubt – für einen guten Zweck?', *Der Tagesspiegel*, 22 July 2001, 10; Marlies Emmerich, 'Holocaust-Plakat soll so

bald wie möglich verschwinden', *Berliner Zeitung*, 4/5 August 2001, 21.
29. 'Über 150 Historiker und Kulturwissenschaftler aus der ganzen Welt protestieren gegen die Werbekampagne "Den Holocaust hat es nie gegeben"', http://hsozkult.geschichte.hu-berlin.de, 6 August 2001.
30. Henryk Broder, 'Die Privatisierung des Holocaust', in www.henryk-broder.de/html/tb_rosh.html, 3 August 2000. See also: 'NPD wirbt in Wahlkampf mit Holocaust-Provokation', *Frankfurter Rundschau*, 9 October 2001.
31. Michael Naumann, 'Hygiene am Bau', *Die Zeit*, 30 October 2003, 1.
32. Siegfried Jäger, *Kritische Diskursanalyse. Eine Einführung*, Duisburg: Duisburger Institut für Sprach- und Sozialforschung, 1993, 156.
33. Perspektive Berlin, 'Aufruf', *Frankfurter Rundschau*, 30 January 1989, 4, and instructions briefing artists, in Senatsverwaltung für Bau- und Wohnungswesen, ed., *Künstlersicher Wettbewerb – Denkmal für die ermordeten Juden Europas*, Berlin: 1995.
34. Perspektive Berlin, 'Aufruf', *Frankfurter Rundschau*, 30 January 1989, 4.
35. Senatsverwaltung für Bau- und Wohnungswesen, ed., *Künstlersicher Wettbewerb – Denkmal für die ermordeten Juden Europas* ('Anlaß und Ziel'), Berlin, 1995.
36. Senatsverwaltung für Bau- und Wohnungswesen, ed., *Künstlerischer Wettbewerb 'Denkmal für die ermordeten Juden Europas'*, Berlin, 1997.
37. 'Kanzler Kohl lehnt Berliner Entwurf ab', *Frankfurter Rundschau*, 1 July 1995, 1.
38. Albrecht Wellmer, 'Architektur und Territorium', in *Endspiele: Die un-versöhnliche Moderne*, Frankfurt am Main: Suhrkamp, 1993, 257–78, 269.
39. Perspektive Berlin, 'Aufruf', *Frankfurter Rundschau*, 30 January 1989, 4.
40. Perspektive Berlin, '2. Aufruf', *Die Tageszeitung*, 2 April 1989.
41. Förderkreis zur Errichtung eines Denkmals für die ermordeten Juden Europas, 'Aufruf', *Süddeutsche Zeitung*, 2/3/4 June 1990, 20.
42. *'Eingerichtet'; 'angelegt'*. Cf. Duden, 8 vols, Mannheim, Leipzig, Vienna, Zürich: Duden Verlag, 1994.
43. Ibid. Detailed interpretations of these terms are proposed in Holger Thünemann, *Das Denkmal für die ermordeten Juden Europas. Dechiffrierung einer Kontroverse*, Münster, Hamburg & London: Lit Verlag, 2003, 14–17.
44. Senatsverwaltung für Bau- und Wohnungswesen, ed., *Künstlersicher Wettbewerb – Denkmal für die ermordeten Juden Europas* ('Aufgabenstellung'), Berlin, 1995.
45. Ibid., ('Anhang').
46. Ibid., ('Teilnahmeberechtigung').
47. Interview with Peter Steinbach, 'Denkmäler laufen Gefahr, Kranzabwurfstellen zu werden', *Stuttgarter Zeitung*, 4 April 1998, 5.
48. Rosh, 'Ein Denkmal im Lande der Täter', in Bürgerinitiative Perspektive Berlin, ed., *Ein Denkmal für die ermordeten Juden Europas. Dokumentation 1988–1995*, 3–7, 3.
49. This is the 'basic idea' behind the monument, according to Jäckel. See E. Jäckel, 'An alle und jeden erinnern', *Die Zeit*, 7 April 1989.
50. Cf. Peter Michalzik, 'Das Gedenken ist frei', *Süddeutsche Zeitung*, 9 December 1997, 16.
51. '… wo die Leute gerne hingehen.' See Ulrich Speck, 'Spielball oder Mitspieler. Zwei Essays zur Politik der Berliner Republik', *Merkur* no. 3, March 2002, 244–49.
52. See Wiedmer, *The Claims of Memory*, 149.
53. *Verhandlungen des Deutschen Bundestages. Stenographischer Bericht – 13. Wahlperiode – 104. Sitzung*, Bonn, 9 May 1996, 9063.

54. Ibid., 9073.
55. Ibid., 9063.
56. Ibid., 9069.
57. Rosh in a panel discussion of proposed models in the Marstall Gallery, Berlin, 20 January 1998; Jäckel in a telephone debate on *Deutschlandfunk* radio, 3 August 1998.
58. Quoted in '"Scham ist ein Moment menschlicher Würde"', *Der Tagesspiegel*, 26 June 1999, 2.
59. Quoted in 'Das Wort steht gegen die Masse', *Der Tagesspiegel*, 26 June 1999, 25.
60. Hermann Rudolf, 'Ein Kraftakt ohne Kraft', *Der Tagesspiegel*, 26 June 1999, 1.
61. Volker Beck, quoted in 'Bundestag bekennt sich zum Mahnmal', *Die Tageszeitung*, 26/28 June 1999, 1.
62. Wolfgang Gerhardt, quoted in ibid.
63. See Andreas Schäfer, '"Vielen Dank für die großzügige Einladung"', *Berliner Zeitung*, 13 January 1998, 11.
64. In response to an advertisement in the *Frankfurter Allgemeine Zeitung*, 8 May 1998, 60. Cf. Jan Hendrik Neumann, 'Mahnmalheur', *Kunstzeitung*, 23 July 1998, 4.
65. See Thomas Lackmann, 'Die Säule der Nation', *Der Tagesspiegel*, 2/3 October 1997, 37.
66. Christina von Braun, 'Würdigen statt mahnen', *Süddeutsche Zeitung*, 23 January 1998, 13.
67. See Andreas Schäfer, '"Vielen Dank für die großzügige Einladung"', 11.
68. Disillusionment over the complexity and long duration of the selection procedure did not deter supporters of the monument from warning of a political 'loss of face' in the event of a cancellation of the project. Cf. Christian Meier, 'Stachel im Fleisch', *Der Tagesspiegel*, 23 January 1998, 23.
69. Klaus Hartung, 'Gedenken – aber wie?', *Die Zeit*, 24 March 1995, 8 (my italics).
70. See 'Stahlträger vermitteln eine unheimliche Last', *Berliner Zeitung*, 18 March 1995, 2.
71. Walter Jens, quoted in 'Opfer werden aus der Anonymität herausgeholt', *Berliner Zeitung*, 18 March 1995, 2.
72. Korn, 'Holocaust-Gedenken: Ein deutsches Dilemma', 28. Details of the Vietnam Veterans Memorial comparable to those of the Holocaust Monument are described in Daniel Abramson, 'Maya Lin and the 1960s: Monuments, Time Lines, and Minimalism', *Critical Inquiry* no. 4, 1996, 679–709.
73. Korn, quoted in Stefanie Flamm, 'Das Holocaust-Denkmal als Erfolgsgeschichte', *Berliner Zeitung*, 11 May 1998, 11.
74. Hartung, 'Gedenken – aber wie?', *Die Zeit*, 24 March 1995, 8.
75. Richard Serra, statement at public presentation of proposed monument in the Marstall Gallery, Berlin, 13 January 1998.
76. Eisenman and Serra, *Materialien für die erste Beurteilungssitzung*, press release, November 1997.
77. Alison Landsberg, 'America, the Holocaust, and the Mass Culture of Memory: Towards a Radical Politics of Empathy', *New German Critique* no. 71, 1997, 63–86, 74. See also Kevin Walsh's discussion of 'folk-life' museums, *The Representation of the Past. Museums and Heritage in the Post-modern World*, London: Routledge, 1992, 121.
78. Eisenman, quoted in Robert von Rimscha, '"Ich will einen Kunden!"', *Der*

Tagesspiegel, 14 June 1998, 3.
79. Quoted in Kluy, 'Der Raum als therapeutisches Gedächtnis', *Frankfurter Rundschau*, 25 October 2003, 16.
80. Eisenman and Serra, *Materialien für die erste Beurteilungssitzung*, 1997.
81. Ibid.
82. Ibid.
83. Jochen Gerz, *Materialien für die erste Beurteilungssitzung*, press release, November 1997.
84. Gerz, interview with Detlev Lücke, 'Wir müssen zur Skulptur werden', *Freitag*, 6 March 1998, 17.
85. A direct reference to a poem by Paul Celan: 'Das aufwärtsstehende Land,/ rissig,/ mit der Flugwurzel, der/ Steinatem zuwächst/ Auch hier/ stürzen die Meere hinzu, aus der Steilschlucht,/ und dein sprach-/ pockiger, panischer/ Ketzer/ kreuzt., in *Atemwende*, Frankfurt am Main: Suhrkamp, 1967, 66.
86. Daniel Libeskind, *Materialien für die erste Beurteilungssitzung*, press release, November 1997.
87. Libeskind, interview with H. Fricke and A. Goldberg, 'Schaun wir mal, was fliegt und was nicht fliegt', *Die Tageszeitung* (Magazin), 17/18 January 1998, ii–iv, iv.
88. Gesine Weinmiller, *Materialien für die erste Beurteilungssitzung*, press release, November 1997.
89. See Udo Becker, *Lexikon der Symbole*, Freiburg, Basel, Vienna: Herder, 1992, 127.
90. Florian von Buttlar and Stefanie Endlich, 'Das Berliner Holocaust-Denkmal. Ablauf des Wettbewerbs und Stand der Diskussion', in Akademie der Künste, ed., *Denkmale und kulturelles Gedächtnis nach dem Ende der Ost-West-Konfrontation*, Berlin: Jovis, 2000, 305–328, esp. 317–23.
91. Gerz, *Materialien für die erste Beurteilungssitzung*, press release, November 1997.
92. Gerz, statement at public presentation of proposed monument in the Marstall Gallery, Berlin, 16 January 1998.
93. Hermann Rudolf, 'Entscheidung über das Trauern', *Der Tagesspiegel*, 13 January 1998, 27.
94. See Michel Friedman, 'Furcht vor abstrakten Pfiffigkeiten', *Berliner Zeitung*, 21/22 March 1998, 9.
95. Libeskind, at the Marstall Gallery, Berlin, 19 January 1998.
96. Eisenman, at the Marstall Gallery, Berlin, 13 January 1998.
97. Eduard Beaucamp, 'Baut Serra!', *Frankfurter Allgemeine Zeitung*, 3 February 1998, 35.
98. Gerz, interview, 'Das dekorative Gemeinwesen', *Die Tageszeitung*, 11 April 1995.
99. See 'Gerz zieht Entwurf zum Mahnmal zurück', *Berliner Zeitung*, 28 July 1998, 11.
100. Only Simon Ungers and Hans Hollein incorporated inscriptions into their proposals for the first competition in 1995. Cf. Jens Jessen, 'Das undeutliche Mahnmal', *Berliner Zeitung*, 20 January 1998, 4.
101. Gert Mattenklott, '"Denk ich an Deutschland ..." Deutsche Denkmäler 1790 bis 1990', Sekretariat für kulturelle Zusammenarbeit Nordrhein-Westfalen, ed., *Deutsche Nationaldenkmale 1790–1990*, Bielefeld: Verlag für Regionalgeschichte, 1993, 17–47, 46.
102. See Young's commentary at the third congress 1997, 'Erinnerung, Gegenerinnerung und das Ende des Monuments', in Senatsverwaltung für

Wissenschaft, Forschung und Kultur, ed., *Colloquium: Denkmal für die ermordeten Juden Europas,* Berlin, 1997, 124–25, 125.
103. See Kudielka's commentary at the third congress, 1997, in ibid., 140–41, 141.
104. Kudielka, 'Das falsche Gewicht der Betroffenheit', *Freitag,* 5 September 1997, 13.
105. See Buddensieg's commentary at the third congress 1997, in Senatsverwaltung für Wissenschaft, Forschung und Kultur, ed., *Colloquium: Denkmal für die ermordeten Juden Europas,* 125–28, 126.
106. Harald Fricke, 'Tote Monumente, lebendige Leere', *Die Tageszeitung* (Magazin), 17/18 January 1998, iv.
107. Hoffmann-Axthelm bases his analysis on the architectural theories of Etienne-Louis Boullée. See 'Die Ästhetik der Nichtzuständigkeit', in Neue Gesellschaft für bildende Kunst, ed., *Der Wettbewerb für das "Denkmal für die ermordeten Juden Europas"',* Berlin: Verlag der Kunst, 1995, 74–83, 79; cf. Konrad Liessmann, 'Auschwitz als Kunstgenuß', *Freitag,* 28 February 1997, 9.
108. Mariam Niroumand, 'Darsteller und Denklöcher', *Die Tageszeitung,* 14 April 1997, 15.
109. Quoted by James Young, 'Was keine andere Nation je versucht hat', *Berliner Zeitung,* 18 December 1998, 13–14.
110. See Elisabeth Noelle-Neumann and Renate Köcher, eds, *Allensbacher Jahrbuch der Demoskopie 1993–1997,* Munich: K. G. Saur, 1997, 516.
111. Cf. Klaus von Beyme, *Hauptstadtsuche,* Frankfurt am Main: Suhrkamp, 1991, 77–111.
112. Jessen, 'Eine Frage der Hauptstadt', *Berliner Zeitung,* 27 August 1998, 9.
113. *'Dauerpräsentation der Schande', 'Einschüchterungsmittel', 'Moralkeule', 'Pflichtübung', 'Moralpistole', 'Meinungssoldaten'.* Martin Walser, 'Erfahrungen beim Verfassen einer Sonntagsrede', *Frankfurter Rundschau,* 12 October 1998, 10.
114. Moshe Zuckermann, 'Perspektiven der Holocaust-Rezeption in Israel und Deutschland', *Aus Politik und Zeitgeschichte* no. 14, 1998, 19–29, 29.
115. See Winfried Speitkamp, ed., 'Denkmalsturz und Symbolkonflikt in der modernen Geschichte', in Speitkamp, ed., *Denkmalsturz. Zur Konfliktgeschichte politischer Symbolik,* Göttingen: Vandenhoeck & Ruprecht, 1997, 5–21, 18.
116. See Gaëlle Pinson, 'La "reconstruction critique" à Berlin, entre formes et idéologie', *Le Visiteur. Ville, territoire, paysage, architecture* no. 6, 2000, 130–155; Harald Bodenschatz, *Berlin. Auf der Suche nach dem verlorenen Zentrum,* Berlin: Junius, 1995, 134ff.
117. Official title: 'Zentrale Gedenkstätte der Bundesrepublik Deutschland', dedicated to 'Den Opfern von Krieg und Gewaltherrschaft'.
118. Cf. Saul Friedlander, ed., *Probing the Limits of Representation. Nazism and the 'Final Solution',* Cambridge, Mass. & London: Harvard University Press, 1992, 6ff.
119. See 'Kanzler Kohl lehnt Berliner Entwurf ab', *Frankfurter Rundschau,* 1 July 1995, 1.
120. See in particular the statements of Volker Beck, Peter Conradi, Ludwig Elm, Anton Pfeifer, Peter Radunski and Rupert Scholz, in *Verhandlungen des Deutschen Bundestages. Stenographischer Bericht – 13. Wahlperiode – 104. Sitzung.* See also Peter Conradi's appeal for consensus over 'a monument of the German people' (*'ein Denkmal des deutschen Volkes'*) to be achieved 'in a broad public discussion' (*'in einer breiten öffentlichen Diskussion'*), in an open

letter to participants in the first colloquium, 10 October 1997.

121. Expressed by Ludwig Elm and Anton Pfeifer in the Bundestag debate of 9 May 1996.
122. Bernard Schulz, 'Strittiges Mahnmal', *Der Tagesspiegel*, 23 March 1998, 1.
123. Peter Radunski, in *Verhandlungen des Deutschen Bundestages. Stenographischer Bericht – 13. Wahlperiode – 104. Sitzung*, 9076.
124. Anton Pfeifer, in ibid., 9071.
125. Mark Haugaard, *The Constitution of Power. A Theoretical Analysis of Power, Knowledge and Structure*, Manchester: Manchester University Press, 1997, 146.
126. See Gerhard Lehmbruch, 'Strukturen ideologischer Konflikte bei Parteienwettbewerb', *Politische Vierteljahresschrift* no. 10, 1969, 285–313, 291f.
127. Among the first advocates of parliamentary intervention was the historian Johannes Willms. See Willms, 'Das leere Machtwort', *Süddeutsche Zeitung*, 10/11 June 1998, 15.
128. Early parliamentary negotiations proposed setting up a foundation to coordinate the construction of a Monument for the Murdered Jews of Europe comprising executive and advisory councils composed of representatives from other Berlin memorial museums, the Central Council of Jews in Germany, Holocaust victim groups and other specialists. See Moritz Müller-Wirth, 'Mahnmal-Stiftung nimmt Gestalt an', *Der Tagesspiegel*, 8 July 1999, 4.
129. Eike Geisel, 'Lebenshilfe von toten Juden', *Junge Welt*, 14 May 1994.
130. Cf. Jay Winter, *Sites of Memory, Sites of Mourning*, 8.
131. Jens, 'In letzter Minute', *Frankfurter Allgemeine Zeitung*, 7 February 1998, 33.

5

The Institutionalisation of Memory in Public Art and Rhetoric

This detailed examination of the evolution of the Vél d'Hiv' and Holocaust Monument reveals discrepancies, but also analogies and overlaps between memory cultures in France and Germany. Memory cultures are not unique and confined in time and space, but are subject to what the sociologist Ulrich Beck calls 'polycentric memory, in which non-state, transnational actors (such as social movements) also play a role'[1] – a model which he perceives to be a key to the constitution of a European memory culture. Beck dismisses Christianity, ethnicity or principles of the welfare state as foundations of either national or European heritages. A multinational and 'slowly dissolving' population, and the traditions of colonialism and genocide are today core elements of European culture that render the conventional national contexts of memory cultures obsolete, and a cosmopolitan revision of memory cultures across national boundaries and open to minorities within these boundaries indispensable.

French–German Analogies

The similarities and dissimilarities between the debates over the Vél' d'Hiv' and Holocaust Monument are highly revealing of the extent to which the Second World War, in particular the persecution and genocide, is both a national and transnational motor of collective memory. Both sites were conceived as national monuments, sharing the organisers' and public's expectation that they represent 'French' or 'German' memory. Since no single monument can fulfill such a condition, however, they became objects of dispute. In fact, disputes over commemorative practices and historical artefacts evoking memories of this period in Paris and Berlin have occurred so frequently that both cities can be conceived as urban archives not only of history but also of present-day perceptions of the past. These urban landscapes may be interpreted in two ways: as networks of pedagogical symbols 'encoding' historical meanings in stone; or as networks of heuristic focal points of dispute giving rise to public negotiation of the very means by which history may be transmitted to future generations via the medium of monuments.

In both France and Germany, public debates over the appropriate symbolisation of the deportation and genocide were central components of the transmission of national memory and production of historical knowledge alongside financial reparations, legal investigations, film productions, and professional historical research and publications. Urban sites, artistic monuments and political rhetoric provided substance for the interaction of politicians, associations, the mass media as well as artists and architects – a dual process of institutionalisation comprising the formation of organisations or social groups representing specific interests, but also the more diffuse, but no less significant 'typification of habitualised actions'[2] with respect to the past. In other words, beyond the immediate group interests such as the call for a presidential speech recognising crimes in France or the call for a central urban memorial in Germany, there are symbolic and rhetorical customs that are shared across national boundaries and which draw on shared reflexes rooted essentially in the national movements of the nineteenth century. This chapter will explore some of the ways in which different nations, taking France and Germany as models, use similar institutionalised customs to evoke the past and legitimise the present in a strictly national sphere of remembrance.

An initial analysis of the objects, issues and actors of the debates suggests that the two monuments have little in common. The site of the Vél' d'Hiv' is small (approximately three square metres), situated in a raised garden not visible at street level to passers-by; it is a figurative sculpture in bronze marking an 'authentic' historical site on which a specific event took place on a precise date; it was erected in conjunction with an annual commemoration, preceded by petitions focusing public attention on a presidential speech rather than on sculptural form. By contrast, the site of the Holocaust Monument is very large and conspicuously located in the heart of the city; it has an abstract sculptural form evoking the genocide against Jews generally rather than a particular historical occurrence associated with a single authentic site; and it was not conceived in conjunction with an annual ceremony but as the object of petitions and public debate. Moreover, the debate in Germany lasted over ten years (in contrast to three years in France), involved a broader section of society, and touched upon fundamental methodological questions concerning the site, form, necessity and political procedure required to realise the project.

In spite of these differences, there exist remarkable analogies between the origins of each monument. Both were initiated by citizens' action groups with petitions published in daily national newspapers, and both campaigns involved the public and highest political representatives, including national parliaments, party leaders, two French presidents and German chancellors. In both cases, petitions appealed for a 'national' symbolic reparation while focusing on representations dedicated to Jewish victims, and both debates were interrupted by elections, followed by a change of president in 1995 in France and a change of government in 1998 in Germany. Both monuments served as sites for annual ritual speeches held on new national days of commemoration – the 'National Day of Commemoration of the Racist and Anti-Semitic Persecutions' from 1993 in France, and the Day of Commemoration of the Victims of National Socialism (Tag des Gedenkens an die Opfer des Nationalsozialismus) held from 27 January 1996 in the German parliament, and on the monumental site for the first time in 2000. Moreover, the monuments gave rise to similar political issues (the role of the state and minorities), commemorative codes (sculptural symbols and commemorative speeches) and levels of discourse (national, regional, local, individual, moral, reflexive and metatheoretical).

Despite the intense politicisation of these monuments, they did not serve as props for social or class identity. Neither monument was the product of a closed community pursuing adversarial identity politics. In France, representatives of the Jewish community such as Serge Klarsfeld and Henri Hadjenberg supported the project alongside non-Jewish colleagues and historians, including members of the Comité Vél' d'Hiv' 42. The Union of Jewish Students of France (UEJF) mounted an independent campaign by staging a mock trial of 'the French people'[3] in front of the Law Courts in Paris in 1992, and by launching its own petition for a speech by President Mitterrand.[4] The Berlin project initially provoked only reserved support from members of the Jewish Community of Berlin, while the World Jewish Congress initially lent support on condition that Jewish representatives were *not* involved in the project.[5] Later, in 1992, the Central Council of Jews in Germany became actively committed to the project in reaction to the campaigning by other victim groups, in particular the Roma and Sinti, for a single collective monument representing all victim groups. Subsequent discussions about the projects took place between journalists, intellectuals and politicians on the occasion of exhibitions, public forums and parliamentary debates – diverse forms of social communication which, once relayed by the mass media, offered platforms for dispute rather than group cohesion. In political circles, the projects incited politicians to formulate informal policies on the monuments that provoked the formation of political factions that cut across and consequently undermined traditional party unity. Divisions arose within the Gaullist RPR party and Socialist Party (PS) in France, for example, and within the SPD and CDU at local and national levels in Germany. These projects did not sustain forms of what the historian Charlotte Tacke calls 'cultural sociability'[6] based on ritual activities of closed groups during the nineteenth century; although the Vél' d'Hiv' and Holocaust Monument both owe their existence to the initiative of citizens' action groups, they were rendered public primarily by countless articles in the mass media, which fostered divisions of opinion and spheres of sociability that surpassed the scope of identifiable social groups. Participation in the emergence of these monuments extended to a broader section of the public, pervaded informal conversation, included state representatives and, particularly in Germany, provoked critical discussion on their form and function. Moreover, participation in these projects was facilitated by a number of associations *other* than those whose sole purpose was to initiate the monuments and commemorations: Protestant organisations such as the Association of the Evangelical Free Churches (VEF: Vereinigung Evangelischer Freikirchen) and the church offices of the Evangelical Church in Germany (EKD: Evangelische Kirche in Deutschland), the association Tree of Life (Lebensbaum), committed to counselling on all kinds of social problems, the left-wing association Initiative Against the Final Stroke (Initiativkreis gegen den Schlußstrich), and the right-wing regional association Alliance of Free Citizens (Bund Freier Bürger) each held independent public meetings on the subject of the Holocaust Monument in 1999.[7]

These monuments also reflect parallel urban developments of the cities of Paris and Berlin. Both monuments functioned as correctives of existing monuments and previous state commemorations: of the Memorial of the Martyrs of Deportation in Paris, and of the Neue Wache in Berlin. In both countries, existent memorials had rendered the commemoration of victims in universal terms as a commemoration of victimisation, and thus discounted the specific political motivations for the persecutions as well as their ethnic, gender, political or religious pretexts. The Gaullist memorial incorporated poetic imagery, contrasted abstract motifs of nature and enclosure, light and darkness, and the shrine of an unknown deportee. The Neue Wache was dedicated to 'victims of war and tyranny' generally and only subsequently, following public protest, amended with a bronze plaque naming specific victim groups.

Perhaps the most enduring analogy between the two projects was the persistence with which arguments over the monuments were overshadowed by conditions established in the initial petitions. These demanded the symbolic reparation of the entire nation and, by implication, broad consensus over the significance of symbolic gestures and monuments. In France, politicians strove for reconciliation over the immediate issue of whether crimes of deportation occurring fifty years earlier should be acknowledged in a speech by the president. In Germany, consensus was consistently sought over the issues of the site, size and form, but also over the procedure for selecting the monument and over its very purpose in a city already endowed with numerous commemorative sites. The discrepancy between discursive ideals of reconciliation and consensus and their social reality ensured long debates in both countries. Although neither monument could be the object of genuine social reconciliation or consensus, petitioners maintained their conviction that monuments or commemorative rituals may guarantee the continuing remembrance of past events, a condition for symbolic reparation. The application of such arguments to the Vél' d'Hiv' and Holocaust Monument was based on the erroneous assumption that there exists a direct proportional relation between representations and collective historical memories. Although petitions evoked such incommensurable political conditions in relation to these monuments, single symbols clearly cannot be binding for entire national communities; the act of naming them as national raises false expectations that a monument should 'represent' or 'reflect' collective memory on the basis of a one-to-one relation between artefacts and historical self-understanding. Yet the fact remains that the conditions raised in the petitions were taken very seriously throughout the debate. The very discourse of reconciliation and consensus in this context demonstrated the central status accorded to symbols as a guarantee of reparation.

In order to understand some of the discursive codes used to articulate a sense of memorial belonging during these debates, one has to look to the nineteenth century. The sociologist Bernhard Giesen identifies three such codes employed in the construction of a notion of collective identity in the nineteenth century that have largely subsisted in the twentieth century as *boundaries, origins* and *differences*.[8] These principal codes recurred in debates over the Vél' d'Hiv' and the Holocaust Monument, which were categorised territorially (with respect to boundaries) as central symbols, which commemorated historical origins or 'founding moments'[9] of each nation (the caesura of the Second World War), and symbolically integrated 'difference' on behalf of Jewish victims of deportation and genocide. Giesen categorises three further codes as 'primordial', which presupposes the perception of the nation as natural; 'conventional', in which in-groups and out-groups are identified in terms of 'us' and 'them'; and 'cultural', referring to the construction of cultural emblems. These codes were also expressed in connection with the Vél' d'Hiv' and the Holocaust Monument. In terms of 'primordiality', the initial petitions established conditions for the types of commemoration (a speech or monument, and their significance as emblems standing for national self-understanding) which were perceived as natural and therefore taken for granted as conditions throughout the ensuing debates. 'Conventional' codes emerged in the polarisation of perceptions of historical actors as two distinct in-groups and out-groups – of perpetrators and their descendants belonging to the nation on the one hand, and victims excluded or not belonging on the other, where the goal of each monument was to reconcile these groups and dissolve the polarity. Finally, both monuments are 'cultural' emblems perpetuating the traditional genre of national monuments, although they were not designed to pay homage to cultural figures of the nation, but to mourn the dead and acknowledge responsibility for their death.

Neither the Vél' d'Hiv' nor Holocaust Monument are inherently national monuments, yet their significance was anticipated and interpreted as such. Both have been criticised for being inapt as national representations: the Vél' d'Hiv' because it is a monument of collaboration with another state;[10] the Holocaust Monument because it is open to multiple interpretations,[11] because it is too big, or because there previously existed a sufficient number of memorials. Yet the fact that the debates nevertheless focused on the quest to propose a speech or sculpture that could fulfil the criteria of a genuinely 'national' monument requires further investigation. How can we explain the mechanisms by which the monuments were construed and perceived as national and thereby won public acceptance?

One reason why these monuments evolved into national monuments in spite of their historical inaptness lies in their formal aptness as sites for public rituals and visual reproduction in photographs. One can easily identify and visually conceive a single site like a cycling stadium or a monument marking its place, which can be seen, photographed, visited, which serves as a stage for political rituals, and about which spectators are able to read or to which they can relate stories from the past. The images and historical narratives associated with the Vél' d'Hiv', for example, were rendered public in the media by the introduction of the a National Day of Commemoration of the Racist and Anti-Semitic Persecutions in 1993, which since 2000 has become the key official event relating to Vichy in the French commemorative calendar. Images relating to the Holocaust Monument were likewise publicised extensively during architectural competitions, featuring models and their designers. Rituals and the mass media were therefore instrumental in entrenching the perception of these monuments as national. In contrast to other fiftieth anniversary commemorations during the 1990s in which several different nations participated simultaneously (for example, on 8 May (capitulation of the National Socialists), 6 June (Normandy landings), 29 August (liberation of Paris)), the Vél' d'Hiv' and Holocaust Monument were constructed within the context of strictly nationwide debates, and with the participation of regional and federal state representatives. The degree to which a site lends itself to commemoration on a national scale is therefore dependent on the visual qualities and associated narratives with which the event may be subsequently represented and communicated to a public which has no direct experience of the period in question.[12] In short, the emergence and political expediency of monuments as sites of collective national memory depends on their formal characteristics and discursive contexts.

A second factor determining whether memorial sites evolve into national sites is the facility with which political issues of the present day may be associated with or 'grafted' onto the site or event being commemorated. The Paris and Berlin monuments became established as central sites of memory due to a partial but growing consensus among individuals and associations that they illustrated moral and political issues relative to both the deportation and genocide of the 1940s and to xenophobia and the integration of minority communities during the 1990s. In France, Chirac's speech of 1995 raised the issue of the legitimacy of Jewish memories of the Second World War in relation to the contemporary problem of racism by associating anti-Semitism under Vichy with the present-day exclusion of ethnic minorities. As a consequence of increased exclusion, variously referred to as the 'cultural fragmentation' or 'ethnocentrism'[13] of French society, where the marginalisation of social groups such as French Algerians undermines the integrative force of republicanism, the Vél' d'Hiv' evolved into a symbol not only of anti-Semitic persecutions under Vichy, but also of the repressive treatment of minorities in general, both past and present. The 'imprescriptible debt' of which president Chirac spoke in 1995 was not only a declaration of legal but also of moral and symbolic debt, which applied primarily to the treatment of Jews under the Vichy regime but also, by association, to the treatment of minorities today. Rhetoric thus served to graft political issues of the 1990s onto those of the 1940s. In Berlin, the Holocaust Monument was also justified by its advocates on moral and pedagogical grounds. This site was not 'grafted' with the issue of the integration of present-day minorities (Turkish, Kurdish, Jewish or eastern European, for example), however, but with speculation over the representative function of the monument – whether it should represent all or only Jewish victim groups, and whether it would incite vandals to use the monument as a surface for political graffiti. The Vél' d'Hiv' and the Holocaust Monument thus both fulfilled pedagogical functions as symbols of past crimes by warning against their repetition in the present and future. But whereas the French case focused on the words of the president and explicitly instrumentalised the memory of war crimes in relation to immediate political issues, the immediate political concerns of opinion-makers in Germany were confined to the quest to establish parity among the representations of memories of victim groups (euthanasia victims, homosexuals, Jews, political prisoners, Roma and Sinti).

A third reason why these symbols emerged as 'national' sites of memory may be ascribed to the involvement of state representatives in a phenomenon which the political scientist John Gaffney calls 'political personalism'[14] – the symbolic personification of the nation in the president and in the acts of presidential leadership. The monuments were closely associated with political personalities, their involvement in commemorations and their expressed understandings of history. Sustained controversy surrounded the participation of political leaders in successive commemorations at the Vél' d'Hiv' site, including President Mitterrand in 1992 and 1994, President Chirac in 1995, and the prime ministers Edouard Balladur, Lionel Jospin and Jean-Pierre Raffarin in 1993, 1997 and 2002 respectively. As a result, commemorative ceremonies and speeches were not always a prop but also an obstacle to political legitimisation. Debate over the Vél' d'Hiv' in 1992, for example, was marked by new biographical revelations about the role of President Mitterrand in Vichy. By contrast, President Chirac's Vél' d'Hiv' speech occurred only ten weeks after his election as president on 7 May, and was applauded as the first major symbolic event of his presidency, followed by the transfer of André Malraux's ashes to the Panthéon in November 1996. Political personalism operated equally in Germany, where debate was punctuated by controversies staged as political duels between individuals, either for or against the project: between the president of the Central Council of Jews in Germany, Ignatz Bubis, and the writer Martin Walser; between Chancellor Kohl and the designated State Minister for Culture Michael Naumann prior to the parliamentary elections of 1998; or between Chancellor Schröder and the governing mayor of Berlin in 1999. In both France and Germany, heads of state played a consistent role in the symbolic construction of monuments.

The Contingency of Monuments

A crucial analogy between the Vél' d'Hiv' and Holocaust Monument is their semantic contingency. Monuments are inherently mute. While standing in front of a monument, one is not privy to its origins and only partly to factual details and complexities of the event being commemorated. This is why monuments are effective projection surfaces for successive (and even contradictory) interpretations of the past. The heuristic value of the monuments and their accompanying debates lies not in their intrinsic artistic significance alone but equally in their extrinsic rhetorical and ritual environment, which incites people to reflect on the event, its forms of transmission and their personal understanding of it – an event which constitutes the most radical rupture in the contemporary history of both France and Germany and which lies at the origin of postwar constitutions. For this reason, the interpretation and manipulation of these commemorations by political leaders were paramount.

In Germany, Gerhard Schröder's and Michael Naumann's decision first to oppose then, following the parliamentary election of 1998, to support the project was a politically motivated manoeuvre calculated to appeal to public opinion, not a decision motivated by historical experience or heuristic intentions. By seeking to put a decisive end to the punctilious debate prior to the 1998 elections, they could expect to win votes on both the right and the left. The extreme right-wing party, the German People's Union (DVU), had campaigned in its journal the *Deutsche National-Zeitung* almost weekly in 1997 and 1998 for the suspension of the project, while prominent intellectuals including Jens and Konrád also called for a suspension, albeit on formal grounds, due to the size of the monument and the anachronistic monumentality of the shortlisted models. Protest by associations and Jewish organisations against right-wing slandering of the monument, and the debate between Walser and Bubis in late 1998, nevertheless convinced the new federal government that the monumental gesture in memory of victims was a political necessity, a bulwark against public sympathy with those, like Walser, who presented themselves as victims of moral intimidation resulting from ritual public acts of remembering war crimes in the 1990s.

In France, Mitterrand justified his refusal to make the speech in 1992 by reasserting the primacy of the founding moment of 1789 and republican tradition, by claiming that the Vichy regime constituted a historical interruption without legal foundation (the republican constitution was suspended from 1940–44), and by recalling the extensive reparations achieved during the purges of 1944–45.[15] Chirac also reasserted the origin of 1789 and republican tradition, albeit while acknowledging the legality of the Vichy regime (the republican parliament voted the dissolution of the constitution in July 1940) and racism generally, where the verbal assertion of republican tradition served as a negation of Vichy. In this way, despite the presidents' different historical interpretations, they pursued similar political strategies with respect to republican ideology, each asserting the primacy of one origin and tradition of the nation over another. The interpretations of the two presidents, though similar in their historical content, differed essentially in their type of historiographical discourse. Chirac adopted a mode of confession and redemption by acknowledging war crimes, making an explicit verbal reference to legal, moral and political continuities linking the republic to the Vichy regime, while at the same time appealing to a transcendental principle of the nation as an expression of universal enlightenment ideas in contrast to Vichy as a momentary historical principle. By contrast, Mitterrand adopted a mode of denial, by making non-verbal symbolic gestures of recognition of deportations without explicit reference to moral lessons to be drawn from the Vichy regime for the Fifth Republic. Whereas Chirac countered the historical principle of Vichy with a political principle of republicanism and a transcendental principle of nationhood, Mitterrand countered the historical principle of Vichy with a political principle of republicanism and a historical principle of the Fourth Republic which, he claimed, had already made amends for damages in the postwar purges.

Hence his emphatic refusal to express acknowledgement of the crimes in the name of the Fifth Republic in 1992.

Discourse over the Holocaust Monument in Berlin was also interpreted in relation to perceived national origins, derived from historical caesuras following the end of the Second World War and the collapse of the East German regime in 1989. Reinhard Rürup, director of the Topography of Terror memorial in Berlin, emphasised the need to preserve memories of National Socialist persecutions in the 1990s not only for people educated in the German Democratic Republic according to a distorted vision of a nation united in anti-fascist resistance, but also within a burgeoning official all-German memory culture marked by symbols of the former communist regime.[16] The fall of the Berlin Wall on 9 November 1989 and the official unification of Germany on 3 October 1990[17] presented the nation with new symbolic origins, new historical and constitutional anniversary days which certainly rivalled those established during the postwar years, including 8 May 1945 (end of the Second World War) and 24 May 1949 (introduction of the constitution of the Federal Republic of Germany) and supplanted other days such as 7 October 1949 (introduction of the constitution of the German Democratic Republic). Within this new context, the campaign to build the Holocaust Monument acquired significance as an attempt to maintain a bold symbol of the genocide of the Second World War within the 'new' Federal Republic of Germany during the 1990s – a means of symbolically complementing the origins of the new state with the memory of the origins of the old state, and thus sustaining 'Holocaust-identity' alongside 'normal-national-identity'.[18] Moreover, it provided a focal point for the renegotiation of the status of the genocide against Jews in the new memory culture. In both cases, the monument was deemed national in so far as it confronted citizens from both East and West Germany with a common symbolic point of reference. Its site, on the former no-man's land dividing East and West Berlin, is today a more poignant symbol of the unity of the new Federal Republic precisely because it was once a symbol of national division.

In sum, both the French and German monuments provided symbolic points of historical orientation for contemporary memory cultures with respect to founding moments of political traditions. Debate over the Vél' d'Hiv' was characterised by the relativisation of republican origins in 1789 and the legacy of the Vichy regime since 1944. Debate over the Holocaust Monument focused on form and procedure, but also on the relative status of war crimes in the memory culture of the Federal Republic since 1945 and 1989 respectively. Both monuments were contingent on the interpretations of national traditions. Commemorative rituals and monuments – narrative, symbolic and artistic entities – cannot prescribe their own meaning, and therefore do not guarantee the maintenance of a given memory culture. At the same time, commemorative artefacts do not reflect mimetically the attitudes and historical experiences of their creators, but serve as a projection surface with which contemporary interpreters explain history discursively, and thereby situate themselves with respect to ideological points of reference such as the years 1789, 1945 or 1989. In short, the meaning of monuments is acquired in a process of interaction between objects and their multiple interpretations; they are contingent on, but not reducible to political interests.

The Rhetorical Construction of Monuments as Symbolic Reparation

The first petition of the Comité Vél' d'Hiv' 42, which initiated the debate in France, established a single condition governing the entire three-year-long debate: that the president officially recognise in a verbal statement the responsibility of the Vichy regime. The presence of the president at the ceremony was considered to be an inadequate gesture, for the petition had called exclusively for a verbal statement, anticipated as the corrective of an 'unsaid thing' ('*non-dit*'), which would symbolically cure 'French collective memory', 'the very idea of the French Republic', and 'its founding principles'.[19] Moreover, the second petition stated explicitly that gestures such as the laying of a wreath or the legal indictment of individuals were unsatisfactory, and that the sole and absolute condition was the president's utterance.[20] The fact that the logic of these petitions governed the subsequent debate and all subsequent commemorative speeches on the site of the Vél' d'Hiv' demonstrates the authority ascribed to petitions and, by implication, the procedural mechanisms governing the institutionalisation of this site – its transformation from a memorial site used primarily by the Jewish community to a site of memory with national significance. Exclusive emphasis on the spoken word, the appointment of the president as a spokesman for the moral conscience of the nation, the suggestion that a solemn declaration may compensate for collective fault, and the fidelity with which the contents of petitions were accepted as a moral authority prescribing the norms of argumentation, shows that the Vél' d'Hiv' commemoration was governed by rules analogous to religious protocol, in so far as Chirac's compliance with demands in 1995 was analogous to a declaration of faith in the conditions of petitions, and therefore in the authority of the presidential word to stand for the collective attitude of the nation. At the same time, it is remarkable that petitioners, including representatives of Jewish institutions, campaigned for the recognition of crimes while insisting that only the president's word could legitimately represent the state as a moral authority; their contestation of the state's previous negligence to perform an act of recognition disclosed a desire for integration within that same state's historical self-image.

Members of Perspektive Berlin likewise justified their campaign for a Holocaust Monument initially as compensation for the lack of a monument and, by implication, as a symbolic form of collective moral reparation. According to the initial organisers Lea Rosh and Eberhard Jäckel, the idea for the project arose on a visit to the Yad Vashem Memorial in Jerusalem, during preparation for a documentary film. Rosh and Jäckel claimed that Germany was not yet in possession of a central, national monument because this event 'is too big, still too close, the guilt too heavy, and the persecutors still among us'.[21] 'In almost every European country there are memorials and monuments for the murdered Jews,' claimed Rosh in 1989, 'in Germany, in the country of the persecutors, there are not.'[22] The initial plan to build this monument was therefore based on the comparison of national forms of commemoration and the equation of the existence of a monument with the moral rectitude of the nation. The equation of the lack of a monument with the lack of collective moral rectitude and even collective ill health (according to petitions in each country) governed the first stages of the campaign. The banner displayed to draw attention to street collections and discussions from 1988, for example, read, 'Perspektive Berlin demands: *At last* a Holocaust Monument on the former Gestapo site!'[23] Petitions published in regional and national newspapers from January 1989 likewise focused on the lack of a central monument, interpreted as a 'disgrace'.[24] Successive petitions in the first half of 1989 began with a moral appeal to compensate this symbolic lack, to put something right which was previously supposed to be wrong. However, the fact that there already existed in 1989 a number of monuments and memorials to the victims of genocide suggests that the lack to which the campaign for the monument repeatedly referred pertained less to the monument itself than to the specific *centrality* of its situation and its status as a national symbol for all citizens. The originality of this monument lay not in the fact that it was the first to commemorate victims, as extolled by petitioners, but solely in its political function as a central national site in the capital city designed to appeal to the historical consciousness of all citizens in the new republic in a nation otherwise still divided socially between east and west. Prior to the campaign of Perspektive Berlin from 1988, discussions about the potential use of the Prince-Albrecht Palace site (the site originally designated for the monument) had already been conducted locally over a period of almost ten years, during which the question of the putative geographical and political centrality of the site had played no role. The essential difference between the campaign of this association to mark the site of the Prince-Albrecht Palace with a monument before and after 1989 lay primarily in the verbally projected status of centrality. The specific centrality of the site, which played a key role in the debate after 1989, was an invention of the petitioners from Perspektive Berlin, though not inherent in the site as such. Although both the Prince-Albrecht site and the site south of the Brandenburg Gate are central to the city, the political status of each site is one of discursive construction and perception which is not given by its geographical position alone. The fact that the former was perceived as a memorial with no exceptional status, and the latter as 'the' central memorial, is proof of this.

The conditions established in both the French and German petitions determined the terms and issues of the ensuing debates. Both appeals overstated the political significance of the sites by suggesting that they were a direct reflection of the moral status of the entire nation. The petitions' expression of indignation over the lack of a public speech or monument therefore implied that the fulfilment of these conditions would be an effective form of reparation for the crime on behalf of the nation as a whole ('the entire nation' in France, and as 'a duty for all Germans' in Germany). Although it was true that state leaders had not previously acknowledged the crimes of Vichy in this solemn fashion, the petition was designed to provoke public indignation by associating this gesture with reparation of the collective conscience of the nation. The petitions also overstated the idea that the nation lacked any monument in memory of victims, suggesting that these monuments were entirely original. Yet the claim that there existed no memorial in Germany commemorating Jewish victims was inaccurate, since it ignored the presence of memorials for Jewish victims in Berlin (in the Grosse Hamburger Strasse (1985), on the site of the former synagogue in the Levetzow Strasse (1988), and at the Grunewald local railway station (plaque installed in 1973, a monument in 1991 and an additional monument in 1998)). Nevertheless the repeated gesture of verbal indictment claiming a lack of monument sufficed to engage the public imagination. The desire to correct a lack – of a presidential speech in France, and of a central national monument for Jewish victims in Germany – was interpreted as an innate shortcoming of national memory in itself. In reality, the originality of these monuments lay less in the fact that they put an end to a lack of a speech, monument or even of collective remembrance, than in their specifically national symbolic significance and the solemnity with which they were carried out. As a consequence, the equation of each site with the collective memory and moral rectitude of the nation was unjustified. Both projects were conducted in the form of a moral litigation on the premise that the fulfilment of these symbolic conditions would morally redeem the nation. The focus of criminality was displaced from deportations and genocide to the lack of a public speech and central monument, the culprits defined as the French and German nations in the 1990s, and the desired reparations conceived as symbols which should fulfil a 'duty' in Germany and 'cure' collective memory in France.

The principle of both petitions, based on the identification of a crime, a responsible collective subject and a rhetorical or monumental act of recognition of victims, is founded on a doctrine of symbolic reparation. However, critics of the Holocaust Monument have already pointed out that the dilemma arising when equating commemorations or monuments with the fulfilment of anticipated collective reparation is that there exists no consensus on the secular moral authority determining the conditions of reparation. The art historian Gabi Dolff-Bonekämper rightly questions whether any worldly authority (the relatives of victims, the state of Israel, moral citizens of the world?) is in a position to judge what form and site is most adequate to symbolically recognise the event or even honour either the German people or those who campaigned for the monument.[25] Other critics like Georges Bensoussan, Michael Bernstein and Micha Brumlik have likened the commemoration of the persecution and genocide to a civil religion.[26] Yet the petitions in France and Germany prescribed not only the fault (the lack of a speech or monument) but also the symbolic authority summoned to guarantee reparation: the word of the president in France, and the most appropriate artistic monument in Germany. While Mitterrand rejected this doctrine by refusing to make the speech, Chirac preached national reparation by making a subtle defence of the republic in his speech of 1995, acknowledging and negating Vichy as a historical principle while reasserting republican ideals and France as an ideal transcendental principle, that is, by praising timeless moral values of a personified yet eternal nation and reiterating de Gaulle's doctrine of 'a certain idea of France'. In Germany, responses to the campaign for the Holocaust Monument also promised reparation by adhering to the terms in which the petition had been formulated. MPs claimed to respect the conditions laid down in petitions by renouncing their personal responsibility to choose a monument, by claiming that it should be a work of art or architecture, and that only specialists in these fields were competent to decide what type of monument should be built. Politicians thus delegated the responsibility for selecting a monument to artists, intervening only when the debate acquired an explicitly political dimension in 1998 on the occasion of the Walser–Bubis debate, the parliamentary election during the same year, and when solicited to intervene in the failed competition process in 1999.

Although both the Vél' d'Hiv' and the Holocaust Monument were initiated by the petitions of citizens' action groups, they each appealed to different media of symbolic reparation. The Comité Vél' d'Hiv' 42 appealed directly to the authority of the rhetoric of state leaders, whereas Perspektive Berlin appealed to the authority of a monument in itself. The acceptance of state authority as a medium of symbolic reparation in France, in contrast to reliance on purely symbolic representation (and only reluctant subsequent intervention of the state) in Germany, constitute the most pronounced difference between the institutional administrations of these commemorative projects.

The literary critic Michael Bernstein argues that the 'Shoah' has acquired the status of a universal ideology, an authority in its own right widely accepted without the medium of a worldly representative authority: the 'ultimate negative truth', a 'single all-encompassing standard'.[27] One might presume that a monument may only weigh upon social beliefs and practices if it is visited, if it has an effect on visitors, or if it is talked about in public. However, the debates accompanying the inception and planning of these monuments showed that much significance was attached to symbolic production in itself, rather than reception, as a condition for national reparation. In these specific cases, moral authority over collective memory did not stem from the Shoah as a general abstract principle, as Bernstein suggests, or from the descendants of victims, the Israeli state or the 'community of the good', as Dolff-Bonekämper suggests, but from its forms of auxiliary mediation: in particular the published petitions in the name of signatories, the mass media, exhibitions, meetings of associations, artists, intellectuals and the state representatives of countries in which the monuments were built. Although the conditions of the petitions – the supposition that the delivery of a speech in France or the possession of a monument in Germany would redeem an entire nation – were arbitrary, they were the initial and single most determinant authority of both debates, and fixed standards to which political and intellectual elites subsequently adhered.

Notes

1. Ulrich Beck, 'Wie Versöhnung möglich werden kann', *Die Zeit*, 10 July 2003, 34.
2. Peter Berger and Thomas Luckmann, *The Social Construction of Reality. A Treatise in the Sociology of Knowledge* (1966), Harmondsworth: Penguin, 1991, 72.
3. See Philippe Bernard, 'Vichy en procès', *Le Monde*, 18 July 1992, 8.
4. See 'Vichy: Les étudiants juifs attendent un geste de Mitterrand', *Libération*, 14 January 1993.
5. See 'Jüdischer Weltkongreß: Wir brauchen kein zentrales Denkmal', *Frankfurter Allgemeine Zeitung*, 26 July 1995, 4.
6. Charlotte Tacke, *Denkmal im sozialen Raum. Nationale Symbole in Deutschland und Frankreich im 19. Jahrhundert*, Göttingen: Vandenhoeck & Ruprecht, 1995, 78.
7. The VEF and EKD held a meeting at the Jewish Cultural Centre in Berlin on 3 March 1999; the Lebensbaum association invited the writer Martin Walser and representatives of religious communities to a hearing on 10 June 1999 within the scope of the project 'History and Tolerance'; the Initiative Against the Final Stroke staged a public discussion on the planned site of the monument on 30 May 1999; the Alliance of Free Citizens held a demonstration against the Holocaust Monument in front of the Neue Wache on 19 June 1999.
8. Bernhard Giesen, *Die Intellektuellen und die Nation*, Frankfurt am Main: Suhrkamp, 1993, 28.

9. Cf. Lyn Spillman, *Nation and Commemoration. Creating National Identities in the United States and Australia*, Cambridge: Cambridge University Press, 1997, 70.
10. Conan and Rousso propose the introduction of anti-Semitic laws on 3 October 1940 in the unoccupied zone as a truly national site of memory. See *Vichy, un passé qui ne passe pas*, 65.
11. Other, less ambiguous, sites were proposed in the report by Urs Kohlbrenner, Günter Schlusche and Bernhard Schneider, 'Standortuntersuchung der im Colloquium benannten Standorte', in Senatsverwaltung für Wissenschaft, Forschung und Kultur, ed., *Colloquium. Denkmal für die ermordeten Juden Europas: Dokumentation*, Berlin, 1997, 65–89.
12. Compare this to Michal Bodemann's analysis of the visual and narrative elements of the Reichskristallnacht, which make it particularly memorable. According to Bodemann, the Reichskristallnacht 'is dramatic because it represents the beginning of the Holocaust, it is emblematic, contains vivid visual aspects, a play of good against evil, and a dash of violence': Bodemann, *Gedächtnistheater. Die jüdische Gemeinschaft und ihre deutsche Erfindung*, Hamburg: Rotbuch Verlag, 1996, 116.
13. Michel Wieviorka, 'Culture, société et démocratie', in Wieviorka, ed., *Une Société fragmenté? Le multiculturalisme en débat*, 11–60, 14, 38ff.
14. John Gaffney, *The French Left and the Fifth Republic. The Discourses of Communism and Socialism in Contemporary France*, London: Macmillan, 1989, 198f.
15. See François Mitterrand's annual presidential declaration of 14 July 1992, '"De mauvaises moeurs se sont répandues partout, y compris dans la justice"', *Le Monde*, 16 July 1992, 6–7.
16. Reinhard Rürup, 'Lebendige Erinnerungskultur in der Demokratie: Gedanken und Erwartungen', unpublished paper presented at the Enquete Commission of the Bundestag on 'Living Memory Culture in Democracy', Berlin, 10 November 1997, 5.
17. Designated the 'Day of German Unity', which displaced 17 June as the national day of commemoration.
18. Cf. Christina von Braun's characteristic appeal to 'maintain the reality of Germany's National Socialist past'. Quoted in Stephanie Endlich, *Die Zukunft des Berliner 'Prinz-Albrecht-Geländes' ('Gestapo-Geländes')*', 34. The terms 'Holocaust-identity' and 'normal-national-identity' were proposed by Edgar Wolfrum to define opposed camps of the Historians' Dispute of 1986. These definitions acquired additional pertinence in light of debate over the Holocaust Monument after unification in 1990. See Wolfrum, 'Geschichtspolitik in der Bundesrepublik Deutschland 1949–1989. Phasen und Kontroversen', *Aus Politik und Zeitgeschichte* no. 45, 1998, 3–15, 15.
19. First petition of the Comité Vél' d'Hiv' 42, 'Un appel est lancé à M. Mitterrand pour que soient reconnus officiellement les "persécutions" et les "crimes de Vichy contre les juifs"', *Le Monde*, 17 June 1992, 10.
20. Second petition of the Comité Vél' d'Hiv' 42, 'Le Comité Vél' d'Hiv' 42 : l'Etat est "sourd"', *Le Monde*, 16 July 1992, 8.
21. Rosh, 'Ein Denkmal im Lande der Täter', in Bürgerinitiative Perspektive Berlin e.V., ed., *Ein Denkmal für die ermordeten Juden Europas. Dokumentation 1988–1995*, 3–7, 3.
22. Quoted in Hartwig Maack, 'Politische Weichen gestellt', *Berliner Volksblatt*, 20 April 1989, 12.
23. My italics. Bürgerinitiative Perspektive Berlin e.V., ed., *Ein Denkmal für die ermordeten Juden Europas. Dokumentation 1988–1995*, 12f.
24. 'Aufruf', *Frankfurter Rundschau*, 30 January 1989, 4.

25. Gabi Dolff-Bonekämper, 'Der geliehene Schmerz', *Frankfurter Allgemeine Zeitung*, 13 February 1997, 36.
26. Georges Bensoussan, 'Histoire, mémoire et commémoration. Vers une religion civile', *Le Débat* no. 82, 1994, 90–97; Michael Bernstein, 'Homage to the Extreme. The Shoah and the Rhetoric of Catastrophe', *The Times Literary Supplement*, 6 March 1998, 6–8; Micha Brumlik, 'Gewissen, Gedenken und anamnetische Solidarität', *Universitas* no. 630, December 1998, 1143–53.
27. Bernstein, 'Homage to the Extreme. The Shoah and the Rhetoric of Catastrophe', 8.

Part III

Dialogic Monuments between Negotiation and State Intervention

The dramatic increase in the number of historical monuments, commemorations and exhibitions since the 1970s is an international phenomenon, as demonstrated by the sociologist Frank Füredi in his extensive study of memory cultures in the U.K., France, Germany, Japan and the United States.[1] In Europe, debates over historical monuments, museums and commemorations have occurred with such frequency and intensity during this period that the debates themselves have become paradigmatic moments if not intellectual monuments of contemporary public understandings of history. Controversy over the cult of the past following the National Heritage Act of 1983 in the U.K., the Historians' Dispute in Germany in 1986, or the debate over the bicentenary celebrations of the French revolution in France in 1989 – though thematically unrelated – were comparable in so far as they all raised essential questions about the historical foundations of national memory. Whether these questions undermine or consolidate memory cultures is an ongoing dispute. I suggest that such monumental public debates first undermine but essentially rearticulate national self-understanding. Consolidation occurs following this process of questioning and rearticulation. Thus the dynamic of political and public communication depends primarily on the relative steadfastness of tradition in any given memory culture, which in turn depends on the willingness of individuals and institutions to repeatedly question and renew collective memorial paradigms.

In her study of *German National Identity after the Holocaust*, the historian Mary Fulbrook exposes the premises upon which national identity was propagated in the postwar Germanys and the influence of diverse state propaganda on historical experience in each case. 'Across both sides of the iron curtain, there were different fractures, different dissonances between public and private, between memories of victims and perpetrators, between collaborators and conformists, between parents and children.'[2] Indeed, in a nation that has only briefly known unity between 1871 and 1945 and from 1989 to the present day, one would expect collective national identity to be a contentious issue. Yet in Germany, as in France, the nation remains to this day the primary framework within which questions of identity are discussed – a 'symbolic disposition'[3] inherited over several generations and adhered to through habit, such that its citizens are still committed to the nation as a reliable political and cultural force of social cohesion. As shown in Part II, the conventional national framework of memory cultures is nevertheless only one level of discourse parallel to local and supranational levels. The terminologies and institutional structures of memory cultures are not unique to each nation, but largely analogical and overlapping. And the use of monuments to commemorate war crimes renews a conventional mode of national commemoration while subverting it from within. It is on the basis of these findings that this part will attempt to explain the specific function of Holocaust monuments in the development of national memory cultures. How did states attempt to forge a coherent public model for remembrance by responding to demands to inaugurate national memorials commemorating the persecution and genocide such as those in Paris and Berlin? Chapter Six traces the institutional and discursive contexts in which the Vél' d'Hiv' and Holocaust Monument emerged, Chapter Seven reexamines the debates over these monuments in relation to existing national discursive and symbolic memorial paradigms, and Chapter Eight proposes a revision of Nora's concept of a 'site of memory' in terms of a dialogic focal point of contemporary memory cultures. Whereas previous studies on political symbolics in contemporary France and Germany have focused on the intentions of political actors and parties (Stavginski, Wolfrum), on processes of collective mourning (Kirsch, Winter), and on the failures of decision-making bodies (Wiedmer), this study concludes with a definition of the specificity of monuments as focal points of dialogue for the continual negotiation of historical self-understanding – a negotiation fuelled by the antagonism between art and politics which is inherent to monuments as a means of representation.

Notes

The text of notes 1–3 appears at the end of Chapter Six.

6

The National Memorial Paradigm

Compensation and Consolidation: Two Paradigms of Contemporary Memory Cultures

The proliferation of monuments and commemorations and the social and political values invested in them since the 1970s are symptomatic of societies that have been actively seeking a symbolic reinforcement of collective memories. Public symbols are neither a cause nor a consequence of the present international preoccupation with memory, however, but the very language with which these societies transmit and negotiate their pasts. What are the historical and political origins and the social consequences of this phenomenon? And how do contemporary societies legitimate their existence on the basis of memory and historical representations? The rise of memory cultures, which is regularly described in terms of impulsive collective emotion – as 'the scramble to appropriate the past'[4] or 'the passion of the past',[5] for example – is manifested primarily at national, but also at local and international levels, and has been a source of intense speculation over reasons why memory in general appears to play such a conspicuous role in assuring social cohesion. The proliferation of historical representations of the Second World War since the 1980s may in part be imputed to the natural succession of generations. According to the historian Annette Wieviorka, the commemorations between 1989 and 1995 were products of a social custom of commemorating fiftieth anniversaries, and an attempt to compensate the anticipated disappearance of the generation of witnesses. They belong to a twofold 'age of witnesses' and 'age of commemorations'[6] which is characterised by the voluntary expression and recording of living memories, the desire to remember the exceptional nature of the original event, to transmit witnesses' memories to subsequent generations, as well as to construct or consolidate consensus among public and scientific communities over the origins, significance and exemplariness of the event.

The multiplication and intensification of commemorations of the Second World War during the 1990s is also a consequence of a more pervasive drive towards commemoration, one which reinforces traditions in the face of rapid historical changes perceived as a source of disorientation. This phenomenon is international yet also rooted largely in national historical narratives. In France, the contemporary interest in the past is often interpreted as a form of refuge from social insecurities resulting from rapid industrial growth, population migration from the countryside to towns, decolonisation and immigration, the weakened legitimacy of republican ideology, as well as cultural and educational reforms.[7] In Germany, prior to unification in 1990, invocations of the past in museums and exhibitions promoted distinct memory cultures in West and East Germany opposed to their ideological rival on the other side of the Iron Curtain. Yet unification reinvigorated public interest in a German national history, exemplified by debates over the extent to which architectural symbols of Berlin such as the central Pariser Platz should be historically reconstructed as they were in the prewar period. In both France and Germany therefore, rapid social or historical change appears to have fuelled interest in history as a form of compensation for a sense of lost identity. This contemporary international proliferation of history and memory is not unique, but one in a chain of historical precedents. The French revolution, the process of urbanisation during periods of rapid industrialisation, and periods of social and political instability and technological progress during the nineteenth century in Europe, were all moments in which history served as a form of national legitimisation. Characteristic examples of this during the nineteenth century were the preservation movements, founded in order to conserve relics of the past like ancient monuments.[8]

Frank Füredi has explored in detail the increase in commemorations during the 1990s as an expedient measure to counteract the elusive nature of the future after 1989, brought about by the loss of political orientation in the West and East since the breakdown of the balance of power at the end of the Cold War. The ideological vacuum following the dissolution of the eastern bloc led a whole spectrum of political parties and minority groups to reinforce either national or particularist identities by seeking to reappropriate the past. The current race to commemorate the past with anniversaries, monuments, films and books may therefore be defined as a symptom of what Füredi identifies as an international revival of the authority of the past as a foil for the crises of national and particularist histories, one which 'reflects a more pervasive ideological and political crisis in society'.[9] The elaborate large-scale D-Day commemorations in 1994 on the coast of Normandy, involving the former Allied powers with the exception of the former Soviet Union and excluding Germany, were one such symptom of the use of the past in order to symbolically evoke a sense of national unity and international solidarity at a time of relative political disorientation.

The cultural historian Andreas Huyssen also suggests that the present 'memory boom' fulfils a compensatory function, albeit one motivated not by a sense of political disorientation following rapid historical change, but by the cognitive disorientation triggered by electronic and information technologies. Huyssen claims that, 'The memory boom … is a potentially healthy sign of contestation: a contestation of the informational hyperspace and an expression of the basic human need to live in extended structures of temporality.'[10] Museums and monuments thus provide a sense of 'permanence' in a 'culture dominated by the fleeting image of the screen and the immateriality of communications'.[11] We should nevertheless guard against imputing the memory boom primarily to a general contestation of technological progress. Although relics of the past, monuments and museum exhibits harbour a 'material quality' to which people may flee for refuge from a sense of the rapid flux of time, Huyssen overlooks the fact that technology is also an indispensable aid to memory. Printing and computer technology facilitate the storage of large quantities of recorded memories to which political representatives have recourse as proof of their cultural legitimacy – a principle demonstrated in 1993 when the French national archives were the object of fierce debate over the inconsistent criteria applied when granting dispensations to historians seeking access to politically sensitive archives.[12] Furthermore, since computerised archives offer the capacity for storing unprecedented quantities of information, they are as much part of the memory boom as monuments and museums. Although the aura of a historical object resulting from its physical presence, as in museums or memorial sites, may evoke a sense of authenticity and therefore provide a place of historical 'refuge' not offered by technological reproductions or archives, it does not follow that the memory boom as such is a reaction against 'informational hyperspace'. Technically reproduced archives or images may also provide access to the historical past, and images on the screen are not necessarily 'fleeting', as Huyssen suggests, but may be fixed and nuanced over a prolonged period of time, as prints, films or via CD-ROM, for example, and thus act as a support of memory. According to the historian Jacques Le Goff, the 'present excesses of memory' may even be considered as a *product* of technology.[13] At the beginning of the twentieth century, new technical facilities for stocking written, audio and visual data arose parallel to discoveries made in the fields of literature, philosophy, sociology, history and psychoanalysis, which equipped societies with material means to master and underpin their social traditions on the basis of cultural memory.[14] Technological facilities and social memory are therefore not necessarily mutually exclusive.

The paradigm of compensation underpins strategies of legitimisation in almost every society in which history and memory play a prominent role in public discourse. The sheer quantity of monuments, museums and commemorations initiated since the 1970s suggests that history plays a central role in securing tradition and social cohesion on the basis of self-understanding, that historical representations compensate for a lost sense of identity at a time of change and insecurity, and that they are manipulated by symbolic gestures in order to achieve political ends. In short, contemporary memory cultures are generated by a heightened awareness of history that consequently becomes a significant support of collective self-understanding.

Such a normative understanding of memory cultures brings with it shortcomings. First, it assumes a coherent set of shared and binding memories. Since history and memory are rather contingent upon constant interpretation and revision – not only by professional historians, but also by politicians, lawyers, teachers and journalists in the public sphere – they offer a platform for the pluralistic negotiation of historical identities. Second, interpretations of the proliferation of memory cultures as a form of compensation – for rapid historical change, lost political stability or technological advances – are based on purely negative premises. They attribute the rise of memory cultures to the collective desire to flee either from an insecure present or an unimaginable future to the illusions of an imagined past which is assumed to be preferable to the present. In reality, as the historian Hermann Lübbe has shown, the cult of memory is an expression not only of flight from an unbearable present, but also a consolidation of traditions. Monuments and commemorations fulfil a specific historical and political role by contributing towards stocks of national cultural symbols designed to guarantee the future memory of the past. Future and past are, according to Lübbe, complementary. We are not faced with a choice between either utopia or nostalgia, but with a balanced evaluation of the interdependency of past and future, both on the level of personal biography and state historiography.[15] Lübbe argues that interest in the past springs from a desire not only to flee from the present and an unknown future, but also to revive or revise a society's shared memories of the past in order to articulate them afresh in the present. The memory boom sustained since the 1970s should therefore not be understood as a form of cultural pessimism compensating for a sense of loss, or as a collective flight into the past, but as a rearticulation of shared memories of the past which are designed to consolidate the cohesion of contemporary society. Hence the need to examine how memory cultures emerge out of the artistic, narrative, rhetorical or ritual forms of this rearticulation within the field of political communication.

Theories of memory cultures since the 1980s appear to have turned social theories of the 1960s on their head by displacing utopian sentiment with a pervasive international social nostalgia. The argument that memory cultures compensate a sense of unfamiliarity with present-day everyday life following rapid political and technological changes is only valid if the events and images of the past are idealised. The politically motivated inventions of historical traditions are almost invariably based on events of the past that are interpreted in a positive manner: 1848 in Germany, 1789 in France, 1688 or even 6 June 1944 in the U.K. By contrast, recent lobbying by single-issue or minority interest groups has given rise to commemorations recalling events that appear detrimental to the cohesion of national memory. In such cases, states have responded by acknowledging embarrassing episodes of the past precisely in order to negate them with moral discourse or appeals to democratic tradition. Under pressure from the lobbying of witnesses and associations in the 1990s, the French and German governments did precisely this by constructing central monuments to deportation and genocide. How do states incorporate memories of state crimes into their otherwise positive national heritages? Since genuine integration of incompatible collective memories is almost impossible, states generally take a complementary approach, arguing that crimes indeed occurred but that one should learn moral lessons from them for the future and remember democratic traditions. Commemorations of the deportations and genocide of the Second World War upheld a negative example, the rejection of which lent legitimacy to the state management of memory cultures in France and in the united Germany.

The Nation as a Vector of Memory

The cultural legitimacy of nations is sustained by the management and sponsoring of social memory on the basis of historical monuments, commemorations, the mass media and even tourism. Governments play a direct role in promoting exhibitions, commemorations, cultural foundations, monuments and museums – forms of political intervention in the organisation of public representations of history which underpin both social pedagogy and leisure activities with commercial interests for the tourist industry.[16] The recognition that monuments, historical relics exhibited in museums, or public commemorations are a pedagogical asset has led to the creation of state institutions designed to administer cultural heritage, if not 'nationalise' historical memory. Since 1978 in France, 1992 in the U.K. and 1998 in Germany, where governmental departments were appointed to oversee the administration of 'patrimony', 'heritage' and 'culture' respectively, the maintenance of national memory cultures has become an integral part of state policy.

France, for example, has a long history of state institutions created to preserve national culture, dating from the appointment of an Inspector of

Historical Monuments in 1830 and a Commission of Historical Monuments seven years later. This tendency continued after the Second World War with the creation of a Ministry of Culture in 1958, a Director of Patrimony under the patronage of the Ministry of Culture in 1978, and a Heritage Foundation to finance the upkeep of historical monuments in 1996.[17] Following the creation of a State Council for the Memory of War Veterans (Haut Conseil de la Mémoire Combattante) in January 1997, President Chirac and representatives of the Ministry of Veterans Affairs also recommended the increased institutionalisation of the memory of the two world wars.[18] The cultural historian Jean-Michel Leniaud describes the responsibility of the state somewhat bombastically as the 'management … of public opinion on the basis of its affective dimensions'.[19] The introduction of events such as 'The Heritage Year' (L'Année du Patrimoine) in 1980 and the annual conference 'Heritage Talks' (Entretiens du patrimoine) in 1988, continue the tradition of representing state interests in public commemorations but also of stimulating scientific and public discussion.

Similar measures to institutionalise national memory on the basis of artefacts, architecture or historical sites exposed in museums or as memorials have been undertaken in the U.K., where the National Heritage Act was passed before parliament in 1983 and ultimately led to the creation of a new government ministry, the Department of National Heritage, in 1992. The first extensive critique of these measures by Robert Hewison in *The Heritage Industry* (1987) fuelled debate over the role of the state in administrating culture and fostering national historical myths. Questions were raised regarding the degree to which institutions should sponsor historical relics from the past rather than contemporary art, the effect of commercialisation on historical exhibitions and education, the extent to which institutions should represent either 'official' national history or an 'unofficial' history of everyday life, and the relative responsibility of political parties in fostering the national conservation movement, which sparked conflict between the Labour and Conservative parties over the methods and their respective claims to be the legitimate representative of patriotic interests.[20]

In Germany, unlike the U.K. and France, the responsibility for administrating historical culture has traditionally fallen on local governments and associations, and only partly on the federal government. In 1996, there existed a total of twenty-seven associations for the preservation of historical monuments (Denkmalpflege) and twenty-four local history (Heimatkunde) associations, as well as numerous local independent associations such as the Historical Berlin Society. Local history associations are nevertheless grouped under the national umbrella organisation German Local History Association (Deutscher Heimatverbund) in Bonn, and foundations such as the German National Museum in Nuremberg are sponsored directly by the federal government, while some memorials German Resistance Memorial, are co-sponsored by both federal a governments. Cultural administration acquired an additionally natio character in 1998, when the newly elected coalition government of the Social Democratic and Green parties created the new post of State Minister for Culture, whose task was to coordinate federal cultural policies and represent Berlin and cultural projects abroad. The same government also introduced a comprehensive national policy on 'democratic memory culture' in April 1999, designed to coordinate the management and financing of memorials and museums of the National Socialist and communist dictatorships.[21] The implementation of cultural policy nevertheless retained its cooperative central and decentralised character in so far as decisions continued to be regularly obstructed by differences of opinion between local and national governments, as in the case of the Holocaust Monument.

The historian Eric Hobsbawm interprets the survival of national memory cultures as a form of compensation or substitution for supra- and subnational political forces, and refers to the reinforcement of national aspirations in the face of the demise of internationalism as 'a substitute for lost dreams'.[22] In light of the cultural and economic globalisation since 1989, one could go a step further and argue that nationalism arises dialectically in response to and parallel to forms of localisation and globalisation. It is essential to distinguish here between the nationalisms of new states of the former Soviet Union and Yugoslavia, and those of existing states such as France, the U.K. or Germany. The former are largely subject to emerging nationalisms in pursuit of territorial and political sovereignty following the demise of a transnational power, whereas the latter pursue what Hobsbawm defines as a 'defensive' maintenance of already-existing national cultures in the face of an anticipated challenge to sovereignty.[23] In both cases, cultural programmes of commemoration have compensated the limitation of the political (and institutional, economic and legal) sovereignty of states. Emergent nations do this by establishing a culture distinct from the former hegemonic power, whereas defensive nations do so in anticipation of a challenge to sovereignty both from the regions below and supranational states like the European Union from above. There therefore appears to be a causal relation not only between forces of globalisation and localisation, but also between the undermining of national sovereignty and the rise of memory cultures. One could argue that the present nationalisation of memorial events by such institutions as the Department of National Heritage in the U.K. (later renamed the Department for Culture, Media and Sport), the Director of Patrimony in France or the State Minister for Culture in Germany is in part a reaction to globalisation and Europeanisation on the one hand and to regional or ethnic identity politics on the other. The programmes to maintain or reconstruct national memory cultures with commemorative projects in the 1990s, including the commemorations of the Second World War in both its heroic and tragic aspects, must be examined within this political context.

Following the appointment of governmental departments to oversee the administration of heritage, patrimony and culture in the U.K., France and Germany, we must inquire into the consequences of the policies of these institutions for contemporary memory cultures, and whether they signal greater state interventionism. In contrast to nation-building of the nineteenth century, based largely on movements either for the emancipation of individual territories from multinational states, for the integration of separate territories or for the conquest of new territories, most established European nations today strive for the consolidation of nationhood in the face of subnational organisations, supranational bodies, or increased communications, travel and economic exchange. The political will of western European states to commemorate national histories is therefore not designed to achieve emancipation from a hegemonic power but to reassert former sovereignty symbolically. Almost all existing nations of Europe are confronted with challenges of this kind. In the 1990s, the U.K. introduced the progressive devolution of Scotland, Wales and Northern Ireland, the unity of Italy was challenged by the separatist party 'Liga Nord', Spain and France continued to face claims of regional independence movements in Catalonia and the Basque region, and in Corsica, Occitania and Brittany, while Germany attempted to reconcile persisting social and political differences between its former eastern and western zones. The memory boom of the 1990s may therefore be defined as a symbolic form of 'reform' nationalism,[24] consisting in the reaffirmation of sovereignty by an existing state as a method of defence against interior or exterior challenges, a process which involves a state's reform or adaptation to new circumstances. A characteristic example of this phenomenon is the annual European Heritage Days event, when museums and historical sites, normally closed to the public, open their doors during one weekend in mid September, and where the term 'European' is used despite the fact that the sites are of strictly local or national interest: castles, factories, old cinemas, museums, archaeological and architectural sites. In similar fashion, Europe-wide commemorations of the end of the Second World War in 1995 were largely national in character, when political leaders marked the event less frequently in common ceremonies than in a series of ceremonies in separate capital cities. Though similar in form and scope, the memorials and rituals of memory cultures are generally administrated under the aegis of national policies.

Although nations do not have an exclusive claim on memory cultures, recent commemorations and new monuments testify to the dominance of national over regional or supranational forms of memorial discourse. In spite of repeated controversies over the administration of national heritage, both supporters and opponents of governmental intervention appear to be caught in debate over the nation, which remains a yardstick of the scope of memory cultures. The principle of nationhood has traditionally been based on competition between states. Military and economic conflicts are obvious manifestations of such competition. However, most contemporary European states continue inadvertently to sustain memory cultures on a national basis without being in a state of conflict, by appealing to public adhesion to commemorations on the basis of a common history. This leads to the somewhat paradoxical situation in which societies sharing the same (national) type of political system are effectively divided by the very system they tacitly agree to share. Although public interest in memory cultures during the 1990s was an international phenomenon, the issues that galvanised public interest in each case were debated in terms of their national relevance. The use of particular national symbolic reference points continues to divide nations, yet also binds them in the pursuit of a common interest of national memorial specificity. This paradox was reinforced by the fact that debates over national memory were generally conducted within a given structure of national terminologies, institutions and mass media. The very interests, languages and modes of communication assured the limited national scope of each debate from the outset. Moreover, while participants in memory debates within any one country often disagreed over specific issues, their very disagreement stemmed from consensus on the nature of the authority (the nation) whose heritage they perceived to be worthy of dispute.

According to Lowenthal, heritage – the cultivation of the past within a given memory culture – is by definition incomparable and inscrutable, 'a jealously unshared possession'.[25] The fact that history since the nineteenth century has been conceived in terms of nation-building and conflicts, opposing one nation against another, means that references to collective historical memories today generally tap into an existent rhetorical and symbolic repertoire which is similarly national in scope. Thus stock symbols and terminologies of memory provide the medium with which national histories are transmitted from one generation to the next. Generic forms of commemoration (monuments, inscriptions, national holidays, speeches by political leaders, and public debates in the national press and television) acquire political significance through association with non-generic national issues, institutions, symbols and terminologies of historical memory. The nation is clearly an ingrained 'symbolic disposition' of memory cultures. However, the Vél' d'Hiv' and Holocaust Monument demonstrate that the national discursive framework is by no means exclusive, as will be seen in Chapter Seven below.

Analytical Terms of Memory Cultures

Terminology provides an indispensable key to understanding memory cultures as spaces of political communication. The very words employed in public by politicians, journalists, artists and historians reveal how political symbols are conceived and how nations 'narrate' their pasts. From one country to another, public attention traditionally focuses on specific political concepts, as reflected in the mass media. Structural analogies exist between national memory cultures, founded not only on shared founding myths but also on shared terminological assumptions. Focus in France during the commemorations of war crimes was on 'reconciliation'. In Germany it focused largely on 'consensus'. Yet the aim of this study is not to trace the historical origins of national founding myths or of dominant conceptual paradigms, but to explore their usage in the present, suggesting that they act as collective discursive paradigms underpinning memory cultures that are currently undergoing a process of integrating war crimes into the national memorial canon. In this section, I will explain some existing terms used during the memorial debates of the 1990s, but also explore the vocabulary of critics, including professional historians, who are equally part of the memory cultures which they interpret for the public. Central to debates over memory cultures in several countries since the 1980s has been the elusive analytical term 'site of memory', which will receive particular attention in the final part of this section.

The debates that have repeatedly flared up in the media and in books and films have left a legacy of concepts that constitute a linguistic and intellectual heritage in their own right. Historians and politicians use memorial concepts to interpret or legitimate certain memories of events or symbols of the past, such as 'heritage' in the U.K., 'patrimony' in France, and 'culture' in Germany. These terms have become so much part of vocabularies that they pervade all levels of public discourse: everyday, educational, media, political and academic.[26] Beyond historical events themselves, debates about commemorations draw on a wealth of concepts to forge, celebrate and mourn, or to describe and analyse the construction of public memory, and therefore reflect the complexity of attitudes to history within political and public spheres. Many commemorations or monuments thus derive their complexity from the speeches and debates which precede them, or which they produce in their wake, so that their social and political significance can only be deduced within the broad context of verbal and visual media beyond the monument or the initial commemorative event.

There is little consistency between the terms used in different languages such as English, French and German to define the increased social prominence of history and memory. Not only are the themes of debates over historical memory in different countries specific to each nation, but linguistic divergences between vocabularies used to express the past also perpetuate the national confines of the cultures from which they were born, such that debates over historical memory often remain impervious and resist comparison. Memory cultures, perpetuated on a national scale via specific themes and vocabularies in which they are expressed, are thus entrenched within both scientific and everyday discourses. The linguistic variations in English, French and German correspond to both institutional divergences and differences in perceptions of the foundations of national memory cultures. Caution is particularly urgent where terms in English are borrowed from other languages and could foster misunderstandings, such as 'coming to terms with the past', the standard translation of the German term *Vergangenheitsbewältigung*.[27]

Three broad categories of terms referring to history and memory may be identified. The first category, of 'affirmative' terminology, describes national memory cultures in broad and positive terms, the most common examples of which are found in English as 'heritage' and in French as 'patrimony'. These almost synonymous terms acquired their present meaning in the 1970s and refer to collective, generally national, cultural inheritance, having previously signified private family inheritance. According to Françoise Choay, patrimony refers to an institution and a mentality, and is sustained by the accumulation of artistic, everyday or industrial objects that belong to the past.[28] In the U.K., heritage has been subject to severe critical analysis. Hewison defines heritage as 'bogus history',[29] which appeals to a sense of nostalgia, while David Lowenthal suggests that heritage is founded on a sense of religious faith in the past.[30] Both patrimony and heritage are, in part, the product of state cultural policies following the foundation of the French Department of Patrimony and the British Department of National Heritage. In Germany, where cultural administration has traditionally been the responsibility of regional governments, and which had no equivalent comprehensive national institution for the administration of heritage prior to the appointment of a Minister for Cultural Affairs in 1999, there is also no agreed linguistic equivalent to 'heritage' or 'patrimony'. These terms are customarily rendered in German as *Kulturerbe*[31] or *Erbgut*,[32] while the political historian M. Rainer Lepsius makes a further distinction between 'cultural heritage' in general, and 'cultural heritage as historical tradition'.[33]

The second category, of 'critical' terminology, has been generated by interpretations of historical events perceived as catastrophes or sources of collective trauma. Again, this terminology is specific to languages in which relevant discussions have taken place, and resists satisfactory translation. Events in Germany such as the Historians' Dispute in 1986 and the debate since 1989 over the legacy of the German Democratic Republic have enhanced the wealth of terminology describing processes of collectively appropriating or negating the legacies of the National Socialist and communist dictatorships. Terms have therefore evolved in the German language which constitute a subtle rhetorical medium for analysing historical memory. The past may, for example, be 'come to terms with' or 'overcome' (*bewältigt*), 'disposed of' (*entsorgt*), 'reappraised' or 'worked up' (*aufgearbeitet*), 'relinquished' or 'divested of' (*entäußert*),[34] 'distorted' (*verbogen*),[35] 'repressed' (*verdrängt*), 'made reparations for' or 'put right' (*wiedergutgemacht*) or 'worked through' (*durchgearbeitet*). A number of terms referring to memory have also emerged in everyday French, often with moralistic overtones, such as 'memory work' (*travail de la mémoire*),[36] 'memory duty' (*devoir de mémoire*),[37] 'memory act' (*acte de mémoire*),[38] 'memory claim' (*revendication mémorielle*),[39] or the verbal phrase 'to engage in memory work' (*faire oeuvre de mémoire*).[40] When memory cultures relating to the Second World War and state crimes are discussed, they are thus consolidated on the basis of terminology borrowed from legal, moral and psychological discourse.

A third category of terminology referring to the past may be described as 'analytical' in so far as it is used in theoretical writings to define the phenomenon of the social and political role of memory and history. Critics regularly refer in English to 'politics of memory' or 'identity politics',[41] while the similar terms '*politique de la mémoire*' or '*politique du patrimoine*' have entered the French language.[42] A broad variety of analytical definitions have also evolved in German, including 'politics of the past' (*Vergangenheitspolitik*),[43] 'history-politics' (*Geschichtspolitik*)[44] or 'politics with memory' (*Politik mit der Erinnerung*).[45] All these terms emphasise the political instrumentalisation of the past, although they each predicate different means with which political aims are pursued: either with identity, the past in general, history, or memory. The use of each of these terms is not gratuitous, but conveys a specific meaning requiring clarification. The term 'identity' implies a specifically western ideology of cultural essentialism based on the boundedness, continuity, uniqueness and homogeneity of collective memory.[46] The meaning of the 'past' in 'politics of the past' is vague, although the historian Norbert Frei uses it to define the legal implementation of amnesty and the professional reintegration of former members of the National Socialist party in the Federal Republic during the late 1940s and 1950s. 'History' in 'history-politics' presupposes that historical knowledge is promoted in public with the aim of legitimising the interests of political representatives.

These three levels of memorial discourse, whether affirmative, critical or analytical, evolved since the 1970s, the second two levels specifically in response to the legacy of the National Socialist and communist dictatorships. Yet discourse is not merely a product of, but also has an impact on our understanding of contemporary memory cultures. And since participants in debates of the 1990s were not only subjects *of* new conceptual interpretations of memory cultures, but also subject to existing interpretations, one should approach these with caution.[47] If we consider the literal sense of the definitions of the 'politics of' either 'identity', 'the past', or 'history', for example, none of these categories encompasses the inevitably ambiguous understandings of history generated by symbolic representations. These terms lend themselves poorly to the specific interpretation of monuments. Representations constitute an element of formal mediation between the interests of political actors, associations, artists, and the public understanding of the past. Monuments and commemorations alone can express neither political interests nor the collective self-understanding or 'identity' of a society, and do not lay claim to historical truth. Instead, their significance is contingent on sculptural forms and on their peripheral rhetorical and ritual forms of mediation. As expressions of heritage rather than history, they may appeal not to a social demand for scientifically grounded historical facts but to a 'faith' (Lowenthal) which relies on an understanding of the past derived from forms in which the past is publicly represented and understood and in which, from a scientific point of view, the past is potentially misrepresented and misunderstood.[48]

The analytical terms of memory named above presuppose a binary relation between present-day political interests on the one hand and the utility of 'the past', 'history', 'memory' or 'patrimony' on the other, and do not offer specific insight into the rhetorical and symbolic *medium* by which this relation takes effect. The cases of the Vél' d'Hiv' and Holocaust Monument were regularly approached with similar terms, indicative of an instrumental understanding of public art. Yet historical and political studies of public symbolics often lose sight of the contingent artistic artefacts at the centre of their analysis. In reality, both the Paris and Berlin monuments acquired symbolic significance as a result of their relation to surrounding architectural sites in Paris and Berlin and as a result of public debate in which political issues were derived directly from rhetoric on art and on modes of commemoration. According to the art historian Walter Grasskamp, the political dimension of conflicts over art in public places has not been given adequate attention. 'If atomic power, disarmament or birth control are the object of conflict', he claims, 'why should highly conflictory art be an exception to this rule?'[49] Following Grasskamp's advice, the public outcries and exchanges of complex arguments on the occasion of the Vél' d'Hiv' and Holocaust Monument merit analysis as discursive events in their own right. Party-political interests were certainly at stake in these debates. Presidential authority (in France) and parliamentary authority (in Germany) were ultimately responsible for settling the disputes. And the monuments alone proved to be ineffective platforms with which to rally cohesive public support. Yet monuments and their accompanying commemorations, that is, media of symbolic and rhetorical *representation*, nevertheless were the original and constant focal points of the debates.

For the purposes of this study, I have used the generic term 'memory culture'[50] to describe the social context in which monuments and commemorations take effect. This expression may easily be translated into most languages, as '*Erinnerungskultur*' or '*culture de la mémoire*' for example, and may refer to any community – local, national or supranational – which shares a repertoire of common memories and which is not closed and static, but permits multiple contiguity between one set of memories and another, and which is inherently conflictory. The case studies of the Vél' d'Hiv' and Holocaust Monument, as well as the relative mutual imperviousness of memorial terminologies in different languages, have shown that the internal openness and transparency of memory cultures (for people versed in the established terms of any one debate) do not prevent or even contradict their external closure (to people not versed in the terms of debate). Lowenthal's suggestion that memory cultures are 'jealously unshared' is corroborated by the historian Jan Assmann's definition of a memory culture as a chosen *community*.[51] Yet both Lowenthal and Assmann overlook the possibility that multiple identities, whether local, national or supranational, may exist simultaneously within one person or group. Memory cultures are not intrinsically mutually exclusive and may subsist parallel to other community bonds such as ethnicity or religion.

This brief survey of the terms describing monuments and memory demonstrates that the very means of debating in each country are largely specific to national memory cultures. If we assume that history, or the past and memory in general, are the object of 'battles over political concepts' between opposing 'communities of interpretation',[52] we must ask in what way not only symbolic, everyday, political and affirmative, but also how critical and analytical concepts of research on memory are subject to the very political functions they are designed to expose and interpret. Do battles between communities of interpretation entrench the closed, exclusive nature of communities participating in them, or do they reveal structural analogies with other memorial communities? And do scientific analyses of memory cultures also entrench the traditional mutual exclusivity of memory cultures? The study of memorial discourses other than one's own necessarily entails a process of translation and comparison which most specialists of memory cultures like Frei, Leniaud, Nora and Reichel have neglected. The present study of memory cultures is an attempt not to entrench but to diffuse the perceived uniqueness of national memory cultures by exposing some patterns common to commemorative processes taking place in different countries.

One of the most prolific concepts and tools of research relevant to the field of memory politics is 'site of memory', most recently employed to analyse the relation between memory and nationhood in contemporary France on the basis of shared historical symbols. This is one of the few terms adopted internationally in analyses of memory cultures, and which is used in both everyday and academic discourses. In the remainder of this chapter, I propose to explain the sense of this complex term with respect to its underlying political premises. At first glance, the Vél' d'Hiv' and Holocaust Monument merit categorisation as 'sites of memory' according to Nora's definition. However, in light of controversies over the crimes of the Second World War in France and Germany, they also require us to redefine some of Nora's presumptions about the function of historical memory as a force of national cohesion.[53]

'Site of Memory': Critique of Pierre Nora's Theory of Memory Cultures

The notion 'site of memory' became known as the title of a seven-volume work edited by the historian Pierre Nora that traces the history of symbols of French national memory. Consistent with the diversity and conflict inherent in French history, *Les Lieux de mémoire* projects a pluralist understanding of memory; not collective memory, therefore, but a collection or constellation of memories which, in various combinations, constitute the memory of French individuals. Paradoxically, however, while Nora's work testifies to the pluralist and fragmented nature of contemporary memory, it also projects a unitary history under the all-encompassing, though elusive, banner of Frenchness.

Since its inception, this term has almost become a commonplace in the French language. President François Mitterrand used it in his inaugural speech of the memorial museum of Izieu, a children's internment camp during the Second World War, promising to transform this place into a 'site of memory and education'.[54] In the annual speech on the a 'National Day of Commemoration of the Racist and Anti-Semitic Persecutions' on 20 July 1997, the French prime minister Lionel Jospin also used the term twice without explaining its meaning,[55] thus assuming that it was well understood by the general public. However, the difficulty in grasping the precise meaning of this term is reflected in the multiple ways in which it is translated into English, including 'place', 'site', or 'realm' of memory.[56] According to its author, a 'site' or 'place' of memory refers to the various symbolic 'sites' or cultural expressions of collective memory such as geographical regions, monuments, commemorative ceremonies, well-known personalities, political movements, professional institutions or social habits described by Nora as the 'focal points of our national heritage'.[57] A site of memory may be defined, therefore, as a cultural support for a particular shared memory. It is not necessarily a topographical site, however, such as a historical monument, for it may be more loosely defined as a focal point of emotional attachment including broad cultural characteristics such as gastronomy or revolution (in France), and Luther or the Weimar Republic (in Germany). In 1993, this term was even introduced into the *Grand Robert* dictionary, which defines a site of memory as a 'significant unit, ideal or material in nature, which the will of people or the effect of time have turned into a symbolic element of a certain community'.[58] The emphasis here on the signification pertaining to a 'symbolic element' of a 'community' brought about by 'will' or the 'effect of time' suggests that a site of memory is essentially a semantic element or tool which renders the self-understanding of a society intelligible on the basis of historical origins ('will' or 'the effect of time') and contemporary political utility (the cohesion of a 'community'). According to definition, therefore, sites of memory act as vehicles for shared memories underpinning social cohesion.

Nora is concerned less with establishing the veracity of historical facts than with the ways in which the past is understood and appropriated within contemporary consciousness. He posits the 'historical present' as a branch of historical study in its own right. Unlike contemporary history, which analyses events and phenomena from the recent past (a period beginning with a given historical rupture such as a revolution or war, or a period measured according to the limits of living memory, for example), the historical present focuses strictly on current or *actual* phenomena (those acting or happening in the present). Its essential medium is therefore memory, an elusive support which lacks the historical legitimacy of documentary evidence available in the practice of contemporary history, and one which focuses on memory as an object of study for its own sake: the medium by which the past is rendered intelligible, and the resulting consciousness it sustains.

It is precisely in their impact on the present day and on the *intelligibility* of the past that monuments play a key role. Monuments are media of historical interpretation that acquire particular effect via the mass media, as in the cases of the Vél' d'Hiv' and Holocaust Monument. They also contribute to a partial displacement of the authority over collective consciousness from professional historians to journalists and public opinion, invited to participate in the process of fixing the present as it becomes past via the mass media. The shift of authority over the meaning of the past has coincided with a radical modification of the supports sustaining collective memory. Historians, according to the positivist nineteenth-century model of historiography, traditionally have recourse to documentary evidence stored in archives and disseminate their work in educational institutions and publications in order to legitimate a specific reconstruction of the facts of the past worthy of social consensus or collective memory. Public opinion, on the other hand, renders its understanding of the present intelligible and legitimate on the basis of significant collective symbols. The Vél' d'Hiv' commemorations from 1992, the official inauguration of the Central Memorial of the Federal Republic of Germany in the Neue Wache in 1993, the project for a Holocaust Monument in Berlin from 1988, or the international fiftieth anniversaries of the Second World War, were all designed to foster national consciousness in this way. They are therefore remarkable examples of the dynamic social force of commemorative events, in which the influence of the mass media and public opinion is paramount, and where the historian's pedagogical role is reduced to that of a critic or moral guardian. Sites of memory thus take over from documentary archives as *symbolic* archives supporting a type of memory which Nora describes as 'archival' – albeit not in order to compare memory to a state archive or data bank, but to underline its dependence on external recorded material foreign to the remembering organism: a 'prosthesis memory', or 'recording memory that delegates to the archive the responsibility of remembering '.[59]

None of the contributions to the collections *Les Lieux de mémoire* and *Deutsche Erinnerungsorte* draws specific attention to the formal and discursive aspects of either ritual means of commemoration (via speeches or monuments, for example) or the public debate about these means. These collections of essays focus on existing sites of memory, those that are assumed to have already become an integral part of the imagination of most French and German citizens. By contrast, a close reading of the discursive and symbolic elaborations of contemporary sites of memory *as they emerge* requires us to dispense with a purely historical account of their genesis. The emergence of the Vél' d'Hiv' and Holocaust Monument has shown that these sites are not natural or given, and that their existence may be imputed less to intrinsic pedagogical qualities than to their formal appeal and extrinsic contextual popularisation.

The criterion common to the memories projected in works on French and German sites of memory remains the nation. While the model of 'national memory' is conceived by Nora as an alternative to coercive republican 'national history',[60] it nevertheless reflects the republican model of cultural integration. According to Nora, memory is all-pervasive and neutralises division. 'Gaullists and Communists', 'The French and Foreigners' or 'Catholics and Laymen' are each presented as *single* sites of memory, as cultural appropriations of a politically inert past. However, some of the most stirring symbols of French culture during the 1980s and 1990s such as the 'Islamic headscarf' or the 'suburb' (resulting from controversies over Muslim schoolgirls claiming the right to wear the veil in secular state schools or over social unrest in the immigrant ghettos of large cities) are absent from *Les Lieux de mémoire*. Likewise,

German citizens of Turkish descent, war refugees and asylum-seekers are absent from the three-volume study of German sites of memory, *Deutsche Erinnerungsorte*, as its editors Etienne François and Hagen Schulze point out. These 'sites' are too contested to be subsumed to 'patrimonial memory' ('*mémoire patrimoine*'), defined by Nora as a cultural bond that has lost its former political or social appeal.[61] Yet these expressions of postcolonial and postwar deviance from French and German cultural uniformity do merit attention as sites of memory, although they challenge the conventional national framework of memory in these projects. Moreover, although the French project contains a chapter on Vichy, and its German counterpart takes ample account of Auschwitz both in the explicit discussion of 'guilt' (to which an entire section is devoted in the first volume) and in the memorial construction of such 'sites' as Nietzsche, Weimar and the Volkswagen motor company, the question remains whether memory cultures and monuments founded in memory of crimes committed during the Second World War can be defined as sites of memory. Can contested symbols build collective memory? And what are the consequences for a national collective if, as the historian Jan-Holger Kirsch argues, 'Declarations of belief in historical guilt and declarations of belief in the nation are no longer perceived to be contradictory'?[62] In the following chapters, I will propose an alternative understanding of sites of memory to that of Nora, François and Schulze, one that suggests that sites of memory owe their existence precisely to the contestedness of the memories associated with them.

Notes

1. See Frank Füredi, *Mythical Past, Elusive Future. History and Society in an Anxious Age*, London: Pluto Press, 1992.
2. Mary Fulbrook, *German National Identity after the Holocaust*, Cambridge: Polity Press, 1999, 178.
3. David Sears, 'Symbolic Politics: A Socio-Psychological Theory', in Shanto Iyengar and William McGuire, eds, *Explorations in Political Psychology*, Durham & London: Duke University Press, 1993, 113–49, 121.
4. Füredi, *Mythical Past, Elusive Future*, 3.
5. 'La passion du passé', editorial of *Le Monde*, 2 February 1995.
6. Annette Wieviorka, '1992. Réflexions sur une commémoration', *Annales ESC* no. 3, 1993, 703–14, 703.
7. Cf. Jean-Michel Leniaud, *L'Utopie française. Essai sur le patrimoine*, Paris: Mengès, 1992, 29–32.
8. Preservationist laws and institutions founded at this time include the Ancient Monuments Protection Act (Britain, 1882), the Loi sur la protection des monuments historiques (France, 1887 and 1913), and the Heimatschutz association (Germany, 1904). Cf. David Lowenthal, *The Past is a Foreign Country*, Cambridge: Cambridge University Press, 1985, 394f.
9. Füredi, *Mythical Past, Elusive Future*, 22, 36. Cf. J. H. Plumb, *The Death of the*

Past, London: Penguin Books, 1969; Wolfrum, 'Geschichte als Politikum – Geschichtspolitik', *Neue politische Literatur* no. 3, 1996, 376–401, 393.
10. Andreas Huyssen, *Twilight Memories. Marking Time in a Culture of Amnesia*, New York & London: Routledge, 1995, 9.
11. Ibid., 255.
12. See Sonia Combe, *Archives interdites. Les peurs françaises face à l'Histoire contemporaine*, Paris: Albin Michel, 1994.
13. Jacques Le Goff, *Histoire et mémoire*, Paris: Gallimard, 1988, 110.
14. Ibid., 175.
15. Hermann Lübbe, *Die Gegenwart der Vergangenheit. Kulturelle und politische Funktionen des historischen Bewußtseins*, Oldenburg: Heinz Holberg Verlag, 1985, 22.
16. Cf. Kevin Walsh, *The Representation of the Past: Museums and Heritage in the Post-modern World*, London: Routledge, 1992, 176.
17. See Françoise Choay, *L'Allégorie du patrimoine*, Paris: Seuil, 1992, 10; 'Castles and Heirs', *The Economist*, 27 July 1996, 28–9.
18. See Jean-Michel Aphatie and Pascale Robert-Diarel, 'Vers la création d'un ministère de la "mémoire"?', *Le Monde*, 18/19 July 1999, 5.
19. Leniaud, *L'Utopie française*, 28.
20. See Raphael Samuel, *Theatres of Memory*, vol. 1, *Past and Present in Contemporary British Culture*, London & New York: Verso, 1994, 291, 297.
21. Policy consisted in the coordination of projects and an increase in the annual federal budget for memorials, essentially original historical sites, from 30 to 50 million deutschmarks. See *Verhandlungen des Deutschen Bundestags. Stenographischer Bericht – 14. Wahlperiode – 35. Sitzung*, 22 April 1999, 2864–75; Christine Tilmann, 'Naumann kündigt mehr Bundesmittel für Gedenkstätten an', *Der Tagesspiegel*, 24 July 1999, 29.
22. Eric Hobsbawm, *Nations and Nationalism Since 1780*, Cambridge: Cambridge University Press, 1990, 178. Hobsbawm reiterates this thesis in the concluding chapter of *The Age of Extremes. The Short Twentieth Century 1914–1991*, London: Michael Joseph, 1994, 576f.
23. Hobsbawm, *The Age of Extremes*, 576.
24. Peter Alter, *Nationalismus*, Frankfurt am Main: Suhrkamp, 1985, 39ff.
25. Lowenthal, 'Identity, Heritage, and History', 48.
26. Levels defined by Siegfried Jäger, *Kritische Diskursanalyse*, 183.
27. See Marc Bloch's comparison of historiographical terminologies in relation to problems arising from translation: 'Pour une histoire comparée des sociétés européennes' (1928), in *Histoire et Historiens*, Paris: Armand Colin, 1995, 94–123.
28. Choay, *L'Allégorie du patrimoine*, 9.
29. Hewison, *The Heritage Industry*, 144.
30. David Lowenthal, *The Heritage Crusade and the Spoils of History*, 2.
31. Joseph Hanimann, 'Das schwierige Erinnern', *Frankfurter Allgemeine Zeitung*, 13 January 1997, 25.
32. Lowenthal, *The Heritage Crusade and the Spoils of History*, 4.
33. '*Kulturelles Erbe als geschichtliche Überlieferung*'. M. Rainer Lepsius, 'Die Teilung Deutschlands und die deutsche Nation', in Lepsius, *Demokratie in Deutschland*, Göttingen: Vandenhoeck & Ruprecht, 1993, 196–228, 219.
34. Brigitte Rauschenbach, ed., *Erinnern, Wiederholen, Durcharbeiten. Zur Psycho-Analyse deutscher Wenden*, Berlin: Aufbau Taschenbuch Verlag, 1992, 115.
35. Hilmar Hoffmann, ed., *Gegen den Versuch, Vergangenheit zu verbiegen*, Frankfurt am Main: Athenäum, 1987.

36. Olivier Abel, *Libération*, 9 October 1997.
37. Used by Lionel Jospin in his speech at the Vél' d'Hiv' commemoration 1997. See 'Un gouvernement, une administration de notre pays, ont alors commis l'irréparable', *Le Monde*, 22 July 1997. See also Rousso's critique of the term '*devoir de mémoire*' in Rousso and Petit, *La Hantise du passé*, 14.
38. Jean Dujardin, *Le Monde*, 1 October 1997.
39. Annette Wieviorka, '1992. Réflexions sur une commémoration', 713.
40. Henri Hajdenberg, *Le Monde*, 1 October 1997.
41. Eric Hobsbawm, 'Identity Politics and the Left', *New Left Review* no. 217, 1996, 38–47.
42. Marc Guillaume, *La Politique du patrimoine*, Paris: Galilée, 1980.
43. Norbert Frei, *Vergangenheitspolitik. Die Anfänge der Bundesrepublik und die NS-Vergangenheit*, Munich: C.H. Beck, 1996, 13f.
44. Reichel, *Politik mit der Erinnerung*, 13ff; Wolfrum, 'Geschichte als Politikum – Geschichtspolitik', *Neue Politische Literatur* no. 3, 1996, 376–401.
45. Reichel, *Politik mit der Erinnerung*.
46. See Richard Handler, 'Is "Identity" a Useful Cross-cultural Concept?' in John Gillis, ed., *Commemorations. The Politics of National Identity*, Princeton: Princeton University Press, 1994, 27–40.
47. Cf. Stuart Hall, 'The Work of Representation', 56; Raoul Girardet, *Mythes et mythologies politiques*, Paris: Seuil, 1986, 182, n. 90.
48. Lowenthal explores modes of error and fabrication inherent to public representations of history. See Lowenthal, 'Fabricating Heritage'.
49. Grasskamp, 'Invasion aus dem Atelier. Kunst als Störfall', in Grasskamp, ed., *Unerwünschte Monumente. Moderne Kunst im Stadtraum*, 141–69, 168.
50. Reichel defines a memory culture as something that is 'rendered present in the media', subjected to 'a varied form of expression', and open to 'controversial interpretations'. Reichel, *Politik mit der Erinnerung*, 18.
51. Jan Assmann, *Das Kulturelle Gedächtnis. Schrift, Erinnerung und politische Identität in frühen Hochkulturen*, Munich: Beck, 1992, 30.
52. Terms used by Wolfrum, 'Die Preußen-Renaissance', in Martin Sabrow, ed., *Verwaltete Vergangenheit. Geschichtskultur und Herrschaftslegitimation in der DDR*, Leipzig: Akademische Verlagsanstalt, 1997, 148, 150; and Alfred Lorenzer, *Sprachspiel und Interaktionsformen*, Frankfurt am Main: Suhrkamp, 1977, 16.
53. For a comprehensive assessment of Nora's work, see Carrier, 'Places, Politics and the Archiving of Contemporary Memory in Pierre Nora's *Les Lieux de mémoire*', in Susannah Radstone, ed., *Memory and Methodology*, Oxford: Berg, 2000, 37–58.
54. *Le Monde*, 24/25 April 1994, 8.
55. *Le Monde*, 22 July 1997, 8.
56. Arthur Goldhammer's translation of this term as 'realm of memory' is rather misleading, since its etymological roots in the old French *reialme* and Latin *regimen* signify 'rule'. The royal connotations of this term suggest a monarchic, prerevolutionary context of French sites of memory, which effectively disregards the wealth of postrevolutionary symbols of national memory in France. See Nora, ed., *The Realms of Memory*.
57. Pierre Nora, 'Das Abenteuer der *Lieux de mémoire*', 83.
58. *Le Grand Robert de la langue française*, 1993.
59. Nora, 'Entre mémoire et histoire', xxviii, xxvi.
60. Nora, 'L'ère de la commémoration', in Nora, ed., *Les Lieux de mémoire*, vol. III, *Les France* 3, Paris: Gallimard, 1993, 977–1012, 1010.

61. Nora, 'La nation-mémoire', in Nora, ed., *Les Lieux de mémoire,* vol. II. *La Nation* 3, Paris: Gallimard, 1986, 647–58, 650.
62. Jan-Holger Kirsch, *Nationaler Mythos oder historische Trauer? Der Streit um ein zentrales 'Holocaust-Mahnmal' für die Berliner Republik,* Cologne & Vienna: Böhlau, 2003, 317.

7

The Postnational Memorial Paradigm

The monumental historiographical projects on sites of memory in France and Germany, *Les Lieux de mémoire* and *Deutsche Erinnerungsorte*, provide pedagogical models for understanding the historical foundations of contemporary memory cultures in these two countries. Both projects are highly informative, thorough in their treatment of historical facts, and theoretically innovative. The notions that collective symbols are today 'patrimonial' instead of partisan foci of collective memory, that we are subjects of 'archival' memory, that 'present time' is a historiographical category in which societies forge a cohesive self-understanding on the basis of shared symbols of the past, and that the mass media have an overwhelming influence on our understandings of history, have enriched research on the transmission and political uses of historical knowledge. Nevertheless, the historical studies of sites of memory contained in these projects seldom venture into the field of the very recent past as it happens, as implied by the category of a history of present time. They also pay scant attention to the forms of rhetorical and artistic *communication* of historical knowledge on which the public understanding of sites of memory depends. Moreover, the chosen historical method – the study of 'expressive forms of collective memory that have been in existence for a certain time and are fully formed'[1] – by definition marginalises sites that constitute the collective memory of ethnic minorities, women or refugees, as indicated in Chapter Six. By appealing for the stabilisation of memory cultures, these projects address sites of memory which already fit into the national framework. Some of the theoretical premises of Nora's work on sites of memory, including the idea that national traditions are now upheld artificially by symbolic props, and that the mass media has partially substituted the authority of historical science over the formation of historical consciousness, are borne out by the memory cultures emerging from Holocaust remembrance. Yet the Vél' d'Hiv' and Holocaust Monument, whose broad public resonance leads us to assume that we are dealing with archetypal sites of memory, violate many of these categories. The Vél' d'Hiv' and Holocaust Monument etched themselves onto public awareness not in retrospect but as they evolved in the present, they were essentially artistic and rhetorical in substance, and addressed an event – state persecution, deportation and genocide – which does not conform to patrimonial or patriotic sentiment. In order to put Nora's concept to the test, the following chapter proposes a revision of the notion of 'sites of memory' in light of the debates over the monumental sites in France and Germany during the 1990s. How does the painful remembrance of the genocide against the Jews of Europe become, via a complex procedure of national, generational, religious and compensatory encodement, incorporated into the national memory cultures of France and Germany? Can nations commemorate their own crimes and, if so, how do they then continue to lay claim to legitimacy as bases for cultural cohesion? Beyond the national memorial paradigms of compensation and consolidation described above, the symbolic and rhetorical constructions of the Vél' d'Hiv' and Holocaust Monument were governed by what may be called 'postnational' paradigms: of negative compensation and transnationality.

'National Monument': a Misnomer?

To what extent are monuments and memory cultures national in scope and appeal? The question whether monuments in the 1990s can legitimately be called 'national', and therefore whether nations are 'capable of monuments' (*'denkmalfähig'*),[2] that is, capable of possessing monuments which fulfil a national representational function, appears to have been answered affirmatively by the prolonged but successful campaigns for the Vél' d'Hiv' and Holocaust Monument. And despite legitimate claims to alternative non-national forms of social adherence, whether regional, ethnic, transnational or cosmopolitan, history continues to be widely understood and projected in the public sphere as the consequence and continuing responsibility of nations. Monuments representing wars, cultural achievements and political figures generally underpin mental structures based on national history that are in turn sustained by national media and languages. Moreover, smaller groups laying claim to regional or ethnic identities, or larger groups representing European, transnational or religious identities, are often defined only in relation to and as negations of existing nation-states in so far as they contest the exclusive legitimacy of the claim of nations to historical memory. Do debates over fiftieth anniversary commemorations of the Second World War, including the Vél' d'Hiv' and Holocaust Monument, continue this trend or do they urge us to redefine national memory cultures in France and Germany? Do these symbolic prisms of public attitudes to history foster conventional national identity and have an integrative effect on memory cultures, or do they undermine national consensus?

It is tempting to deduce the aptitude of monuments for national commemorations from their form. Abstraction, for example, can be socially binding, since it appeals to the greatest number of people who may interpret an abstract sign in a way that corresponds to their own interests. However, abstract signs are less emotionally binding than figurative images of national heroes, for example. A quantitative increase in consensus entails a qualitative decline in the value of consensus associated with a historical monument. Moreover, although almost all shortlisted models for the Holocaust Monument were abstract and controversial, whereas the Vél' d'Hiv' model was figurative and not controversial, we cannot conclude from this that the greater public approval of the Vél' d'Hiv' resulted from its higher degree of figuration. The omission of public discussion over the form of this monument does not reflect an anachronistic public approval of figurative art in France, but rather the suppression of information in a debate that focused primarily on the issue of a presidential speech. By contrast, the prolonged failure to implement a decision over the Berlin project was provoked not by disorientation resulting from people's incapacity to 'identify' with abstract symbols, but by a fundamental scepticism towards the very process of commemorating and erecting a central, national monument to the genocide. This scepticism was further aggravated by the artistic means of commemoration under discussion. Whereas the Vél' d'Hiv' is located on an original historical site, a physical trace of the past with documentary value, the Holocaust Monument was deliberately projected as a purely artistic form of commemoration. It encouraged active participation not in the process of understanding historical traces, as advocated by the association Active Museum in Berlin, but of understanding purely artistic forms of commemoration detached from the historical significance of a specific site. Dispute was provoked partially by the challenge of selecting an appropriate form, but essentially by the question whether the artistic monumental genre in itself was an adequate means of commemoration.

Nations emerge and thrive on the basis of a number of concomitant factors. The political scientist Anthony Smith defines nationhood as 'a named human population sharing an historic territory, common myths and historical memories, a mass, public culture, a common economy and common legal rights, and duties for all members'.[3] Additional cultural linchpins of nationhood include the perceived cohesion of in- and out-groups, ethnic identity, a common religion, a common language, and collectively recognised symbols with which historical origins, myths, and narratives are associated. Each of these factors is more or less dependent on a public opinion informed by the mass media. Although culture is indispensable to social identity, neither collective symbols nor the audiences to which they appeal can be assumed to be strictly national in scope. Does prolonged public dispute over historical symbols such as the Vél' d'Hiv' or Holocaust Monument suffice to define these symbols as national? What proportion of the French or German populations can be said to harbour shared historical memories relating directly to single symbols or commemorations? In reality, neither the Vél' d'Hiv' nor Holocaust Monument embody the criterion of sharedness underscored in Smith's definition of nationhood. Memories of the Second World War are a constant source of disagreement, suggesting that, although many people share memories of the historical event, the meanings and moral and emotional attitudes associated with them are anything but shared. It is for this reason that the strategies employed by political representatives with respect to rhetorical or symbolic forms were rather intended to neutralise conflicting opinions by projecting an alternative consensual basis for a national community, one founded on a largely abstract *idea* of nationhood. The rhetoric used in the commemorative speeches on the site of the Vél' d'Hiv' and the search for an ideal monumental form in Berlin were essentially designed to appeal to a sense of nationhood grounded not in a strict consensus among individuals, but in a tacit agreement to prioritise collective memory of the persecution and genocide without urging agreement over interpretations of this event. One cannot underestimate the political potency of what the historian David Kertzer calls 'solidarity without ... uniformity of belief' on which national communities continue to build cohesion. 'Ritual,' claims Kertzer, 'is a means by which we express our social dependence; what is important in ritual is our common participation and emotional involvement, not the specific rationalizations by which we account for the rites. ... Ritual can serve political organizations by producing bonds of solidarity without requiring uniformity of belief.'[4]

One of the pioneering studies on nationalism by Karl Deutsch, *Nationalism and Social Communication* (1953), explores the formation of national consciousness on the basis of social communication. Deutsch argues that national consciousness is expressed in the form of actions, cultural artefacts or institutions that are qualified verbally with symbolic political values. Character attributes such as wit, thoroughness, ingenuity, or the possession of a language, a country or state are items of information which people habitually qualify with secondary symbolic information like 'French', 'German' or 'American'. Nationalities are thus conceived as symbolic or somewhat unreal because they are generally defined but naturally cannot be equated with qualities such as individual character attributes, languages or states. 'The symbols of nationality are all in the last analysis adverbs or adjectives: they are not things or acts, but labels added to objects or actions. The words "German" or "Argentine" or "English" mean nothing in themselves; they mean something only if they are understood as being added to the words "persons", or "language", or "country", or "habits and customs", or "state".'[5] In light of Deutsch's definition of national consciousness, historical events could also be considered as primary actions which are rendered national by their association with adjectives of nationality such as 'French' or 'German' and their transmission via national channels of communication such as the mass media, a monument situated in the capital city, or commemorations attended by political representatives.

Deutsch's insistence on the linguistic constructedness of nationhood exposes the error of assuming too readily that symbols are truly national. The Vél' d'Hiv' and Holocaust Monument are two such examples of linguistic labelling, revealed to be not inherently national but *named* as such in the interest of interpreting history with respect to political aims of the 1990s. Responsibility for the round-ups at the Vél' d'Hiv' in 1942 was not national in scope, for they were ordered by German, not French authorities, and the participation of French people in the round-ups was local, involving the Parisian police force and public transport.[6] A similar argument may be applied to the Holocaust Monument, whose organisers overstated (in the initial petition) its national political significance as 'a duty for all Germans in East and West'. The fact that an opinion poll conducted in August 1995 stated that only 35 per cent of interviewees 'had heard about the debate'[7] suggests that remembrance was not in reality performed as a national group action as a result of this one central monument. Public appeals to lessons to be learnt from history and to moral responsibility are justified, but it is questionable whether such responsibility should or can be conceived in national terms, and whether single monuments are adequate supports for such pedagogical aims. In order to define these monuments literally as national today, one would have to perform a leap of faith linking a particular historical event, embodied in a single monumental site, to a group of people who understand themselves collectively as members of a socially homogeneous and historically continuous nation. Such a link between a single symbol and a nation necessitates a process of dual sublimation in which first the symbol, as a channel of social communication, is perceived as an emblem for a historical event to which, second, a label of (French or German) nationality is attached in order to lend it collective appeal in the present.

The social construction of the Vél' d'Hiv' and Holocaust Monument as national historical symbols may clearly be attributed to national channels of social communication arising as a result of controversy. But these monuments did not only acquire national significance by being named as such, their political significance was also established by means of additional formal mediation: the national mass media, the use of capital cities as a symbolic backdrop, and the involvement of state leaders. The reason why these monuments, rather than one of the numerous existing monuments, historical sites or commemorative dates, were designated as key national symbols in the 1990s also lies in the intensity and duration of public controversies conducted on their behalf and in the elaborate forms of their supplementary communication via emblems, speeches, exhibitions, media debates and petitions. It is unlikely that the site in Paris would have taken on monumental political significance if the Comité Vél' d'Hiv' 42 association had not initially urged Mitterrand to make a formal verbal declaration, if he had not refused their request, and if Chirac had not subsequently acquiesced. Likewise, the Holocaust Monument acquired national significance due to the stringent conditions of petitions, the initial resistance of victim associations and political factions at local and national levels, and the irresolvable challenge of selecting a single artistic form. The quality of these sites of memory derives from their capacity to focus public attention on a single symbol. In this way, the Vél' d'Hiv' and Holocaust Monument evolved into two of the most expressive and politically explosive historical sites of memory of the Second World War. They convey not history, but perceptions and interpretations of history pertinent to the 1990s.

The reason why the misnomer 'national monument' continues to have a rhetorically persuasive impact in the public sphere stems from the residual symbolic disposition according to which monuments are conceived as focal points of social consensus. The relation between a monument and a nation implied by the rhetoric of national monuments is not essentially rhetorical, however; monuments do not possess a metaphorical or even synechdochic value, for there exists no resemblance between a monument and a nation, and the smaller symbolic part cannot be understood to stand for the whole. In other words, the consensus to which advocates of monuments regularly appeal, and on which the legitimacy of a monument depends, resides in the shared received conviction that a monument renders the past collectively intelligible for a group known as the 'nation'. National monuments fulfil a role akin to that of political myths, which traditionally reinforce a sense of common identity and social cohesion on the basis of an imagined fusion of individual and collective memories.[8]

It is precisely to myths of ideal and holistic conceptions of nationhood that petitions for the Vél' d'Hiv' and Holocaust Monument appealed. The suggestion in the first petition of June 1992 that the president's speech may cure 'ill French collective memory' and repair 'the very idea of the French Republic' won presidential approval when Chirac responded by vowing to uphold 'a certain idea of France' and 'humanist values'. The petition for the Holocaust Monument similarly promised to repair the moral 'disgrace' and fulfil the 'duty' of a collectivity conceived in imprecise terms as 'all Germans'. Echoes of these stock definitions of ideal or holistic nationhood during the discussions over these sites further reinforced their authority. Implicit in much public discourse about the crimes of the Second World War in Germany is the idea that the 'Germans' whose duty it is to build the monument are those who share a common descent from perpetrators – an exclusive conception of a memory culture which perpetuates an ethnic notion of nationhood not unlike that upheld by the very state whose crimes 'Germans' today seek to symbolically repair. The historian Hanno Loewy has demonstrated how public discourse on the Second World War in contemporary Germany draws on a 'tragic consciousness' evoking an identity 'based on a common national fate'. More significantly, argues Loewy, 'such a definition of the German nation excludes all those who do not belong to the German community of fate because they can't be confronted with German "disgrace": Jews, immigrant workers, refugees.'[9] It is the force of such ideal and holistic or even ethnic models of nationhood that determined the criteria on which the quest for consensus and reconciliation with respect to the monuments was based, precisely because these models were long-term conventions that predated the Second World War and onto which memories of this event were rhetorically grafted.

Negative Compensation

The drive to build monuments in memory of victims of the persecution and genocide of the Second World War has different causes in each country. In France, this trend may be explained as a reaction to the earlier occultation of memories of Jewish victims under de Gaulle, exemplified by the Memorial of the Martyrs of Deportation in Paris. Here, victimhood is conceived in universal and national terms, symbolised in a tomb containing an unknown victim within a monumental complex dedicated to 'French' deportees. In Germany, the Holocaust Monument may also be understood as a reaction to previously inadequate distinctions made between the identity of perpetrators and victims, exemplified by the Neue Wache memorial, whose inscription, 'To the Victims of War and Tyranny', symbolically amalgamates all categories of victims, as if victims of perpetration and fallen soldiers were reconciled in death. Both the Vél' d'Hiv' and Holocaust Monument, by refocusing attention on the identity of victims and thus the motivations for war crimes, compensate the historical fallacies of previous monuments which blur differences between victims.

Sybil Milton suggests that the central Memorial of the Martyrs of Deportation in Paris, which universalises the notion of victimhood by making no specific mention of the identity of deportees or motivations of perpetrators, is a symbolic 'obfuscation of Jewish victims'.[10] The Vél' d'Hiv' memorial could therefore be interpreted as the compensation for an urban, monumental obfuscation, since it redresses the balance of previous memorials by referring explicitly to the identity of one group of victims. It therefore subverts standard narratives of twentieth-century war memorials, both the tragic heroism depicted in memorials of the First World War and the universalisation of victimhood in memorials of the Second World War. At the same time, this new type of compensatory war memorial does not abandon national ideology. Both the Vél' d'Hiv' and Holocaust Monument afforded recognition of victims while at the same time enhancing the self-image of the nation. The accolades received by President Chirac following his Vél' d'Hiv' speech of 1995 show that commemoration of the nation's war crimes did not undermine national self-understanding, for war crimes were interpreted, by negation, as a source of moral redemption for the nation. Memories of historical crimes, which potentially subvert the moral legitimacy of the nation, were thus integrated and neutralised within a larger framework of positive events or values in what the political scientist Rainer Lepsius calls a 'negatively valued event of historical reference'.[11]

Conventional structures of national self-understanding are founded on a sense of 'us' and 'them', on in-groups and out-groups[12] which mutually identify themselves as the negation of an imagined other or enemy beyond their boundaries. In war memorials of the nineteenth century and early twentieth century following the First World War, victims were generally soldiers injured or who died in defence of their own nation and who were mourned by members of the same group that perceived itself as a victim of foreign aggression. The monumental representation of victimhood has undergone a transformation during the twentieth century, in particular since the Second World War, from victims belonging to the in-group to those belonging to an out-group. While the Buchenwald national memorial, erected in 1958 in the German Democratic Republic to honour victims of fascism, adhered to the conventional positive identification of victims belonging to the in-group, plans for a national 'Memorial in Honour of the Dead' (Mahnmal zur Ehrung der Toten) in the Federal Republic in Bonn in 1985 had to be deferred due to dispute over the unspecific dedication to 'the dead', which again made no distinction between dead victims and dead perpetrators.[13] The redesign and new inauguration of the Neue Wache in 1993 in Berlin marked a turning point in the representation of victims in the Federal Republic. Having first been dedicated in universal terms to 'victims of war and tyranny', public protest spurred the government to add a bronze plaque naming victims in terms of their membership of a group, whether Jews, Roma and Sinti, euthanasia victims, homosexuals or political dissidents. The Neue Wache thus represents a transition from self-stylisation as victim to recognition of the other as victim. One of the reasons for the suspension of the Holocaust Monument project in 1995 and 1998 was likewise confusion over the question whether it would be more appropriate to build a single monument for both Jewish and for Roma and Sinti victims, or even for all victim groups collectively, or whether such a site would not detract from the historical specificity of the victimisation of each of these groups.

One of the shortcomings of the Vél' d'Hiv' and Holocaust Monument is that they project an image of Judaism that is exclusively one of victimisation. However, monuments are not only dedicated to events or people, but also by and in the name of people. The novelty of these monuments lies in their parallel focus on victims and perpetrators, and in the fact that the commemorations were inaugurated in the name of the successor states of the Axis powers in which the monuments are situated. They embody the symbolic integration of what Habermas calls the 'injured other' into a repertoire of national commemorations, and thereby represent an innovative trend in commemorative policy that ushers in 'the postnational constellation'.[14] Both monuments are designated as central and national, but nevertheless commemorate the nation's persecution of victims. A formerly archetypal out-group, and the moral depravity of the nation, is thereby given a central visible sign by means of a commemorative convention traditionally reserved for a national *cult*, whether of national triumphs, heroes or dead soldiers. These symbols do not reverse history by transforming the former out-group into an in-group, but represent a symbolic gesture of recognition and compensation and thereby subvert the conventional function of monuments as focal points of positive identification.

In psychological terms, a 'compensation' is a mechanism by which individuals conceal a weakness or defect. In historical terms, memory cultures and their supporting symbols compensate present-day disorientation by recalling a glorious past or by satisfying nostalgia with a sense of security offered by relics from the past. Representations of national histories likewise testify to a simplification or manipulation of the past in order to sustain myths in the present.[15] A similar principle underlies the state promotion of 'heritage' in the U.K. and 'patrimony' in France, in which historical artefacts offer a source of leisure activity to satisfy a demand for escapism from the present to the past and participation in tradition via historical tourism.[16] Memory cultures since the 1970s have almost invariably been interpreted in these terms, as a form of affirmative compensation for political disorientation in the present, but also as the selective rearticulation and consolidation of tradition (see Chapter Six). However, the Vél' d'Hiv' and Holocaust Monument disrupt the conventional principles of compensation and consolidation. They offer no immediate consolation in the past or support for positive memories. Only by means of elaborate mechanisms of interpretation on the basis of speeches, exhibitions, petitions, media reports and public forums were these unorthodox sites of memory rendered publicly acceptable and thus accommodated to existing memory cultures. These prolonged discursive processes of symbolic integration of the victimised other into a repertoire of national commemorations were not provoked by the inherent nature of the monuments, but induced by those who engaged publicly in the interpretation of their commemorative transmission.

In spite of their unorthodox symbolic value as sites of disturbing memories in the urban landscapes of Paris and Berlin, these monuments were enhanced as sites of national memory on the basis of universalist and exclusionary discourse. By defining the community of mourners as 'French' or 'German', petitions and speeches entrenched a conception of in- and out-groups that echoed distinctions propagated during the 1940s. The utterances of French representatives in relation to the Vél' d'Hiv' testify to a universalist assimilationist approach towards the injured other, while petitions and political statements in Germany testified to an exclusionary approach. When President Chirac, in his historic speech of 1995, affirmed the compatibility of Jewish and French remembrance ('the Jewish community remembers, and the whole of France along with it'), but particularly when Prime Minister Raffarin, in his Vél' d'Hiv' speech of 2002, equated Jewish and French interests ('an aggression against the Jewish community is an aggression against France'), their evocations of empathy with victims revealed motivations for the commemorations bordering on the assimilation of the victims to the national community. When Lea Rosh or Martin Walser evoked the Holocaust Monument as an icon of what Loewy calls Germany's 'national fate' and of 'common descent' from the perpetrators, they effectively upheld an exclusionary model of national self-understanding.

The fact that the Vél' d'Hiv' and Holocaust Monument redress an apparent lack of monuments to Jewish victims, that they are novel in so far as they integrate war crimes into an existent repertoire of symbolic elements and therefore modify the conventional compensatory and consolidatory function of commemorations, suggests that these sites are not national but negative national sites of memory. According to Walter Reese-Schäfer, negative nationalism is a latent sense of national belonging or 'covert nationalism'[17] underlying the willing acceptance of the division of Germany before 1989 as a just form of punishment for crimes committed by the National Socialists. 'Division could be perceived as a form of punishment by someone who still wished for unity. For someone who had accepted dual statehood as a matter of fact, division was no longer a form of punishment. The conception of division as punishment presupposed the idea or sense of unity. It was a sort of negative nation-state thinking.'[18] Reese-Schäfer goes on to question why the moral legacy of genocide is consistently interpreted and taken for granted as a *national* legacy rather than as that of a movement, party or individuals, and concludes that moral inheritance is primarily an individual responsibility, shouldered by all individuals with a sense of social belonging, not only by descendants of perpetrators. This pattern of the commemorative reception of war crimes, described by Reese-Schäfer as a mechanical assumption that moral responsibility for historical events is inherited collectively by nations while less emphasis is laid on individual responsibility, is reflected in the public interpretations of the Vél' d'Hiv' and Holocaust Monument. Mitterrand and Chirac both understood the conditions of the petitions literally, in which the commemorative speech was anticipated as reparation for the collective moral status of the nation, and acted accordingly in their handling of the commemorations. By contrast, Jospin rejected the basic premise of the petitions, insisting that moral responsibility is not transmitted biologically by national, collective organisms, but by an 'administration, ... responsible political agents, administrators, judges, policemen, gendarmes'.[19] Although French people were not subjected to the 'punishment' of state division after 1945 as in Germany, the Vél' d'Hiv' commemoration also constituted a 'negatively valued event of historical reference' against which politicians projected a positive holistic notion of nationhood.

A further example of negative compensation, whereby commemorations and monuments serve not to evoke an ideal past that compensates for present-day insecurities, but to symbolically repair errors of the past, is corroborated by Lea Rosh's understanding of the Holocaust Monument as an expression of an 'anti-nationalist attitude' among people who had 'faced up to history'.[20] Rosh's apparently contradictory appeal for a central, *national* monument testifying to an *anti*-nationalist standpoint may be understood in political and historical terms. In political terms, Rosh saw the commemoration of the persecution and genocide as a national collective duty, and thus attacked members of right-wing parties who had objected to the monument as an expression of unpatriotic sentiment. In historical terms, she understood the monument as anti-nationalist because it recognised victims of crimes of extreme nationalism and thus integrated symbolically the negation of criminal nationalism as a positive moral and political legacy for the postwar democratic nation. However, whereas Rosh apprehended the monument in a positive manner as a symbolic negation of the period of National Socialist rule in Germany, critics on the left interpreted it as an expression of a new national ideology. Eike Geisel opposed the Holocaust Monument project on the grounds that it exploited a symbol of genocide as the foundation of a sense of national community, such that 'the ash of the dead has become the stuff with which the new nationalism secures its clear conscience.'[21]

The contradiction between interpretations of the Holocaust Monument, as either a support for or infringement of national self-understanding, divided intellectuals and politicians and remained unresolved throughout the debate. Is the symbolic recognition of victims of past nationalism, as Rosh claims, tantamount to an anti-nationalist attitude in the present? Or does the public condemnation of past wrongs underpin a sense of complacent national identity in the present? These apparently insurmountable contradictions even caused several intellectuals to change camps, by supporting the project in its early stages and opposing it after the escalation of public interest in 1995.[22] They justified their position in similar terms to those expressed by Geisel and Habermas, albeit by combining political and formal arguments, calling for a smaller, politically and artistically 'modest' monument which might foster memory and enlightenment rather than act as 'a site rather of distraction, withdrawal from reality, and cold abstraction'.[23] The designated SPD Federal Cultural Representative, Michael Naumann, followed this argumentation by rejecting the project as a 'gigantic-monumental petrifaction'.[24] Formal arguments against the project suggested that large monuments relating to historical traces did not induce people to remember but to forget. Jens even compared the site and size of the Holocaust Monument with examples of National Socialist architecture, and called instead for a more modest memorial site. 'Shouting cannot be out-shouted, but only given precise expression with a whisper, even voicelessly.'[25]

The accumulation of insurmountably contradictory interpretations of this monument project is the prime reason why controversy over this monument remained irresolvable for over ten years. It was welcomed as an official symbolic recognition of Jewish victims of genocide yet opposed on account of its monumental size. It recalled crimes yet was cast in a conventional commemorative genre. And it was, according to its initiator Rosh, a national duty yet anti-nationalist in spirit. As the educationalist Micha Brumlik points out, the dilemma was simultaneously artistic, political and moral. Only art, claimed Brumlik, could adequately express emotions, but no artistic form was adequate to the event. While opting for the monument might be interpreted as an ultimate act of remembrance that might relieve people of the duty to remember, opting for no monument at all would appear as a sign of reluctance to remember at all. And while its limitation to the remembrance of Jewish victims echoed the very selective discrimination of the persecutors, a collective monument would eclipse the specificity of victimisation policies of the National Socialists.[26]

The ambiguities underlying the Vél' d'Hiv' and, in particular, the Holocaust Monument, provided the very substance of public debate which turned them into sites of memory. The date of the annual Vél' d'Hiv' commemoration and the urban site of the Holocaust Monument both embody poignantly the irresolvable contradictions innate to these memorials, as simultaneously 'negative' and 'positive' sites of memory with which conventional codes and national discourses were expressed and articulated anew. The Vél' d'Hiv' is commemorated on the first Sunday following 16 July each year, that is, two days after the national day of commemoration on 14 July, and thus juxtaposes the positive founding moment of 1789 with its symbolic negation of 1940–44. The

Holocaust Monument symbolically sustains the memory of the genocide on the site of the former no-man's land between East and West Berlin which, having served national division now symbolises national unity. Both monuments incorporate negative memories in proximity to each nation's positive repertoire of commemorations, 1789 in France and 1989 in Germany. In light of Reese-Schäfer's definition of 'negative nationalism', the Berlin monument could be interpreted on the basis of its urban site as a symbolic convergence of the national founding moment of crime with that of its historical consequence, division, as a focal point of self-understanding common to citizens of both former German states. However, since unification in 1990, both the crime and its alleged 'punishment' may be equally relegated to the realm of memory and commemorative representations. As a pure symbol of former crimes and division, this monument also effectively symbolises unity today, as the negation or overcoming of division.

Trans- and Postnational Sites of Memory

International wars such as the First, Second and Cold War provided common cornerstones of separate national memory cultures during the twentieth century. Although the Cold War, by far the most prolonged, had a more profound influence on social attitudes over several generations and although the First World War caused unprecedented human suffering and an upheaval of social and political structures, the intensity and scale of destruction of the Second World War as well as the persecution and genocide were the most conspicuous focal point of memory cultures of the late twentieth century. Largely coherent collective narratives were produced after 1945, including military heroism in the U.K. and the cult of Churchill, de Gaulle's myth of the Resistance, a nation of anti-fascist resistance in East Germany and of anti-communism and victimhood in West Germany.[27] Most European capital cities contain official sites for national rituals of remembrance for victims of the world wars that document these myths in public memorial 'archives' (Nora). The Cenotaph in London, the tomb of the unknown soldier at the Arc de Triomphe in Paris, the Neue Wache in Berlin are all sites at which memories of military victims of the First World War have been supplemented symbolically by memories of victims of the Second World War.

Two conclusions may be drawn from this trend. Although these countries played different roles in the Second World War, this event represents a common historical and political caesura and a founding moment of multiple contemporary memory cultures. Commemorative rituals and popular discourses (of heroic victory in the U.K., of resistance in France, or of anti-fascist resistance, responsibility and victimhood in the two

Germanys) differed, but fulfilled similar political functions by appealing for political legitimacy and consensus in each country. More recently, the fiftieth anniversary commemorations of the end of hostilities staged in Europe in 1995 continued to fulfil a common function in each country by putting a symbolic seal not only on the end of the war, but also on the end of the prolonged and intense series of fiftieth anniversary commemorations themselves, as if these marked the demise of the Second World War as a key vector of postwar memory cultures. Yet commemorations of the Second World War clearly did not end in 1995. In some respects, they even increased as, for example, the commemorations of the persecution and genocide became an ever more international affair. The trials of Vichy officials in France, the rise of the right in Austria, gradual demythification of Swiss neutrality, the high number of state apologies,[28] and even the introduction of a Holocaust Memorial Day in the U.K. on 27 January from 2001 and a 'National Day of Commemoration of the Racist and Anti-Semitic Persecutions' in France from 1993, mean that Germany no longer has a monopoly over the moral accountability for the genocide committed during the Second World War. The analogies between the complex symbolic representations of the Holocaust in Paris and Berlin, demonstrating efforts undertaken to inaugurate alternative national war memorials which do not mourn the nation's victims but victims of the nation's perpetration, exemplify the internationalisation of critical metatheoretical memorial practices.

Unlike the nationally framed historical studies of political agency and interests responsible for the implementation of commemorations and the cultivation of public memories of the Second World War,[29] this comparison of French and German memory cultures aims rather to identify structural and discursive parallels between them in direct relation to symbolic forms. In spite of the national confines of memory cultures, sustained largely by the diffusion of historical information via national languages and national mass media, the Vél' d'Hiv' and Holocaust Monument largely conform to patterns of historical commemoration, discourse and interpretation which are shared by different nations. The focal event of the Second World War conforms to what we may define as a principle of commemorative *subsidiarity*. The type and theme of commemoration in each country were not selected according to scientific principle by a single governing authority, but resulted from the clash and negotiation of multiple interests and factors (ranging from the wording of petitions, the nature of the chosen urban site, the biographies of political leaders, the varying cohesion of political parties and selection procedures), each offering opportunities to discuss memories of international historical events of the 1930s and 1940s on a local and national level.

The fact that specific national understandings of the legacy of the Second World War are transmitted with analogous forms and patterns of commemoration (monuments, speeches, and deliberation in different countries) reveals the inadequacy of a purely national apprehension of this event. Although different nations share common cultural and historical references derived from this event, their local and national narratives combine to form, as the historian Michael Geyer observes, a 'contestatory mesh of narratives', a metaphor suggesting that each narrative possesses a distinct thread which is nevertheless dependent on adjacent and even antagonistic threads within the transnational postwar memory culture.[30] Given the essentially contestatory nature of Holocaust remembrance, postwar memory cultures no longer conform to a pattern established during the nineteenth century, when nations depended upon mutual enmity in order to fuel a sense of identity in opposition to their neighbours. Non-exclusive forms of commemoration are becoming more apparent. An example of transnational solidarity was expressed in the 1990s when French people protested at the decision to not invite Chancellor Kohl to attend the fiftieth anniversary commemoration of the Allied Normandy landings in 1994. As historical prisms of contemporary memory cultures, the Vél' d'Hiv' and the Holocaust Monument were often perceived as symbols of national cohesion, supported by the 'certain idea' of French identity or the 'tragic' exclusiveness of German responsibility. However, they also opened opportunities for the public negotiation of and reconciliation with an imagined religious, ethnic or political victim within the nation. The traditional pattern of identifying nations in binary oppositions between an in-group and an out-group was thus supplanted by a more complex process of identification in which the in-group is no longer homogeneous and defined territorially, ideally or ethnically, but subverted from within by the remembrance and recognition of its own crimes against a former victim or out-group.

This ambiguous combination of 'positive' (present national) and 'negative' (past criminal) national discourses corroborates Nora's dialectic conception of archival memory. Nora claims that sites of memory sustain parallel complementary forms of affective and critical memory serving to either 'construct' or 'deconstruct' a sense of identity.[31] On the one hand, both the Vél' d'Hiv' and Holocaust Monument served to fix a historical event in conventional ritual and sculptural forms as publicly visible points of historical reference in each capital city. On the other hand, the prolonged and complex public debates detracted from and therefore subverted the effect of rhetorical and sculptural forms in which events were commemorated as focal points of emotional identification. The debates offered a focal point of national memory but also a platform for a complex exchange of memories, a local 'contestatory mesh of narratives'. These monuments may therefore be categorised as sites of memory, whereas their resultant debates are sites of plural memories in conflict, operating as a platform for intersubjective communication about history rather than as a point of identification with history. The Vél' d'Hiv' and Holocaust Monument do not conform to Nora's normative notion of memory as 'patrimonial memory', which neutralises the political divisiveness of historical memories; according to Nora, 'patrimonial memory' celebrates the past as 'pastness', that is, the past for its own sake, without regard for historical details, and thereby diffuses conflict in a process which Nora refers to as the 'exhaustion of classic conflicts' (*'l'épuisement des oppositions classiques'*).[32] Instead, as sources of reflection *on* the very function of national commemorations, expressed particularly during discussion over the Holocaust Monument, these debates are an expression of what Habermas defines as 'posttraditional identity',[33] in which the past does not offer a model for behaviour in the present but a source of critical and even conflictory discussion on questions of political self-understanding.

In practice, participation in the interpretation of the Vél' d'Hiv' and Holocaust Monument and the construction of commemorative narratives is not confined to political and intellectual opinion-makers. Moreover, membership of a memory culture cannot be adequately defined in legal or ethnic terms corresponding to traditional conditions of nationality. As objects of political communication occupying urban space and rendered popular via the mass media, these monuments are effectively accessible to all passers-by or readers of newspapers whose participation, whether in terms of vociferous protest or silent acquiescence, is party to a public memorial discourse without which the decisions of associations and politicians would lack legitimation. It is significant that pioneering research done on the teaching of Second World War history for pupils of immigrant origin in Germany has focused on the behaviour of pupils during visits to historical exhibitions.[34] For it is precisely the heuristic value of museums, exhibitions, or memorials that facilitates broad social participation in the formation and understanding of memory cultures. Although national identities are often perceived to be natural, unquestionable, monolithic and exclusive – inherited from a given common past, language, religion or ethnicity – effective communication about the past can open membership of a memory culture to any participants who are versed in the issues and language of that memory culture, in so far as public negotiation of the past is inevitably also a negotiation of models of behaviour and values in the present. In this respect, while the individual memory of the Second World War derives from witnesses' direct experiences of events and their subsequent interpretations, public memory of this event is inherited entirely indirectly via symbolic and rhetorical communication, and may therefore be acquired by all those who relate to the history of the Second World War via images, symbols, words and resulting exchanges of ideas about these media and the events to which they refer.

Notes

1. Etienne François and Hagen Schulze, 'Einleitung', in François and Schulze, eds, *Deutsche Erinnerungsorte* vol. 1, 9–24, 22.
2. Wolfgang Eberl, 'Sind Denkmäler heute möglich?', in Ekkehard Mai and Gisela Schmirber, eds, *Denkmal – Zeichen – Monument. Skulptur und öffentlicher Raum heute*, Munich: Prestel Verlag, 1989, 35–37, 36.
3. Anthony Smith, *National Identity*, Harmondsworth: Penguin, 1991, 14.
4. David Kertzer, *Ritual, Politics and Power*, New Haven & London: Yale University Press 1988, 67. In similar vein, François and Schulze refer to 'subliminal solidarity' ('*unterschwellige Solidarität*'), 'Das emotionale Fundament der Nationen', in Monika Flacke, ed., *Mythen der Nationen. Ein europäisches Panorama*, Berlin: Deutsches Historisches Museum, 1998, 17–32, 28.
5. Karl Deutsch, *Nationalism and Social Communication. An Inquiry into the Foundations of Nationality*, Cambridge, Mass.: MIT Press, 1953, 173.
6. Cf. Conan and Rousso, *Vichy, un passé qui ne passe pas*, 64f.
7. See Elizabeth Noelle-Neumann and Renate Köcher, eds, *Allensbacher Jahrbuch der Demoskopie* 1993–1997, Munich: K. G. Saur, 1997, 516.
8. Raoul Girardet, *Mythes et mythologies politiques*, 181f.
9. Hanno Loewy, 'A History of Ambivalence: postreunification German Identity and the Holocaust', *Patterns of Prejudice* no. 2, 2002, 3–13, 10, 11. See also Raphael Gross and Werner Konitzer, 'Zum Fortwirken der nationalsozialistischen Moral', *Mittelweg 36* no. 4, 1999, 44–67; and Viola Georgi, *Entliehene Erinnerung. Geschichtsbilder junger Migranten in Deutschland*, Hamburg: HIS Verlag, 2003.
10. Sybil Milton, *In Fitting Memory. The Art and Politics of Holocaust Memorials*, Detroit: Wayne State University Press, 1991, 9.
11. *'Negativ bewertetes Bezugsereignis'*. M. Rainer Lepsius, 'Das Erbe des Nationalsozialismus und die politische Kultur der Nachfolgestaaten des "Großdeutschen Reiches"', in Lepsius, *Demokratie in Deutschland*, Göttingen: Vandenhoeck & Ruprecht, 1993, 229–45, 229.
12. Michael Billig, 'Nationalism as an International Ideology: Imagining the Nation, Others and the World of Nations', in Glynis Breakwell and Evanthia Lyons, eds, *Changing European Identities: Social Psychological Analyses of Social Change*, Oxford: Buttersworth-Heinemann, 1996, 181–94, 187; and Billig, *Banal Nationalism*, London: Sage, 1995, Chapter 4.
13. See Michael Jeismann, 'Zeichenlehre', in Jeismann, ed., *Mahnmal Mitte: Eine Kontroverse*, Cologne: DuMont, 1999, 7–31, 13.
14. Jürgen Habermas, 'Der Zeigefinger. Die Deutschen und ihr Denkmal', *Die Zeit*, 31 March 1999, 42–44, 44.
15. The promotion of a simplified and mythical past in nineteenth-century historicist art as compensation for present insecurities is dealt with by Stefan Germer, 'Retrovision: die rückblickende Erfindung der Nationen durch die Kunst', in Monika Flacke, ed., *Mythen der Nationen. Ein europäisches Panorama*, Berlin: Deutsches Historisches Museum, 1998, 32–52, 34. See also Raoul Girardet's discussion of the compensatory function of myths, in *Mythes et mythologies politiques*, 187.
16. Lowenthal, *The Heritage Crusade and the Spoils of History*, 6f; Lowenthal, *The Past is a Foreign Country*, 384–89.
17. Walter Reese-Schäfer, 'Universalismus, negativer Nationalismus und die neue Einheit der Deutschen', in Petra Braitling and Walter Reese-Schäfer, eds, *Universalismus, negativer Nationalismus und die neue Einheit der Deutschen*, Frankfurt am Main: Fischer Verlag, 1991, 39–54, 46.

18. Ibid.
19. Jospin, 'Un gouvernement, une administration de notre pays, ont alors commis l'irréparable', *Le Monde,* 22 July 1997, 8.
20. Lea Rosh, 'Ein Denkmal im Lande der Täter', 7.
21. Eike Geisel, 'Lebenshilfe von toten Juden', *Junge Welt,* 14 May 1994. See also Karl Wilds, 'Identity Creation and the Culture of Contrition: Recasting Normality in the Berlin Republic', *German Politics* no. 1, 2000, 83–102, 95.
22. The former chairman of the selection jury for the monument, Jens, and his successor as president of the Academy of Arts, Konrád, both revoked their support of the project in an open letter in February 1998, signed by eighteen intellectuals: '"Aus Einsicht verzichten"', *Der Tagesspiegel,* 4 February 1998, 25. See also: Jens, 'In letzte Minute. Mein Widerruf zum Holocaust-Mahnmal', *Frankfurter Allgemeine Zeitung,* 7 February 1998, 33; Konrád, 'Abschied von der Chimäre. Wider das Holocaust-Denkmal', *Frankfurter Allgemeine Zeitung,* 26 November 1997, 41.
23. See the open letter, '"Aus Einsicht verzichten"', *Der Tagesspiegel,* 4 February 1998, 25.
24. Naumann, inteviewed on Deutschlandradio, 21 July 1998.
25. Jens, 'In letzter Minute', *Frankfurter Allgemeine Zeitung,* 7 February 1998, 33.
26. Micha Brumlik, 'Gewissen, Gedenken und anamnetische Solidarität', 1152–53.
27. Cf. Norbert Frei, *Vergangenheitspolitik. Die Anfänge der Bundesrepublik und die NS-Vergangenheit,* Munich: C.H. Beck, 1996.
28. See Lübbe, *'Ich entschuldige mich.' Das neue politische Bußritual,* Berlin: Siedler, 2001.
29. See, for example, Peter Reichel, *Politik mit der Erinnerung;* and Norbert Frei, *Vergangenheitspolitik.*
30. Michael Geyer, 'The Place of the Second World War in German Memory and History', 39.
31. Nora, 'La nation-mémoire', 650.
32. Ibid., 650f.
33. Jürgen Habermas, *Die nachholende Revolution,* Frankfurt am Main: Suhrkamp, 1990, 220; idem, *Eine Art Schadensabwicklung,* Frankfurt am Main: Suhrkamp, 1987, 173.
34. See, for example, Bernd Fechler, 'Zwischen Tradierung und Konfliktvermittlung. Über den Umgang mit "problematischen" Aneignungsformen der NS-Geschichte in multikulturellen Schulklassen. Ein Praxisbericht', in Bernd Fechler, Gottfried Kößler and Till Lieberz-Groß, eds, *'Erziehung nach Auschwitz' in der multikulturellen Gesellschaft. Pädagogische und soziologische Annäherungen,* Weinheim & Munich: Juventa Verlag, 2000, 207–227.

8
Dialogic Monuments

The Vél' d'Hiv' and Holocaust Monument are examples of a new kind of war memorial. They commemorate neither military victory nor glorious defeat, customary following national campaigns of the nineteenth century and following the First World War, but war crimes. Consequently, there is no all-embracing notion that captures either the style or function of contemporary monuments. Several existent terms, such as 'ephemeral' or 'objectless' monuments, pinpoint essential formal features of monumental art, but are normative and partial (see Introduction). Other concepts have pinpointed the reactive function of monuments in relation to existing monuments and traditions, including 'counter-monuments' and monuments erected 'with reference to existing public memorials'.[1] Jay Winter proposes a comprehensive definition of war memorials of the First World War as sacred 'cultural codes' aiding the process of mourning war victims.[2] Kirsch similarly interprets the Holocaust Monument as a focal point of collective mourning rituals in the unified Germany.[3] Most specialists agree that traditional forms of monumental art could not be adopted after the Second World War and focus their attention entirely on a functionalist definition. Jochen Spielmann characterises the period since 1945 in Germany as one in which monuments were treated as focal points for debates over the interpretation of National Socialism on the one hand, and as instruments for making known and implementing the political intentions of minorities on the other.[4] Aleida and Jan Assmann likewise define a threefold 'personal', 'social' and 'political' function of monuments.[5] All these definitions certainly spotlight but do not explain the precise mechanisms by which the interrelation between monuments and their political context is articulated in the public sphere.

There are several reasons why there today exists no single concept with which to define monuments, in particular those designed to commemorate the persecution and genocide of the Second World War. First, the scale and nature of the event defies traditional forms of representation and commemoration. The language of archways, busts, columns and inscriptions has been rendered obsolete by the apparently unbridgeable gap between the event being commemorated and the existing iconic repertoire. Second, forms of monumental art have been enriched and diversified by the language of contemporary art, including elements of conceptual art, installations, happenings and even multimedia. Third, the public and political acceptance of new monuments is obstructed by resistance to innovation, in particular the tendency to judge monuments according to the anachronistic criterion of national representativeness. Moreover, the ideological abuse of public art during the dictatorships of the twentieth century has promoted scepticism towards monumental art as such.

The historian Winfried Speitkamp has suggested that innovative monumental buildings such as the new Jewish Museum in Berlin do not, in spite of their radical forms, provoke and undermine conventional monumentality but rather reinforce or even normalise the 'certainty of disturbance'.[6] Speitkamp implies that the force of traditional forms of communication such as monuments and monumental architecture effectively normalises the memory of genocide by turning an apparently disturbing memory into a force of social cohesion. However, the fact that monuments are inevitably subject to repeated reinterpretations at successive moments in time, and that each new interpretation depends on the interests and perspective of the individual or group in whose name the interpretation is made (whether members of an ethnic group, a national community, immigrants or tourists, for example), suggests that their meanings are in fact contingent.

Several critics including Spielmann and Christoph Heinrich locate the meaning of monuments not in what they embody or represent, but in their effects. Heinrich argues that their essential function is to 'give impetus to critical debate, as a source of friction for public discussion'. Young develops a similarly comprehensive definition of monuments as objects of public dialogue over the meaning of monuments and of the past rather than as artistic representations offering models for collective identification. According to Young, they stimulate 'the activity of remembering together, ... make visible the activity of memory', and expose the very 'memorial-making process'.[7] This concept of monuments as an object of dialogue between individuals and groups derives from the inherent contingency of public monuments as sources of public participation in the discursive construction of historical self-understanding. In what way do these diagnoses of monuments as *essentially* debated, dialogic sites of memory help us to grasp the significance of the Vél' d'Hiv' and Holocaust Monument? Critics agree that neither of these monuments is the product of fair, transparent and open debate. The essayist Eduard Beaucamp argues that the Holocaust Monument is a product of bureaucracy and haste, an unclear initial concept, disregard for competition procedure and political intervention.[8] Caroline Wiedmer similarly argues that institutional inconsistencies and the breaking of competition rules marred the debate over the Holocaust Monument, and that alternative artistic proposals for the Vél' d'Hiv' monument were stifled from the outset. These criticisms are, in light of institutional procedures in each case, justified. However, the preceding chapters have demonstrated that, although the meanings of these monuments were certainly shaped by the rhetoric of petitions and subsequent, often unfair, dialogue between politicians and artists, they cannot be reduced to these alone. Like political myths, monuments are not only 'products of social reality, but also producers of social reality'.[9] And to both these realities belong not only prize-winning monuments and presidential speeches, but also the public responses, proposals for alternative models, exhibitions, books and even private discussion. This final chapter therefore proposes some parameters for an understanding of the specific function of monuments as a form of political communication about the past that is contingent on but also constitutive of contemporary memory cultures.

The case studies of the Vél' d'Hiv' and Holocaust Monument demonstrate that forms of contemporary monuments are multiple and *open*, that their social context renders them impracticable or *inexpedient* as media of political intentions, and that they may only be interpreted in light of *procedures* governing debates over monuments. Moreover, these monuments occupy a unique point of intersection between artistic and political forms of representation, which will be addressed in the penultimate section of this chapter. The prolonged and complex nature of the commemorative debates over the Vél' d'Hiv' and Holocaust Monument confirms the suggestion proposed by the philosopher Jean-Marc Ferry that sites of memory not only rally collective emotions behind a charismatic figure or historical event, but also spur intersubjective communication about the very significance and function of symbols. Both these monuments stimulated what may be called metadiscussion on the present-day political function of historical symbols, such that they were not only forces of social cohesion or identity, but also sources of critiques of historical symbols and processes of identity formation. According to Ferry, 'commemoration is characterised initially not by the subjective level of affective memory nor by the objective level of factual description, but by the intersubjective level.'[10] In addition to the 'affective' appeal of symbols and their 'factual' historical content, such disputed sites of memory thus offer a basis for the public negotiation of historical memories and their political function.

In short, the meaning of monuments is not located in monuments themselves. During the debates over the Vél' d'Hiv' and Holocaust Monument, they were appropriated variously in terms of the historical significance of their sites, their political expediency in light of parliamentary elections and in relation to xenophobia and violent attacks on Jewish cultural sites. These sites were used as a platform to debate issues of social ethics, the appropriateness of various ritual and artistic forms, the social status of public art and of political rhetoric, and even the means of financing and administrating the commemorations. These monuments are channels for the production of cultural meaning whose openness, inexpediency and procedural character invite individuals to construct meanings out of the traces of the past.

Open Forms: Monumental Disputes as a Genre

Given the formal and functional heterogeneity of war memorials since the Second World War, is it possible to categorise the Vél' d'Hiv' and Holocaust Monument in relation to earlier and existing memorial categories? Since the nineteenth century, figurative monuments made of stone have been a standard feature of public places in European cities. In France and Germany, for example, monuments to cultural and historical figures, to events such as the French revolution, but also to the Napoleonic wars, the Franco-Prussian War and the two world wars, have been systematically erected, restored, neglected, removed or replaced according to their political expediency. As foci of public and political attention, they testify to the tradition of the use of tangible symbols set in urban and rural landscapes by associations or nation-states in order to sustain memory cultures. Today, a large number of these monuments still adorn city landscapes. The Arc de Triomphe in Paris, Nelson's Column in London or the Völkerschlachtdenkmal in Leipzig are three obvious examples relating to the Napoleonic wars.

Monuments to the two world wars of the twentieth century differ from those of the nineteenth century. Following the First World War, war memorials were no longer designed to celebrate heroic victims in triumphal arches or victory columns characteristic of the Napoleonic Wars or the Franco-Prussian War, but to mourn the dead who were often perceived as national martyrs. These monuments took the form of figurative sculptures of religious motifs such as the pietà, or tombs containing the remains of unknown soldiers, eternal flames, mass cemeteries and cenotaphs. Such monuments sustained the cult of victims with sacred but also universal appeal, in so far as they were often used as sites of civic commemorations. As Winter observes, war memorials of the First World War were generally '*both* noble and uplifting *and* tragic and unendurably sad'.[11] Yet the persecution and genocide of the Second World War is clearly not a source of uplifting or sad emotions, and states were understandably reluctant to inaugurate monuments immediately after 1945 with the traditional iconography of heroism and martyrdom.[12] The events of

1933–45 posed a far greater challenge to the practice of commemoration than did those of 1914–18. Local monuments erected after 1945 often included plaques, inscriptions added to memorials for victims of the First World War, or memorial museums on historically significant sites. While the first central memorials appeared in France and the German Democratic Republic in the late 1950s and early 1960s, the Federal Republic began discussions for such a monument in Bonn only in the mid 1970s, and finally inaugurated one after unification in 1993 (Neue Wache) and will inaugurate another in 2005 (Holocaust Monument). Since the 1960s, forms of monuments were invented that not only explored new types of expression but challenged the very tradition of marking historical events with monuments in order to commemorate the past in the present. Crucial to this development were the works of the American and German artists Edward Kienholz and Jochen Gerz. Kienholz's 'anti-monument',[13] the *Portable War Memorial* of 1968, comprises a blackboard and chalk with which spectators are invited to record the names of victims of future wars, while Gerz's much debated 'counter-monument' of the 1980s and 1990s is based on the principle that monuments that renounce symbolism draw spectators into an active questioning of their relation to the past and its representations.[14] The inscription on the plaque marking the site of Gerz's invisible 'Monument Against Fascism' in Harburg near Hamburg reads, 'For nothing can with duration rise against injustice in our place' (*Denn nichts kann auf Dauer an unserer Stelle sich gegen das Unrecht erheben*). The abandonment of symbolism not only echoes the ban on divine images in Jewish theology, but testifies to what Hubertus Tim Adam calls the 'capitulation' of artistic representation and its incapacity to function as a 'social corrective'.[15] Moreover, it implies a displacement of the responsibility to represent or give meaning to the past from the artistic object itself to the perceiver of that object. Young, in his early essays, also favours a radical renunciation of representation by calling for the suspension of monuments in order to sustain discussion over the very means of commemorating. Commenting the project to build a permanent memorial Topography of Terror on the former site of the Gestapo headquarters in Berlin, Young suggests that 'left unresolved, the memorial project at the Gestapo-Gelände flourishes precisely because it contests memory – because it continues to challenge, exasperate, edify, and invite visitors into a dialogue between themselves and their past.'[16]

The eclecticism of available styles, the lack of consensus over appropriate commemorative rituals, the wording of commemorative speeches, the process of selecting a monument, and the use of historical evidence in monuments are characteristic sources of contemporary memorial debates. Yet the fact that these debates accompany conventional sculptural monuments, as well as those employing innovative memorial techniques, suggests that the source of dispute lies not only in the type of monument but also in people's very different preconceptions of the purpose and function of monuments. In spite of radical doubts about the pertinence and adequacy of monuments as a form of commemoration (by Richard Serra and Jay Winter, for example), the analogies between issues debated in relation to the Vél' d'Hiv' and Holocaust Monument testify to a common politically motivated consensus over the pertinence of monuments. This consensus does not relate to monumental forms or to decision-making procedures, but to underlying conditions for the monuments: that they should mark a central site in the capital city, be permanent, commemorate victims of crimes, and amend shortcomings of existing monuments. These monuments testify to the significance still imputed to monuments as a *genre*, and to the continued attempts to voluntarily cultivate collective self-understanding on the basis of shared memories and values associated directly with symbolic historical sites. Monuments are still expected to fulfil a pedagogical function in the transmission and maintenance of historical memories. As the number of surviving witnesses of the Second World War dwindles, forms of historical media, including film, literature, monuments and television or digital recordings play an increasingly central role in the transmission of knowledge of this event. However, the makers of monuments can no longer rely on what Mona Ozouf calls the 'docility' of citizens towards the pedagogical goals of public symbols.[17] It is therefore questionable whether monuments continue to appeal to a sense of national belonging among generations that did not participate in or witness these events. Although they continue to serve as a backdrop for state rituals and commemorations, or even as topographical landmarks, their immediate political function today is obscure. The lack of consensus, coupled with verbal insistence on consensus and reconciliation was, paradoxically, the most constant feature of debates over both the Vél' d'Hiv' and Holocaust Monument, such that we may even define disputed monuments as a genre in its own right. The dialogue provoked by these monuments is perhaps their defining feature, one which facilitates the open exchange of plural interpretations of history and of the function of historical memories in relation to their representations and forms of transmission.

Inexpedient Intentions: the Inaptness of Monuments as Media for the Implementation of Political Objectives

Although the petitions of citizens' action groups in both France and Germany predetermined neither the precise wording of the speech nor the sculptural form of the monument, they imposed conditions on the types of medium to be used and their significance: a presidential speech and a monument, which were required to symbolise a collective national attitude. These conditions determined the terms of debate on the false assumption that monuments should *stand* for national memory. In practice, monuments proved to be inefficient and inexpedient conveyors of political messages. The intentions of organisers were inevitably subject to the mediation of artists, and to artistic or rhetorical forms that were in turn contingent upon multiple receptions and reinterpretations. The complexity of the symbolic forms, ritual procedures and rhetoric with which the Vél' d'Hiv' and Holocaust Monument were implemented also rendered these monuments contingent upon the often arbitrary influence of associations, politicians or parties whose aims and interests obscured the significance of the sites. In France, debate focused on the biographies, behaviour and rhetoric of the presidents, excluded discussion on the form of the monument, and engaged journalists, historians, politicians and representatives of Jewish institutions. In Germany, debate focused initially on monumental form as a definitive gesture of national reparation and engaged journalists, historians, politicians and artists, but provoked additional dispute between the cultural representatives of the organising and sponsoring bodies, the Berlin Senate and the federal government, as well as non-Jewish victim associations, such that the multiplication of decision-making authorities resulted in a multiplication of grounds for dispute.

Moreover, dissent within political parties hindered administrative measures undertaken to forge a cohesive public opinion. In France, dispute over Mitterrand's refusal to hold a speech split the PS. And when President Chirac officially recognised the deportations in his Vél' d'Hiv' speech of July 1995, the Front National launched a defamatory campaign designed to lure voters from the right of the Gaullist RPR party, which in turn led Philippe Séguin to dissociate the RPR from President Chirac and thus also split that party. In Germany, the discordant positions within the SPD and CDU parties at national and local levels thwarted the authority of individual members of parliament, the parliamentary cultural committee and ministers to promote public consensus on the issue of the monument. For this reason, the campaigns for both monuments sapped the capacity of the governmental apparatus to implement decision-making processes. The political significance of these monuments may be reduced to neither party nor individual interests expressed in relation to them, nor to inherent formal qualities of the sites, for they may be better understood on the basis of the codes and discursive paradigms invested in their interpretation by participants in the debates.

The relation between art and politics exemplified in disputes over the Vél' d'Hiv' and Holocaust Monument may not be defined as one of 'instrumentalisation'. This term would suggest that political intentions are developed then sequentially 'encoded' and communicated via a commemorative medium, which may subsequently be 'decoded' by spectators. In practice, people do not identify directly with a monument, for its significance is contingent upon meanings acquired by its interactions with and translation via secondary media of speeches, rituals, reports, forums, conferences, exhibitions and political statements. Monuments are rather catalysts of complex social and political communication. Moreover, the inconclusive and often contradictory standpoints of participants in debates over these monuments testified to the resistance of monuments to political instrumentalisation. Whereas Günter Grass, Jens and Konrád doubted the efficacy of the monument as a support for historical memories,[18] for example, Bubis and Walser interpreted it as a mimetic reflection of national memory and thus adopted the restrictive conditions of the petition, which had supposed a causal relation between monuments and national self-understanding. Attempts to politically 'instrumentalise' these monuments were founded on the erroneous assumption that there exists a direct relation between monumental representation and the moral state of the nation as an organic whole. The political instrumentality of monuments appears even less credible if we attempt to systematise the connection between political interests of participants in the memorial debates and their understandings of the symbolic media required to shape memory cultures, because the stated attitude towards the monuments gives no indication of the political position of individuals or the type of remembrance they advocate. Philippe Séguin, Martin Walser, and representatives of extreme right-wing parties in both countries opposed the projects, whereas Jacques Chirac, Ignatz Bubis and Willy Brandt approved them. Yet it is significant that both these groups, of strict opponents and strict supporters of the commemorations, shared the common assumption that the gesture of representation stands for the nation's collective remembrance of war crimes, and that an act of symbolic remembrance would secure a corresponding act of social remembrance. In reality, however, the issues and interests at stake – the representation of national memory and the remembrance of victims – surpass the capacity of any one object, museum or commemoration to embody or represent them. The impulse to commemorate therefore appears to have emerged from a confusion of symbolic and political categories, based on the false assumption that the authority of symbolic representation is a substitute for the authority of political representation.[19]

The binary categorisation of approaches to these monuments, in which participants were expected to be either 'for' or 'against', characterised the media debates in both France and Germany. Such either-or argumentation was politically expedient, but detracted from the specific function of the monuments. Both Mitterrand and Chirac were in favour of the commemoration and the construction of a monument and both staunchly supported republican tradition, while their differences arose in relation to the interpretation of the verbal gesture demanded by the Vél' d'Hiv' Comité

42. An analogous pattern occurred in Germany, where standpoints towards the Holocaust Monument crystallised during the parliamentary election campaign of 1998 in terms of supporters versus opponents of the project, and came to a head in June 1999 prior to the Bundestag vote on the list of five motions. But political decision-makers with immediate political interests at heart rarely took the contextual dimension of monuments and commemorations as objects of social intercourse seriously, such that formal questions were either subordinated to political interests or eclipsed altogether. Instead of deducing the meaning of monuments solely from their extrinsic political utility, in terms of those 'for' and those 'against', one must take into account the dual contingency of monuments which derives from their extrinsic political utility in relation to intrinsic qualities of form, size, urban situation, and to existing commemorations.

Procedural Context: the Displacement of the Function of Monuments from Representation to Participation

The petitions of the associations Comité Vél' d'Hiv' 42 and Perspektive Berlin each stipulated conditions which, if fulfilled, were to be valid for an entire nation. Arguments aired in the ensuing debates adopted the criteria of petitions, such that the success or failure of each project, judged according to whether each nation was capable of implementing rhetorical or sculptural forms of commemoration (their '*Denkmalfähigkeit*'), was perceived as a litmus test for the moral and historical consciousness of the nation. These conditions were fulfilled more effectively in the case of the Vél' d'Hiv' than the Holocaust Monument for three reasons: in his speech, President Chirac counterbalanced the memory of deportations with positive traditions of the Enlightenment and Gaullist values; the 'authentic' historical site of the Vél' d'Hiv' provided a concise narrative and historical justification of the commemoration; and decision-making procedures (the legitimacy of the conditions of the petition, and the symbolic authority of the president) were largely excluded from public discussion until after the event. The conditions for the national memorial in Germany were more difficult to fulfil. Commemoration of the genocide could not be readily counterbalanced by a single alternative positive tradition, especially where no nationwide consensus had previously been established over the exclusive authority of one national founding moment, whether the 1848 or 1918 revolutions, for example, the Weimar Republic, or the popular uprising against the East German regime on 17 June 1953. The decision-making procedure in Germany was also prolonged by the unrealistic claim that the Holocaust Monument should commemorate the genocide in general and in the name of all Germans, a claim that overestimated the semantic capacity of a single site and sculptural artefact. It was likewise prolonged by the complex and plebiscitary nature of the debate, which offered regular opportunities for public involvement in exhibitions and conferences, attracted extensive press coverage, provoked statements by political leaders, and guaranteed the involvement of three organising bodies and an advisory jury. In spite of similar conditions contained in the petitions in Paris and Berlin, dissimilar procedures used to implement each commemoration meant that the debate in Germany lasted longer than that in France.

The negative memories associated with the Vél' d'Hiv' and Holocaust Monument defied the erection of a figurative object with which the nation could identify in a traditional, affirmative manner. None of the shortlisted projects in Berlin had recourse to representation of a cultural figure or event, but demanded instead the active participation of spectators in their interpretation. Even the figurative, three-dimensional Vél' d'Hiv' monument, appealing to the identification of spectators with victims of the nation, was interpreted in elaborate speeches and debates in relation to alternative political traditions. Both monuments testify to a displacement of their artistic representational function to a participatory function. The network of semiotic references in Libeskind's proposal for the Holocaust Monument offered a set of references to historical events and existing symbols which spectators were invited to decode. The counter-monument by Jochen Gerz dispensed with symbolic elements in order to induce spectators to question and write about their relation to historical media and the means by which historical understanding is acquired. Weinmiller claimed that her Star of David offered an opportunity for meditation in a 'stone garden'. Likewise, the experiential monument proposed by Eisenman was to arouse a sense of anxiety in spectators when they walked between the steles, a means of connecting with experiences of the past that should cancel out awareness of the monument as a representation of history. These memorials were intended to encourage solitary and cognitive rather than ritual group participation based, according to Kertzer's terms, on 'emotional involvement' beyond 'specific rationalisations'.[20]

In this study of the function of monuments in contemporary memory cultures, I have examined monuments which are conventional in so far as they mark urban sites with stone, but whose significance is not determined by figurative form alone, and which do not embody unambiguous coded narrative renderings of politically motivated messages about history. They are products of conflicting opinions and interests projected through complex and multiple forms of visual, rhetorical, spatial and ritual media. The process by which these monuments became central, national monuments was contingent upon conditions stipulated in the petitions of citizens' action groups, artistic and architectural competitions, structures of cultural administration, the intervention of state leaders, and the participation of journalists and members of the public. Debate over the Holocaust Monument focused initially on the quest to select a sculptural form, but increasingly on issues of its political legitimacy as well. Debate over the Vél' d'Hiv' focused on the presidential speech and political protocol, but not on sculptural form. Yet both monuments served as catalysts for discussion by intellectuals, politicians and government leaders about the political and heuristic function of commemorations and monuments in relation to their site, and on the question of how to reach a common decision. They were often mistakenly understood and interpreted as representations standing directly for national self-understanding, based on a convention of mimesis prescribed by conditions of the petitions. In reality, however, they fulfilled a catalytic function for public negotiation of the complex *medium* with which history is understood, represented and appropriated in the public sphere.

One could argue, using terms proposed by Nora, that the 'ethnographical' function of these sites of memory, fostering a critical apprehension of supports of historical understanding, outweighs their 'sentimental' function as supports of individuals' emotional attachment to shared memories,[21] for they offer a rich opportunity for participation in an ongoing negotiation of the modes of historical commemoration. First, they provoke controversy inviting us to participate in discussion about forms and about the purpose of commemoration as such. Second, they invite individuals to participate in the monuments – in the 'experiential' event presented by Eisenman, in the decoding of symbols constructed by Libeskind, or in the collection of written statements in Gerz's countermonument, for example. They are not merely normative supports of an 'imagined community' which, according to Benedict Anderson, presupposes a collective but vague sense of sharing a common language, history or cultural bonds within a limited and sovereign nation.[22] Rather, they are also obstacles to a cohesive collective identity, which stimulate open dialogue about the transmission and contemporary meaning of a difficult heritage. The quest for reconciliation (in France) or consensus (in Germany) over the issues of these monuments did not bring about the common agreement of the greatest number of individuals on the specific wording of a commemorative speech or on the sculptural form of a monument, but the common act of participating in the ongoing negotiation, construction and interpretation of historical media.

Monuments at the Intersection of Political and Artistic Representation

One of the aims of this study has been to explore the specific role of monuments in the constitution of memory cultures at a time when public memories of the persecution and genocide of the Second World War have been subjected to a process of symbolisation parallel to processes of judiciarisation, internationalisation, historicisation, politicisation and even commercialisation. The contemporary rhetoric of 'national monuments' is just one expression of the continuing relevance of public art as a vector, that is, as one of the agents of the formation of collective memory whose mechanisms require serious attention alongside those of historiography, legal procedure, financial reparation and the restitution of cultural property.

The Vél' d'Hiv' and the Holocaust Monument show how the spheres of political and artistic representation intersect as a result of the commitment of the highest political authorities and of artists and architects to forms of reparation for victims via the mass media. Although monuments engage three or more collective agents in a symbolic contract, between those who build a monument (in this case, the French and German states), those for whom it is built (Jewish victims of the genocide), and those in whose name it is built (French and German people), they are primarily an expression of the first of these categories, the 'clients' of a monument. In practice, the procedure by which this contract was fulfilled met with fewer obstacles in France than in Germany. There existed broad fundamental consensus in France over the central symbolic status of the president and his words. Broad, unspoken consensus also existed in Germany over the central symbolic status of public art, but dissent over the appropriate procedure for its implementation led to a slow and complex but also more plural exchange of ideas. In other words, state representation was taken for granted in France and shunned in Germany where, at least prior to the intervention of parliament in 1999, the exclusive authority of public art was sought. These representational paradigms were echoed in each of the petitions, which commanded extraordinary authority over the unfolding of the debates. The petitions in France calling for a verbal expression by the president presupposed that symbolic representation and political representation were concurrent; the petitions in Germany calling for a monument for 'all Germans' presupposed that the symbolic representation should be a direct expression of national consciousness, without an intermediary political representative body.

A systematic examination of the rhetoric and institutional procedures used to implement the Vél' d'Hiv' and Holocaust Monument suggests that each monument is an expression of a system of symbolic practice characteristic of its respective national memory culture. In the history of both republics, public art and architecture have played a key role in the construction of national memory cultures, drawing on a Romantic tradition in which art, art historians, exhibitions, public festivals and rituals were focal points for the formation of national consciousness. The art historian Hans Belting claims that the search for German national identity found expression during the nineteenth century not in political unity but in the collective perception of a specific artistic style. 'Art became important in the Romantic period', claims Belting, 'because people wanted art to provide what the political reality of their times could not – a distinctive expression of that emotional affinity for nature that the Romantics saw in themselves and in the German people in general.'[23] The perception of the Vél' d'Hiv' and the Holocaust Monument as mediators of national history and of public discourse about history shows that we are today confronted with an analogous phenomenon. But can memories of war crimes in countries like France and Germany be subsumed to or 'grafted' onto a genre of national representation inherited from the nineteenth century? Advocates of these monuments appear to have been motivated by the desire to overcome the difficulty of founding a positive historical identity on the basis of memories of war crimes by couching this potential source of social discord in a familiar genre recollecting the promise of social concord. In response, the sociologists Stephanie Endlich and Willi Goetschel repeatedly warned against the assumption that artistic representations such as monuments *stand for* national remembrance and that, by deduction, they relieve individuals of the responsibility for individual remembrance. Endlich and Goetschel argued that the initial campaigners for the Holocaust Monument had sought to invest the monument with a political and moral 'alibi function' for the nation, and that they had 'delegated' the task of remembrance to the monument such that it became a 'substitute memory' for genuine historical memory.[24]

The confusion of political and artistic representational practices derives from a common terminology and from the assumption that symbols can be identified directly with the collectives on behalf of which and in whose name they are built. Both political and artistic representations presuppose what the political scientist Hanna Pitkin calls 'correspondence'. Political representation is the exercise of power by a delegate or trustee on behalf of a person or nation, founded on correspondence between the representative body on the one hand and the people represented on the other; artistic representation involves an image or object standing as an equivalent of something that is not present, founded on correspondence between the representative object or symbol and a represented object.[25] Although a monument is in essence a point of convergence between artistic and political representational practices, closer analysis of the assumptions underlying our understanding of 'national monuments' or even 'national Holocaust monuments' reveals an irreconcilable relation between the expectations evoked by the terms themselves and the effective practice of public commemoration with monuments. This is not to say that a symbol cannot be political, or that a nation has no legitimate claim to symbols, but that these distinct representational practices are by definition antagonistic. There can be no direct correspondence between the monument and the nation. And since there is no language to describe the objects of either 'national' or Holocaust monuments (they are built for only an idea of 'the nation' as a collective subject, and for an idea of 'the Holocaust'), their meanings cannot be deduced from the monuments themselves but only induced extraneously from processes of production and reception, as seen in the case studies of the Vél' d'Hiv' and the Holocaust Monument.

Although formulated as appeals and protests from the grassroots, petitions for the Vél' d'Hiv' and Holocaust Monument in fact adopted and corroborated existent representational practices. The insistence by the Comité Vél' d'Hiv' 42 that nothing less than the president's word pronounced in a commemorative speech 'in an official capacity' (*'à titre officiel'*) would be a valid form of reparation, implicitly legitimised the constitution of the Fifth Republic of 1958, in which de Gaulle accorded unprecedented executive and symbolic powers to the presidency. Forms of political and artistic representation were interdependent, such that the condition for the success of the Vél' d'Hiv' campaign was the symbolic convergence of the head of state with words of recognition pronounced on a historical site on the anniversary date. The campaign for the Holocaust Monument similarly hinged on gaining acceptance for the constitutional rights of the citizens' action group or *Bürgerinitiative*, an established form of association frequently used during the 1960s and 1970s in West Germany in order to voice demands in relation to single issues of social concern, and which effectively gave expression to a form of direct democracy fostering the development of an informed public opinion. In both France and Germany, associations protested against the perceived lack of a commemoration in order to promote conventional political and artistic representations that upheld a holistic notion of the nation's symbolic unity.

It is often suggested that memories of the persecution and genocide of the Second World War should today serve to promote humanist ethical values. This is one consequence of the increasingly international recourse to monuments, museums, ritual commemorations and the introduction of Holocaust studies into school curricula. Yet the specific contribution of public art to the consolidation of ethical values amounts to more than the ritual proclamations of such values in commemorative speeches on memorial sites, whose universalistic rhetoric often detracts from historical detail and appropriates the genocide as a means to legitimise political interests such as national or European social cohesion. In reality, monuments facilitate what the sociologists Daniel Levy and Natan Sznaider call a 'contextually determined universal memory',[26] a memory that results from an individual's or group's encounter with a phenomenon of worldwide relevance such as persecution and genocide, which is understood in relation to a local context and particular experiences. Monuments thus engage spectators in dialogue with the past by means of dialogue with the site itself, that is, with the specific historical significance of the site (the events that took place on it, or the genesis of the memorial itself), and with the spectators' individual relation to history via their participation in the monumental site.

If we assume, as stated above, that the meaning of a monument lies not in the monument itself but in each spectator's contextual interpretation of it, it follows that the Vél' d'Hiv' and Holocaust Monument do not belong exclusively to the Romantic tradition of national memorials to which Belting refers. Monuments today play an integrative but also critical role within memory cultures. Rürup suggested at a meeting of the Enquete Commission of the Bundestag on 'Living Memory Culture in Democracy' in November 1997, that democracy is not compatible with a singular and binding version of collective memory, but that a democratic memory culture should thrive on 'a combination of openness, plurality and the ability to sustain conflict on the one hand, and basic democratic consensus on the other'.[27] This idea is echoed in the statutes of the Support Group for the Holocaust Monument, which states that 'memory of the murder of European Jews adheres directly to civic democratic legal and ethical goals under the rule of law.'[28] But can a public monument fulfil these conditions or somehow guarantee that legal and ethical goals or values may be sustained via collective remembrance of the persecution and genocide of the Second World War? If we expect monuments to 'stand for' national historical self-understanding, the answer to this question is clearly no. A monument is a poor symbolic representation of a national memory culture, since it forges a plurality of opinion so irreconcilable that, in practice, disputes abate only when state institutions (the French presidency and the German parliament, for example) intervene in the process of representation. The representational function of monuments is in reality twofold, as suggested by Rürup in his speech at the Enquete Commission: they sustain open, plural and even conflictory public discourse about historical events and representations alongside a more fundamental consensus over the democratic values that permit such discourse. It is on this procedural level, rather than via political statements directly negating genocide and applauding democratic traditions, that historical symbols such as Holocaust monuments are politically representative. Both Holocaust monuments examined in this study were accompanied by deliberative representation. Mitterrand's contention of the symbolic links between the Vichy regime and the Fifth Republic triggered debate over alternative commemorative rites, symbols and rhetoric and over the legal implications of the Vél' d'Hiv' commemoration. In Germany, contestation of the very necessity of a national Holocaust monument placed methods of artistic and political representation at the centre of debate. The metatheoretical aspects of these disputes thus confirm Jean-Marc Ferry's hypothesis that sites of memory forge not only social consensus but also dialogue and deliberation. It is for similar reasons that Habermas welcomed the dispute over the Holocaust Monument in Berlin on the grounds that it demonstrated a questioning of national consciousness in Germany, the articulation of particularism within universalism, and therefore contained in germ the 'postnational constellation'.[29]

The symbolic function of monuments is twofold: the Vél' d'Hiv' and Holocaust Monument continued a national symbolic convention instituted in the nineteenth century while simultaneously stimulating criticism of the principle of monumental commemoration in itself; the debates unfolded within national contexts but fostered open plural exchange of opinion; they also invested the conventional war memorial genre with symbols of criminality. In light of the public impact of discourse about these monuments, one could enquire what status they merit within ongoing international research into the influence of public symbols on the constitution of collective memory. The recent projects on 'sites of memory' in France and Germany, *Les Lieux de mémoire* and *Deutsche Erinnerungsorte,* draw attention to focal points of collective memory that are inherently ambiguous, in so far as they appeal to social cohesion but also to contention and disunity. These works promote a dual affirmative and participatory interpretation of national memory cultures. On the one hand, the editors of both collections justify the selection of sites contained in these studies in terms of their national representativeness. The German project, for example, contains sites that 'cannot be translated',[30] while both projects embody representative functions as literary models of historiographical pedagogy. On the other hand, the editors promise a degree of openness within these national frameworks. Nora understands the selection of sites metaphorically as 'à la carte' and invites readers to freely select essays from the volumes to be read.[31] In a similarly metaphorical way, François and Schulze describe the selection of German sites as a 'labyrinth' offering readers an open choice of paths of historical discovery.[32] The editorial policies of these projects are thus underpinned by theoretical models for national memory cultures, governed by openness within (according to the metaphors of menu and labyrinth) and closure without (according to the criterion of being untranslatable). The Vél' d'Hiv' and Holocaust Monument correspond only partially to this given model. They were certainly perceived as national sites of memory during the debates, but the procedural, participatory and dialogic nature of debate, their contingent and contextual (often local) significance, their ineffectiveness as objects of political or historical representation, their incompatibility with conventional oppositions of in-groups and out-groups, the metatheoretical element of debate bearing on methods of representation and deliberation, as well as implicit transnational analogies undermined the putative nationality of these sites of memory.

Beyond Musil: Making Monuments Visible with Words

The banality of monuments standing on street corners, their apparent insignificance in comparison to the overwhelming presence of media advertising, and the fact that the pasts they evoke are often detached from present-day concerns, all reinforce the topicality of Robert Musil's famous suggestion in 1927, that there is 'nothing in the world so invisible as a monument'.[33] Yet this study of two monuments on the basis of symbolic and rhetorical discourse elaborated during the course of their conception, production and reception in the public sphere, has attempted to disprove Musil's thesis as a maxim for the invisibility of public monuments in the late twentieth century. The abundance of words and images produced as a result of the Vél' d'Hiv' and Holocaust Monument projects suggests that these monuments, as sites of memory, are not only not invisible but perhaps more visible than ever. The real monument is not the stone object but the debate itself.

The lessons to be learnt from these monuments may be summarised as follows. In spite of their different artistic forms and the different historical contexts in which the Vél' d'Hiv' and Holocaust Monument emerged, these sites acquired analogous symbolic functions as national monuments due to structural parallels between institutions, political agents and the conditions established in petitions by citizens' action groups. Both debates were initiated by groups that collected signatures and published petitions in the press calling for a symbolic commemoration of Jewish victims of deportation and genocide. They were both conducted between intellectual, political and artistic elites in the form of articles, speeches, exhibitions, public conferences or parliamentary debates. Moreover, both petitions provoked the response and engagement of the mass media, associations representing other victim groups, and national political leaders. Both debates were interrupted and influenced by changes of political leadership, following presidential and parliamentary elections in France and Germany respectively. And in both countries, these monuments were called for in order to compensate for the perceived lack of an appropriate central memorial to victims of war crimes and, by deduction, in order to guarantee national redemption via symbolic reparation. Finally, language employed during the debates hinged on analogous interpretations of the monuments as reminders of war crimes, the negation of which was used to legitimise national cohesion.

As the case studies of the Vél' d'Hiv' and the Holocaust Monument have shown, it is not possible to define the significance of contemporary monuments with one comprehensive concept. We may nevertheless conclude that monuments are essentially contingent: that sculptural forms are eclectic or open; that they operate as focal points of political controversy although, being subjected to multiple and changing interpretations, they are ineffective or inexpedient as supports for political messages; and that their significance derives only partially from their representative function as sculptural forms in urban settings, and essentially from public participation in the procedural negotiation of forms and purposes of historical commemoration. Reconciliation over the Vél' d'Hiv' and consensus over the Holocaust Monument were tenuous, because stringent conditions imposed in petitions (conceiving of the monument as a national 'duty' in Germany and as a prerequisite for a national 'cure' in France) could hardly be matched by adequate commemorative measures. In both countries, these measures were ultimately fulfilled symbolically by the state: by the president in France and by parliament in Germany.

Yet neither monument is representative of state interests alone. The combined commitment of associations and states to the construction of the Vél' d'Hiv' and Holocaust Monument, and the explicit appeal within petitions to the national representative function of these monuments, suggests that they are products of both social *and* state enterprise rather than a particular local, ethnic, party or state vision of the past. The claim that the social impact of monuments is regularly overestimated[34] therefore does not apply to the Vél' d'Hiv' and Holocaust Monument. The debates over these monuments were not confined to any one association or social sphere, or to intellectual, political and artistic circles, but involved the numerous mediating institutions implicated in their construction, including the mass media, political parties, parliamentary committees, pressure groups, several associations and educational establishments. They therefore broadened opportunities for both the active and passive participation of the public in these debates, and extended the reception of the monuments beyond the strictly institutional spheres of public communication. Monuments do not symbolically embody national memory, and may not be interpreted as fixed sets of coded public archives. Rather, they are focal points of an ongoing process of public dialogue operating on the basis of artistic, historical, journalistic and political appropriations of the past.

This study began by probing the relationship between art and politics. How do stone artefacts acquire the status of national memorials, and how do they impinge upon historical consciousness? Any inquiry into the relationship between national memory cultures and Holocaust monuments begs the question to what degree such monuments can or should be considered 'national', and to what degree a national memory culture can be considered monumental, that is, socially cohesive for a population. The very term 'national monument' is a misnomer because no work of public art can represent all members of a nation collectively. Monuments are not built by nations, but by artists, with the aid of associations, citizens' initiatives, journalists, historians and politicians. Moreover, once built, the symbolic and conceptual language of a monument stimulates responses in the form of a synchronic dialogue between the site and its spectators on the basis of a diachronic dialogue between the historical significance of the site itself and subsequent artistic and rhetorical transformations of the site. The essential significance of monuments in contemporary memory cultures may therefore be sketched as follows: as non-prescriptive heuristic stimuli that enable individuals to encounter and understand both the past and their relation to the past via representations of it.

The multidisciplinary facets of art in public space confute the common dichotomy according to which monuments are treated either as vehicles of political pedagogy or as forms of purely artistic experience. Monuments are rather meeting points of different spheres of communication, that is, communication projected both by the art and onto the art during public discussion. The Vél' d'Hiv' and Holocaust Monument show that their accompanying debates often had little to do with artistic quality but with party conflict, the symbolism of their sites, with finance and with moral values. Above all, they sustained the poignant expression of a historical dialectic in remembrance of the nation but also a criminal nation in the extreme. Yet neither debate could have taken place effectively in the absence of the artistic project and the challenge of institutionalising memory symbolically on a central national site. The impossible task of symbolising the nation underpinned both debates, and was exacerbated by the challenge of commemorating deportation and genocide. The capacity of monuments to resist unequivocal interpretation may thus sustain dispute over the past and over the means by which we witness and interpret it.

Notes

1. Herbert Jochmann, *Öffentliche Kunst als Denkmalkritik. Studien zur Spezifik zeitgenössischer Kunst in Bezugnahme auf öffentliche Erinnerungszeichen*, Weimar: Verlag und Datenbank für Geisteswissenschaften, 2001.
2. Jay Winter, *Sites of Memory, Sites of Mourning*, 5ff, 225.
3. See Jan-Holger Kirsch, *Nationaler Mythos oder historische Trauer?*
4. Jochen Spielmann, 'Steine des Anstoßes - Denkmale in Erinnerung an den Nationalsozialismus in der Bundesrepublik Deutschland', *Kritische Berichte* no. 3, 1988, 5–16, 13.
5. Interview with Aleida and Jan Assmann, 'Niemand lebt im Augenblick', *Die Zeit*, 3 December 1998, 43–44, 44.
6. Winfried Speitkamp, review of James Young, *At Memory's Edge. After-images of the Holocaust in Contemporary Art and Literature*, New Haven & London: Yale University Press, 2000, in Sehpunkte 9, 2002, www.sehpunkte.historicum.net/2002/09/3930908700.html, 15 September 2002.
7. James Young, *The Texture of Memory*, 7, 11.
8. Eduard Beaucamp, 'Kunst in der Falle. Das Holocaust-Denkmal und das Scheitern der Künstler', in *Der verstrickte Künstler. Wider die Legende von der unbefleckten Avantgarde*, Cologne: DuMont, 1998, 42–47, 45. See also Stavginski's critique of the competition procedure, in which 'legitimisation via

chancellor-decisionism prevailed over legitimisation via prodecure', in Stavginski, *Das Holocaust-Denkmal*, 113f.

9. Raoul Girardet, *Mythes et mythologies politiques*, 182.
10. Jean-Marc Ferry, *L'Ethique reconstructive*, Paris: Cerf, 1996, 44.
11. Winter, *Sites of Memory, Sites of Mourning*, 85.
12. See Axel Lapp, 'Monumentales Schweigen: keine Kriegsdenkmale in Großbritannien nach dem Zweiten Weltkrieg', in Akademie der Künste, ed., *Denkmale und kulturelles Gedächtnis nach dem Ende der Ost-West-Konfrontation*, Berlin: Jovis Verlag, 2000, 293–304.
13. Koselleck, 'Kriegerdenkmale als Identitätsstiftungen der Überlebenden', 274.
14. See Young, 'The Counter-monument: Memory against Itself in Germany Today', 274.
15. Hubertus Tim Adam, 'Kämpfe um die Erinnerung. Die Neue Wache im diskursiven Streit', in Thomas Schmidt et al., eds, *Nationaler Totenkult. Die Neue Wache. Eine Streitschrift zur zentralen deutschen Gedenkstätte*, Berlin: Karin Kramer Verlag, 1995, 43–65, 60f.
16. Young, *The Texture of Memory*, 90.
17. Mona Ozouf, 'Le Panthéon', in Pierre Nora, ed., *Les Lieux de mémoire*, vol. I, *La République*, Paris: Gallimard, 1984, 139–66, 163.
18. See the open letter, '"Aus Einsicht verzichten"', *Der Tagesspiegel*, 4 February 1998, 25.
19. See Frank Ankersmit's analysis of the interrelation between political and artistic representation, in *Aesthetic Politics. Political Philosophy Beyond Fact and Value*, Stanford: Stanford University Press, 1996, Chapter I. Harry Redner makes further distinctions between aesthetic, bureaucratic, economic, legal and political forms of representation, in Redner, *A New Science of Representation*, Boulder, San Francisco & Oxford: Westview Press, 1994, 37, 46.
20. See Chapter 7, note 4.
21. Nora, 'L'ère de la commémoration', 977; idem, 'Das Abenteuer der *Lieux de mémoire*', 89.
22. Benedict Anderson, *Imagined Communities*, 7.
23. Hans Belting, *The Germans and their Art. A Troublesome Relationship*, trans. Scott Kleager, New Haven & London: Yale University Press, 1998, 27.
24. On the function of symbols as 'alibis' 'standing for' something else, or to which we 'delegate' the responsibility of remembering, see Anthony Cohen, *The Symbolic Construction of Community*, 18; Stefanie Endlich, 'Gedenkstätten und Gedenkorte in Berlin', in Endlich and Lutz, eds, *Gedenken und Lernen an historischen Orten*, 14; Willi Goetschel, 'Ab/Deckerinnerung im großen Stil', in Neue Gesellschaft für bildende Kunst, ed., *Der Wettbewerb für das 'Denkmal für die ermordeten Juden Europas'*, Berlin: Verlag der Kunst, 1995, 52–56, 56; Korn, 'Holocaust-Gedenken: Ein deutsches Dilemma', 23; Lowenthal, *The Heritage Crusade and the Spoils of History*, 12; Christian Meier, 'Das Problem eines Berliner Denkmals', *Die neue Gesellschaft/Frankfurter Hefte* no. 8, 1997, 733–43, 733; Nora, 'Entre mémoire et histoire', xxvi; Redner, *A New Science of Representation*, 25f.; Paul Ricoeur, *Temps et récit*, Paris: Seuil, vol. 3, *Le temps raconté*, 1985, 253f; Ruth Wodack et al., eds, *Die Sprachen der Vergangenheiten. Öffentliches Gedenken in österreichischen und deutschen Medien*, Frankfurt am Main: Suhrkamp, 1994, 105.
25. Cf. Hanna Pitkin, *The Concept of Representation*, Berkeley: University of California Press, 1967, 8.
26. Daniel Levy and Natan Sznaider, *Erinnerung im globalen Zeitalter: Der Holocaust*, Frankfurt am Main: Suhrkamp, 2001, 30.

27. Rürup, 'Lebendige Erinnerungskultur in der Demokratie', 2.
28. See the statutes of the Support Group for the Construction of a Monument for the Murdered Jews of Europe: 'Satzung', in Ute Heimrod et al., eds, *Der Denkmalstreit – das Denkmal. Die Debatte um das 'Denkmal für die ermordeten Juden Europas'*, Berlin: Philo Verlag, 1999, 69.
29. Jürgen Habermas, 'Der Zeigefinger. Die Deutschen und ihr Denkmal', 44.
30. François and Schulze, 'Einleitung', in François and Schulze, eds, *Deutsche Erinnerungsorte*, vol. 1, 9–24, 20.
31. Nora, 'Comment écrire l'histoire de France?', in Nora, ed., *Les Lieux de mémoire* III, Les France 1, Paris: Gallimard, 1993, 11–32, 30.
32. François and Schulze, 'Einleitung', in François and Schulze, eds, *Deutsche Erinnerungsorte*, vol. 1, 9–24, 21f.
33. See note 16.
34. Cf. Peter Burke, 'Two Crises of Historical Consciousness', *Storia della Storiografia* no. 33, 1998, 3–16, 3; Jay Winter and Emmanuel Sivan, 'Setting the Framework', 29.

Appendix

Speech by President Jacques Chirac at the ceremony commemorating the round-ups of 16 and 17 July 1942, held at the Vél' d'Hiv' monument in Paris, 16 July 1995 (English Translation)

Mayor,
President,
Ambassador,
Chief Rabbi,
Ladies and Gentlemen,

There are, in the life of a nation, moments which offend the memory and the idea one has of one's country.

It is difficult to recall these moments, because one does not always know how to find the right words with which to evoke the horror, to express the sorrow of those who lived through the tragedy. Those women and men who, in their souls and in their flesh, have been for ever marked by the memory of those days of tears and shame.

It is difficult to recall them, moreover, because those dark hours indelibly soil our history, and are an insult to our past and to our traditions. Yes, the criminal lunacy of the occupying forces was assisted by French people, by the French State.

Fifty-three years ago, on 16 July 1942, 450 French police officers and gendarmes, acting under the authority of their superiors, responded to the demands of the Nazis.

On that day, in the capital city and in the Paris area, almost ten thousand Jewish men, women and children were arrested at their homes in the early hours of the day and assembled in police stations.

Atrocious scenes were to be seen: families torn apart, mothers separated from their children, elderly people–some of whom, ex-servicemen from the Great War, had spilt blood for France–thrown brutally into Parisian buses and vans of the Paris police headquarters.

Some police officers were also to be seen turning a blind eye, allowing some people to escape.

For all those who were arrested, this was the beginning of a long and painful journey towards hell. How many of them were never to see their homes again? And how many of them, at that moment, felt betrayed? What was their distress?

France, home of the Enlightenment and of the Rights of Man, the land of welcome and refuge, on that day, accomplished irreparable acts. Failing to keep its word, it handed over its protégés to their executioners.

Having been taken to the Winter Cycling Stadium, the victims had to wait for several days in dreadful conditions, as we know, before being taken to one of the transit camps–Pithiviers or Beaune-la-Rolande–which had been set up by the authorities in Vichy.

Yet this was only the beginning of the horror.

More round-ups were to follow, more arrests. In Paris and in the provinces. Seventy-four trains left for Auschwitz. Seventy-six thousand Jewish deportees from France were never to return.

We still owe an imprescriptible debt to them.

The Torah makes it the duty of all Jews to remember. One phrase recurs time and again, which says, "Always remember that you were a slave in the land of Egypt".

Fifty years later, faithful to its law, but without a spirit of hatred or vengeance, the Jewish community remembers, and the whole of France along with it. So that six million martyrs of the Shoah can live on. So that such atrocities may never be repeated. So that the blood of the Holocaust becomes, in the words of Samuel Pisar, one "of blood and hope".

When the spirit of hatred makes itself felt, aroused here by fundamentalisms, fuelled there by fear and exclusion; and when even here, before our very doors, certain small groups, certain publications, certain teachings, and certain political parties are proving, more or less overtly, to be purveyors of racist and antisemitic ideology, then this spirit of vigilance which drives you on, which drives us on, needs to express itself more forcefully than ever before.

This is a subject for which nothing is insignificant, nothing is banal, and everything is connected. Racist crimes, the defence of revisionist arguments, all kinds of provocations–little expressions, witty remarks–derive from the same sources.

Transmitting the memory of the Jewish people, of the suffering and of the camps; bearing witness again and again; recognising the faults of the past, and the faults committed by the State; hiding nothing from the dark hours of our history, simply means defending an idea of Mankind, of its free-

dom and its dignity. It means struggling against obscure forces continually at work.
Younger people among us, I'm happy to say, are sensitive to everything relating to the Shoah. They want to know. And along with them, from now on, there are more and more French people determined to look their past squarely in the face.
France, as we all know, is not in the least an antisemitic country.
At this moment of contemplation and recollection, I want to make a choice, for hope.
I want to remember that the summer of 1942, which reveals the true face of collaboration (there remained no doubt about its racist character following the anti-Jewish laws of 1940), came, for a lot of our compatriots, as a brusque surprise, the starting point of a huge resistance movement.
I want to remember all the Jewish families, tracked down, but shielded from the ruthless investigations of the occupier and the Milice by the heroic and fraternal action of numerous French families.
I like to recall that, one month earlier, at Bir Hakeim, the Free French Forces under General Koenig had heroically held out against the German and Italian divisions for two weeks.
Of course, mistakes are made, there are faults, there is a collective fault; but there is also France, a certain idea of France, honest, generous, faithful to its traditions, to its genius. This France has never been in Vichy. And for a long time, it has not been in Paris. It is in the sands of Libya and wherever the Free French are fighting. It is in London, embodied in General de Gaulle. It is present, one and indivisible, in the heart of these French people, these "righteous among the nations" who, at the darkest moment of agony, as Serge Klarsfeld writes, at the risk of their life, save three-quarters of the Jewish community resident in France, and give life to its better qualities: humanist values, the values of freedom, justice, and tolerance on which French identity is founded, and to which we remain bound in the future.
These values, which form the basis of our democracies, are being held up to ridicule today, even in Europe, under our very eyes, by those who support ethnic purification. May we learn to draw lessons from history. Let's not accept to be passive witnesses, or accomplices, of what is unacceptable. This is the meaning of the appeal I have launched to our main partners in London, Washington and Bonn. If we wish, together, we can put a check on an undertaking which is destroying our values and which, step by step, might threaten the whole of Europe.'

Bibliography

1. Primary Sources

a. Newspapers and magazines

Allgemeine Jüdische Wochenzeitung
Berliner Volksblatt
Berliner Zeitung
Deutsche National-Zeitung
Le Figaro
Frankfurter Allgemeine Zeitung
Frankfurter Rundschau
Freitag
Jüdische Korrespondenz
Jüdisches Berlin
Jüdisches Museum Berlin
Junge Welt
Kunstzeitung
Libération
Le Monde
Le Quotidien de Paris
Der Spiegel
Stuttgarter Zeitung
Süddeutsche Zeitung
Der Tagesspiegel
Die Tageszeitung
Tribune Juive
Die Woche
Zeichen
Die Zeit

b. Brochures, Open Letters, Pamphlets, Press Releases

Akademie der Künste, *Diskussion zum Umgang mit dem 'Gestapo-Gelände'. Dokumentation*, Berlin: Akademie der Künste, 1986: protocol.

Bürgerinitiative Perpektive Berlin, ed., *Ein Denkmal für die ermordeten Juden Europas. Dokumentation 1988–1995*, Berlin, 1995: brochure and press cuttings.

Commission du Souvenir du C.R.I.F., *Inauguration de la Place des Martyrs Juifs du Vélodrome d'Hiver. Grande Rafle des 16 et 17 juillet 1942*, July 1986: brochure & protocol.

Conradi, Peter, Das 1. *Kolloquium zum Denkmal für die ermordeten Juden Europas am 10.1.97 in Berlin*, 10 January 1997: open letter.

Deutscher Bundestag, *Verhandlungen des Deutschen Bundestages. Stenographischer Bericht*, Bonn, 25 June 1999: protocol.

Duve, Freimut, ed., *Mahnmal für die Opfer des Krieges und der Gewaltherrschaft in Bonn*, Bonn: SPD Bundestagsfraktion, 1985.

Endlich, Stephanie, 'Überlegungen zur Kunst im öffentlichen Raum', *Berlin Stadtforum. Programm für die 21. Sitzung des Stadtforums am 19/20.6.1992*: brochure.

Initiativkreis gegen den Schlußstrich, *Zum Holocaust-Mahnmal in Berlin*, May 1999: pamphlet.

Kommission zum Umgang mit den politischen Denkmälern der Nachkriegszeit im ehemaligen Ost-Berlin, *Bericht*, Berlin, 15 February 1993.

Materialien für die erste Beurteilungssitzung, November 1997: press releases on artists' blueprints for a 'Holocaust Monument'.

Materialien für die zweite Beurteilungssitzung, August 1998: press releases on artists' blueprints for a 'Holocaust Monument'.

Ministère des Anciens Combattants et Victimes de Guerre. Délégation à la Mémoire et à l'Information Historique, *Le Mémorial des Martyrs de la Déportation (Paris – Ile de la Cité)*, Paris, 1995: brochure.

Reichel, Peter, *Geschichtspolitik und Erinnerungskultur in Deutschland*, 10 November 1997: statement at Enquete-Kommission of the Bundestag 'Demokratische Erinnerungskultur', Berlin.

Rürup, Reinhard, *Lebendige Erinnerungskultur in der Demokratie: Gedanken und Erwartungen*, 10 November 1997: statement at Enquete-Kommission of the Bundestag 'Demokratische Erinnerungskultur', Berlin.

Senatsverwaltung für Bau- und Wohnungswesen, ed., *Künstlersicher Wettbewerb – Denkmal für die ermordeten Juden Europas*, Berlin, 1995 & 1997: briefings for architectural competitions in 1995 and 1997.

Senatsverwaltung für Wissenschaft, Forschung und Kultur, ed., *Colloquium: Denkmal für die ermordeten Juden Europas*, Berlin, 1997: protocol.

Sigurdsson, Sigrid, *Deutschland. Ein Denkmal. Ein Forschungsauftrag 1996 bis…*, www.keom.de/denkmal, 1998–2000: database, maps, installations in progress.

Stiftung Denkmal für die ermordeten Juden Europas, *Wir können uns unserer Geschichte nicht entziehen*, 1995: pamphlet calling for donations.

Zech, Mechthild, and Andreas Kühler, eds, *Ein Zentrales Denkmal für die ermordeten Juden Europas?* Berlin: Berliner Institut für Lehrerfort- und -weiterbildung und Schulentwicklung, 1997: exhibition catalogue.

2. Secondary Sources

Abramson, Daniel, 'Maya Lin and the 1960s: Monuments, Time Lines, and Minimalism', *Critical Inquiry* no. 4, 1996, 679–709.

Adam, Hubertus Tim, 'Kämpfe um die Erinnerung. Die Neue Wache im diskursiven Streit', in Thomas Schmidt et al., eds, *Nationaler Totenkult. Die Neue Wache. Eine Streitschrift zur zentralen deutschen Gedenkstätte*, Berlin: Karin Kramer Verlag, 1995.

Agamben, Giorgio, *Remnants of Auschwitz. The Witness and the Archive*. trans. Daniel Heller-Roazen, New York: Zone Books, 2000.

Agulhon, Maurice, 'De Gaulle et l'histoire de France', *Vingtième Siècle* no. 53, January–March 1997, 3–12.

Alter, Peter, *Nationalismus*, Frankfurt am Main: Suhrkamp, 1985.

Anderson, Benedict, *Imagined Communities. Reflections on the Origin and Spread of Nationalism* (1983), London & New York: Verso, 1991.

Ankersmit, Frank, *Aesthetic Politics. Political Philosophy Beyond Fact and Value*, Stanford: Stanford University Press, 1996.

Arnheim, Rudolf, *The Power of the Center. A Study of Composition in the Visual Arts*, Berkeley, Los Angeles & London: University of California Press, 1988.

Assmann, Aleida, *Erinnerungsräume. Formen und Wandlungen des kulturellen Gedächtnisses*, Munich: C. H. Beck, 1999.

____, 'Individuelles und kollektives Gedächtnis – Formen, Funktionen und Medien', in Kurt Wettengel, ed., *Das Gedächtnis der Kunst. Geschichte und Erinnerung in der Kunst der Gegenwart*, Frankfurt am Main: Hatje Cantz Verlag, 2000.

Assmann, Aleida, and Ute Frevert, *Geschichtsvergessenheit – Geschichtsversessenheit. Vom Umgang mit deutschen Vergangenheiten nach 1945*. Stuttgart: Deutsche Verlags-Anstalt, 1999.

Assmann, Jan, *Das Kulturelle Gedächtnis. Schrift, Erinnerung und politische Identität in frühen Hochkulturen*, Munich: C. H. Beck, 1992.

Augé, Marc, *Non-lieux. Introduction à une anthropologie de la surmodernité*, Paris: Seuil, 1992.

Azéma, Jean-Pierre, and François Bédarida, eds, *La France des années noires*, 2 vols, Paris: Seuil, 1993.

____, eds, *Vichy et les français*, Paris: Fayard, 1992.

Barcellini, Serge, and Annette Wieviorka, *Passant, souviens-toi! Les lieux du souvenir de la Seconde Guerre mondiale en France*, Paris: Plon, 1995.

Barou, Jacques et al., *Mémoire et intégration*, Paris: Syros, 1993.

Bauer, Yehuda, 'Geschichtsschreibung und Gedächtnis am Beispiel des Holocaust', *Transit* no. 22, 2002, 178–92.

Beaucamp, Eduard, *Der verstrickte Künstler. Wider die Legende von der unbefleckten Avantgarde*, Cologne: DuMont, 1998.

Becker, Udo, *Lexikon der Symbole*, Freiburg, Basel, Vienna: Herder, 1992.

Bédarida, François, ed., *L'histoire et le métier d'historien en France 1945–1995*, Paris: Editions de la maison des sciences de l'homme, 1995.

Belting, Hans, *The Germans and their Art: A Troublesome Relationship*, trans. Scott Kleager, New Haven & London: Yale University Press, 1998.

Benbassa, Esther, *The Jews of France. A History from Antiquity to the Present*, trans. M. DeBevoise, Princeton: Princeton University Press, 1999.

Bensoussan, Georges, 'Histoire, mémoire et commémoration. Vers une religion civile', *Le Débat* no. 82, 1994, 90–97.

Benton, Sarah, 'The 1945 "Republic"', *History Workshop Journal* no. 43, 1997, 249–57.

Berger, Peter, and Thomas Luckmann, *The Social Construction of Reality. A Treatise in the Sociology of Knowledge* (1966), Harmondsworth: Penguin, 1991.
Bernstein, Michael, 'Homage to the Extreme. The Shoah and the Rhetoric of Catastrophe', *The Times Literary Supplement*, 6 March 1998, 6–8.
Bernstein, Serge, 'Le retour de la culture républicaine', *Vingtième Siècle* no. 44, 1994, 113–20.
Beyme, Klaus von, *Hauptstadtsuche*, Frankfurt am Main: Suhrkamp, 1991.
Billig, Michael, *Banal Nationalism*, London: Sage, 1995.
____, 'Nationalism as an International Ideology: Imagining the Nation, Others and the World of Nations', in Glynis Breakwell and Evanthia Lyons, eds, *Changing European Identities: Social Psychological Analyses of Social Change*, Oxford: Buttersworth-Heinemann, 1996, 181–94.
Blänkner, Reinhard, 'Integration durch Verfassung? Die "Verfassung" in den institutionellen Symbolordnungen des 19. Jahrhunderts in Deutschland', in Hans Vorländer, ed., *Integration durch Verfassung*, Wiesbaden: Westdeutscher Verlag, 2002, 213–36.
Bloch, Marc, (1928) 'Pour une histoire comparée des sociétés européennes', in *Histoire et Historiens*, Paris: Armand Colin, 1995, 94–123.
____, *The Historian's Craft*, trans. Peter Putnam, Manchester: Manchester University Press, 1954.
Bodemann, Michael, *Gedächtnistheater. Die jüdische Gemeinschaft und ihre deutsche Erfindung*, Hamburg: Rotbuch Verlag, 1996.
Bodenschatz, Harald, *Berlin. Auf der Suche nach dem verlorenen Zentrum*, Berlin: Junius, 1995.
den Boer, Pim, and Willem Frijhoff, eds, *Lieux de mémoire et identités nationales*, Amsterdam: Amsterdam University Press, 1993.
Borg, Alan, *War Memorials from Antiquity to the Present*, London: Leo Cooper, 1991.
Bourdieu, Pierre, 'Espace social et genèse des "classes"', *Actes de la recherche en sciences sociales* no. 52–53, 1984, 3–12.
____, *The Rules of Art*, trans. Susan Emanuel, Cambridge: Polity Press, 1996.
____, *Langage et pouvoir symbolique*, Paris: Fayard, 2001.
Braitling, Petra, and Walter Reese-Schäfer, eds, *Universalismus, negativer Nationalismus und die neue Einheit der Deutschen*, Frankfurt am Main: Fischer, 1991.
Brenner, Michael, *After the Holocaust. Rebuilding Jewish Lives in Postwar Germany*, trans. Barbara Harshar, Princeton: Princeton University Press, 1977.
Bruendel, Steffen, and Nicole Grochowina, eds, *Kulturelle Identität*, Berlin: Centre Marc Bloch, 2000.
Brumlik, Micha, 'Gewissen, Gedenken und anamnetische Solidarität', *Universitas* no. 630, December 1998, 1143–53.
Bruner, M. Lane, *Strategies of Remembrance: The Rhetorical Dimensions of National Identity Construction*, Columbia: University of South Carolina Press, 2002.
Burke, Peter, 'French Historians and their Cultural Identities', in E. Tonkin et al., eds, *History and Ethnicity*, London: Routledge, 1989, 157–67.
____, 'Two Crises of Historical Consciousness', *Storia della Storiografia* no. 33, 1998, 3–16.
Buttlar, Florian von, and Stefanie Endlich, 'Das Berliner Holocaust-Denkmal. Ablauf des Wettbewerbs und Stand der Diskussion', in Akademie der Künste, ed., *Denkmale und kulturelles Gedächtnis nach dem Ende der Ost-West-Konfrontation*, Berlin: Jovis, 2000, 305–28.
Carr, Edward, *What is History?* (1961), Harmondsworth: Penguin, 1964.
Carrier, Peter, 'Historical Traces of the Present: the Uses of Commemoration', *Historical Reflections/Réflexions Historiques* no. 2, 1996, 431–45.

____, 'Places, Politics and the Archiving of Contemporary Memory in Pierre Nora's *Les Lieux de mémoire*', in Susannah Radstone, ed., *Memory and Methodology*, Oxford: Berg, 2000, 37–58.

Carrozza, Gianni, *Le Nationalisme de l'entre-deux-guerres: quelques références classiques et la production récente. Bibliographie*, Nanterre: Bibliothèque de Documentation Internationale Contemporaine, 1995.

Cassirer, Ernst, *Philosophie der symbolischen Formen*, Darmstadt: Primus Verlag, 1977.

Celan, Paul, *Atemwende*, Frankfurt am Main: Suhrkamp, 1967.

Charlot, Jean, *Pourquoi Jacques Chirac?* Paris: Fallois, 1995.

Chauveau, Agnès, and Philippe Tétart, eds, *Questions à l'histoire des temps présents*, Brussels: Editions Complexe, 1992.

Choay, Françoise, *The Invention of the Historical Monument*, trans. Lauren O'Connell, Cambridge: Cambridge University Press, 2001.

Citron, Susanne, *Le mythe national. L'histoire de France en question*, Paris: Editions Ouvrières, 1989.

Cohen, Anthony, *The Symbolic Construction of Community*, Chichester, London & New York: Ellis Horwood & Tavistock Publishers, 1985.

Combe, Sonia, *Archives interdites. Les peurs françaises face à l'Histoire contemporaine*, Paris: Albin Michel, 1994.

Conan, Eric, and Henry Rousso, *Vichy, un passé qui ne passe pas*, Paris: Fayard, 1994.

Confino, Alon, 'Collective Memory and Cultural History: Problems of Method', *The American Historical Review* no. 5, December 1997, 1386–403.

Connerton, Paul, *How Societies Remember*, Cambridge: Cambridge University Press, 1989.

Cullen, Michael, ed., *Das Holocaust-Mahnmal. Dokumentation einer Debatte*, Zürich & Munich: Pendo Verlag, 1999.

Desquesnes, Rémy, '1994: Echos des commémorations de la deuxième guerre mondiale: 1990–1995', *Contemporary French Civilization* no. 2, 1995, 148–98.

Deutsch, Karl, *Nationalism and Social Communication. An Inquiry into the Foundations of Nationality*, Cambridge, Mass.: MIT Press, 1953.

Diers, Michael, ed., *Mon(u)mente. Formen und Funktionen ephemerer Denkmäler*, Berlin: Akademie Verlag, 1993.

____, 'Politik und Denkmäler. Allianzen – Mesalliancen', *Zeitschrift für Kunsttechnologie und Konservierung* no. 1, 1995, 5–17.

Dörner, Andreas, *Politischer Mythos und symbolische Politik. Sinnstiftung durch symbolische Formen*, Opladen: Westdeutscher Verlag, 1994.

Duhamel, Olivier, and Jérôme Jaffré, eds, *L'Etat de l'opinion 1995*, Paris: SOFRES, Seuil, 1995.

Eberl, Wolfgang, 'Sind Denkmäler heute möglich?', in Ekkehard Mai and Gisela Schmirber, eds, *Denkmal – Zeichen – Monument. Skulptur und öffentlicher Raum heute*, Munich: Prestel Verlag, 1989, 35–37.

Eco, Umberto, *The Open Work*, trans. Anna Cancogni, London: Hutchinson, 1989.

Edelman, Murray, *The Symbolic Uses of Politics*, Urbana, Chicago & London: University of Illinois Press, 1964.

____, *Political Language. Words That Succeed and Policies That Fail*, New York: Academic Press, 1977.

____, *Constructing the Political Spectacle*, Chicago & London: University of Chicago Press 1988.

Elias, Norbert, *The Symbol Theory*, London, Newbury Park & New Delhi: Sage, 1989.

Endlich, Stephanie, *Die Zukunft des Berliner 'Prinz-Albrecht-Geländes' ('Gestapo-*

Geländes'), Berlin: Senatsverwaltung für Kulturelle Angelegenheiten & Berliner Festspiele, 1990.
Endlich, Stephanie, and Thomas Lutz, eds, *Gedenken und Lernen an historischen Orten*, Berlin: Landeszentrale für politische Bildung, 1995.
Evans, Martin, and Ken Lunn, eds, *War and Memory in the Twentieth Century*, London: Berg, 1997.
Fechler, Bernd, 'Zwischen Tradierung und Konfliktvermittlung. Über den Umgang mit "problematischen" Aneignungsformen der NS-Geschichte in multikulturellen Schulklassen. Ein Praxisbericht', in Bernd Fechler, Gottfried Kößler and Till Lieberz-Groß, eds, *'Erziehung nach Auschwitz' in der multikulturellen Gesellschaft. Pädagogische und soziologische Annäherungen*, Weinheim & Munich: Juventa Verlag, 2000, 207–27.
Ferry, Jean-Marc, *L'Ethique reconstructive*, Paris: Cerf, 1996.
Flacke, Monika, ed., *Mythen der Nationen. Ein europäisches Panorama*, Berlin: Deutsches Historisches Museum, 1998.
Flood, Christopher, and Hugo Frey, 'The Vichy Syndrome Revisited', *Contemporary French Civilization* no. 2, 1995, 231–49.
Forever in the Shadow of Hitler, trans. James Knowlton and Truett Cates, Atlantic Highlands: Humanities Press International, 1993.
Fowler, Robert, 'Community: Reflections on Definition', in Amitai Etzioni, ed., *New Communitarian Thinking*, Charlottesville & London: University Press of Virginia, 1995, 88–98.
François, Etienne, ed., *Lieux de mémoire: d'un modèle français à un projet allemand*, Berlin: Centre Marc Bloch, 1996.
François, Etienne et al., eds, *Nation und Emotion*, Göttingen: Vandenhoeck & Ruprecht, 1995.
François, Etienne, and Hagen Schulze, 'Das emotionale Fundament der Nationen', in Monika Flacke, ed., *Mythen der Nationen. Ein europäisches Panorama*, Berlin: Deutsches Historisches Museum, 1998, 17–32.
____, eds, *Deutsche Erinnerungsorte*, 3 vols, Munich: C.H. Beck, 2001.
Frank, Robert, 'A propos des commémorations françaises de la deuxième guerre mondiale', in Alfred Wahl, ed., *Mémoire de la Seconde Guerre Mondiale*, Metz: Centre de Recherche Histoire et Civilisation de l'Europe Occidentale, 1984, 281–90.
Frei, Norbert, *Vergangenheitspolitik. Die Anfänge der Bundesrepublik und die NS-Vergangenheit*, Munich: C.H. Beck, 1996.
Frey, Hugo, 'Rebuilding France. Gaullist Historiography, the Rise-fall Myth and French Identity 1945–58', in Stefan Berger et al., eds, *Writing National Histories. Western Europe since 1800*, London: Routledge, 1999, 205–16.
Friedlander, Saul, ed., *Probing the Limits of Representation*, Cambridge, Mass. & London: Harvard University Press, 1992.
Friedrich, Jörg, *Der Brand. Deutschland im Bombenkrieg*, Berlin: Propyläen, 2002.
Fulbrook, Mary, *German National Identity after the Holocaust*, Cambridge: Polity Press, 1999.
Füredi, Frank, *Mythical Past, Elusive Future*, London: Pluto Press, 1992.
Gaffney, John, *The French Left and the Fifth Republic. The Discourses of Communism and Socialism in Contemporary France*, London: Macmillan, 1989.
Gaffney, John, and E. Kolinsky, eds, *Political Culture in France and Germany*, London: Routledge, 1991.
Gall, Lothar, 'Brauchen wir eine Mitte?', in Helmut Engel and Wolfgang Ribbe, eds, *Hauptstadt Berlin – Wohin mit der Mitte? Historische, städtebauliche und architektonische Wurzeln des Stadtzentrums*, Berlin: Akademie Verlag, 1993,

229–36.
Gaspard, Françoise, and Farhad Khosrokhavar, *Le Foulard et la République*, Paris: La Découverte, 1995.
Gaulle, Charles de, *Mémoires de guerre*, 6 vols, Paris: Plon: vol. 1, L'Appel 1940–1942, 1976.
Georgi, Viola, *Entliehene Erinnerung. Geschichtsbilder junger Migranten in Deutschland*, Hamburg: HIS Verlag, 2003.
Germer, Stefan, 'Retrovision: die rückblickende Erfindung der Nationen durch die Kunst', in Monika Flacke, ed., *Mythen der Nationen. Ein europäisches Panorama*, Berlin: Deutsches Historisches Museum, 1998, 32–52.
Geyer, Michael, 'The Place of the Second World War in German Memory and History', *New German Critique* no. 71, 1997, 5–40.
Giesen, Bernhard, *Die Intellektuellen und die Nation*, Frankfurt am Main: Suhrkamp, 1993.
Giesen, Bernhard, and Kay Junge, 'Der Mythos des Universalismus', in Helmut Berding, ed., *Mythos und Nation*, Frankfurt am Main: Suhrkamp, 1996, 34–64.
Gillis, J.R., ed., *Commemorations. The Politics of National Identity*, Princeton: Princeton University Press, 1994.
Gilman, Sander, *Jews in Today's German Culture*, Bloomington: Indiana University Press, 1995.
Girardet, Raoul, ed., *Le nationalisme français*, Paris: Seuil, 1983.
____, *Mythes et mythologies politiques*, Paris: Seuil, 1986.
Gombrich, Ernst, *The Uses of Images. Studies in the Social Function of Art and Visual Communication*, London: Phaidon, 1999.
Grasskamp, Walter, ed., *Unerwünschte Monumente. Moderne Kunst im Stadtraum*, Munich: Verlag Silke Schreiber, 1992.
Gross, Raphael, and Werner Konitzer, 'Zum Fortwirken der nationalsozialistischen Moral', *Mittelweg 36* no. 4, 1999, 44–67.
Grosse, Frieder, *Zentrale nationale Holocaust-Gedenkstätte in Berlin. Ein Plädoyer für Toleranz*, Bremen: WMIT-Druck und Verlags-GmbH, 2001.
Guillaume, Marc, *La Politique du patrimoine*, Paris: Galilée, 1980.
Habermas, Jürgen, *Eine Art Schadensabwicklung*, Frankfurt am Main: Suhrkamp, 1987.
____, *Die nachholende Revolution*, Frankfurt am Main: Suhrkamp, 1990.
____, 'Der Zeigefinger. Die Deutschen und ihr Denkmal', *Die Zeit*, 31 March 1999, 42–44.
Halbwachs, Maurice, *Les Cadres sociaux de la mémoire* (1925), Paris: Albin Michel, 1994.
____, *La mémoire collective* (1950), Paris: Albin Michel, 1997.
Hall, Stuart, 'The Work of Representation', in Hall, ed., *Representation. Cultural Representations and Signifying Practices*, London, Thousand Oaks & New Delhi: Sage, Open University Press, 1997, 13–64
Hamburger Kunstverein, ed., *Richard Serra: Zum Holocaust-Mahnmal in Berlin*, trans. Barbara Uppenkamp, Hamburg: Hamburger Kunstverein, 1998.
Handler, Richard, 'Is "Identity" a Useful Cross-cultural Concept?' in John Gillis, ed., *Commemorations. The Politics of National Identity*, Princeton: Princeton University Press, 1994, 27–40.
Hartog, François, 'Temps et histoire. "Comment écrire l'histoire de France?"', *Annales* HSS no. 6, 1995, 1219–36.
Haupt, Heinz-Gerhard, and Jürgen Kocka, eds, Geschichte und Vergleich. *Ansätze und Ergebnisse international vergleichender Geschichtsschreibung*, Frankfurt am Main: Campus Verlag, 1996.

Heimrod, Ute, Günter Schlusche and Horst Seferens, eds, *Der Denkmalstreit – das Denkmal? Die Debatte um das 'Denkmal für die ermordeten Juden Europas'*. Eine Dokumentation, Berlin: Philo Verlag, 1999.

Heinich, Nathalie, 'Sortir du silence: justice ou pardon?', *Le Débat* no. 89, 191–97.

____, 'En guise de clarification', *Le Débat* no. 89, 205–6.

Heinrich, Christoph, *Strategien des Erinnerns. Der veränderte Denkmalbegriff in der Kunst der achtziger Jahre*, Munich: Verlag Silke Schreiber, 1993.

Herz, Rudolf, and Reinhard Matz, *Zwei Entwürfe zum Holocaust-Denkmal*, Nuremberg: Verlag für moderne Kunst, 2001.

Hewison, Robert, *The Heritage Industry. Britain in a Climate of Decline*, London: Methuen, 1987.

Hobsbawm, Eric, *Nations and Nationalism since 1780. Programme, Myth, Reality*, Cambridge: Cambridge University Press, 1990.

____, *The Age of Extremes. The Short Twentieth Century 1914–1991*, London: Michael Joseph, 1994.

____, 'Identity Politics and the Left', *New Left Review* no. 217, 1996, 38–47.

Hobsbawm, Eric, and Terence Ranger, eds, *The Invention of Tradition*, Cambridge: Cambridge University Press, 1983.

Hoffmann, Detlef, and Karl Ermert, eds, Kunst und Holocaust. *Bildliche Zeugen vom Ende der westlichen Kultur*, Rehburg-Loccum: Evangelische Akademie Loccum, 1990.

Hoffmann, Hilmar, ed., *Gegen den Versuch, Vergangenheit zu verbiegen*, Frankfurt am Main: Athenäum, 1987.

Hübner, Holger, *Das Gedächtnis der Stadt. Gedenktafeln in Berlin*, Berlin: Argon Verlag, 1997.

Hutton, Patrick, *History as an Art of Memory*, Hanover & London: University of Vermont Press, 1993.

Huyssen, Andreas, *Twilight Memories. Marking Time in a Culture of Amnesia*, New York & London: Routledge, 1995.

____, 'Monumental Seduction', *New German Critique* no. 69, 1996, 181–200.

Hyman, Paula, *The Jews of Modern France*, Berkeley: University of California Press, 1998.

Iggers, Georg, *Geschichtswissenschaft im 20. Jahrhundert*, Göttingen: Vandenhoeck & Ruprecht, 1993.

Inglis, Ken, 'Entombing Unknown Soldiers: From London and Paris to Baghdad', *History & Memory* no. 5, 1993, 7–31.

Institut d'Histoire du Temps Présent, ed., *Ecrire l'histoire du temps présent*. Paris: CNRS Editions, 1993.

Jäger, Siegfried, *Kritische Diskursanalyse. Eine Einführung*, Duisburg: Duisburger Institut für Sprach- und Sozialforschung, 1993.

____, *Text- und Diskursanalyse. Eine Anleitung zur Analyse politischer Texte*, Duisburg: D.I.S.S., 1993.

James, Paul, *Nation Formation. Towards a Theory of Abstract Community*, London, Thousand Oaks & New Delhi: Sage, 1996.

Jeismann, Michael, ed., *Mahnmal Mitte: Eine Kontroverse*, Cologne: DuMont, 1999.

Jochmann, Herbert, *Öffentliche Kunst als Denkmalkritik. Studien zur Spezifik zeitgenössischer Kunst in Bezugnahme auf öffentliche Erinnerungszeichen*, Weimar: Verlag und Datenbank für Geisteswissenschaften, 2001.

Kertzer, David, *Ritual, Politics and Power*, New Haven & London: Yale University Press, 1988.

Kirsch, Jan-Holger, *Nationaler Mythos oder historische Trauer? Der Streit um ein zentrales 'Holocaust-Mahnmal' für die Berliner Republik*, Cologne & Vienna: Böhlau,

2003.
Klarsfeld, Serge, *Le Mémorial de la déportation des juifs de France*, Paris: Centre de Documentation Juive Contemporaine de Paris, 1979.
____, ed., *Mémoire du génocide*, Paris: Centre de Documentation Juive Contemporaine and Association 'Fils et Filles des Déportés Juifs de France', 1987.
Klein, Théo, 'Une manière d'être juif', interview with Théo Klein, *Le Débat* no. 82, 1994, 117–28.
Klother, Eva-Maria, *Denkmalplastik nach 1945 bis 1989 in Ost- und West-Berlin*, Münster: Lit Verlag, 1996.
Koch, Heinz, Nationale *Mahn- und Gedenkstätte Buchenwald. Geschichte ihrer Entstehung*, Weimar: Druckhaus Weimar, 1988.
Kocka, Jürgen, 'Geteilte Erinnerungen. Zweierlei Geschichtsbewußtsein im vereinten Deutschland', *Blätter für deutsche und internationale Politik* no. 1, 1998, 104–11.
Korn, Salomon, 'Holocaust-Gedenken: Ein deutsches Dilemma', *Aus Politik und Zeitgeschichte* no. 4, 1997, 23–30.
Koselleck, Reinhart, 'Kriegerdenkmale als Identitätsstiftungen der Überlebenden', in Odo Marquard and Karlheinz Stierle, eds, *Identität*, Munich: Wilhelm Fink Verlag, 1979, 255–76.
Koselleck, Reinhart, and Michael Jeismann, eds, *Der politische Totenkult. Kriegerdenkmäler in der Moderne*, Munich: Wilhelm Fink Verlag, 1994.
Kruse, Irène, 'Le Mémorial de l'Holocauste à Berlin', *Vingtième Siècle* no. 67, 2000, 21–32.
Kunstamt Schöneberg, ed. *Orte des Erinnerns*, vol. 1, *Das Denkmal im Bayerischen Viertel: Kontext und Rezeption des Kunstprojekts von Renata Stih und Frieder Schnock*; vol. 2, *Jüdisches Alltagsleben im Bayrischen Viertel. Eine Dokumentation*, Berlin: Kunstamt Schöneberg, 1994.
LaGrou, Pieter, *The Legacy of Nazi Occupation: Patriotic Memory and National Recovery in Western Europe, 1945–1965*, Cambridge: Cambridge University Press, 2000.
Landsberg, Alison, 'America, the Holocaust, and the Mass Culture of Memory: Towards a Radical Politics of Empathy', *New German Critique* no. 71, 1997, 63–86.
Lapp, Axel, 'Monumentales Schweigen: keine Kriegsdenkmale in Großbritannien nach dem Zweiten Weltkrieg', in Akademie der Künste, ed., *Denkmale und kulturelles Gedächtnis nach dem Ende der Ost-West-Konfrontation*, Berlin: Jovis Verlag, 2000.
Lavabre, Marie-Claire, 'Usages du passé, usages de la mémoire', *Revue Française de Science Politique* no. 3, 1994, 480–93.
Le Goff, Jacques, 'Documento / monumento', in *Enciclopedia Einaudi*, vol. 5, Turin, 1978, 38–48.
____, *Histoire et mémoire*, Paris: Gallimard, 1988.
Le Goff, Jacques et al., eds, *Dictionnaire de la nouvelle histoire*, Paris: Bibliothèque du C.E.P.L., 1978.
Lehmbruch, Gerhard, 'Strukturen ideologischer Konflikte bei Parteienwettbewerb', *Politische Vierteljahresschrift* no. 10, 1969, 285–313.
Leniaud, Jean-Michel, *L'Utopie française. Essai sur le patrimoine*, Paris: Mengès, 1992.
Lepsius, M. Rainer, *Demokratie in Deutschland*, Göttingen: Vandenhoeck & Ruprecht, 1993.
Levy, Claude, and André Tillard, *La Grande rafle du Vel' d'Hiv'*, Paris: Laffont, 1967.

Levy, Daniel, and Natan Sznaider, *Erinnerung im globalen Zeitalter: Der Holocaust*, Frankfurt am Main: Suhrkamp, 2001.
Levy, Margot, ed., *Remembering for the Future. The Holocaust in an Age of Genocide*, 3 vols, Basingstoke: Palgrave, 2001.
Link, Jürgen, *Versuch über Normalismus. Wie Normalität produziert wird*, Opladen: Westdeutscher Verlag, 1996.
Link, Jürgen, and Wulf Wülfing, eds, *Nationale Mythen und Symbole in der zweiten Hälfte des 19. Jahrhunderts. Strukturen und Funktionen von Konzepten nationaler Identität*, Stuttgart: Klett-Cotta, 1991.
Lochak, Danièle, 'Usages et mésusages d'une notion polémique. La référence à l'identité nationale dans le débat sur la réforme du code de la nationalité 1985–1993', in C.R.I.S.P.A. and C.U.R.A.P.P., eds, *L'Identité politique*, Paris: Presses Universitaires de France, 1994, 306–23.
Loewy, Hanno, ed., *Holocaust: Die Grenzen des Vestehens. Eine Debatte über die Besetzung der Geschichte*, Reinbek: Rowohlt, 1992.
____, 'A History of Ambivalence: postreunification German Identity and the Holocaust', *Patterns of Prejudice* no. 2, 2002, 3–13.
Loewy, Hanno, and Werner Schneider, 'Wir Deutsche und die Ehre des Vaterlandes. Über Klaus von Dohnanyis Rede zur Ausstellung "Aufstand des Gewissens" in der Paulskirche', *Blätter für deutsche und internationale Politik* no. 3, 1998, 359–70.
Lorenzer, Alfred, *Sprachspiel und Interaktionsformen*, Frankfurt am Main: Suhrkamp, 1977.
Lowenthal, David, *The Past is a Foreign Country*, Cambridge: Cambridge University Press, 1985.
____, 'Identity, Heritage, and History', in John Gillis, ed., *Commemorations. The Politics of National Identity*, Princeton: Princeton University Press, 1994, 41–57.
____, *The Heritage Crusade and the Spoils of History*, London: Viking, 1997.
____, 'Fabricating Heritage', *History & Memory* no. 1, 1998, 5–24.
Lübbe, Hermann, *Die Gegenwart der Vergangenheit. Kulturelle und politische Funktionen des historischen Bewußtseins*, Oldenburg: Heinz Holberg Verlag, 1985.
____, *'Ich entschuldige mich.' Das neue politische Bußritual*, Berlin: Siedler, 2001.
Mai, Ekkehard, and Gisela Schmirber, eds, *Denkmal – Zeichen – Monument. Skulptur und öffentlicher Raum heute*, Munich: Prestel Verlag, 1989.
Marcus, Jonathan, 'Advance or Consolidation? The French National Front and the 1995 Elections', *West European Politics* no. 2, 1996, 303–20.
Marquard, Odo, and Karlheinz Stierle, eds, *Identität*, Munich: Wilhelm Fink Verlag, 1979.
Mattenklott, Gert, 'Denkmal/Memorial', *Daidalos* no. 49, 1993, 26–35.
____, '"Denk ich an Deutschland..." Deutsche Denkmäler 1790 bis 1990', in Sekretariat für kulturelle Zusammenarbeit Nordrhein-Westfalen, ed., *Deutsche Nationaldenkmale 1790–1990*, Bielefeld: Verlag für Regionalgeschichte, 1993, 17–47.
Meadow, Robert, *Politics as Communication*, New Jersey: Ablex Publishing Corp., 1980.
Meier, Christian, 'Erinnern – Verdrängen – Vergessen', *Merkur* no. 570/571, 1996, 937–52.
____, 'Das Problem eines Berliner Denkmals', *Die neue Gesellschaft/Frankfurter Hefte* no. 8, 1997, 733–43.
Menkovic, Biljana, *Politische Gedenkkultur. Denkmäler – die Visualisierung politischer Macht im öffentlichen Raum*, Vienna: Braumüller, 1999.
Michalski, Sergiusz, *Public Monuments. Art in Political Bondage 1870–1997*, London:

Reaktion Books, 1998.
Milton, Sybil, *In Fitting Memory. The Art and Politics of Holocaust Memorials*, Detroit: Wayne State University Press, 1991.
Ministerium für Wissenschaft, Forschung und Kultur des Landes Brandenburg and Brandenburgische Landeszentrale für politische Bildung, eds, *Brandenburgische Gedenkstätten für die Verfolgten des NS-Regimes*, Berlin: Hentrich, 1992.
Mouré, Kenneth, and Martin Alexander, eds, *Crisis and Renewal in France 1918–1962*, New York & Oxford: Berghahn, 2002.
Münkler, Herfried, *Politische Bilder, Politik der Metaphern*, Frankfurt am Main: Fischer, 1994.
Musil, Robert, 'Denkmale', in *Gesammelte Werke* II, Hamburg: Rowohlt, 1978, 506–9.
Namer, Gérard, *Mémoire et société*, Paris: Méridiens Klincksieck, 1987.
Neue Gesellschaft für Bildende Kunst, ed., *Der Wettbewerb für das 'Denkmal für die ermordeten Juden Europas'*, Berlin: Verlag der Kunst, 1995.
Noelle-Neumann, Elisabeth, and Renate Köcher, eds, *Allensbacher Jahrbuch der Demoskopie 1993–1997*, Munich: K.G. Saur, 1997.
Nohlen, Dieter, ed., *Lexikon der Politik*, 2 vols, Munich: C. H. Beck, 1994.
Nora, Pierre, ed. *Les Lieux de mémoire*, 7 vols, vol. I, *La République*, 1984; vol. II, *La Nation* (1, 2, 3), 1986; vol. III, *Les France* (1, 2, 3), 1993, Paris: Gallimard.
____, 'Le Retour de l'événement', in Jacques Le Goff and Pierre Nora, eds, *Faire de l'histoire*, vol. 1, Paris: Gallimard, 1974, 210–28.
____, 'Mémoire collective', in Jacques Le Goff et al., eds, *La nouvelle histoire*, Paris: Editions C.E.P.L., 1978, 398–401.
____, 'Histoire nationale', in André Burguière, ed., *Dictionnaire des Sciences Historiques*, Paris: Presses Universitaires de France, 1986, 487–90.
____, 'De l'histoire contemporaine au présent historique', in Institut d'Histoire du Temps Présent, ed., *Ecrire l'histoire du temps présent*, Paris: CNRS Editions, 1993, 43–47.
____, 'Das Abenteuer der *Lieux de mémoire*', in Etienne François et al., eds, *Nation und Emotion*, Göttingen: Vandenhoeck & Ruprecht, 1995, 83–92.
____, 'Gedächtniskonjunktur', *Transit* no. 22, 2002, 38–49.
Novick, Peter, *The Resistance versus Vichy. The Purge of Collaborators in Liberated France*, London: Chatto & Windus, 1968.
Odermatt, Peter, 'The Use of Symbols in the Drive for European Integration', in J. Leerssen and M. Spiering, eds, *Yearbook of European Studies*, 'National Identity – Symbols and Representations', Amsterdam & Atlanta: 1991, 217–38.
Ortevola, Peppino, 'Storia e mass media', in Nicola Gallerano, ed., *L'uso pubblico della storia*, Milan: Franco Angeli, 1995, 63–82.
Overesch, Manfred, *Buchenwald und die DDR, oder Die Suche nach Selbstlegitimation*, Göttingen: Vandenhoeck & Ruprecht, 1995.
Paxton, Robert, *Vichy France. Old Guard and New Order*, London: Barrie & Jenkins, 1972.
Perelman, Chaim, *The Realm of Rhetoric*, trans. William Kluback, Notre Dame: University of Notre Dame Press, 1982.
Petitfils, Jean-Christian, *Le Gaullisme*, Paris: Presses Universitaires de France, 1977.
Pinson, Gaëlle, 'La "reconstruction critique" à Berlin, entre formes et idéologie', *Le Visiteur. Ville, territoire, paysage, architecture* no. 6, 2000, 130–55.
Pitkin, Hanna, *The Concept of Representation*, Berkeley: University of California Press, 1967.
Poulot, Dominique, *De l'héritage monumental à l'entreprise de patrimoine. Pour une histoire de la transmission culturelle en France, XVIII–XX*ᵉ, Bada Fiesolana:

European University Institute, 1991.
Puvogel, Ulrike, and Martin Stankowski, *Gedenkstätten für die Opfer des Nationalsozialismus. Eine Dokumentation*, 2 vols, Bonn: Bundeszentrale für politische Bildung, 1995 & 1999.
Quack, Sybille, ed., *Auf dem Weg zur Realisierung. Das Denkmal für die ermordeten Juden Europas und der Ort der Information. Architektur und historisches Konzept*, Stuttgart: Deutsche Verlags-Anstalt, 2002.
____, ed., *Dimensionen der Verfolgung. Neue Perspektiven auf Opfer und Opfergruppen im Nationalsozialismus*, Stuttgart: Deutsche Verlags-Anstalt, 2003.
Rabbow, Arnold, *dtv-Lexikon politischer Symbole*, Munich: Deutscher Taschenbuch Verlag, 1970.
Rapaport, Lynn, *Jews in Germany after the Holocaust. Memory, Identity, and Jewish–German Relations*, Cambridge: Cambridge University Press, 1997.
Rauschenbach, Brigitte, ed., *Erinnern, Wiederholen, Durcharbeiten. Zur Psycho-Analyse deutscher Wenden*, Berlin: Aufbau Taschenbuch Verlag, 1992.
Redner, Harry, *A New Science of Representation*, Boulder, San Francisco, Oxford: Westview Press, 1994.
Reichel, Peter, *Politik mit der Erinnerung. Gedächtnisorte im Streit um die nationalsozialistische Vergangenheit*, Munich: Hanser, 1995.
Reuße, Felix, *Das Denkmal an der Grenze seiner Sprachfähigkeit*, Stuttgart: Klett-Cotta, 1995.
Richard, Lionel, *L'art et la guerre. Les artistes confrontés à la Seconde Guerre mondiale.* Paris: Flammarion, 1995.
Ricoeur, Paul, *Temps et récit*, 3 vols, vol 1, *L'intrigue et le récit historique*, 1983; vol. 2, *La Configuration dans le récit de fiction*, 1984; vol. 3, *Le Temps raconté*, 1985, Paris: Seuil.
Riegl, Aloïs, *Der moderne Denkmalkultus*, Vienna & Leipzig: Braumüller, 1903.
Rosenau, James, 'The Dynamics of Globalization: Toward an Operational Formulation', *Security Dialogue* no. 3, 1997, 247–62.
Rosh, Lea, 'Ein Denkmal im Lande der Täter', in Bürgerinitiative Perpektive Berlin, ed., *Ein Denkmal für die ermordeten Juden Europas. Dokumentation 1988–1995*, 3–7.
Rosh, Lea, and Eberhard Jäckel, *'Der Tod ist ein Meister aus Deutschland'. Deportation und Ermordung der Juden, Kollaboration und Verweigerung in Europa*, Hamburg: Hoffmann und Campe, 1990.
Rousso, Henry, *Le Syndrome de Vichy*, Paris: Seuil, 1987.
____, 'Sortir du dilemme: Pétain, est-ce la France?', *Le Débat* no. 89, 1996, 198–204.
____, 'Le débat continue…', *Le Débat* no. 89, 1996, 206–7.
____, *Vichy. L'événement, la mémoire, l'histoire*, Paris: Gallimard, 2001.
Rousso, Henry, and Philippe Petit, *La Hantise du passé*, Paris: Les éditions Textuel, 1998.
Samuel, Raphael, *Theatres of Memory*, 2 vols, vol. I, *Past and Present in Contemporary British Culture*, 1994; vol. 2, *Island Stories. Unravelling Britain*, 1998, London & New York: Verso.
Sarasin, Philipp, *Geschichtswissenschaft und Diskursanalyse*, Frankfurt am Main: Suhrkamp, 2003.
Scharf, Helmut, *Kleine Kunstgeschichte des deutschen Denkmals*, Darmstadt: Wissenschaftliche Buchgesellschaft, 1984.
Schiller, Dietmar, '"Geschichtsbilder" im Fernsehen: Zur Militarisierung des öffentlichen Raums im vereinten Deutschland durch staatlich inszenierte Symbolpolitik', *Kritische Berichte* no. 1, 1997, 39–54.
Schlaffer, Heinz, 'Gedenktage', *Merkur* no. 479, 1989, 81–84.
Schmidt, Bernhard et al., eds, *Frankreich Lexikon*, Berlin: Erich Schmidt Verlag,

1981.

Schmidt, Hans-Werner, *Edward Kienholz. The Portable War Memorial. Moralischer Appell und politische Kritik*, Frankfurt am Main: Fischer, 1988.

Schmidt, Thomas et al., eds, *Nationaler Totenkult. Die Neue Wache. Eine Streitschrift zur zentralen deutschen Gedenkstätte*, Berlin: Karin Kramer Verlag, 1995.

Schönfeld, Martin, *Gedenktafeln in Ost-Berlin*, 9 vols, Berlin: Aktives Museum, 1991–1993.

Schoeps, Julius, *Leiden an Deutschland. Vom antisemitischen Wahn und der Last der Erinnerung*, Munich & Zürich: Piper Verlag, 1990.

____, *Das Gewaltsyndrom. Verformungen und Brüche im deutsch-jüdischen Verhältnis*, Berlin: Argon Verlag, 1998.

Schwan, Gesine, *Politik und Schuld. Die zerstörerische Macht des Schweigens*, Frankfurt am Main: Fischer, 1997.

Sears, David, 'Symbolic Politics: A Socio-Psychological Theory', in Shanto Iyengar and William McGuire, eds, *Explorations in Political Psychology*, Durham & London: Duke University Press, 1993, 113–49.

Sigurdsson, Sigrid, *Deutschland – ein Denkmal – ein Forschungsauftrag 1996–1998*, Hagen: Neuer Folkwang Verlag, 1998.

Smith, Anthony, *National Identity*, Harmondsworth: Penguin, 1991.

Sontheimer, Kurt, *Grundzüge des politischen Systems der Bundesrepublik Deutschland*, Munich: Piper, 1984.

Speitkamp, Winfried, ed., *Denkmalsturz. Zur Konfliktgeschichte politischer Symbolik*, Göttingen: Vandenhoeck & Ruprecht, 1997.

Spielmann, Jochen, 'Gedenken und Denkmal', in Berlinische Galerie and Senatsverwaltung für Bau- und Wohnungswesen, eds, *Gedenken und Denkmal. Entwürfe zur Erinnerung an die Deportation und Vernichtung der jüdischen Bevölkerung Berlins*, Berlin: Berlinische Galerie, 1988, 7–46.

____, 'Steine des Anstoßes – Denkmale in Erinnerung an den Nationalsozialismus in der Bundesrepublik Deutschland', *Kritische Berichte* no. 3, 1988, 5–16.

____, *Entwürfe zur Sinngebung des Sinnlosen. Zu einer Theorie des Denkmals als Manifestation des 'kulturellen Gedächtnisses'. Der Wettbewerb dür ein Denkmal für Auschwitz*, Ph.D. dissertation, Freie Universität Berlin, 1990.

Spillman, Lyn, *Nation and Commemoration. Creating National Identities in the United States and Australia*, Cambridge: Cambridge University Press, 1997.

Stavginski, Hans-Georg, *Das Holocaust-Denkmal: der Streit um das 'Denkmal für die ermordeten Juden Europas' in Berlin (1988–1999)*, Paderborn: Schöningh, 2002.

Steinbach, Peter, 'Erinnerung und Geschichtspolitik', interview, *Universitas* no. 50, 1995, 181–94.

____, 'Die Vergegenwärtigung von Vergangenem. Zum Spannungsverhältnis zwischen individueller Erinnerung und öffentlichem Gedenken', *Aus Politik und Zeitgeschichte* no. 4, 1997, 3–13.

Stih, Renata, and Frieder Schnock, *Bus Stop. Fahrplan*, Berlin: Neue Gesellschaft für Bildende Kunst, 1995.

Tacke, Charlotte, *Denkmal im sozialen Raum. Nationale Symbole in Deutschland und Frankreich im 19. Jahrhundert*, Göttingen: Vandenhoeck & Ruprecht, 1995.

Taguieff, Pierre-André, *La Nouvelle judéophobie*, Paris: Fondation du 2 mars/Mille et une nuit, 2002.

Throm, Danny, 'Frankreich. Die gespaltene Erinnerung', in Monika Flacke, ed., *Mythen der Nationen. Ein europäisches Panorama*, Berlin: Deutsches Historisches Museum, 1998, 129–51.

Thünemann, Holger, *Das Denkmal für die ermordeten Juden Europas. Dechiffrierung einer Kontroverse*, Münster, Hamburg & London: Lit Verlag, 2003.

Tombs, Robert, review of Pierre Nora, ed., *The Realms of Memory*, vol. I, in *Times*

Higher Education Supplement, 18 April 1997.
Vallet, Odon, 'Des mots en politique: Les noms de l'innommable', *Mots/Les langages du politique* no. 56, Sept. 1998, 138–41.
Vidal-Naquet, Pierre, *Les Assassins de la mémoire*, Paris: La Découverte, 1991.
Voigt, Rüdiger, 'Politische Symbolik und postnationale Identität', in Angsar Klein, ed., *Kunst, Symbolik und Politik. Die Reichstagverhüllung als Denkanlaß*, Opladen: Leske und Budrich, 1995, 283–98.
Walsh, Kevin, *The Representation of the Past. Museums and Heritage in the Post-modern World*, London: Routledge, 1992.
Wellers, Georges, 'Le déroulement de la Rafle des 16 et 17 juillet 1942', *Le Monde Juif* no. 46, 1967.
____, *La Journée tragique des 16 et 17 juillet 1942*, Paris: Centre de Documentation Juive Contemporaine, 1962.
Wellmer, Albrecht, *Endspiele: Die unversöhnliche Moderne*, Frankfurt am Main: Suhrkamp, 1993.
Welzer, Harald, Sabine Moller, and Karoline Tschuggnall, *Opa war kein Nazi. Nationalsozialismus und Holocaust im Familiengedächtnis*, Frankfurt am Main: Fischer, 2002.
Wewer, Heinz, ed. *May '45 – Remembrance and the Future. On the Representation of the Non-representable in the Arts*. Glasgow: Network for International Cooperation in the Arts, 2001.
Wiedmer, Caroline, *The Claims of Memory. Representations of the Holocaust in Germany and France*, Ithaca: Cornell University Press, 1999.
Wieviorka, Annette, *Déportation et génocide: entre la mémoire et l'oubli*, Paris: Plon, 1992.
____, '1992. Réflexions sur une commémoration', *Annales ESC* no. 3, 1993, 703–14.
____, *L'Ere du témoin*, Paris: Plon, 1998.
Wieviorka, Michel, ed., *Une société fragmentée? Le multiculturalisme en débat*, Paris: La Découverte, 1996.
____, 'La transformation des juifs', *Le Débat* no. 98, 1998, 177–80.
Wieviorka, Olivier, *Nous entrerons dans la carrière. De la Résistance à l'exercise du pouvoir*, Paris: Seuil, 1994.
Wilds, Karl, 'Identity Creation and the Culture of Contrition: Recasting Normality in the Berlin Republic', *German Politics* no. 1, 2000, 83–102.
Winter, Jay, *Sites of Memory, Sites of Mourning: The Great War in European Cultural History*, Cambridge: Cambridge University Press, 1995.
Winter Jay, and Emmanuel Sivan, 'Setting the Framework', in Winter and Sivan, eds, *War and Remembrance in the Twentieth Century*, Cambridge: Cambridge University Press, 1999, 6–39.
Wise, Michael, *Capital Dilemma. Germany's Search for a New Architecture of Democracy*, New York: Princeton Architectural Press, 1998.
Wodack, Ruth et al., eds, *Die Sprachen der Vergangenheiten. Öffentliches Gedenken in österreichischen und deutschen Medien*, Frankfurt am Main: Suhrkamp, 1994.
Wolfrum, Edgar, 'Geschichte als Politikum – Geschichtspolitik', *Neue politische Literatur* no. 3, 1996, 376–401.
____, 'Geschichtspolitik in der Bundesrepublik Deutschland 1949–1989. Phasen und Kontroversen', *Aus Politik und Zeitgeschichte* no. 45, 1998, 3–15.
Wood, Nancy, 'Memory's Remains: *Les Lieux de mémoire*', *History and Memory* no. 1, 1994, 123–49.
Young, James, *Writing and Rewriting the Holocaust. Narrative and the Consequences of Interpretation*, Bloomington & Indianopolis: Indianopolis University Press, 1988.
____, 'The Counter-Monument: Memory Against Itself in Germany Today',

Critical Inquiry no. 2, 1992, 267–86.

____, *The Texture of Memory*, New Haven & London: Yale University Press, 1993.

____, *At Memory's Edge. After-images of the Holocaust in Contemporary Art and Literature*, New Haven & London: Yale University Press, 2000.

Zima, Pierre, '"Rezeption" und "Produktion" als ideologische Begriffe', in Zima, *Kritik der Literatursoziologie*, Frankfurt am Main: Suhrkamp, 1978, 72–112.

Zimmermann, Hans-Dieter, 'Holokauston, holocaustum, holocaust. Die Bedeutung des Wortes "Holocaust"', *Die Neue Gesellschaft/Frankfurter Hefte* no. 12, 1997, 1120–23.

Zuckermann, Moshe, 'Perspektiven der Holocaust-Rezeption in Israel und Deutschland', *Aus Politik und Zeitgeschichte* no. 14, 1998, 19–29.

Index